S0-AHJ-904

¡Presente!

American Catholic Identities
A Documentary History
Christopher J. Kauffman, General Editor

American Catholic Identities is a nine-volume series that makes available to the general reader, the student, and the scholar seminal documents in the history of American Catholicism. Subjects are wide-ranging and topically ordered within periods to encounter the richly textured experiences of American Catholics from the earliest years to the present day. The twenty-six editors of these volumes reveal a command of trends in historiography since the publication of John Tracy Ellis's three-volume work, *Documents of American Catholic History*. Hence the American Catholic Identities series shows developments in our understanding of social history — the significance of gender, race, regionalism, ethnicity, and spirituality, as well as Catholic thought and practice before and since the Second Vatican Council.

The series elucidates myriad meanings of the American Catholic experience by working with the marker of religious identity. It brings into relief the historical formations of religious self-understandings of a wide variety of Catholics in a society characterized by the principles of religious liberty, separation of church and state, religious pluralism, and voluntarism.

American Catholic Identities is united by such dominant factors in American history as waves of immigration, nativism, anti-Catholicism, racism, sexism, and several other social and ideological trends. Other aspects of unity are derived from American Catholic history: styles of episcopal leadership, multiple and various types of Catholic institutions, and the dynamic intellectual interaction between the United States and various national centers of Catholic thought. Woven into the themes of this documentary history are the protean meanings of what constitutes being American and Catholic in relation to the formations of religious identities.

Titles of books in the series are:

Public Voices: Catholics in the American Context, Steven M. Avella and Elizabeth McKeown

The Frontiers and Catholic Identities, Anne M. Butler, Michael E. Engh, S.J., and Thomas W. Spalding, C.F.X.

Creative Fidelity: U.S. Catholic Intellectual Identities, Scott Appleby, Patricia Byrne, C.S.J., and William Portier

Keeping Faith: European and Asian Catholic Immigrants, Jeffrey M. Burns, Ellen Skerrett, and Joseph M. White

Prayer and Practice in the American Catholic Community, Joseph P. Chinnici, O.F.M., and Angelyn Dries, O.S.F.

Gender Identities in American Catholicism, Paula Kane, James Kenneally, and Karen Kennelly, C.S.J.

"Stamped with the Image of God": African-Americans as God's Image in Black, Cyprian Davis, O.S.B., and Jamie Phelps, O.P.

¡Presente! U.S. Latino Catholics from Colonial Origins to the Present, Timothy Matovina and Gerald E. Poyo, in collaboration with Cecilia González-Andrieu, Steven P. Rodríguez, and Jaime R. Vidal.

The Crossing of Two Roads: Being Catholic and Native in the United States, Marie Therese Archambault, O.S.F., Mark Thiel, and Christopher Vecsey

A workshop for the editors of these books was entirely funded by a generous grant from the Louisville Institute.

American Catholic Identities
A Documentary History
Christopher J. Kauffman, General Editor

¡Presente!

U.S. Latino Catholics from Colonial Origins to the Present

Timothy Matovina
Gerald E. Poyo
Editors

In Collaboration with
Cecilia González-Andrieu
Steven P. Rodríguez
Jaime R. Vidal

ORBIS BOOKS

Maryknoll, New York 10545

✗44701938

Third Printing, September 2005

The Catholic Foreign Mission Society of America (Maryknoll) recruits and trains people for overseas missionary service. Through Orbis Books, Maryknoll aims to foster the international dialogue that is essential to mission. The books published, however, reflect the opinions of their authors and are not meant to represent the official position of the society. To obtain more information about Maryknoll and Orbis Books, visit our website at www.maryknoll.org.

Copyright © 2000 by Timothy Matovina and Gerald E. Poyo

Published by Orbis Books, Maryknoll, New York, U.S.A.

All rights reserved. No part of this publication may be reproduced or transmitted in any form or by any means, electronic or mechanical, including photocopying, recording, or any information storage or retrieval system, without prior permission in writing from Orbis Books, P.O. Box 308, Maryknoll, NY 10545-0308, U.S.A.

Manufactured in the United States of America

Library of Congress Cataloging-in-Publication Data

Presente! : U.S. Latino Catholics from colonial origins to the present / Timothy Matovina, Gerald E. Poyo, editors ; in collaboration with Cecilia González-Andrieu, Steven P. Rodríguez, Jaime R. Vidal.
     p. cm. – (American Catholic identities)
   Includes bibliographical references and index.
   ISBN 1-57075-347-4 – ISBN 1-57075-328-8 (pbk.)
   1. Hispanic American Catholics–History–Sources. 2. Catholic Church–United States–History–Sources. 3. United States–Church history–Sources. I. Matovina, Timothy M., 1955–   II. Poyo, Gerald Eugene, 1950–   III. Series.
BX1407.H55 P74 2000
282′.73′08968 – dc21
                                          00-060673

CONTENTS

Part 2
ENDURING COMMUNITIES OF FAITH
IN THE SOUTHWEST

Part 3
CROSSING BORDERS:
THE IMMIGRANT EXPERIENCE

Part 4
EXILES, FAITH, AND THE HOMELAND

Part 5
TWENTIETH-CENTURY
STRUGGLES FOR JUSTICE

Part 6
CONTEMPORARY THEOLOGICAL VOICES

FOREWORD
Christopher J. Kauffman

Timothy Matovina, Gerald E. Poyo, and their collaborators have drawn from their extensive research experience in several archives to gather together a book that is characterized by originality, imagination, and scholarly expertise.

Hispanic religious identities have to varying degrees achieved historical significance in their dynamic encounters with non-Hispanic groups and within their specific economic, political, social, and regional contexts. Working from this knowledge, the editors of the current work have chosen documents from an exceedingly large pool of accessible primary sources on several principles of selectivity: the point of view of the author(s) of the letter, memoir, constitution, and so forth, and the clarity of its religious identity-formation within the various historical situations of conflict, encounter, or a participant's witness of a religious devotion. There are several examples of the diversity and specificity of these kinds of documents: a Protestant's description of a Hispanic celebration of the traditional Christmas; a Mexican priest's conflict with his French bishop in Santa Fe; Tejano celebration of the feast of Our Lady of Guadalupe shortly after the American annexation of Texas. Such documents show a sharpening of the religious identities of the historical characters as well as the authors' appreciation of the formation of these self-understandings.

Crucial to our contemporary understanding of these identities are the introductions to the book, the parts, and the documents, which together outline the shape of the Hispanic presence in the United States. Characterized by rhetorical clarity, a command of historical contexts, and a rich background in several disciplines, the introductions are particularly helpful because they provide necessary context for those students unfamiliar with the history of Hispanics in the United States. The introductions to the documents deepen the reader's perspective; without such background the documents might seem one-dimensional or not clearly related to the salient themes. Even those students familiar with Chicano and Latino studies may not have incorporated the Catholic dimension into their course work. And religion may not have been considered other than as a factor in systems of oppression. However, as the editors point out, the formation of religious identities is gaining recognition, particularly as these self-understandings were manifested in the everyday lives of the diverse peoples. In part 2, "Enduring Communities of Faith in the Southwest," as well as in other parts of the book, there is an abundance of documents on folk or popular religion from the participants' point of view.

Students eager to become engaged in the quotidian religious lives of Hispanic peoples will be enriched by immersing themselves in these documents.

Parts 3, 4, and 5 integrate the encounters, conflicts, and adaptations of immigrants of several generations not only of the larger groups of Hispanics represented in the United States — Mexicans, Cubans, and Puerto Ricans — but also of smaller groups, such as the Guatemalans, Salvadorans, Peruvians, and others.

The topical organization and integration of diverse groups allow the editors to arrange the documents over a long time period from the late sixteenth to the late twentieth century. The emphasis here is on the depiction of historical developments within various theoretical frameworks. During this time, the Hispanic presence became almost nationwide: Puerto Ricans settled in the urban areas of the Northwest and even in the Midwest; the Sanctuary movement for exiles from San Salvador and Honduras extended to the Northwest; Mexican immigrants migrated beyond the southern rim of the nation into various towns and cities of the country.

United in a cultivation of their ethnoreligious identities in confrontation with Americanizing prelates and priests, immigrants of all national origins have shared in the struggle for their parish communities, where they may foster and preserve their popular religious feasts that are significant to their identities in a pluralist society. For example, the Cuban exiles introduced the devotion to Our Lady of Charity in Miami, where they built a shrine for their community. This devotion functions to foster continuity, survival, and hope for the return home. In part 5 we encounter various documents on reform, including the prophets' cries for the pursuit of justice within the church and society; examples of these groups are the Hermanas and the Padres and the various movements of solidarity (e.g., the farmworkers movement led by César Chávez).

The editors' originality is evident in selecting documents and in framing and elucidating the meanings and significances of those texts. Another distinctive mark is part 6, "Contemporary Theological Voices." By placing these voices immediately after the texts on struggles for justice, the editors provide the reader with the praxis–theological reflection methodology of liberation theology. In any event, this part on theological voices does not constitute an epilogue but rather is in continuity with the previous part and is an appropriate conclusion for the book. The final part, then, certainly represents the editors' commitment to theology's role in discovering new meanings in many documents.

Readers will note that the editors have a feel for the documents. They have all made a personal pilgrimage through these five centuries of Hispanic life. By participating in these encounters, conflicts, and cries for justice, as well as the festivals and feasts of the popular religion, they have developed a passion for the meanings of their documents, no doubt derived from their own experiences with those on the margins and beyond the limits. Their creative introductions to each part, moreover, convey their sense of the poetic. Their scholarship is matched by a sense of pilgrimage, passion, and poetry.

ACKNOWLEDGMENTS

We offer our deepest gratitude to Christopher J. Kauffman, the general editor for the American Catholic Identities documentary history series. His confidence in us and his patience and support during this project have been a continuous source of inspiration. Many thanks also to Bill Burrows and his colleagues at Orbis Books, who did an outstanding job editing the book and seeing it through to publication.

The Louisville Institute provided generous financial assistance for our work and that of the other collaborators in this nine-volume series. A 1998 Collaborative Research Assistance Grant from the American Academy of Religion enabled us to hold an additional editorial meeting at a crucial moment in the development of the book. During spring 1998, a Rockefeller Fellowship in the Humanities from Florida International University enabled Gerald Poyo to pursue essential research at the University of Miami Library. We greatly appreciate these organizations, their directors, and their staffs for supporting our scholarship.

Numerous colleagues collaborated on this project. We are especially grateful to David A. Badillo, Mario T. García, and Lara Medina, each of whom contributed documents and accompanying introductions from their current research. Special thanks also to Ana María Díaz-Stevens and Antonio M. Stevens-Arroyo, whose extensive knowledge of Puerto Rican history and abundant kindness in opening their research files to us enhanced this volume significantly. Thomas J. Steele, SJ, was equally generous in making available his expertise and files of primary materials on Colorado and New Mexican Catholicism. Allan Figueroa Deck, SJ, offered insightful comments on critical portions of the manuscript, as well as wise counsel in our search for various documents and illustrations. Dora Elizondo Guerra provided expert translations for nearly two dozen documents in a most timely manner. Miryam Bujanda reviewed and edited translations and helped identify documents for the collection. Other colleagues, archivists, and librarians assisted us in locating, selecting, and translating documents and in editing various sections of the book. For this gracious assistance, we thank Adán Benavides Jr., Jeffrey M. Burns, Rudy Busto, Araceli Cantero, Alfredo G. Cardentey, Antonia Castañeda, Ron Cruz, Kenneth G. Davis, Uva de Aragón, Anita de Luna, MCDP, Esperanza B. de Varona, Lesbia de Varona, OFM Conv, Lissette Elguezabal, Father Virgilio Elizondo, Michael Engh, SJ, Eduardo C. Fernández, SJ, Gabriel Gutiérrez, José Roberto Gutiérrez, Jane Hotstream, RSM, Nicolás Kanellos, Edward Loch, SM, Salvador Miranda, Marina Ochoa, Lisandro Pérez, Alberto L. Pulido, Gladys Ramos, Hal Recinos, Guillermo

Romagosa, Monsignor Agustín Román, Father Juan Romero, Vicki L. Ruiz, Rosa Sánchez, Moises Sandoval, Lois Stanford, Yolanda Tarango, CCVI, Mary D. Taylor, Rosie Torres, María Teresa Venegas, IHM, Monsignor Bryan Walsh, and Bob Wright, OMI.

The ninety-one documents in this volume come from a wide array of previously published works, library holdings, archives, and private papers and collections. We gratefully acknowledge all those who granted us permission to reprint selections from translated works and primary materials; citations identifying those who gave us such permissions appear at the end of individual documents throughout this volume.

Loyola Marymount University generously supported Timothy Matovina's work with a one-semester writing fellowship from the College of Liberal Arts and a summer research grant, both in 1998. The university also provided funding for various student research assistants: Daniel Chavira, Teresa Derrick, Richard Grijalva, D. J. Mitchell, Cecilia Rendón, and Martha I. Saldaña. In spring 1998 Matovina had the privilege to team-teach a seminar on American Catholic identities with history professor Michael Engh, SJ. The following participants in that course each helped draft an introduction for a document included in this volume: Rachael Aguirre, Augusto J. Castañeda, David García Viramontes, D. J. Mitchell, and Matthew W. Thompson. Stephen J. Thacker, the head of interlibrary loans at Loyola Marymount's main library, consistently procured rare books and other materials in a timely manner.

St. Mary's University awarded Gerald Poyo faculty grants to conduct research at the University of Miami Otto G. Richter Library during the summers of 1997 and 1999. Additionally, the university graduate school provided a graduate assistantship and the history department funded a work-study student, Rubén Castro, who worked on obtaining publication permissions for the documents.

Elida Matovina Yañez and and Jean-Paul Andrieu also supported the project in many ways, from sorting through documents and identifying possible candidates for inclusion in the volume to offering wise counsel and moral support when the task seemed too overwhelming. Above all, we feel a great sense of debt and admiration for the Latina and Latino Catholics whose faith, courage, struggle, and living historical legacy have inspired and fascinated us throughout this project. To them and their ancestors and descendants, we gratefully dedicate this book.

CECILIA GONZÁLEZ-ANDRIEU
TIMOTHY MATOVINA
GERALD E. POYO
STEVEN P. RODRÍGUEZ
JAIME R. VIDAL

INTRODUCTION

Spanish-speaking Catholics have been continuously *presente* in what is now the continental United States for almost twice as long as the nation has existed. Subjects of the Spanish Crown founded the first permanent European settlement within the current borders of the fifty states at St. Augustine, Florida, in 1565, four decades before the establishment of Jamestown, Virginia, the first British colony. Before the end of the sixteenth century, Spanish Jesuits and Franciscans initiated missionary activities in present-day Georgia and even as far north as Virginia (Hennesey 10–12). Meanwhile, in 1598 at present-day El Paso, Texas, eight Franciscans and other Spanish subjects established the permanent foundation of Catholicism in what is now the Southwest (Almaráz).

While Hispanics were the first Catholic (as well as first European) inhabitants to establish settlements in territories now under U.S. control, for much of U.S. history Hispanics have constituted a relatively small and frequently overlooked group within U.S. Catholicism. But in the last half-century their numbers and their influence have increased dramatically. An influx of newcomers from such diverse locales as Puerto Rico, Cuba, the Dominican Republic, El Salvador, Guatemala, Nicaragua, Colombia, Peru, Ecuador, and Argentina, along with ongoing Mexican immigration, added to the ranks of an established Hispanic population comprised primarily of Mexican-descent Catholics. Today, Hispanics comprise the largest group of U.S. Catholics as well as the largest group of recent Catholic arrivals. For example, although notoriously inaccurate, census figures indicate that, while Cubans have resided in this nation since the first decades of the nineteenth century, in the three decades following Fidel Castro's 1959 rise to power the Cuban population in the United States increased eightfold. Thousands of Guatemalans and Salvadorans fled civil wars in their homelands that escalated during the 1970s and 1980s; 1990 census statistics indicated that more than three-fourths of Guatemalans and Salvadorans were foreign-born. That same census showed similar figures for foreign-born Colombians and Peruvians in the United States; more than half of them had entered the country during the previous decade.

These few examples illuminate both the long-standing presence and recent arrival of Latina and Latino Catholics in the United States; their history is a wide-ranging and fascinating story of colonial origins and new beginnings, struggle and endurance, immigration and exile, unity and diversity, triumph and resistance. This book explores the complex and multiple ways Hispanic

Catholics have forged and expressed identities in the midst of these varied experiences that comprise the mosaic of U.S. Catholicism.

Scholarly Contribution

This volume is the first compilation of primary documents that encompasses U.S. Hispanic Catholicism from colonial times to the present. It is also the first book-length work to address explicitly the role of religion in the formation of Latina and Latino identities. A significant feature of the book is that Mexicans and Mexican Americans, Puerto Ricans, Cubans, Dominicans, and various other groups from Central and South America are treated concurrently rather than in isolation. This approach implies that certain affinities exist among the many and diverse people of Latin American extraction living in the United States and that these affinities provide the basis for an integrated examination of Latino history. While not all Latinos are Catholic, of course, Catholicism is a central feature of the Latin American historical experience that continues to influence the vast majority of Latinos in the United States at one level or another. At the same time, it is important to emphasize that Latino Catholic identities are not homogenous and must be viewed in all their rich diversity. Diversity among Latinos is a historical reality and includes national, cultural, racial, class, gender, and regional differences, among others. This volume, then, treats the history of Latino Catholics as a story shaped by the tension inherent in the dynamics between diversity and commonality. The historiography of Latin American–origin populations in the United States is generally a literature defined by national origin: Mexican American, Puerto Rican, Cuban, and others. Another approach is to tell a more integrated Latino story which points to the commonalties across groups. This approach, however, should not be understood as an effort to homogenize Latino history or discourage the continuing focus on national group histories, which will inevitably continue to grow as new communities form and develop. In fact, a Latino historiography is absolutely dependent on the continuing development of national-group historiographies, and, in the end, the goal is to offer not a competing approach but a complementary vision and analysis.

   ¡Presente! adds to the growing body of literature on U.S. Latino Catholic history and complements the groundbreaking works of Antonio Stevens-Arroyo, Moises Sandoval, and the three-volume study sponsored by the Cushwa Center for the Study of American Catholicism at the University of Notre Dame (Dolan and Hinojosa; Dolan and Vidal; Dolan and Figueroa Deck). Stevens-Arroyo's *Prophets Denied Honor* (1980) presents one hundred select documents, almost all of them from the twentieth century, and focuses on the genesis and development of a distinctly "Hispano church" in the United States. Mexicans, Puerto Ricans, and Mexican Americans produced the documents in that study. Since only five documents from that work are republished in this collection, the two books are excellent companion volumes. Moises Sandoval's *On the Move* (1990) remains a standard text for readers who

desire a relatively brief overview of U.S. Latino Catholicism; it identifies more people, events, and organizations than this study, which is focused more specifically on Latino Catholic identities. The earlier volume that Sandoval edited, *Fronteras* (1983), provides more detailed information on various topics treated in *On the Move*. The three-volume Cushwa study (1994) adds to Sandoval's work by exploring the regional differences among Mexican Americans as well as offering a more in-depth examination of Puerto Ricans and Cubans. Despite its stated focus on twentieth-century U.S. Hispanic Catholicism, the Cushwa study also contains valuable analysis on the historical context of earlier time periods.

In addition to these more general works, various books and articles examine specific time periods, regions, and locales that are part of the U.S. Hispanic Catholic story. Many of these writings are cited in the chapters that follow and listed in this book's bibliography. Of particular note is the winter/spring 1990 issue of *U.S. Catholic Historian*, which contains fourteen articles on diverse aspects of Latino Catholic history in the United States. This issue, as well as the aforementioned 1983 volume edited by Moises Sandoval, were primarily the work of CEHILA (Comisión para el Estudio de la Historia de la Iglesia en Latinoamerica), a group of historians dedicated to writing Latin American church history "from the perspective of the poor." Since the establishment of the U.S. branch of CEHILA in 1975, Moises Sandoval, Bishop Ricardo Ramírez, CSB, and other organization leaders have facilitated a growing effort to explore the historical contours of Hispanic Catholicism in the United States.

Besides complementing the work of CEHILA colleagues and other historians of U.S. Latino religion, this book on Latino Catholic identities contributes to U.S. Catholic studies, a discipline in which Latino religion is frequently treated inadequately. To be sure, in recent decades some general histories of U.S. Catholicism have offered a more detailed examination of Hispanics. But frequently these works rely on secondary sources that lead to biased and unfounded conclusions. For example, in his *American Catholics* (1981), James Hennesey states that, after the secularization of the California missions in 1834, the Californios were "innocent of cultural influence" and that "religion declined" in the region (21). He further claims that, during this same period in New Mexico, the church was "decadent," "sacramental life was virtually non-existent," native priests like Antonio José Martínez were corrupt and "extorted exorbitant fees," and religious culture was plagued by "ignorance, neglect, and permissiveness" (137). As the part introductions and documents that follow demonstrate (especially in part 2), such sweeping generalizations are not consistent with extant primary sources.

Finally, this book enhances the work of scholars in Latino studies, who evidence a growing interest in religion and its role. While religion continues to be a peripheral topic in many general, regional, and local histories of Chicanos, Puerto Ricans, Cubans, and other Latino groups, other studies increasingly examine religion as an important element in the analysis of topics such as migration, women, and identity formation (e.g., Díaz-Stevens 1993a; Ruiz 138–43; G. Sánchez 151–70). Some general histories include sections or chapters on religion (e.g., Acuña 430–37; Fitzpatrick 117–38; Gonzales esp. 241–44; Samora and Vandel Simon 223–34). These general works often explore Latino Catholics' efforts to engage their faith as a resource for cultural survival and social change; they also frequently criticize Catholicism as institutionally negligent or as a mechanism of social control among Latinos. *¡Presente!* provides primary documents and an analysis of Latina and Latino Catholic identities that will enable colleagues in Latino studies to examine religion in greater depth and with a stronger grasp of its significance and complexity.

Document Selection and Editing

Primary sources for this study encompass diaries, journals, memoirs, reminiscences, travelogues, testimonials, correspondence, press releases, newspaper accounts, essays, speeches, sermons, parish and diocesan records, and other official documents. In the selection of documents, we gave priority to sources produced by Latinas and Latinos themselves. Since documents from marginalized groups like women and the economically poor were the most difficult to find, we gave these documents the highest priority in our research efforts and selection process. As the title of this documentary series suggests, the primary criterion was that documents deal with the issue of identity formation. Because of space limitations, we omitted official documents that are readily available like the conclusions from the three National Hispanic Pastoral Encuentros (1972, 1977, 1985), the U.S. bishops pastoral letter on Hispanic ministry (1983), and the National Pastoral Plan for Hispanic Ministry (1987), as well as most of the documents already published in the aforementioned book by Antonio Stevens-Arroyo. The sheer volume of material also prevented us from including all regions, time periods, issues, organizations, groups, and significant individuals.

The most difficult decision in developing a schema for this volume was whether to include documents from the island of Puerto Rico. On the one hand, Puerto Rico has been under U.S. jurisdiction since the 1898 Treaty of Paris, which ended the war between the United States and Spain. Moreover, all Puerto Ricans have legally been U.S. citizens since the Jones Act of 1917. On the other hand, unlike conquered territories on the mainland, to date the island has not been granted statehood — nor asked for it. Instead, in a 1952 vote the Puerto Rican population agreed with U.S. officials on the status of a commonwealth for the island or, as it is known in Spanish, an *estado libre asociado,* a free state voluntarily associated with the United States. This compromise position between statehood and independence allows for a political alliance with the United States while enabling island residents to retain important elements of autonomy and identity like the Puerto Rican flag and anthem, as well as the parity of Spanish with English as the island's official languages (Fitzpatrick 29–31). Given Puerto Rico's unique political situation as a semiautonomous state, we decided to focus on Puerto Rican migrants to the mainland who, like other Latinos, forge and express their identities in a U.S. milieu that is far more pluralistic than their homeland. Of course, as various documents in this collection illustrate, Puerto Ricans on the mainland consistently refer to the island in statements that express their identity; these documents provide a look at island life and events from the lens of Puerto Ricans living on the mainland.

The documents in this volume illuminate the diversity of nationalities among U.S. Hispanics. Spanish is a primary language in at least twenty countries; the United States has the fifth largest Spanish-speaking population, composed of a diverse cross-section of nations. Spanish-speaking people share a common Iberian heritage, a heritage in which Roman Catholicism plays a significant role. At the same time, indigenous and African roots influence Spanish-speaking populations to varying degrees. In the Caribbean, for example, where Spanish colonizers decimated native populations and forcibly resettled numerous African slaves, the African influence remains particularly strong. In places like Peru, Guatemala, and Mexico where many significant elements of the Inca, Maya, and Aztec civilizations survived the Spanish conquest, these and other ancient indigenous cultures continue to shape contemporary life. The mixing or *mestizaje* of Iberian, African, and indigenous cultures is a complex process with numerous local, regional, and national variations. Variations in national background are reflected in our selection of documents, although most of the documents come from the three largest U.S. Hispanic groups: Mexicans, Puerto Ricans, and Cubans, respectively. Nonetheless, select documents also illuminate the experience of Catholics from the Dominican Republic and several countries in Central and South America.

Besides revealing distinctions of nationality, this volume contains a variety of documents that collectively illuminate differences of region, time periods, age, gender, social class, and the perspectives of laity, religious, and clergy. The book also highlights elements of the Latino Catholic story that are often overlooked or forgotten. For example, we are delighted to present documentary evidence that South and Central Americans promoted Hispanic ministry in the United States as early as 1871 (document 27). Similarly, the nineteenth-century primary sources (documents 41, 42) that relate the story of Father Félix Varela and Cuban Catholic activity in Key West demonstrate that the Cuban exile experience antedates Fidel Castro's 1959 rise to power by well over a century. We hope our readers will be as fascinated as we are with these and numerous other episodes and historical figures that illuminate the story of U.S. Latino Catholics and their expressions of identity.

Where possible, we have transcribed documents from original sources, but we also cite secondary materials because they are more accessible to readers. We made some minor editorial changes in spelling and punctuation to render the documents more readable. Other corrections of errors and omissions are inserted in brackets, as are translations of Spanish or Latin words and phrases. Although we use inclusive language in our own analysis and commentaries, we have retained the gender-exclusive language that appears in various cited documents. In this regard and in our selection of excerpts from longer documents or works, we have made every attempt to avoid editorial changes that alter the original tone and meaning of a passage.

Language and Self-Expressions of Identity

The persons who produced the various documents in this volume used diverse terms to describe themselves. Since the names people call themselves express their sense of identity, this diverse terminology is obviously a central concern for this study. Some people who produced documents in the book name themselves by their nation of origin, for example, Dominican, Puerto Rican, Cuban, Bolivian, Chilean, Peruvian, Colombian, Nicaraguan, Costa Rican, Salvadoran, Mexican. Others attest to their U.S. residence or citizenship by employing terms like "Mexican American." Although many Spanish-speaking people from the Americas decry the tendency of U.S. citizens to monopolize the term "American," in this collection several U.S. citizens of Mexican descent identify themselves as "American [U.S.] citizens" or simply "Americans" as part of a strategy for demanding equal treatment in the United States. Other persons of Mexican heritage embrace the term "Chicana" or "Chicano," usually to highlight their justice orientation. A few people who produced documents in this book claim a Latino identity even though they have only one Hispanic parent; these claims illuminate the growing complexity of identity formation as contemporary Latinas and Latinos increasingly marry non-Hispanics or Latinos of other national groups.

The documents in this book also reveal that, as Puerto Ricans, Cubans, Mexicans, and other groups came into contact and worked collaboratively, they more frequently adopted terms like "Spanish-speaking," "Hispanic," "Latina," and "Latino" to reflect and promote perceptions of a common heritage and a common struggle adapting to life in the United States. To be sure, not all persons who use these terms explicitly express a collective identity for all groups of native Spanish speakers and their descendants. Moreover, while "Spanish speaking" is rarely used in contemporary parlance and there is evidence that "Latino" and the gender-inclusive "Latina/o" are gaining popularity in written works (Díaz-Stevens and Stevens-Arroyo 1998: 13–14), the appearance of all these terms in this compilation of documents illustrates the lack of a clear consensus on any one term. Nonetheless, the increased use of these terms over the past three decades reflects a growing sense of solidarity among U.S. residents who originate from countries where Spanish is a primary language.

Several documents in this volume illuminate the plurality of names that some Latinos use to identify themselves. For example, Peruvians will proudly acclaim their national heritage on a Peruvian feast day or civic holiday, but the same persons may also call themselves Latinos or Hispanics at an ecclesial, political, or social gathering where they interact with Puerto Ricans, Cubans,

Venezuelans, Ecuadorians, Colombians, or other groups. This phenomenon of expressing "multiple identities" is not uncommon in pluralistic societies; among Latinos it is a growing trend as they seek to express both pride in their unique heritage and solidarity with others who share a similar language, history, culture, and life struggle in the United States.

Besides employing different terms to name themselves, the persons who produced the documents in this book have different visions of what it means to be Catholic. As can easily be imagined, this also allows for a tremendous amount of variation and diversity. For example, some of the people we examined see Catholicism as a set of rituals and traditions, others as a body of doctrines and teachings. Still others perceive Catholicism essentially as part of their heritage. A few view the church primarily as an institution, while others insist that the "church" is also lived out in ordinary people's prayers, devotions, faith expressions, and struggle for justice. Not surprisingly, most people who produced documents in this volume see Catholicism as some combination of these (and other) elements. With regard to their assessment of the church vis-à-vis ministry with Hispanics, their perspectives range from defense of the institutional church to sharp accusations of institutional neglect and even racism, although most documents in this collection reflect a stance somewhere in-between these two positions.

The intersection of diverse perspectives on Catholicism and their own ethnic background accounts for the tremendous complexity and variety in Latino Catholic expressions of identity. Throughout this work we reflect that complexity and variety by mirroring the language used in primary sources. In this way, we respect both the diversity of terminology among individuals and the general shifts in language usage (and ethnic consciousness) among Latinas and Latinos, as well as the self-expression of each person or group with regard to their vision or understanding of Catholicism.

Plan of This Work

This book encompasses six parts, each of which includes a general introduction and a series of select documents with accompanying statements that identify the document's source, the context in which it was written, and other information pertinent to understanding its meaning and significance. Where possible, document introductions include the year of birth and death for persons mentioned who are already deceased. Additionally, each part begins with an illustration and a meditative text that illuminate the part's theme and contents. While the documents are presented in parts that reflect the chronology of U.S. Latino Catholicism, the presentation is primarily thematic. This thematic presentation will enable the reader to note the uniqueness of Mexican Americans, Puerto Ricans, Cubans, and other Latino groups, as well as the affinities in their backgrounds and their strategies for adaptation to life in the United States.

The first part, "Colonial Foundations," spans the Spanish colonial and Mexican republic periods in territories from Florida to California. It encompasses Spanish expeditions into these territories beginning in the early sixteenth century, the foundation of Catholic missions and parishes, the eventual secularization of the missions, and the ongoing practice of Catholicism up to the outbreak of war between the United States and Mexico in 1846. While this part is a prologue to the formation of Latino Catholic identities *in the United States,* this exploration into the colonial origins of Latino Catholicism is essential for understanding subsequent events, time periods, and expressions of identity.

Part 2, "Enduring Communities of Faith in the Southwest," examines Mexican communities incorporated into the United States as a result of the war between Mexico and the United States (1846–1848), particularly local initiatives to resist the effects of conquest and celebrate faith traditions that were a primary means for Mexican communities to forge and express their collective identities. This part spans the six decades from the U.S.-Mexican War to the dawn of the Mexican Revolution in the early twentieth century, when accelerated migration from Mexico significantly altered demographic and social conditions in the Southwest and other regions across the United States.

Part 3 treats the experiences of immigrants and part 4 that of exiles, both ranging from the nineteenth century to the present. For the purposes of this study, an "immigrant" is someone who came to the United States seeking reunification with family members, economic or educational opportunity, or some other personal goal. Exiles, on the other hand, are those who fled political and social forces in their homeland; whether they eventually act on their desire or not, they usually arrive with a firm resolve to return home at the earliest possible opportunity. To be sure, Hispanics who arrive in the United States often do not fit neatly into either of these categories. Some who came as exiles, for example, later decide to stay, shifting their attitude toward the United States and adapting to life in an adopted homeland. Nonetheless, many exiles differ from immigrants both in their experience of resettlement and in their approach to self-identity after arriving in the United States. In order to examine these differences, documents that *primarily* express an immigrant identity and those that *primarily* express an exile identity are treated in separate parts.

While parts 2, 3, and 4 illuminate the diverse Latino experiences of entry into U.S. society (conquest, immigration, and exile), the final two parts explore Latinos' common struggle to survive, adapt, and understand their life in a new country. Part 5, "Twentieth-Century Struggles for Justice," examines the ways twentieth-century Latino Catholics have formulated their identities in the process of demanding justice in both U.S. church and society. While there is divergence in the issues they address and the positions they espouse, there are also noticeable similarities in the identities expressed as different individuals and groups struggle for justice. The final part surveys Latina and Latino theologies as they have emerged in the past three decades. This theological reflection illuminates the distinct heritage and experience of various

Hispanic groups in the United States, but also reveals that theological analysis of their situation has enabled Latinas and Latinos to articulate groundbreaking theological insights and forge common bonds by critically examining their personal and collective histories.

The six major themes addressed in this volume's six parts do not comprehensively encompass the Latino Catholic experience, of course; nor are the documents presented in this volume exhaustive of the living legacy that comprises U.S. Latino Catholicism. Our hope is that, besides enlightening the reader and sparking conversation and debate, this book will inspire further research and animate the ongoing process of uncovering and celebrating the rich Hispanic Catholic heritage in the United States.

Nineteenth-century photo taken from the back of San Fernando Church (document 4) in San Antonio, Texas. Wanda Graham Ford Collection, San Antonio Conservation Society. Courtesy the Institute of Texan Cultures, San Antonio.

Part 1

COLONIAL FOUNDATIONS

ALABANZA A NUESTRA SEÑORA DE GUADALUPE

Juan Diego quedo al mirado	Juan Diego stood transfixed
de tan linda que la bido	by the beauty there before him.
I luego subio a la cumbre	He climbed to the top of the hill
a ber lo que le queria	to see what it was she wanted.
en el Serro de Tepallan	On the hill of Tepeyac
me ablo la birgen maria	the Virgin spoke to me.
dise que le formes un templo	She wants you to build her a church
para bibir con bosotros	so she may live among us.
Bide una birtuosa nube	I saw a glorious cloud.
me causo mucha alegria	It filled me with unspeakable joy.
y en un arco de colores	And there, in the midst of a rainbow of hues,
vide a la birgen maria	I saw the Virgin Mary.

Book of chants of the mission San Juan Capistrano, California, San Juan Capistrano Records, Bancroft Library, University of California, Berkeley. Trans. Dora Elizondo Guerra. Printed by permission.

Introduction

The origins of Hispanic Catholicism in what is today the continental United States are found in the communities planted during the sixteenth through early nineteenth centuries in the regions from Florida to California. Of course, subsequent immigration from Latin America in the nineteenth and twentieth centuries deepened and brought new vibrancy and expansion to this religious tradition in the United States, but the story must begin with the foundational communities. The planting and development of Hispanic Catholic communities in the borderlands regions by Spanish, Indian, African, and *mestizo* (mixed-heritage) peoples constituted a highly conflictive and coercive but also cooperative and integrative imperial enterprise; it was a story of conquest, violence, cultural confrontations, accommodations, change, and emergence of new traditions.

The establishment of Christianity in the "New World" initially involved conquest and destruction of indigenous and African religious traditions. In studying contemporary Latino Catholicism, the immensity of this painful experience should not be underestimated or forgotten: a historical process often driven by greed, racial and cultural oppression, and exploitation gave birth to

1

new societies that to this day live with the legacy. Many Europeans offered religious justifications for their colonialism, but others, driven by a sincere desire to spread the gospel, often understood and decried the hypocrisy of utilizing religious doctrine to justify conquest, enslavement, and exploitation. Indeed, seeing the injustices of these emerging colonial communities, many evangelizers spoke up in defense of the Indians, and less often of African slaves, but generally to no avail. This experience represents a difficult moral dilemma for Christians of all kinds that can never be fully resolved.

While it is important to keep this painful legacy in mind, it is also the case that indigenous civilizations and African slaves contributed to the diverse cultures and traditions that are encompassed in the history of Hispanic American Catholicism. Throughout the Western Hemisphere, indigenous cultures had thrived for thousands of years before the Spanish arrived. Sometime between 50,000 B.C.E. and 10,000 B.C.E., Asiatic peoples migrated across the Bering Straits to settle what is presently known as North, Central, and South America. Some of these nomadic groups developed into the indigenous civilizations of the Mayas, Olmecs, Toltecs, Incas, and Aztecs. Although these cultures rose and fell at different times throughout the Pre-Columbian period, they each built on their predecessors' accomplishments. Before the arrival of the Europeans, the Incas and Aztecs had already established splendid societies with sophisticated forms of art, language, architecture, mathematics, economics, spirituality, and sociopolitical organization. Though conquered by the Spanish, indigenous civilizations, along with Africans who arrived in the Americas as slaves, joined in creating Hispanic Catholic traditions.

The Spanish established their first American communities in the Caribbean. From Hispaniola, Cuba, and Puerto Rico, Spanish explorers and *conquistadores* launched their incursions into the mainland. Juan Ponce de León landed in Florida in 1513, initiating Spain's exploration of the North American continent. Six years later Hernán Cortés set out to conquer Mexico, defeating the Aztecs within three years. This was followed by expeditions to Peru and the taking of the Inca capital by 1532. Part of this Spanish imperial design included staking claims to the northern regions of the Americas, which occurred during the next three centuries, establishing a Spanish presence in present-day Florida, Louisiana, New Mexico, Texas, Arizona, and California.

The church was a crucial component in the spread of Spain's civilization in the Americas. From the very beginning the Spanish enterprise was defined by secular and religious goals; the church became intimately incorporated into the process of spreading Spain's interests. The Bulls of Pope Alexander VI in 1493 sanctioned the Spanish colonial enterprise, giving Spain title to the Indies with the condition that the peoples encountered would be converted to Christianity. In 1508, Pope Julius II conceded royal patronage to the Spanish monarchs, giving them the right to administer the church in the Indies, with powers ranging from naming the church hierarchy to collecting tithes, and in general establishing civil authority over most religious activities. This cemented the church's role as an arm of Spain's conquest and colonization in the Americas (Scholes 19–21).

While territorial acquisition and accumulation of wealth defined the Crown's primary secular goals, maintaining Catholicism among Spanish settlers and converting the Indians became the fundamental spiritual goals. Soon after Christopher Columbus's first voyage, Spain initiated the Christianization of the Indies, sending priests and introducing Catholicism's symbols and institutions. The construction of the first Catholic church in the New World began at the settlement of Santo Domingo on the island of Hispaniola in 1503. In 1511 Pope Julius II established the first three dioceses in the Americas, two in Hispaniola and another, San Juan Bautista, at Puerto Rico under the direction of Bishop Alonso Manso. Two years later a bishop was sent to Darién (in present-day Panama), another to Mexico in 1522, yet another to Peru in 1534. By the end of the century five archbishops and twenty-seven bishops ministered in Spanish America (Kanellos and Ryan 21–22). These traditional church structures and institutions ensured religious continuity for the settlers arriving from Spain, but the church also embarked on evangelizing the indigenous peoples.

The evangelizing fervor was a natural consequence of the church's *reconquista* history on the Iberian peninsula during the previous four centuries. The retaking and Christianizing of the territories taken by the Muslims, who had invaded Iberia in 711, were central goals of Spain's Christians. By 1492, Spain's crusading religiosity led to the forced conversion of Moors and Jews; those who refused were expelled. Spain's very identity became synonymous with Catholicism. This crusading spirit, which remained in close partnership with the highly developed fighting skills of Spanish soldiers, became a defining aspect of Spain's enterprise in the Americas (see document 1b).

Throughout the colonial era (sixteenth through early nineteenth centuries), Hispanic culture and civilization made their way into territories that are today within the borders of the United States. The "arrival" of Christianity began with the first explorations (documents 1a–1c) but became a permanent element of the landscape with the establishment of Hispanic population centers. Founded to stake territorial claims for the Spanish Crown as well as to advance Christendom's boundaries, small towns formed around the basic institutions of the state and church. *Pueblos* (towns) with formal civil and church institutions, military garrisons, and missions provided historically tested structures around which Hispanic frontier communities emerged. These communities developed grassroots traditions that came to define their very existence.

The Missions

From the start, friars accompanied expeditions of exploration and were an integral part of Spanish efforts to establish settlements. Sometimes the friars founded missions within or near settled Indian communities; in other cases, they induced nomadic peoples to settle down at newly established missions, usually near Spanish *pueblos* and military garrisons. While initially the prospect of entering the missions to stave off enemies, starvation, and harsh winters seemed attractive to some Indians (see document 1c), many eventually found mission life too alien and coercive. Not only were they not accustomed to the Spanish work routines and religious lifestyles, but they also found unacceptable the friars' demands that they shed their traditional ways. A number of Indians made the transition into these new lives and eventually embraced Christianity, but many others became resentful and left the missions at the earliest opportunity. In some cases outright rebellion ensued.

The period between 1680 and 1706 was a crucial time for the missions. In New Mexico and Florida the missions collapsed mainly because of Indian resistance to Spanish hegemony. The Pueblo revolt of 1680 in New Mexico demonstrated the shortcomings of Spanish policies in relation to the Indians (documents 2, 3). Although elements such as drought, famine, and rivalries for resources among the various Indian groups fueled resentments and dissatisfaction, it seems clear that Spanish efforts to destroy Pueblo traditional religious beliefs played a central role in fomenting rebellion. Indian resistance became particularly acute when Catholicism failed to resolve fundamental concerns like starvation and disease. Whenever Indians returned to their traditional belief systems for relief, the Spanish response was swift. In 1675, for example, Spanish authorities hung three Pueblo priests and whipped forty-three others as an incentive for the natives to remain loyal Catholics (Weber 1992: 134). In short, the Spanish effort to reshape Native American life took the form of congregating nomadic or seminomadic groups into communities, often subjecting them to forced labor, religious intolerance, and personal abuses and exploitation, sexual and otherwise. The natives built and maintained the missions with their labor, and many rebelled when they tired of answering to soldiers, priests, settlers, and government officials. In New Mexico, Spanish forces initiated the reconquest of the Pueblo Indians in 1692, but in the case of Florida the collapse of the missions was permanent. The Spanish never managed to reestablish a viable mission system in that region.

Despite the drawbacks and difficulties of mission life that often encouraged Native Americans to rebel or simply return to familiar ways, others remained within the world of the missions, accepted Christianity, and took on Hispanic and Catholic identities. For the missionaries, Hispanicizing the Indians entailed creating living spaces for their charges around impressive churches and chapels that became the center of everyday life. The missionaries worked diligently inculcating Catholicism, defining work regimes, establishing predictable daily-life routines, teaching the Spanish language, overseeing social interactions, enforcing Christian-appropriate gender relations, and generally changing or modifying any and all cultural practices among the Indians that were contrary to Christianity.

One strategy was to exert maximum influence over the Native American children, including, as was the case in the San Antonio missions, attempts to ensure they learned Spanish by isolating them from their parents (document

7). However, while missionary strategy generally involved language acculturation of the Indians, a number of religious failed to embrace or implement this strategy. In 1760, for example, Bishop Pedro Tamaron y Romeral of Durango visited New Mexico. He observed that the Indians spoke little Spanish and the Franciscans had no command of the Indian languages. Communications about religious matters took place with translators. The bishop observed "it is a shame that most of those Indians lack the benefit of confession. I take little satisfaction in these confessions through an interpreter when the latter is an Indian or a Negro" (document 5). He complained to the Franciscan priests about this problem and ordered them to learn the Indian languages. Nonetheless, in practice the missionaries usually concentrated on teaching Spanish whenever possible. They hoped that, within a generation, mission Indians would not only speak Spanish and act as Hispanics but also understand and practice Catholicism. At the same time, the mission Indians usually maintained economic and social relations with the Hispanic world around them, enhancing the likelihood that they would eventually join those neighboring communities (documents 5, 6, 7, 12a). As Bishop Tamaron also observed, "In trade and temporal business where profit is involved, the Indians and Spaniards of New Mexico understand one another completely" (document 5).

The Spanish Crown viewed the missions as temporary institutions whose role was to prepare Native Americans to become good Spanish subjects. From as early as the 1570s Spanish authorities had instituted a policy of secularization (transferring the missions to civil authority) once the friars completed the work of Hispanicizing the Indians (Weber 1992: 94–95). In the 1750s and 1760s missions were already being secularized in New Spain's northern regions. The secularization process in Texas began in 1793 after a period of decline and when Native Americans could no longer be persuaded to join the missions. At the same time, however, new mission establishments emerged in California that were not secularized until the 1830s. Secularization, then, varied from region to region, depending on government policies, interests of local officials, the socioeconomic realities of the communities and the missions, the level of cooperation among the Indians, and the interests of the missionaries themselves (document 8; Weber 1982: 50)

Often the missions became *pueblos,* and diocesan priests took the place of the friars in ministering to the former mission communities. In theory, the mission Indians were to receive individual land allotments and other assets in the secularization process; these material possessions would aid them in their transition to a new status as Hispanicized Catholics. In some cases this occurred and they maintained cohesive communities. However, in other cases the Indians simply lost everything in their former missions to unscrupulous officials or other Hispanic residents; subsequently many Indians moved into the Hispanic *pueblos,* usually occupying the bottom of a social structure that gave the advantage to Spanish and *mestizo* residents. However the mission Indians fared, the secularization process transformed their communities from corporate entities under the authority and protection of specific missionary orders to independent communities that became another element of Hispanic civil society. This was the final step in the incorporation of the Indians into the already long-established diocesan church (document 12b).

Parishes

Parishes also played a crucial role in establishing and maintaining Catholicism in the Spanish and *mestizo* population centers from Florida to California. The diocesan church, through its local parishes, provided for the spiritual welfare of Hispanic civilian and military settlers and their descendants, as well for some Indians who eventually joined these communities. Parishes first appeared with the establishment of formal civilian *municipios,* or chartered towns, and they grew as missions were secularized and became parishes. The parishes in frontier towns usually formed through the initiative of the local residents, often with encouragement but little financial support from Spanish authorities. Residents built the churches, and in time they hoped to obtain priests from the diocesan church.

In 1565, Pedro Ménendez de Avilés founded the town of San Agustín and the first parish in what is today the United States. Established to secure Spain's claims on La Florida and to protect Spanish shipping, San Agustín was also the center from which the missionizing efforts in the region were launched. At the same time, however, a parish church, Nuestra Señora de Soledad (Our Lady of Solitude), was founded to meet the needs of the Spanish settlers and was part of the Diocese of Cuba (Koch 98, 102–4). In the eighteenth century, the curate at San Agustín's parochial church of San Francisco administered the sacraments and oversaw the spiritual needs of the settlers. He was assisted by a sacristan, an organist, and later in the century by two altar boys. A chaplain served the chapel at the nearby fortress, Castillo San Marcos de Apalachee (TePaske 160–62). In 1763, at the end of the Seven Years War, Spain ceded the colony to England but regained it twenty years later at the end of the U.S. War of Independence. Florida remained a colony of Spain until the Adams-Onis Treaty of 1819, when the Spanish Crown ceded it to the United States.

Across the continent some fifty years after the founding of San Agustín, Juan de Oñate entered New Mexico and established the Villa de Santa Fe as the province's capital. As part of the founding of the town a modest chapel was built for the Hispanic settlers. By the 1620s, Fray Alonso Benavides, the head of the Franciscan missions in the region, had overseen the construction of a parish church and convent. After the reconquest of New Mexico beginning in 1692, San Francisco de Asís, an adobe church built between 1714 and 1721, served as Santa Fe's parish church (Cruz 29). Parishes were also established among the Hispanic settlers in Albuquerque, Santa Cruz, and subsequently in other communities, including Indian communities that were secularized.

In Texas, Spanish subjects from the Canary Islands founded the Villa de San Fernando in 1731 adjacent to an already established military garrison. At first they held religious services in a makeshift chapel, but in 1738 the Canary Islands settlers and the military families initiated the construction of a parish church (Matovina 1997a: 20–26). In 1759, the bishop of Guadalajara visited the town of Laredo, founded four years earlier, where he baptized children and confirmed over one hundred settlers. He later reported to the viceroy that the community had no priest and did not receive formal instruction in the faith. Finally, after persistent pleas from the settlers, a priest went to Laredo, though royal funds were not available for his support or the construction of a church. In 1769, the governor wrote Laredo's *alcalde* (mayor) that the residents should construct a church with their own funds; a report some twenty years later confirmed that the community did indeed have a church with a resident priest (Cruz 98–99).

As in Laredo and San Antonio the development of parishes in California also fell on the shoulders of the local communities. In 1802 settlers at San Jose, which had been founded in 1783, petitioned for permission to construct a chapel. From its foundation the community had relied on mission Santa Clara about three leagues away for their spiritual needs. When they received the required permission the 217 settlers immediately began work building their church. In 1804 an earthquake destroyed their newly completed chapel, but the community persisted and they rebuilt it, at one juncture receiving help from the military commander at Monterey, who sent individuals under judicial sanction to work for a month on the church building. Once the chapel was built, the settlers negotiated with the Franciscans at Mission Santa Clara for their spiritual services. Other California towns reveal similar stories. Los Angeles (founded in 1781) had the beginnings of a chapel by 1790, but, as in San Jose, finding a priest was difficult. The community looked to San Gabriel mission, some three and one-half leagues away, for a part-time priest (document 18; Cruz 124–25).

The late eighteenth century also saw the creation of Hispanic parishes in Louisiana and Florida, which would be incorporated into the United States well before the communities in Texas, New Mexico, Arizona, and California. In 1763, at the end of the Seven Years War, France ceded Louisiana to the Spanish, just as the Spanish ceded Florida to the British. The church in Louisiana initially fell under the jurisdiction of the bishop of Havana, but in 1793 the region, including Florida, became an independent diocese, the Diocese of Louisiana and the Two Floridas. The first bishop, Cuban-born Luis Peñalver y Cárdenas, arrived in 1795 (Din 1996: 97).

On taking control of Louisiana, the Spanish Crown hoped to Hispanicize the province by recruiting some two thousand Canary Islanders to settle there beginning in 1777. Though it turned out not to be an effective strategy for decisively influencing the region culturally, the Isleños that did arrive established their communities and practiced their religion. One group of Isleños founded the town of Valenzuela, on Bayou Lafourche, just southeast of Baton Rouge. While attending a nearby parish church, the Canary Islanders sought their own church and announced that they had adopted St. Bernard as their patron saint. In 1793, Valenzuela received its first priest and later attained the status of a parish, establishing a church called Asunción de Nuestra Señora de La Fourche de Chetimachas de Valenzuela, which Bishop Peñalver visited briefly in 1796 (Din 1988: 15–27, 64–65, 69–79).

Meanwhile, with the return of Florida to Spain in 1783, the Spanish government, encouraged by San Agustín's Hispanic and recently arrived Minorcan residents who had maintained their faith traditions, built a new church; the previous one had collapsed from neglect during the English occupation. The cornerstone was laid in 1793, the same year Bishop Peñalver of New Orleans became the spiritual leader of Florida and Louisiana, and the church was completed in 1797.

Parishes in Louisiana, Florida, and east Texas were the first Hispanic congregations who confronted the onslaught of North American culture and Protestantism. As early as 1795, Bishop Peñalver of New Orleans noted the danger to Catholicism's integrity in a city of Spanish and French residents whom he perceived to be unschooled in basic church teachings, rituals, and celebrations. He also warned his superiors about the dangers of Protestantism, which Anglo-American settlers and merchants had introduced, assuring his fellow Catholic leaders that "I am putting into operation human means to remedy these evils" (document 9). In 1803, with the Louisiana Purchase, the region's Hispanic Catholics became part of the United States. Nonetheless, the small Isleño community in Valenzuela continued its local traditions relatively undisturbed and maintains elements of its Hispanic Catholic identity to this day, though in isolation and without much possibility of a cultural expansion and reinvigoration (Din 1988: 75, 162). The Hispanic and Minorcan community in San Agustín experienced a similar situation after the transfer of Florida from Spain to the United States in 1819. Faced with considerable obstacles and little support from a predominantly Protestant civil community that arrived with North American sovereignty, the Hispanic and Minorcan residents appealed to the bishop of Havana for help to reconstruct their church (document 11; Quinn 91–100). Like Louisiana's Hispanic Catholics, those in San Agustín managed to maintain a sense of their religious and cultural traditions though in a context of overwhelming Anglo-American and Protestant influence and pressure for cultural assimilation.

Meanwhile, at the beginning of the nineteenth century, the diocesan church in New Mexico slowly displaced the Franciscan missionaries who had served in the region since the late sixteenth century. This was, of course, a natural and predictable course of events since the missions had always been viewed as temporary institutions dedicated to preparing the indigenous communities for parish life as Hispanic citizens. At the beginning of the New Mexican experience, the Franciscans not only operated the extensive mission system among the Pueblos, but also ministered to the Hispanic parish communities. It was not until 1798 that the Diocese of Durango, which encompassed New Mexico, finally introduced diocesan pastors to the region. In that year two secular priests took over the parishes of Santa Fe and Santa Cruz, but the presence of diocesan priests in New Mexico was sporadic due to conflicts with the Franciscans and other complications (Wright 1998: 225–26).

Beginning in 1816–1818, the Diocese of Durango finally established a permanent presence in New Mexico by once again staffing the parishes of Santa Fe, Albuquerque, and Santa Cruz. As the Franciscan numbers declined, the secular priests increased thanks to recruitment of local youth who went to seminary in Durango. Between 1823 and 1826, four Nuevomexicanos completed their training and returned home to begin their ministries; they were joined by another priest from Puebla (southeast of Mexico City). The diocesan presence continued to grow as the missions were secularized and local youth entered training for the priesthood. By the end of the 1840s, the Franciscans had all left or died and some seventeen or eighteen secular priests (mostly recruited locally) served the spiritual needs of New Mexico's parish communities. In the end, the church's viability in New Mexico depended on the communities themselves, especially their ability to recruit their youth into the priesthood (Wright 1998: 239–40).

Though New Mexico was the most successful of the Spanish and, later, Mexican northern borderlands territories in training priests for staffing the local churches, parishes across the region developed grassroots cultural ways and traditions that included a fervent Catholic religious expression. Communities drew on rituals, devotions, and celebrations that their ancestors initiated and fostered for generations. In 1755, for example, the residents of San Antonio pledged to celebrate annually the feasts of Our Lady of Guadalupe and other local patron saints, initiating a tradition of saint devotions that continues to the present (document 4). Good Friday services at Santa Fe in 1821 (document 10) further illuminate the rich and diverse religious life that Hispanic congregations established and maintained. These and countless other religious expressions that defined Hispanic Catholic identity within borderlands communities endured and represent the living legacy of Hispanic colonial foundations in what is now the United States.

1. First Encounters

Throughout the sixteenth and seventeenth centuries explorers authorized by the Spanish Crown, accompanied by Jesuits and Franciscan friars, traversed the regions from Florida to California. While the explorers sought mineral wealth, exploited and often enslaved the Indians, and established territorial claims for the Spanish king, the missionaries hoped to Christianize and Hispanicize the Indian peoples and convert them into productive Spanish subjects. Native Americans responded in multiple ways to the missionary zeal of the newcomers. Often the Indians demonstrated an initial friendliness, curiosity, and willingness to engage a cautious relationship. Just as frequently, however, and at different times, the native peoples developed a skepticism, distrust, and resentment of these aggressive people who carried a crucifix in one hand and a weapon in the other. The experiences of early encounters between Spaniards and Indians were diverse, but they all illuminate the joys and difficulties that confront people of radically different cultures and faiths.

1a. Texas, 1534

In 1528, Alvar Núñez Cabeza de Vaca (1490–1557) arrived on the coast of Florida near Tampa Bay with the Pánfilo de Narváez (1480?-1528) expedition. Composed of four hundred men, the expedition set out to conquer and settle these lands for Spain. Poorly led and ignorant of the land and its inhabitants, the explorers lost their way, and only a handful of them survived the harsh conditions. Although captured and initially enslaved by the Indians, Cabeza de Vaca and several companions completed an epic trek across what became the U.S. Southwest, eventually reaching New Spain in 1536. The Indians befriended them and helped them along the journey after the Spaniards began healing their captors (Weber 1992: 42–45). In the following passage, Cabeza de Vaca relates how in the region now known as Texas he and his companions used Christian symbolism to heal; he was convinced of God's desire to see them survive. These Spaniards were among the first to introduce some aspects of Christianity in the region.

The very night we arrived, some Indians came to Castillo telling him that their heads hurt a great deal; and begging him to cure them. After he made the sign of the cross on them and commended them to God, they immediately said that all their pain was gone. They went to their lodges and brought many prickly pears and a piece of venison, which we did not recognize. Since news of this spread among them, many other sick people came to him that night to be healed. Each one brought a piece of venison and we had so much we did not know where to put the meat. We thanked God heartily because his mercy and kindness grew every day. After the healings were finished, they began to dance and perform their *areítos* [dances and songs] and festivities until sunrise. The merrymaking caused by our arrival lasted three days....

The following morning many Indians gathered there, bringing five sick persons who were crippled and in a very poor condition, looking for Castillo to heal them. Each one of the sick persons offered his bow and arrows, which he accepted. At sunset he made the sign of the cross on them and commended them to God our Lord, and we all asked God as best we could, to restore their health, since He knew that was the only way for those people to help us, so that we might escape from such a miserable life. And God was so merciful that the following morning they all awakened well and healthy. They went away as strong as if they had never been sick. This caused great astonishment among them and caused us to thank our Lord heartily for showing us his kindness ever more fully and giving us the sure hope that He was going to free us and bring us to a place where we could serve Him. For myself I can say that I always had hope in his mercy and knew that He would bring me out of captivity, and I always said this to my companions.

Excerpt from Martin A. Favata and José B. Fernández, eds. and trans., *The Account: Alvar Núñez Cabeza de Vaca's Relación* (Houston: Arte Público Press — University of Houston, 1993), 77, 79. Reprinted with permission from the publisher.

1b. Florida, 1587

In September 1565, Pedro Menéndez de Avilés (1519–1574) founded San Agustín, the first permanent European settlement in what is today the continental United States. The following month he requested Jesuit missionaries to commence the project of converting the Indians to Christianity. By the next year a small band had arrived, many of whom quickly became martyrs. Discouraged with the difficulties, the Jesuits abandoned the Florida mission field in 1572 and were replaced by Franciscans, who initiated their evangelizing efforts in 1587 (Gannon 38). The following account by Fray Alonso Escobedo, a member of the 1587 group that began Franciscan work in the area, describes the journey of a subsequent group of Franciscans to Florida in 1595. This excerpt, from Escobedo's narrative, "La Florida," was probably written after he left Florida. It illustrates the sense of "divine mandate" they carried and suggests how "divine intervention" brought them safely to their destination so they could show the Indians "the light of eternal life for their own lives were full of errors and follies" (Gannon 38; Covington v–vi, 14, 21).

Thirteen apostolic friars sailed from the Holy Province of Castille to preach to the pagans of *La Florida.* . . .

Christ told his disciples, "Go forth and preach to all creatures the Ten Commandments of my Divine Law — a definite and sure chart of navigation through life. The grace of faith and the sacrament of baptism belong to the perfect and, to each one who is in the state of grace God promises his salvation but to the person who does not believe, eternal damnation when he dies" [paraphrase of Mark 16:15–16].

Thirteen Franciscan friars from Castile obeyed this divine mandate and went forth to propagate the Christian faith among the barbarous pagans. Silva, their leader, was able to stimulate a fine spirit of comradeship among his fellow Franciscans and even greater talents were disclosed when he was able to provide both food and spiritual guidance for his charges.

The Franciscan superior had made a wise decision when he appointed Silva to conduct the missionary band to America. He possessed evident skills of expression and education, but at the same time displayed charity and proper humility toward his fellow creatures. Although Silva was a native of an obscure village in Toledo, he was recognized for his capacity in leadership and was selected to command the expedition of the twelve other Franciscans in the voyage across the stormy and boundless sea. . . .

The thirteen friars embarked at Sanlucar for the New World and after traveling one month approached the coast of Puerto Rico. Suddenly the waves began to rise higher, the sky darkened, and it became apparent that a squall would strike the vessel. The captain, pilot, and crew became frightened and prepared themselves for any eventuality by confessing their sins and calling upon God with fervent hearts.

The strong winds buffeted the craft and it made slow headway against the heavy waves. When the storm was at its peak, the pilot cried out to the crew, "Let us all pray so that when we drown, we shall die praying." The frail boat, however, successfully withstood the heavy blows of the wind and water and the fury of the wind gradually diminished. When the travelers realized that their lives had been spared, they offered thanks to God — the goal of a rational soul — and were grateful to the friars for their prayers.

After leaving the storm the ship made good time but while approaching the flat Florida coastline, it ran aground and all the headway ceased. When the pilot found himself on the shoal which was two leagues in length he recognized the dangerous situation and cried, "Only in You, God, do I trust. Free our ship from the pounding waves. Only you, all powerful God, can help." With the tenseness showing in his face, for he knew that no one could swim ashore, he turned to the friars and requested their prayers, "Ask for assistance to the Son of Mary — for if He does not help us, our sepulcher will be the ocean."

Now, a wonderful event occurred which saved our vessel from destruction and allowed us to resume the voyage to San Agustín. While the friars were praying for aid, the vessel shifted its position and, drifting into deeper water, resumed the journey. When the ship had passed into the harbor of the port called San Agustín, everyone gave thanks to the Lord for having rescued them from disaster and allowing us to go free.

The thirteen Franciscans were warmly received in the Province of La Florida but, realizing the purpose of their trip, they did not tarry and, within the brief span of twenty days, they were living among the idolatrous and lost people who welcomed them. They recognized that these good men would show them the light of eternal life for their own lives were full of errors and follies.

> James W. Covington, ed., *Pirates, Indians, and Spaniards: Father Escobedo's "La Florida,"* trans. A. F. Falcones (St. Petersburg, Fla.: Great Outdoors Publishing, 1963), 18, 20–21. Printed by permission.

1c. New Mexico, 1630

At the end of April 1598, Juan de Oñate (1550?–1630) proclaimed Spanish dominion over the region of New Mexico, founding its capital, Santa Fe, in 1608. The Franciscans who accompanied Oñate immediately began building missions and attempting to Christianize the Indians. By 1629 they had already constructed some fifty churches and friaries when an additional contingent of Franciscans accelerated the missionization process (Weber 1992: 96). Among the Franciscans was Fray Alonso de Benavides (1578?–1635), the chief administrator of the New Mexican missions, who returned to Spain in 1630 and published a memorial on the successful conversions among the indigenous peoples of New Mexico. In the following account of Benavides's memorial of 1630, the friar describes his initial meeting with Navajo Apache caciques whom he set out to convert with the aid of already converted Indians.

I awaited him at the church, which on my instructions had been arranged nicely, with many lights burning because it was already night when they arrived. And as this nation is proud and spirited, I judged it better to receive this captain and those accompanying him in a manner different from that in which we received other nations, with whom, at the beginning, we sit on the ground, thus conforming ourselves to their simple ways until we can teach them better manners. But since the Apache nation is so haughty, I thought it better to deviate from this practice. So I ordered a chair placed on a rug close to the altar and, seated there, I received him.

All the people of the pueblo came along ahead of him, and among the Christian captains came the Apache captain with four other of his captains. As soon as they had entered the church and recited a prayer at the altar, the chief captain of the Christians came up to me and kissed my feet — a thing which did not much displease me, although I had not anticipated it — and the strangers, following his example, did in like manner. After greeting me, the chief said that those (our) captains had gone to offer him peace on my behalf and on behalf of their own captains; and to be more certain of this, he had come personally to investigate. Immediately the chief captain of the pueblo arose and offered his own bow and arrows to the Apache, saying that there, before God present on that altar and before me, His priest, he was giving him those weapons as a pledge of his word that he would never violate the peace; and so he placed them on the altar. In order that he (the Apache) might see that all were of like opinion, he (the chief captain) asked the people if they all agreed to what he had said. With a loud cry, they replied that they did. Then the Apache captain selected from his quiver the arrow he considered most suitable, made of white flint and very sharp; and in the presence of all he pronounced these words in a loud voice: "I do not know who this one is whom you call God, but since you invoke him as witness and assurance of your promise that you will not, under any condition, break your word, he must be a person of great power, authority and goodness. So to that God, whoever he may be, I also, with this arrow in the hands of this priest, give my word and promise in the name of all my people, that on my part and on the part of my people peace and friendship will never be lacking." Accepting the arrow from him, I said that if he wished me to tell him who God was, he would enjoy hearing me, and all the more so after pledging to Him his word. He told me that he would.

So in very few words and in his own manner, I explained who God was: the Creator and Lord of all created things, Who had died on the cross in order to redeem us from eternal sufferings. I demonstrated all this to him by means of the painting on the altar, and I told him that whoever did not adore Him and was not baptized would be condemned and go to burn in those eternal torments. Because the word of God is so efficacious, and because it touched his heart so deeply, he turned with great emotion toward all the people; heaving a deep sigh, he said to them in a very loud voice: "O Teoas, how I envy you! You have here one who teaches you who God is, and things so good; while we have no such one, but live and die, going about these fields and mountains like deer and jackrabbits. Herewith I declare that I adore this God of Whom this priest speaks; and now that I know Him, I offer peace and give my word that I shall maintain it with greater determination."

Tears flowing from his eyes, he fell upon his knees to kiss my feet. Whereupon I raised him up and embraced him with all the kindness I could, and then all the Christian captains also embraced him. I took this opportunity to have the bells rung and the trumpets and flageolets sounded — a thing which he enjoyed very much because it was the first time he had heard it. I immediately hung those arrows there on the altar as trophies of the divine word, even though it was announced by so humble a minister, and in this manner I declared it to the people of the pueblo so that they might render thanks to the divine Majesty for everything. Then the Christian captains took the guests away in order to lodge them in their homes, and I gave them what gifts I could.

Peter P. Forrestal, trans., Cyprian J. Lynch, annot., *Benavides' Memorial of 1630* (Washington, D.C.: Academy of American Franciscan History, 1954), 48–50. Reprinted courtesy of the Academy of American Franciscan History.

2. Testimony on Indian Rebellion in New Mexico, 1681

Spanish conquest and imposition of mission systems from Florida to California did not occur without resistance and violence. While many Indians conformed and agreed to live in the missions, in time, control, abuse, and loss of autonomy and tradition deepened Indian resentments that led to outright rebellion. New Mexico's Pueblo Indians exploded into open violence in 1680, driving the Spaniards and their loyal Indian subjects from the region. Calling upon traditional values, the insurgents especially turned their wrath on the church (Weber 1992: 134–37). The following document is an account of the New Mexico rebellion given under interrogation to Spanish officials on 19 December 1681. In this text, Pedro Naranjo of the Queres nation, a participant in the rebellion whom Spanish forces had captured, provides details about how the Indians organized and communicated their resistance (Weber 1999: 81–82). He describes the Catholic symbols upon which they focused their attack in an effort to purge themselves of everything Spanish. Furthermore, it describes their shaman, or spiritual organizer and leader, Popé, whose actions provided the divine sanction for their rebellion. Above all, this document allows the reader to sense the importance given to symbols in all aspects of the New World, as in various places and circumstances Spanish and Native American spiritualities coexisted, clashed, and overlapped. Despite the Pueblos' successes, the Spanish reconquered them beginning in 1692. Franciscan missionaries returned and resumed their efforts to convert the Indians throughout the eighteenth century.

In the said *plaza de armas* [military plaza] on the said day, month, and year, for the prosecution of the judicial proceedings of this case his lordship caused to appear before him an Indian prisoner named Pedro Naranjo, a native of the pueblo of San Felipe, of the Queres nation, who was captured in the advance and attack upon the pueblo of La Isleta. He makes himself understood very well in the Castilian language and speaks his mother tongue and the Tegua. He took the oath in due legal form in the name of God, our Lord, and a sign of the cross, under charge of which he promised to tell the truth concerning what he knows and as he might be questioned, and having understood the seriousness of the oath and so signified through the interpreters, he spoke as indicated by the contents of the *autos* [judicial decree].

Asked whether he knows the reason or motives which the Indians of this kingdom had for rebelling, forsaking the law of God and obedience to his Majesty, and committing such grave and atrocious crimes, and who were the leaders and principal movers, and by whom and how it was ordered; and why they burned the images, temples, crosses, rosaries, and things of divine worship, committing such atrocities as killing priests, Spaniards, women, and children, and the rest that he might know touching the question, he said that since the government of Señor General Hernando Ugarte y la Concha they have planned to rebel on various occasions through conspiracies of the Indian sorcerers, and that although in some pueblos the messages were accepted, in other parts they would not agree to it; and that it is true that during the government of the said Señor General seven or eight Indians were hanged for this same cause, whereupon the unrest subsided. Some time thereafter they (the conspirators) sent from the pueblo of Los Taos through the pueblos of the *custodia* [jurisdiction] two deerskins with some pictures on them signifying conspiracy after their manner, in order to convoke the people to a new rebellion, and the said deerskins passed to the province of Moqui, where they refused to accept them. The pact which they had been forming ceased for the time being, but they always kept in their hearts the desire to carry it out, so as to live as they are living today. Finally, in the past years, at the summons of an Indian named Popé who is said to have communication with the devil, it happened that in an *estufa* [hothouse or sweat room] of the pueblo of Los Taos there appeared to the said Popé three figures of Indians who never came out of the *estufa*. They gave the said Popé to understand that they were going underground to the lake of Copala. He saw these figures emit fire from all the extremities of their bodies, and that one of them was called Caudi, another Tilini, and the other Tleume; and these three beings spoke to the said Popé, who was in hiding from the secretary, Francisco Xavier, who wished to punish him as a sorcerer. They told him to make a cord of maguey fiber and tie some knots in it which would signify the number of days that they must wait before the rebellion. He said that the cord was passed through all the pueblos of the kingdom so that the ones which agreed to it (the rebellion) might untie one knot in sign of obedience, and by the other knots they would know the days which were lacking; and this was to be done on pain of death to those who refused to agree to it. As a sign of agreement and notice of having concurred in the treason and perfidy they were to send up smoke signals to that effect in each one of the pueblos singly. The said cord was taken from pueblo to pueblo by the swiftest youths under the penalty of death if they revealed the secret. Everything being thus arranged, two days before the time set for its execution, because his lordship had learned of it and had imprisoned two Indian accomplices from the pueblo of Tesuque, it was carried out prematurely that night, because it seemed to them that they were now discovered; and they killed religious, Spaniards, women, and children. This being done, it was proclaimed in all the pueblos that everyone in common should obey the commands of their father whom they did not know, which would be given through El Caydi or El Popé. This was heard by Alonso Catití, who came to the pueblo of this declarant to say that everyone must unite to go to the *villa* to kill the governor and the Spaniards who had remained with him, and that he who did not obey would, on their return, be beheaded; and in fear of this they agreed to it. Finally the Señor Governor and those who were with him escaped from the siege, and later this declarant saw that as soon as the Spaniards had left the kingdom an order came from the said Indian, Popé, in which he commanded all the Indians to break the lands and enlarge their cultivated fields, saying that now they were as they had been in ancient times, free from the labor they had performed for the religious and the Spaniards, who could not now be alive. He said that this is the legitimate cause and the reason they had for rebelling, because they had always desired to live as they had when they came out of the lake of Copala. Thus he replies to the question.

Asked for what reason they so blindly burned the images, temples, crosses, and other things of divine worship, he stated that the said Indian, Popé, came down in person, and with him El Saca and El Chato from the pueblo of Los Taos, and other captains and leaders and many people who were in his train, and he ordered in all the pueblos through which he passed that they instantly break up and burn the images of the holy Christ, the Virgin Mary and the other saints, the crosses, and everything pertaining to Christianity, and that they burn the temples, break up the bells, and separate from the wives whom God had given them in marriage and take those whom they desired. In order to take away their baptismal names, the water, and the holy oils, they were to plunge into the rivers and wash themselves with *amole*, which is a root native to the country, washing even their clothing, with the understanding that there would thus be taken from them the character of the holy sacraments. They did this, and also many other things which he does not recall, given to understand that this mandate had come from the Caydi and the other two who emitted fire from their extremities in the said *estufa* of Taos, and that they thereby returned to the state of their antiquity, as when they came from the lake of Copala; that this was the better life and the one they desired, because the God of the Spaniards was worth nothing and theirs was very strong, the Spaniard's God being rotten wood. These things were observed and obeyed by all except some who, moved by the zeal of Christians, opposed it, and such persons the said Popé caused to be killed immediately. He saw to it that they at once erected and rebuilt their houses of idolatry which they call *estufas*, and made very ugly masks in imitation of the devil in order to dance the dance of *Cacina* [a Pueblo Indian deity]; and he said likewise that the devil had given them to understand that living thus in accordance with the law of their ancestors, they would harvest a great deal of maize, many beans, a great abundance of cotton, calabashes, and very large watermelons and cantaloupes; and that they could erect their houses and enjoy abundant health and leisure. As he has said, the people were very much pleased, living at their ease in this life of their antiquity, which was the chief cause of their falling into such laxity. Following what has already been stated, in order to terrorize them further and cause them to observe the diabolical commands, there came to them a pronouncement from the three demons already described, and from El Popé, to the effect that he who might still keep in his heart a regard for the priests, the governor, and the Spaniards would be known from his unclean face and clothes, and would be punished. And he stated that the said four persons stopped at nothing to have their commands obeyed. Thus he replies to the question.

Asked what arrangements and plans they had made for the contingency of the Spaniards' return, he said that what he knows concerning the question is that they were always saying they would have to fight to the death, for they do not wish to live in any other way than they are living at present; and the demons in the *estufa* of Taos had given them to understand that as soon as the Spaniards began to move toward this kingdom they would warn them so that they might unite, and none of them would be caught. He having been questioned further and repeatedly touching the case, he said that he has nothing more to say except that they should be always on the alert, because the said Indians were continually planning to follow the Spaniards and fight with them by night, in order to drive off the horses and catch them afoot, although they might have to follow them for many leagues. What he has said is the truth, and what happened, on the word of a Christian who confesses his guilt. He said that he has come to the pueblos through fear to lead in idolatrous dances, in which he greatly fears in his heart that he may have offended God, and that now having been absolved and returned to the fold of the church, he has spoken the truth in everything he has been asked. His declaration being read to him, he affirmed and ratified all of it. He declared himself to be eighty years of age, and he signed it with his lordship and the interpreters and assisting witnesses, before me, the secretary. Antonio de Otermín (rubric); Pedro Naranjo; Nicolás Rodríguez Rey (rubric); Juan Lucero de Godoy (rubric); Juan Ruiz de Casares (rubric); Pedro de Leiva (rubric); Sebastían de Herrera (rubric); Juan de Noriega García (rubric); Luis de Granillo (rubric); Juan de Luna y Padilla (rubric). Before me, Francisco Xavier, secretary of government and war (rubric).

"Declaration of Pedro Naranjo of the Queres Nation (Place of the Río del Norte, December 19, 1681)," in Charles Wilson Hackett, ed., *Revolt of the Pueblo Indians of New Mexico and Otermín's Attempted Reconquest, 1680–1682*, trans. Charmion Clair Shelby (Albuquerque: University of New Mexico Press, 1970), 245–49. Printed by permission.

3. Report on Mission Collapse in Florida, 1707

During the seventeenth century, Franciscan missionary activity in Florida expanded considerably. By midcentury seventy friars ministered to some twenty-six thousand Indians in four mission provinces from the Atlantic coast across much of the Florida panhandle (Weber 1992: 100–105). These successes did not last into the eighteenth century, however. By 1706, the Florida mission system had

*collapsed in the face of Indian resistance and hostility, as well as English at-
tacks from their base at Charleston. In alliance with neighboring Indians, the
English raided the missions, often killed the friars, and enslaved the neophytes.
The following overview of missionary activities in Florida, written by Franciscan
missionaries in 1707, traces the demise of the mission system (Gannon 68–83).*

This province of Your Majesty in the spiritual realm has always, since the
beginning, been administered in its conversions and administrations by the religious of our seraphic religion, the first cultivators of this evangelic vineyard.
The first laborers that sowed the seeds of this church of Florida were the sons
of Our Seraphic Father San Francisco, who have continued with great labor,
[despite] obstacles, nakedness, hunger, and even the shedding of their blood
on occasion, sacrificing their lives in the apostolic employment of evangelic
preaching, without being intimidated by the tyranny and severity of the idolatrous enemies of the faith, and continuing their labors at the sight of hardships
and threats by which they were terrorized at the beginning of the conversions.
By the years [15]50 and [15]97, in the Province of Guale, one of the provinces
of this government, there had died at the hands of pagan Indians and some of
the recently converted who had forsaken the faith, in defense of the Catholic
religion, five missionary fathers and one lay brother. One other priest, son
of that Holy Province of Castile, escaped with his life by divine intervention,
although he suffered a prolonged martyrdom, since they had him for a slave,
stripped of his holy habit. He served them for about two years by carrying
wood and water to their pavilions [*bujios*], which are their community houses
where they have their meetings, dances, and feasts, and [he] attended [the Indian occupying] the seat near the fire, when they made their *cassina*, the usual
drink of the Indians, which they make from some leaves of a small tree that is
[placed] in a small vessel, roasted at a strong fire, and then boiled. This poor
professor and priest tended the fire and served the dais on his knees according
to the custom of the country, where he suffered intolerable hardships, which is
submitted to the exalted comprehension of Your Majesty. When Divine Providence was pleased to liberate him from heavy and continuous labor, full of
labors and years, he retired to that Province of Castile, where he finished his
life in one of its convents.

In the year [1]647 three other professed priests, missionaries in the Province of Apalachee, died a violent death at the hands of pagans and of some
recent converts who were incited to revolt against the Spaniards and Fathers
at the beginning of the conversion of the said province, although they shortly
returned to the faith. These [Christians] have prevailed, although nearly anni-
hilated by the many plagues and illnesses which have consumed them, and by
the continued incursions of the pagan Indians, their enemies, until, since the
year [1]702 and subsequently, the said province was destroyed from the continued persecution of the pagan enemies. Of the few that have remained in
the said province, some are refugees in the vicinity of this *presidio* [garrison];
these are the fewest; others [have gone] to the shelter of the *presidio* of Pen-
sacola, and others to that of Mobile, *presidio* of the Most Christian King, most

illustrious progenitor of Your Majesty. Still others, as is known, are settled in the vicinity of the pagan enemy, giving obedience to force and violence, until the Divine Majesty may be pleased to give them liberty. Many others of the said province, [as well as of] Timuqua [and] Guale, as has been learned from captives who have escaped from Carolina and villages of the pagan enemies, have surrendered and passed to the islands of the dominion of the Queen of England. In the year [1]696, the rebellious of the mission of [J]ororo took the life of a missionary priest, the minister of those villages, of which an account was given to Your Majesty. In the past invasion of the enemy in the year [1]702, the English of Carolina and the pagan Indians, their confederates, captured three missionaries, who for nearly three years had been in the power of the said English before they were restored to their liberty, where they suffered many penalties, some of them being obliged for their decent subsistence to accept menial service, according to their account.

With the continued incursions of the enemies in the said year of [1]702 and subsequently, [there furthermore] have suffered and died at the hands of the said enemies, the Fathers Fray Juan de Parga Araujo, and Fray Manuel de Mendoza, professors, priests, and evangelical ministers and apostolic missionaries, as has been related to Your Majesty by the Field Master General Don Joseph de Zuñiga y Zerda, formerly governor of this province. The first of the said priests was a son of the Holy Province of Santiago; the second, of the Province of Concepción in those kingdoms; and the last had participated in these conversions, administrations, and teachings [for] about twenty-six years, and the first nearly ten, having shown much zeal, the one as well as the other, in preaching and in teaching the Indians, and, during the invasion of the Province of Apalachee, in stimulating and encouraging the soldiers and Catholic Indians, marching with much bravery among them until he was killed by the enemy. Father Mendoza, encouraging and stimulating the Indians of the mission of his charge, was wounded by a shot, and was burned half alive within the *Conventico de Su C... taz.* We are hoping that because of their lives and professed conduct, both are enjoying the Divine Presence, as is also Fray Agustín Ponce de León, professed priest, native of this *presidio,* who, at the beginning of September [1]705, went in company with Captain Don Joseph Begambre, who was acting governor of this *presidio* by Your Majesty, with a group of infantry and Christian Indians with their arms, in pursuit of the enemy Indians that carried off as captives all the women with all their children and others of minor age of the village in charge of the said Fray Agustín Ponce. The said captain and his force having encountered the enemy at dawn on the 3rd of September, [Fray Agustín] fought with them until several shots made him surrender his soul to his creator, as the others of his force also did. Fighting with all bravery and effort, they defeated the enemy, although at the sacrifice of their lives; by this means he [thought he] might liberate the women and infants, except for a few who did not have the fortune to escape; and the said Fray Agustín, who went along to encourage the Spaniards and Indians of his force, seeking [the places] where the need to administer the sacrament of repentance to the wounded might exist, without exhibiting fear that they might kill him. As a good shepherd, he surrendered his soul in defense of his sheep and children of the mission in his charge because, although he lost his life in pursuit and redemption of his children, as a consequence of his admonitions he succeeded in the recovery of the greater part of them, even though he could not effect it for all.

Three other priests in the said year of [1]705, wandered in the forests, experiencing much hardship, need, want, hunger, and punishment, because they would not leave the sheep in their charge; they followed the poor Indians, their children, who wandered in the woods fleeing from the continuous incursions of the enemies wherever they went, until one of them, called Fray Domingo Criado, was captured. Nearly all the Indians of his village, who were settled in a wood on the banks of a rapid stream, a matter of ten or twelve leagues from this *presidio*, were killed; and [Fray Domingo was] carried off a captive. It is supposed by some captives who have escaped from the enemy [that], stripped of his holy habit, and experiencing much inhumanity and mockery, [he was carried] to their village, where in prolonged martyrdom he served the enemy Indians as their slave; at the end of some months he died, according to accounts from Christian Indians who have escaped from the said enemies and returned to this *presidio*, and who have given individual reports.

> "Summary of the Martyrdoms Experienced in Florida by the Franciscans: Letter of Franciscan Fathers to the King: San Agustín, May 7, 1707," in Mark Frederick Boyd, Hale G. Smith, and John W. Green, eds., *Here They Once Stood: The Tragic End of the Apalachee Missions* (Gainesville: University of Florida Press, 1951), 85–88. Reprinted with the permission of the University Press of Florida.

4. Pledge to Commemorate Local Patron Saints, San Antonio, 1755

Spanish subjects from the Canary Islands founded the villa *(town) of San Fernando in 1731 on a site adjacent to the* presidio *(garrison) of San Antonio. The new settlers joined with the military families already there to build a parish church, which they initially dedicated to Nuestra Señora de la Candelaria (Our Lady of Candlemas, the patroness of the Canary Islands) and Nuestra Señora de Guadalupe. Upon completion of the church in 1755, town council members vowed to annually celebrate with special solemnity the feast days of the patrons for their* villa *and parish church. In celebrating these patronal feasts local residents followed the Spanish custom of designating celestial companions deemed to have a particular relationship with a town or village (Matovina 1997a: 20–26).*

In the Name of the Holy Trinity, Father, Son, and Holy Spirit, three distinct persons and one true God, and of the Most Blessed Virgin Mary, Mother of God and Our Lady conceived without original sin.

Eucharistic Lord of heaven and earth, even though totally unworthy to appear before Your Divine Reverence, we, Captain don Toribio de Urrutia as magistrate and the municipal councilors named below, desire to continue the pious observances that in the Catholic Monarchy of New Spain have been sworn and vowed with joyful approbation and religious acclamations to celebrate annually the feast day of the Empress of Angels, Mary, Our Blessed Lady, with the name of Guadalupe. We recognize that this obligation is the responsibility of the residents of this Villa of San Fernando for [she is the] Universal Patroness of this New World under whose protection the roots of Our Holy Catholic Faith have spread and [by which] we live protected and free from the snares of our common enemy. By this name [of Guadalupe] we profess and name ourselves slaves of such a Holy Mother. Inasmuch as it is a proper obligation and just relationship that faithful slaves swear themselves to the great honor of their lady, we so pledge.

Captain don Toribio de Urrutia, magistrate, before God Almighty, and Jesus Christ, His Only Son, Our Eucharistic Lord, and the Most Serene Queen of Angels, Our Lady, and of all the Heavenly Court, and of the presently assembled faithful, all of whom we make witnesses of this our vow and oath, today, Friday, the twelfth of December of this year of 1755 in the parish church of the Villa of San Fernando. In the hands of our curate and vicar bachiller Don Juan Ignacio de Cárdenas y Ramos, placing our [hands] on the Holy Cross and over the Holy Gospel we promise, vow, and swear to God, Our Lord, that now and forever we shall celebrate the feast of Blessed Mary of Guadalupe. Thus, this *cabildo* [council] remains obligated to her annual rituals.

And, this Villa of San Fernando has for special patroness of its church, Blessed Mary, Our Lady, with the name of Candelaria under whose protection we have lived since the creation of the foundations of the church. Consequently, we ought to serve such a High Queen as our special patroness. As a result, desirous of her rituals, we make the same promise that we have made above. We who compose this town council vow, by ourselves and without obligation of the community, [to observe] her annual rituals.

And, since it is necessary to celebrate annually [the feast] of the patron of this villa [as it is customary in every place] and under whose wing everyone in this community lives protected, in the name of each and every one of us, the community remains obligated to what we have done at the hands of our curate and vicar. With the same ceremonies above of the Holy Cross and Sacred Gospel, we vow and promise to celebrate with the greatest Christian solemnity the feast of San Fernando, King of Spain, [who] by our good fortune we recognize as the patron of this villa and in whom we entrust his greatest increases in times of great prosperity in spiritual treasures and temporal relief.

We beg Our Lady, the Queen of Angels, and San Fernando and, what is more, Our Eucharistic Lord Jesus Christ to accept this our sacrifice as a gift that is worthy of His mercy, the most holy tranquillity of our Holy Faith. And to the Catholic Church prosperity in its monarchy. To our Catholic Monarch Fernando VI spiritual and temporal wealth. To all of those of this villa fervor, increase, and help from heaven in all of its spiritual and temporal adversities. So that thus safe from the snares of the infernal enemy, they will succeed in joining You in the mansions of heaven. Amen. Amen. Amen.

"Town Council of the Villa de San Fernando and Others: Statement on Feast Days, 12 December 1755," Nacogdoches Archives (typescript), 5:46a–46c, the Center for American History, University of Texas at Austin. Trans. Adán Benavides Jr. Printed by permission.

5. Bishop's Concerns about Language in New Mexico, 1760

From the time of their arrival in the Americas at the end of the fifteenth century, missionaries faced the issue of how to evangelize across the cultural divide of language. Many friars became talented linguists and produced catechisms and confessionals in native tongues, but the large number of Indian languages made this difficult, and relatively few missionaries learned indigenous languages. As a practical matter, the missionaries concentrated on teaching in Spanish since this was viewed as a central feature of their ultimate goal of Hispanicizing the Indians (Weber 1992: 109–10). In 1760, Bishop Pedro Tamaron y Romeral (1695?–1768), sixteenth bishop of Durango, made a pastoral visit to New Mexico, the most northern and remote region within his jurisdiction. In his report of the visit, Tamaron dedicated a great deal of space to the problem of language. He believed that evangelization among the Indians was superficial and that their grasp of the Spanish language was not sufficient to understand the fundamental doctrines of the church. In his visit to the town of Pecos, New Mexico, he lamented the inhibiting effect of language barriers on the spiritual growth of Native Americans.

A Franciscan missionary parish priest resides in this Indian pueblo. It is eight leagues from Santa Fe to the southeast. There are 168 families, with 344 persons, and 192 persons were confirmed.

Here the failure of the Indians to confess except at the point of death is more noticeable, because they do not know the Spanish language and the missionaries do not know those of the Indians. They have one or two interpreters in each pueblo, with whose aid the missionaries manage to confess them when they are in danger of dying. And although they recite some of the Christian doctrine in Spanish, since they do not understand the language, they might as well not know it.

This point saddened and upset me more in that kingdom than in any other, and I felt scruples about confirming adults. I remonstrated vehemently with the Father Custos and the missionaries, who tried to excuse themselves by claiming that they could not learn those languages. In my writs of visitation I ordered them to learn them, and I repeatedly urged them to apply themselves to this and to formulate catechisms and guides to confession, of which I would pay the printing costs. I asked the Father Custos to give me a report about this in writing, and he gave me the one contained in a paragraph of a letter dated November 7, 1761, which reads as follows:

Father Fray Tomás Murciano has worked hard on the formulation of an aid to confession in the native language, but so far he has had no success because the interpreters have confused him so greatly by the variety of terms in which they express things that he assured me that he had found no road to follow. And I told him to write it all down and learn it, and then to try to observe with great care the ordinary manner of speaking among them, and that in this way he would succeed. Nevertheless, in many pueblos this year it did come about that a number of people made their confessions, and I am in no way relaxing my efforts in this regard, and, for my part, I am doing all I can. Perhaps it may be God's will that there will be success.

It is a shame that most of those Indians lack the benefit of confession. I take little satisfaction in these confessions through an interpreter when the latter is an Indian or a Negro. I had experience of this when I was a parish priest in Caracas with the Negroes brought there under the English contract [slave trade]. Many died soon after they arrived. I made repeated experiments with those of their own nation who had been in the land for some time. Although we granted confession, I never felt reassurance when this means was used. And I attempted to accomplish something in New Mexico by using interpreters, and their version is nothing but confusion on the subject of catechism and confession. In trade and temporal business where profit is involved, the Indians and Spaniards of New Mexico understand one another completely. In such matters they are knowing and avaricious. This does not extend to the spiritual realm, with regard to which they display great tepidity and indifference.

Eleanor B. Adams, ed., *Bishop Tamaron's Visitation of New Mexico, 1760* (Albuquerque: University of New Mexico Press, 1954), 48–53. Printed by permission.

6. Inauguration of the Church at Mission Santa Clara, California, 1784

The last of the mission enterprises in Spain's northern territories was in California. In 1769, the viceroy of New Spain, José de Gálvez (1720–1787), dispatched Captain Gaspar de Portolá (1723–1784) and Franciscan Fray Junípero Serra (1713–1784) to begin the settlement of Alta California. Over the next six decades, the Franciscans established twenty-one missions from San Diego to Sonoma (north of San Francisco), with over twenty-one thousand Indian residents. With an Indian population of some three hundred thousand the most densely populated region in North America, California proved a fertile ground for the establishment of a prosperous mission system (Weber 1992: 258–65). Just months before his death in August 1784, Serra participated in the inauguration of the church at Mission Santa Clara, near present-day San José. The following description of the inauguration ceremony highlights the architectural substance of the mission buildings, the importance of procedure and ritual, and the interdependence of church and military in the efforts to Christianize and Hispanicize the Indian peoples of the region.

On the fifth Sunday after Easter, consecrated (throughout the whole Seraphic Order) to the Declaration of the Patriarchal Basilica and Papal Chapel of the

Hill of Paradise, in Assisi, in which the sacred body of our Seraphic Father St. Francis rests upright, there was held and celebrated in this Mission of the Seraphic Mother St. Clare, the dedication and inauguration of the new church. The record of its beginning and cornerstone is given on page 59 of this book. The church walls are one vara and a half thick, of adobe, on stone foundations, supported by buttresses one vara thicker. Its dimensions inside are eight vara high, forty and one-half long, and nine vara wide. The sacristy, which is in the rear of the chancel, has the same height and thickness of walls as the church; its length is equal to the width of the church, and its width is six vara. A portico measuring five vara extends, as regards the roof, along the entire length of the building. In the church and the sacristy there is a flat ceiling of wooden beams on brackets with a planking of the wood of *alerche,* commonly called redwood. Above this flat ceiling there is a pavement of adobe flags, and above all there is a slanting roof well adapted for drainage. The brackets extend beyond the walls as also the thatch of the roof, to protect the walls from the rains, which are very abundant. The main door and the cloister door, or side door, each having two leaves, are made of cedar and redwood, respectively, and each is provided with a lock. The two doors of the sacristy are of the same material (redwood), each having one leaf, and provided with locks. The church is whitewashed inside and outside. The walls inside are painted with a border above and below. The entire chancel and a great part of the ceiling are also painted. The whole floor is a pavement of adobe flags.

We began first Vespers of the feast on Saturday, May 15, 1784. The celebrant, vested in alb, stole, and cope, was the Rev. Fr. President of the Missions, Fr. Junípero Serra, assisted by the Fr. Francisco Palóu and Fr. Thomás de la Peña, the former the Minister of the Mission of our Holy Father St. Francis, and the latter of this Mission of Santa Clara. Fr. de la Peña was alone, as Fr. Jos. Antonio de Murguía, the principal builder of this beautiful church, had died four days before (Benedictus Deus!). Everything being prepared for the function, and acolytes bearing the cross, candles, and other things necessary, the key of the church was handed to Don Pedro Fages, Lieutenant-Colonel of the Royal Army and Military and Civil Governor of both Californias, as patron of the ceremony, an office which he gladly accepted. With him was Lieutenant-Commandant of the Royal Presidio of St. Francis, Don Joseph Joaquín Moraga. All arranged in order, we proceeded to the main door of the church, which was locked, and we began the blessing of the church. Everything was conducted according to the prescriptions of the Roman Ritual. The celebration was carried on amid the ringing of bells, salutes from the muskets of the soldiers, and with the fireworks of the Mission.

The celebration was concluded in the evening with a solemn *Te Deum* [a religious chant of praise for God's wondrous deeds]. On the following day, which was the said Sunday, the 16th, of the said month, the dedicated church was inaugurated with the Holy Sacrifice of the Mass. The said Rev. Fr. President sang the Mass, during which he preached a stirring sermon, exhorting the people to give glory to God for their new church. At the close of the

Mass, and as a fitting ending to the festival, he administered the Sacrament of Confirmation with all possible solemnity. In order that all may be recorded for the greater glory of God, this account has been written in this book and we all, who have attended and helped this celebration, affix our signatures.

(*Signed*)

Don Pedro Fages

Fr. Francisco Palóu

Fr. Junípero Serra

Fr. Thomás de la Peña

Don Joseph Moraga

"The Most Beautiful Church," in Arthur Dunning Spearman, ed., *The Five Franciscan Churches of Mission Santa Clara, 1777–1825* (Palo Alto, Calif.: National Press, 1963), 34–36.

7. Guidelines for a Texas Mission, 1786–1787

The permanent settlement of Texas by the Spanish began with the founding of four missions among the Hasinai Confederacy of east Texas in 1716. To bolster the missions and facilitate their resupply, the Spanish established a mission and presidio (garrison) on the San Antonio River two years later. By 1731, three of the east Texas missions had relocated to the San Antonio River, increasing the number of missions along the river to five and making the missions, presidio, and a civilian settlement (see document 4) the heart of the Spanish presence in Texas (Chipman 113–17, 132–33). Despite conflicts between Hispanic settlers and independent Indians in the central Texas region, the mission communities thrived for several decades. As the following document reveals, Indians were Hispanicized and learned to worship in the Spanish Catholic way, but they also practiced their own traditions even if at times they had to do so secretly. Missionaries knew of the neophytes' continuing attraction to their traditional ways and had to determine when and under what circumstances to allow them to practice their customs. The collections of guidelines are quite extensive, but the following selections focus on holiday practices, socializing neophyte children, and advising the friars regarding when to allow neophytes to practice their traditional dances and games.

To hold divine services during Holy Week is left up to the judgment of the missionaries. It is always good to have them to further the devotion of the people and to forestall other activities. When Holy Week services are held, the superintendent is delegated to appoint twelve men who are to act as the twelve Apostles at the washing of the feet. On Holy Thursday toward evening, the procession takes place and the statue of Jesus of Nazareth, bearing the cross, and the statue of Our Lady of Sorrows are carried on a portable stand. On their shoulders, the Indians carry crosses that have been preserved for this occasion. At night, the missionary preaches on the mysteries of the day or the Passion. While the procession is in progress, the rosary is recited, and the missionary leads the choir. On Good Friday, the procession again takes place, carrying an image of Jesus despoiled of his garments and tied to a pillar, the holy burial, and the Virgin clothed in black. During this, the Way of the Cross is prayed. As soon as the procession enters the church, the services continue and end with a sermon on the Passion, unless the Descent from the Cross is conducted [see document 10]. While the Most Blessed Sacrament is in the tabernacle, two men with weapons are to be in the sanctuary as sentinels, and two more at the door of the church. The fiscal has the care of relieving them during the day and night until the services of Holy Saturday begin....

On Christmas Eve, the Indians do the dance of the *matachines* and go on dancing at the entrance of the friary as long as the missionary allows it. He generally gives them a drink of wine if there is enough on hand. On Christmas Day, they go and dance at the *presidio,* at the governor's house, and other places. In some missions, they wear outfits in keeping with the spirit of the feast. When these are not available, they use the women's scarves and shifts. This dance is regularly performed also in the procession of Corpus Christi instead of using the giant figures [as were used for similar processions in Spain].

On the afternoon of the principal festivity of the mission, it is customary to permit them to put a bull in the Mission Plaza, and they amuse themselves with him; and it all goes off with a lot of running and shouting.

The men find their diversion in games such as *patolo y chueca* and, though sometimes these games are permitted, the missionary must not permit residents of the *presidio* or of another mission to play these games with the Indians, because they are so taken up with the game that they would forfeit their blankets, their clothing, and whatever they may have. This is quite common in the mission, and the Indians try to hide from the missionary while playing them. The women are different, because they do not gamble away their clothing very readily, but they do their beads. The game called *palillo* is permitted them even with the women of other missions but not with the women from the *presidio.* They are not permitted to play *chueca* even with their own group, because this game is like that of *pelota.* It is not becoming for them to run and exercise in the manner the game demands, especially the infirm, for this kind of diversion intensifies their infirmity. For this reason, the missionary is solicitous to banish such abuse from the mission.

Regarding the lawfulness of the dance called the *mitote* performed by the Indians, whatever one can say about it, this much is certain, that they consider it evil, and therefore they hide it from the missionary. The Indians have their superstitious practices, and for them this dance is like the *fandangos* and *soirées* among the Spaniards. Therefore, the missionary must be alert to prevent wrongdoing in the mission. Still, it is my conviction that when no superstition, no question of celebrating an enemy's death or any sinful motive is present, then the *mitote* is not unlawful when done for mere diversion, because among the Indians it is the same as the *fandango* among the Spaniards....

In the past, the missionaries have kept the boys in the [missionaries'] cell, inviting them when they have grown up a little, not only to have them work, as has been said, nor employ them personally, but to educate them, civilize them, and make them genuinely human. Therefore, they always live in the friary, eat from the missionary's kitchen, and sleep in his cell, not having to go to their homes except for breakfast, to be washed and deloused. Growing up within the friary is a very laudable custom, because otherwise they generally end up wild, rebellious, and vicious, since they lack instruction by the missionaries and the communication and dealing with them, which is to their benefit. The missionary takes care that they learn the catechism, are taught to serve Mass, to subdue their bad inclinations, correcting what is bad and showing them what is good. As soon as they are able to work in the field, he sends them there. They return to eat and sleep in the cell of the missionary until they marry or have grown and are no longer children. They then may go home and are counted as bachelors.

The missionary should see to it also that the small children speak Spanish in order to meet the demands of various decrees and because of the facility it promotes both for the missionary to understand what they are saying and for the Indians to understand him. At this mission, the missionary has worked so hard on this that it is a pleasure to listen to the Indian children, even the tiniest ones, speaking Spanish. In general, the men and women speak it now, except some who have remained untamed, for the missionary spares no effort in helping them understand the language.

Benedict Leutenegger, trans. and annot., *Guidelines for a Texas Mission: Instructions for the Missionary of Mission Concepción in San Antonio, Texas,* rev. Carmelita Casso and Margaret Rose Warburton, Documentary Series no. 1 (San Antonio: Old Spanish Missions Historical Research Library at Our Lady of the Lake University, 1976), 2–3, 35–38, 42–43. Printed by permission.

8. A Franciscan View on Secularizing Missions in San Antonio, 1792

The friars had always understood their missions to be temporary institutions, no longer necessary once the Indian populations had been Christianized and Hispanicized (Poyo and Hinojosa 64–83). Generally, the secularization of the missions proceeded according to local conditions and circumstances. The growth of Hispanic communities in the vicinity of the missions and competition for land and resources by settlers led to political intrigue and pressure for secularization. As mission Indians entered the cultural world of their Hispanic neighbors, they established social and economic relationships with surrounding communities. In time, marriage, work, and other life activities integrated these diverse peoples into unified though socially stratified mestizo (mixed-blood) towns (Poyo and Hinojosa). By the end of the Spanish period in 1821 the missions in Texas, New Mexico, and what later became Arizona were well on their way to extinction, and during the next decade they disappeared as functional institutions. In the following 1792 report on the San Antonio missions, Father José Francisco López (1699?-1788), president of the Texas missions, argued that the goal of Christianizing the Indians had been completed and that the time

*had arrived to secularize Mission San Antonio de Valerio and place the other
missions in the vicinity under the administration of civil authorities. The following year Mission San Antonio de Valero was secularized; the secularization of
other local missions was complete by 1824.*

Report of Father President, José Francisco López, to Reverend Father
Guardian and the Venerable Board of Counselors of the College of Our
Lady of Guadalupe of Zacatecas, on the Mission in His care.

Since the main purpose of the apostolic institute and its only goal, as
proposed by the Sacred Congregation for the erection of the Colleges of
the Propagation of the Faith, which our Sovereign in his Catholic zeal has
founded in North America, is the conversion of the infidels by establishing
new settlements and making new conquests, there is no doubt that it is very
foreign to our sacred ministry and contrary to the mind of the Holy Pon-
tiff and opposed to the will of our Catholic Monarch that the missionaries of
the Propagation of the Faith, whose maintenance and transportation to this
province are a source of expense to the royal treasury, be drawn away from
this vast pagan field to other projects and objectives, which are not exactly
the conversion of Indians and the spiritual nourishing of the new converts.
Once they have been firmly grounded in faith and have passed the stage when
they are judged to be neophytes, they are to be consigned in conformity with
our sacred Bulls to their respective Ordinary, so that they be incorporated
into the fold of his diocese, and shepherds be assigned for them, who will be
pastors and teachers and will preserve and strengthen them every day in the
faith they received from the missionaries or first instructors. They will be able
then, freed from the care of souls, which is now the task of the new pastors, to
devote themselves to making new conversions, which is the only reason why
they left the monastery.

In view of this high purpose and to satisfy the obligations of my conscience, I bring to the consideration of your Reverences several facts. This
Mission of San Antonio de Valero, which I administer, offers no proximate
and founded hopes that in the future new gentiles will congregate, so that
missionary activity could be exercised; nor can it be said truthfully that the
faith will be spread among the few individuals in the mission, for they are
so instructed in the Christian dogmas and gospel teaching, in the obedience
due our Mother Church and the commandments of the Supreme Shepherd,
in the respect due to priests and missionaries, and in just submission to our
Sovereign and his royal courts and officials, that they are not now, nor can
they be called neophytes, or even Indians, since most of them, being children
of marriages between Indians and white women, are mulattoes or half-breeds,
as can be seen in the census list, sent to the viceroy by the Lord Conde de la
Sierra Gorda, interim governor of this province, and by me to the Guardian
Father of the Apostolic College. It can therefore be inferred that this mission
cannot be called a mission of Indians but a gathering of white people. The few
pure Indians who remain are, in trading and communication, as intelligent as

the others. Consequently, the College ought to disassociate itself and give the mission over to the bishop so that he takes care of their souls.

The first point I make is obvious from the fact that in the sixty and more leagues surrounding these missions of Béjar there is no nation of pagan Indians which can be converted. Those who are at a greater distance to the east, north, and south cannot be taken out of their land without violence to their nature, without offending the laws of humanity, the pontifical regulations, and repeated decrees of his Majesty, nor has it been possible for the missionaries to win them over by favors and kindness, so that they freely leave their lands and congregate in one of the missions. At different times from 1703 till the present year of 1792 various and costly experiments have been made in vain toward this end.

Secondly, it is evidently true, shown not only by the long time of eighty-nine years since the mission of San Antonio was founded, but felt also in the trade and communication with those Indians, that although they have not given up entirely the traits that are proper to and inseparable from their natural low way of living and their fickleness, they nevertheless are seen to be more civilized and cultured than many other Indians and pueblos in lands beyond.

Finally, the experience of so many years has taught us that the best fruit we can promise ourselves for the future of these Indians will be only to preserve in them the faith and Christianity they have received, just as it is preserved in the other Christian pueblos by the help and preaching of their pastors. But no apostolic increase in spreading the faith can be made among them, and yet this is the proper and special office of the missionaries, to which alone our efforts ought to be directed.

In carrying out this resolution, which Your Reverences will judge always to be fitting and in conformity with the decisions of higher government, it does not appear that any difficulty will arise, either from the Indians (they have tried again to free themselves from the economic management of the missionary and, because of this, or because of other motives, the General Commandant had drawn up in 1780 a plan, which had no results, by which the care of these souls would come under the Ordinary), or from the Ordinary, since the Mission of San Antonio is so close to the *presidio* [garrison] and Villa of San Fernando, divided only by the river, that the pastor of the Spaniards can take charge also of the spiritual care of the Indians....

The most zealous, prudent, and holy missionaries, who have been in these Indies from the beginning of the conquest up to this day, as we know from history and as can be seen in the abundant fruit obtained by their evangelical preaching in all the converted pueblos, thought undoubtedly that they fulfilled their task of preaching and exercised their apostolic zeal by instructing the Indians in the Catholic religion, by teaching them to live as Christians, as obedient sons of the holy Church and true subjects of our Sovereign. The true charity, which impelled them to win so many souls, did not influence them to draw the Indians from their natural place of abode, to help them in their bodily miseries, to lift them up from their humble dejection, and to throw on their shoulders the duty of protecting and defending these helpless men, except in so far as these duties were conducive to the teaching and instruction by which they tried to educate them. And when, through the goodness of God our Lord we can say that in these four missions [in the San Antonio area] of which we speak our missionaries have now done all the duties imposed by the apostolic institute, having all the Indians in their care (except a few who have come recently) well instructed and nourished in Christianity, and in all that is required by necessity and precept to reach salvation if they want to be saved.

Benedict Leutenegger and Marion A. Habig, trans. and annots., "Report on the San Antonio Mission in 1792," *Southwestern Historical Quarterly* 77 (April 1974): 489–91, 495. Reprinted courtesy of the Texas State Historical Association. All rights reserved.

9. Report on Catholic Life in New Orleans, 1795

Established in 1793, the Diocese of Louisiana and the Two Floridas included a mix of people and religions that the first bishop of the diocese, Cuban-born Luis Ignacio Maria de Peñalver y Cardenas (1749–1810), had to contend with upon his arrival in 1795. Peñalver y Cardenas's 1795 report to his superiors reveals the influence of Louisiana's political turmoil, socioeconomic situation, and cultural milieu on the region's religious life at the end of the eighteenth century. This report pointed out the "corrupting" influence of Protestantism, but also spoke of the general malaise that existed in New Orleans regarding religious worship and practice. The bishop and other clergy continually reminded the population, including members of the elite and cabildo (city council), of their obligations to the church and their God, but often with little effect. In fact, when Father Antonio de Sedella (1748–1824), commissary of the Holy Office of the Inquisition for Louisiana, was about to invoke his power as inquisitor, he was arrested by the governor and sent to Spain. Apparently, the inquisitor's activities interfered with the governor's policies of encouraging Protestant immigration into Louisiana to increase economic development and strengthen the Crown's claim on the region (Din 1996: 98–99).

Since my arrival in this town, on the 17th of July, I have been studying with the keenest attention the character of its inhabitants, in order to regulate by ecclesiastical government in accordance with the information which I may obtain on this important subject.

On the 2nd of August, I began the discharge of my pastoral functions. I took possession without any difficulty of all the buildings appertaining to the church, and examined all the books, accounts, and other matters thereto relating. But as to re-establishing the purity of religion, and reforming the manners of the people, which are the chief objects El Tridentino [the Tridentine reforms] has in view, I have encountered many obstacles.

The inhabitants do not listen to, or if they do, they disregard, all exhortations to maintain in its orthodoxy the Catholic faith, and to preserve the innocence of life. But without ceasing to pray the Father of all mercies to send his light into the darkness which surrounds these people, I am putting into operation human means to remedy these evils, and I will submit to your

Excellency those which I deem conducive to the interests of religion and of the state.

Because his Majesty tolerates here the Protestants, for sound reasons of state, the bad Christians, who are in large numbers in this colony, think that they are authorized to live without any religion at all. Many adults die without having received the sacrament of communion. Out of the eleven thousand souls composing this parish, hardly three to four hundred comply with the precept of partaking at least once a year of the Lord's supper. Of the regiment of Louisiana, there are not above thirty, including officers and soldiers, who have discharged this sacred duty for the last three years. No more than about the fourth part of the population of the town ever attends Mass, and on Sundays only, and on those great holydays which require it imperiously. To do so on the other holydays they consider as a superfluous act of devotion to which they are not bound. Most of the married and unmarried men live in a state of concubinage, and there are fathers who procure courtesans for the use of their sons, whom they thus intentionally prevent from getting lawful wives. The marriage contract is one which, from a universal custom, admitting only a few accidental exceptions, is never entered into among the slaves. Fasting on Fridays, in Lent, and during *vigilas y temporas* (vigils of feasts and ember days), is a thing unknown; and there are other mal-practices which denote the little of religion existing here among the inhabitants, and which demonstrate that there remains in their bosoms but a slight spark of the faith instilled into them at the baptismal font.

I presume that a large portion of these people are vassals of the king, because they live in his domain, and accept his favors. But I must speak the truth. His Majesty possesses their bodies and not their souls. Rebellion is in their hearts, and their minds are imbued with the maxims of democracy; and had they not for their chief so active and energetic a man as the present governor, there would long since have been an eruption of the pent-up volcano; and should another less sagacious chief ever forget the fermenting elements which are at work under ground, there can be no doubt but that there would be an explosion.

Their houses are full of books written against religion and the state. They are permitted to read them with impunity and, at the dinner table, they make use of the most shameful, lascivious, and sacrilegious songs.

This melancholy sketch of the religious and moral customs and condition of the flock that has fallen to my lot, will make you understand the cause of whatever act of scandal may suddenly break out which, however, I shall strive to prevent; and the better to do so, I have used and am still using some means, which I intend as remedies, and which I am going to communicate to your Excellency.

The Spanish school, which has been established here at the expense of the Crown, is kept as it ought to be; but as there are others which are French, and of which one alone is opened by authority and with the regular license, and as I was ignorant of the faith professed by the teachers and of their morality,

I have prescribed for them such regulations as are in conformity with the provisions of our legislation.

Excellent results are obtained from the convent of the Ursulines, in which a good many girls are educated; but their inclinations are so decidedly French, that they have even refused to admit among them Spanish women who wished to become nuns, so long as these applicants should remain ignorant of the French idiom, and they have shed many tears on account of their being obliged to read their spiritual exercises in Spanish books, and to comply with the other duties of their community in the manner prescribed to them.

This is the nursery of those future matrons who will inculcate on their children the principles which they here imbibe. The education which they receive in this institution is the cause of their being less vicious than the other sex. As to what the boys are taught in the Spanish school, it is soon forgotten. Should their education be continued in a college, they would be confirmed in their religious principles, in the good habits given to them, and in their loyalty as faithful vassals to the Crown. But they leave the school when still very young, and return to the houses of their parents mostly situated in the country, where they hear neither the name of God nor of King, but daily witness the corrupt morals of their parents.

John Tracy Ellis, ed., *Documents of American Catholic History, 1493–1865*
(Wilmington, Del.: Michael Glazier, 1987), 1:177–79. Printed by permission.

10. Good Friday Service in Santa Fe, New Mexico, 1821

One of the annual rituals at the parish church, San Francisco de Asís, in Santa Fe was the Sermón de la Soledad (Sermon of Solitude), a Good Friday afternoon or evening service in which devotees removed Jesus' body from the cross, placed it in the arms of his grieving mother, and then accompanied the corpse through the streets in a solemn procession. The church sanctuary served as the hill of Calvary for this occasion, with the statue of Our Lady of Solitude placed prominently to depict Mary at the foot of the cross. As the following sermon of Franciscan Fray Manuel Antonio García del Valle (1784?–1834) reveals, two other priests played the roles of Nicodemus and Joseph of Arimathea. They removed the following instruments of the passion from the cross and presented them to the Marian image: Pilate's inscription, the crown of thorns, three nails, and Jesus' body. García del Valle's sermon is typical of his era in its treatment of God's justice and mercy and in its anti-Semitic polemic. When the sermon ended with the words "I have finished," the preacher became the stage manager for the brief passion ritual which followed (Steele 19–21).

"One of the soldiers opened his side with his lance, and immediately there came forth blood and water" (John 19:34).

What recollections, my fellow Christians, these words of my text introduce into our minds! Jesus suffering and hanging dead on the tree of the cross! Let us travel by meditation and contemplation to Golgotha, also called Mount Calvary. What do our eyes see in this sad, ill-fated, and mournful place? From every direction come the cries, laments, and voices of sorrow. Here the blood, tears, and cruel sorrows of the best Son, the compassion of one of the Marys, the finest of them, the fury of enemies, scribes and Pharisees, the lamentations of a few pious women, the consternation of the disciples, the blasphemies and insults....

Should we not be surprised at these prodigies of love and mercy which Christ demonstrated in that final hour, ending his race while consummating his charity toward sinners? The nearer he came to the end of his life, the more his heart softened; it breathed only mercy.

And indeed, what were his final words immediately before he gave his spirit into the hands of his eternal Father? He begged pardon for his tormentors; he granted with a few words of solemn promise to the good thief who asked him...in his kingdom, acknowledging his divinity: "'Remember me when you come into your kingdom,' — 'Amen I say to you that you will be with me in paradise.'" He left those sinners as a legacy to his own mother, the person he loved most in this world: "Behold your mother. Behold your son." He showed that he still desired to suffer further as a remedy for the wretched children of Eve.

Are not all of these convincing proofs of his charity, love, and mercy toward those children of the disobedient Adam? In this manner, dear people, God loved the world. He did not hesitate to give his only-begotten true Son as Mediator, even though on him would fall all the fury of the divine wrath, for God saw him laden and overcome under the burden of the many sins of so many others. "God so loved them that (he gave) his (only-begotten) Son etc."

See if, in effect, in this most sorrowful death of my divine Master Jesus there is not found both the Eternal Father's vengeance against sin, which he vindicates in the person of his Son, and this most patient Nazarene's clemency on behalf of mankind. I have finished.

[At this point, the preacher turned to the cross with the life-size figure of Christ hanging upon it and to the bulto of *Nuestra Señora de la Soledad* (Our Lady of Solitude) standing nearby, beginning a text for the deposition from the cross during which the two other priests present, don Francisco Ignacio Madariaga and fray Francisco Hozio, took the parts of Joseph of Arimathea and Nicodemus and removed the various *Arma Christi* — the weapons of Christ, the implements of the passion which he allowed to be used against himself — and placed them one by one onto the cloth hanging over Mary's arms. García continues from the pulpit:]

There remains for me only to say some words to you, most afflicted Lady Mother and Virgin Immaculate, the creature most full of grace but at the same time the fullest of torment and sorrow. Your greatest distress is to see that divine body of your Son hanging on that cross and have neither a way to take him down, nor a shroud to wrap him with, nor a grave to lay him in. Oh what anguish! Oh what conflicts surround you on all sides!

But Divine Queen, Mother of Sinners, behold! I present you these faithful ministers of the sanctuary so that with your permission their sacred hands will place into your hands those instruments which have served in their way as your ransom. [Fray Manuel speaks here to the two priests:] Do not tarry. Quickly ascend those steps. Tear down that inscription, the cause or publication against our adorable Master which nailed to this tree the insolent and sacrilegious ignorance of the venomous scribes. [Then when they have brought it and placed it on the cloth lying over Mary's outstretched arms, he again speaks to *Nuestra Señora:*] Lady, that is the inscription which, in spite of the resistance of the rebellious people, nevertheless announces by a high and particular providence that he who died on this cross is the true and rightful Lord of this rebellious Hebrew people: "Jesus of Nazareth, King of the Jews." The fearful President Pilate, unaware of the cause of the movement of his heart, has given the most authoritative testimony of the deicide and regicide the treacherous Pharisees and leaders of this people have perpetrated. [The two priests remove the crown of thorns:]

This crown, woven of marine reeds, is the one that the executioners, to deride your most patient Jesus with mockery, placed on the sacred head of the King of kings, the Lord of lords. I said incorrectly "Sorrowing Virgin." We ourselves accomplished it by our disordered, vain, proud, and presumptuous thoughts — we, yes, we are the cause why these thorns penetrated the skull, hair, brain, and forehead of that countenance which the angels desire to look upon. [They tie the arms to the crossbar with pieces of cloth to support the body, then they remove the three nails:]

Those nails — which one day will be the fastening either of eternal salvation or, for impious men, of eternal condemnation — have pierced these holy hands which worked miracles by the thousands, offended those feet which traveled so readily to bestow graces, benefits, and spectacular miracles not only upon feeble and perishing bodies but also and even more to bestow benefits upon souls oppressed either with afflictions or with culpable ignorance and the disgrace of refusing to know their proper duties. [Finally the two priests remove the body of Jesus and hold it above the outstretched arms of the Lady of Solitude:]

And finally, my Mother and Lady, Co-Redemptrix of the human race as Father Saint Bernard titled you, ready yourself to receive the stroke of the sword, more cruel for your pure, chaste, living, and all-suffering heart. Take in your arms the lifeless body of the best of all the sons of all mothers. Give him the final embrace of farewell, for this is the final chance to touch with your adorable hands the humanity of that most holy body. [Now at this point, the preacher speaks in the person of the Lady of Solitude, expressing, as best he can, her feelings at this poignant moment of her life:]

Oh dead life! Oh obscured light! Oh defaced beauty! And what hands were they that have done so to your divine form? What crown is this that my eyes see on your head? What other wound do I see in your side? Oh High Priest of the world! Who has disfigured the mirror and beauty of heaven? Who has disfigured the countenance of all graces? Are these the eyes that blinded the sun with their beauty? Are these the hands that raised to life the dead they touched? Is this the mouth from whence the four rivers of paradise flowed? Have human hands such power against God? My Son and my blood, whence rose this powerful storm? What kind of day has this been that you should be taken from me? My Son, what shall I do without you? Where shall I go? Who will care for me? Fathers and brothers came in their affliction to beg for their dead sons and brothers, and you with your infinite virtue and clemency consoled and assisted them. But I who see my Son and my Father, my Brother and my Lord lying in death — whom can I implore to help him? Who will console me? Where is the good Jesus the Nazarene, Son of the living God, that he might console the living and grant life to the dead? Where is that great Prophet, powerful in works and words?

My Son, formerly you were my repose, and now you are the sword of my sorrow. What have you done that the Jews [*sic*] should crucify you? What need was there to kill you? Is this the reward for your many good works? Is this the payment for so much teaching? Has the world's wickedness come to this? Has the devil's malice come to this? Have God's goodness and clemency come to this? Does God have such a great abhorrence for sin? Was it so necessary to make satisfaction for sin? Is such the severity of the divine justice? Does God set so high a value on the salvation of the human race?

Oh sweetest Son of mine, what shall I do without you? You were my Son, my Father, my Spouse, my Master, and my only companion. Today I am left like an orphan without a parent, a widow without a husband; I am alone without such a teacher or so dear a companion. From now on I shall never again see you come through the door, tired from your teaching and your preaching of the Gospel. Never again shall I wipe away the sweat from your face, sunburnt and tired from walking and working. Never again shall I see you eating at my table while I feed my soul with your divine presence.

My glory is now dead. Today my happiness has ended and my solitude begins. [Mary's apostrophe ends, and the preacher resumes in his own person:]

Do not continue further, Mother most sweet. Allow the venerable ministers of the Lord of Hosts to exhibit that mutilated body of my Master and Savior to this people. [At this point the two priests carry the body to the front of the sanctuary, turn it so it faces the congregation, and hold it up in full view of the people.] Now seeing it, they will see what our disorders, our trespasses, and the wickedness of our sins have come to. [And he speaks to all the people:]

Sinners, here you have before your eyes the fruit you have pursued with your sins etc. [Next, the body is placed in an open latticework coffin which some pallbearers raise to their shoulders, a funeral cortege forms, and the congregation files out of the church, walks in procession through some nearby streets, and returns to the church for a brief burial ritual.]

"Good Friday Sermon Preached in the Parish Church of the Villa de Santa Fe in the Province of New Mexico, 20 April 1821," in Thomas J.Steele, ed. and trans., *New Mexican Spanish Religious Oratory, 1800–1900* (Albuquerque: University of New Mexico Press, 1997), 23, 33–39. Printed by permission.

11. Plea to the Bishop of Havana for Support, St. Augustine, 1836

*After the incorporation of Florida into the United States with the Adams-Onis
Treaty of 1819, the Hispanic Catholics who remained struggled to maintain their
religious identity in the face of arriving Protestants with political power and
superior economic resources. During the English occupation of Florida (1763–
1783), Minorcan settlers who had relocated in New Smyrna, Florida, to work
as laborers on English plantations maintained their Catholic traditions and, in
1769, sought to establish a formal and recognized parish under the oversight of
the Diocese of Cuba. Three years after the Minorcans formed the St. Peter parish
community word arrived from Havana that the Spanish Crown had authorized
their endeavor. In 1777 this parish community moved to San Agustín (which
was deemed "St. Augustine" after U.S. occupation) and was there to receive
the new Spanish governor, who arrived to take possession from the British in
1783 (Quinn 55–60). The following document reveals that St. Augustine's Hispanic parishioners continued to seek solace and support from Spain and Cuba
during difficult times in the life of their parish more than a decade after U.S. occupation. Though it is not clear that this letter ever reached Havana, it did reflect
a continuing Catholic Hispanic identity among these former Spanish citizens.*

Your Excellency, the Bishop of Havana

The undersigned residents and Catholic parishioners of the parish church
of Saint Augustine, East Florida, for themselves and in the name of their fellow members, with the most humble and profound respect, appear and say
to Your Excellency: That being full of love and zeal for the Apostolic Roman
Catholic Religion that they profess and considering their obligation to protect
and sustain that divine faith with the proper and necessary decency, they find
themselves urgently impelled to bring to Your Excellency's attention that the
church and other property of this parish are rapidly approaching total ruin,
hoping thereby to call Your Excellency's most magnanimous attention to the
indigent state of this parish and consequently to the lack of means or funds for
its repair. This circumstance recalls to them the justness and care with which
the divine faith was conducted in this city under the protection of the government of His Catholic Majesty. As true Spanish Catholics or, for the most
part, their descendants, they now cannot but see the baneful fate to which our
religion is exposed unless effective measures are undertaken for the complete
repair, adornment, and preservation that this sanctuary so desperately needs.

Your Excellency must surely know that the system of the United States is to
permit and tolerate all faiths. In this city there are various Protestant denominations whose churches are kept in the best and most proper condition and
whose adherents strive to make converts. Our Catholic youth are rapidly increasing, and would it not be painful if, their fathers having failed them, they
should turn to those churches, because the practice of their own holy religion
was not available to them? This unfortunate consequence, Your Excellency,
must surely result from the great poverty in which we find ourselves.

Since this unhappy population was ceded to the United States, we have
experienced nothing but mishaps and misfortunes. The severe and, in this climate, unheard-of freezes of last winter utterly destroyed our luxuriant orange

trees, whose fruit was the only means many of us had, besides our own labor, to support and educate our families with some comfort. Our church has
shared in this general misfortune, for she has suffered an annual loss of some
four hundred pesos, whose sum was almost the only income she had available
to attend to her indispensable ministries and to liquidate, in part, the debts she
had contracted for the repair of two houses in her possession.

And as the culmination of our unhappiness and ruin, we presently find
ourselves under arms night and day, protecting our lives and homes against the
savage Indians that have risen *en masse* against the government, burning and
committing all kinds of attacks, plunderings, and murders in the countryside
and even in the vicinity of this city, because of which the inhabitants have
seen fit to abandon their estates to the fury of the savages and to save their
lives by taking refuge in the towns.

These last two calamities have put an end to our hopes for future remedy. Consequently we find ourselves, in our critical and indigent situation,
compelled to seek, with all humility and respect, the protection of Your Excellency in order that, by means of your benevolent intercession and guidance,
our brothers in religion of that diocese be asked to make a pecuniary, charitable contribution in order that our church building be properly repaired and
decorated. Our parish priest, Don Claudio Rampón, the bearer of this petition, has voluntarily offered to collect it, for which he has all power and
authority to that effect.

Permit us, your Excellency being satisfied and hopeful of the success of our
humble and reverent petition, to pray to the Supreme Being to preserve Your
Excellency's life for many years to come.

St. Augustine, Florida
16 January 1836
(followed by 76 signatures)

> Jane Quinn, *Minorcans in Florida: Their History and Heritage* (St. Augustine:
> Mission Press, 1975), 105–7.

12. Accounts of Mission Life in California, 1820s–1840s

*After Mexico's independence from Spain in 1821, mission life in California
continued to be vibrant. Unlike their brethren in Texas and New Mexico, the
Franciscans in California still saw a need for their services, a perspective influenced in part by the prosperity of the missions. At the same time, because
the missions controlled so much land and resources, government leaders and
Californio (California Hispanic) ranchers saw them as obstacles to the general
economic development of the territory. Some years of debate about the missions culminated in an 1834 decision to secularize the missions and appoint a
government administrator to oversee their dismantling. Taking advantage of the
situation, the overseers often confiscated lands, cattle, and other resources that
by right belonged to the Indians. The initial plan of converting the missions into
pueblos where the Indians would go on living as independent citizens quickly
faded before a rush by Californios to appropriate the resources. In most cases*

the Indians left the missions altogether and moved to Hispanic settlements,
joined independent Indian communities, or worked for ranchers in the surround-
ing areas (Weber 1982: 60–68). The following accounts describe mission life
during the final decades before the North American occupation of California.

12a. Eulalia Pérez

A native of Loreto, Baja California, Eulalia Pérez moved to San Diego around
1800 with her husband, who was assigned to the presidio (garrison) and then
as a guard at Mission San Gabriel (near Los Angeles). After her husband's death,
Pérez lived at the mission with her son and five daughters; there she became
the head housekeeper (llavera), a leadership position in the mission community
that grew increasingly significant as the number of friars decreased. Her duties
included overseeing supplies and their distribution, as well as supervising Indian
workers in their varied domestic tasks. She dictated her memoir in 1877, when,
it is estimated, she was 104 years old (Sánchez, Pita, and Reyes 32).

The priests then held a meeting at which they agreed to place me in charge of
the keys to the mission. If memory serves me, this took place in 1821 because
I remember that my daughter María Rosario was seven years old. She was very
ill at the time, and Father José Sánchez ministered to her with such devotion
that we had the joy of witnessing her recovery. By then, I was already the
mistress of the keys.

The mistress of the keys was responsible for a variety of duties. Primarily
her charge consisted of the daily distribution of rations from the kitchen. To
achieve this, she had to count the number of "nuns" [single women], single
men, field hands, cowboys who rode with saddles, and those who rode bare
back. Furthermore, she was responsible for doling out rations to the married
couples. In a word, it was her duty to distribute rations for the Indians as well
as for the missionaries' kitchen.

She also kept the key to the clothing storehouse from where cloth was
distributed for making dresses for the single and married women as well as
the children. In addition she supervised the cutting of cloth for the men's
clothing.

She also supervised the cutting and sewing of the full dress and other accouterments for the cowboys who rode saddle. Those who rode bare back
received only their calico cloth, their blanket, and their loincloth. Saddle riders dressed like the Spanish-speaking residents. They received a shirt, vest,
jacket, pants, hat, herding boots, a rope, and shoes and spurs. For their horses
they got a saddle, bridle, and, in addition, each cowboy got a large silk or cotton handkerchief as well as a waist band made of wool or silk or whatever else
could be found in the storehouse.

Under my supervision, my daughters did everything having to do with
clothing. I cut and arranged the cloth and my five daughters sewed the garments. When they were unable to keep up, I would inform the priest who
would then hire and pay women from the town of Los Angeles.

I was also in charge of the soap factory, which was very large, and of the grape and olive farms as well as supervising the mashing of grapes and pressing of olives. Olives were pressed for their oil, a task at which I personally worked. Under my supervision and responsibility, Domingo Romero oversaw the fermentation process. Luis, the soap maker, was in charge of the soap factory, but I ran everything.

I oversaw the distribution of hides, leather strips, chamois, bandannas, strips of morocco leather, canvas cloth, tacks, fine cloth, silk, etc. — everything having to do with the manufacture of saddles, shoes, and all the supplies needed in a leather workshop for the making of shoes and sword belts.

Once a week I would distribute rations to the workforce and to the regular Spanish-speaking servants, consisting of beans, corn, chickpeas, lentils, candles, soap, and lard. An Indian named Lucio, who was trusted by the priests, helped me with this.

When necessary, one or the other of my daughters would lend a hand when I was unable to keep up. Usually the one who was always at my side and went everywhere with me was my daughter María Rosario.

After all my daughters married, Rita being the last, it was around 1832 or 1833, Father Sánchez became insistent that I marry a Spaniard — First Lieutenant Juan Mariné. He was a Catalán who had served in the artillery and was a widower with children. I didn't want to marry, but Father explained that Mariné was an excellent person, which indeed he did turn out to be, and that, besides, he had money — a fortune, although he never allowed me to take charge of the cash-box. I finally gave in to Father's wishes because it was impossible for me to deny him anything. Father Sánchez had been father and mother to me and to my entire family....

At Mission San Gabriel there was a very large number of neophytes. Those who were married lived in their camps [rancherias] while their children were small.

The unmarried neophytes were divided into two groups, one for the women, called a cloister or nunnery, and another for the young men.

Little girls from ages seven, eight, and nine were brought to the cloister for rearing, after which they left to go marry. In the cloister they were under the care of an Indian nun, whose name was Polonia; they called her "Mother Abbess."

The young men's apartment was under the charge of the mayor.

Every night the gates to both apartments were locked and the keys were turned over to me and I would then turn them over to the priests.

There was a blind Indian by the name of Andresillo who stood at the door of the cloister and called roll. Each girl entered the cloister as Andresillo called her name. If any girl turned up missing at roll call, she would be sought after on the following day, brought back to the cloister, and, if the girl had a mother, she too would be brought there and punished for having detained her daughter. The girl would then be locked up for her part in not showing up on time.

First thing in the morning, the girls were taken to Father Zalvidea's Mass. Fr. Zalvidea spoke the Indian language. After Mass they were then taken to the kitchen for breakfast that sometimes consisted of corn gruel (or of cornmeal and chocolate porridge). On festive days there were also sweets and bread, and on ordinary days there was hominy stew. After breakfast each girl was directed to their assigned duties whether it was weaving, unloading, sewing, or whatever their charge might be.

At eleven o'clock in the morning, those in charge of unloading were responsible for readying one or two wagons to distribute refreshments to the Indians who worked the fields. The drink was a mixture of water, vinegar, and sugar. Other times it was lemonade. I was in charge of preparing and sending the refreshments. The priests explained that the measure was intended to keep the Indians from dehydrating.

All work stopped at 11:00 a.m. and at twelve everyone came to the kitchen for their hominy stew with meat and vegetables. At 1:00 p.m. they returned to their labors. Work ended at sundown, at which time the Indians came to the kitchen for their supper consisting of meat and cornmeal porridge, or sometimes of just plain corn gruel.

Each Indian man and woman would bring his or her own bowl, which was then filled by an attendant.

The Indian cowboys and the others who were married and whose work was distant ate in their homes. In general, most of the Indians came to the kitchen.

Those Indians who showed promise were taught particular skills, while the others were taken to work either in the fields, to herd and guard the horses or the stock, etc. Still others drove wagons, oxherds, etc.

Wool horse blankets, serapes, and regular blankets were manufactured at the mission.

Saddles, bridles, boots, shoes, and other like items were also manufactured at the mission. There was a soap factory as well as a large and a small carpentry shop. In the latter, beginners were apprenticed before they were transferred to the larger.

Wine, olive oil, brick, and adobe were also made.

Chocolate was made from imported cocoa.

Candy was also manufactured. Much of it, personally made by me, was even sent to Spain by Father Sánchez.

Each workshop was led by an Indian artisan who had been previously educated and properly trained. There had been a white person in charge of the textile factory, but he left once the Indians had been satisfactorily trained.

My daughters and I personally made all the chocolate, olive oil, candy, lemonades, and other such things. I made huge amounts of lemonade, some of which was bottled and sent to Spain.

The Indians were also instructed in prayer. The brighter ones were taught to read and write. Father Zaldivea taught the Indians to pray in their own language. Several Indians learned music and played instruments and sang at Mass.

The sextons and pages that helped with the Mass were Indians from the mission.

Punishment consisted of the pillory, solitary confinement, or, when an offense was serious enough, the culprit was taken to the guardhouse where he was tied to a post or a cannon and flogged twenty to twenty-five times or more, depending on the crime. Sometimes a culprit was placed in the pillory, other times a musket was passed from one leg to the other and fastened, and they also tied their hands. That punishment was called the "Penalty of Bayonne" and it was extremely harsh.

Nevertheless, Father Sánchez and Zaldivea were always very considerate with the Indians. I would not want to say what others did because they did not live at the mission.

> "Eulalia Pérez: Una vieja y sus recuerdos," in Rosaura Sánchez, Beatrice Pita,
> and Bárbara Reyes, eds., *Nineteenth Century Californio Testimonials* (San Diego:
> Crítica Monograph Series, UCSD Ethnic Studies/Third World Studies, 1994),
> 36–39. Trans. Dora Elizondo Guerra. Printed by permission.

12b. Julio César

Born at Mission San Luís Rey (near San Diego), Julio César resided at the mission for many years. He later moved to Tres Pinos, in San Benito County, where at the age of fifty-four he dictated his recollections of life at San Luís Rey.

I am a pure-blooded Indian, born at San Luís Rey in the year 1824. At that time, as I have been informed, Padre Ventura was minister; but when I took service in the mission I was about fourteen years old, and the minister then was Padre Francisco. I do not recollect his surname, but the Indians called him "Tequedeuma," an Indian word which signified that the padre was very sympathetic and considerate toward the Indians; in fact, he was very loving and good.

When I first entered the mission to take service, they employed me to sing in the choir for the sung Masses. The administrator of the mission was Don Pío Pico. When he left, soon after I entered, for I never served under Señor Pico, the administrator was Don José Antonio Estudillo, who was followed by Don José Joaquín Ortega, who in his turn was succeeded by Don Juan María Marron.

When I began to serve there were still a great many Indians at the mission and it was very rich. At that time it had the following ranchos:

Ranchos San Mateo, cattle, and Las Flores, cattle. At the last named, there was a sort of little Indian town, with a small chapel where the *padre* said Mass for the Indians every week. *Rancho* Santa Margarita, which had a large orchard, immense fields of wheat, corn, and other grain, besides cattle; San Juan, cattle *rancho;* Pala, which had a large orchard, the same as Santa Margarita, besides a corner set off for planting beans and corn. In this *rancho* there was a large number of Indians, who had their chapel, where the *padre* came to officiate every week. Temécula, wheat corn, etc., besides cattle. This *rancho* also had a large body of Indians, with their chapel, where the *padre* came once a month. San Jacinto, cattle; San Marcos, sheep; Pamuza, sheep; Potrero, the present Indian town. Wild Indians lived there, and although the *rancho* belonged to the mission the latter made no use of it. Agua Hedionda was a sheep *rancho*, as was Buena Vista.

When Don Pío Pico left the administration of San Luís Rey he bought Santa Margarita *Rancho*, paying for it with the same cattle which he had appropriated from the mission. I believe he gave 500 head of cattle for that *rancho*. After buying Santa Margarita he took two more *ranchos* — San Mateo and Las Flores. Don José Antonio Estudillo, when he ceased to be administrator, took a *rancho*, San Jacinto, with cattle and everything, and it was no longer known as belonging to the Indians.

Don José Joaquín Ortega, during his administration, appropriated to himself nearly all the mission cattle, but did not take any of its land. It was said that Señor Ortega left the mission stripped bare, making an end of everything, even to the plates and cups. I was not at the mission when Señor Marron entered as administrator, but I heard that he found scarcely any furniture in the house and that in the storehouses there was nothing at all.

When Señor Ortega was administrator I was a good-sized boy and worked in the fields, serving as his stirrup boy. I went everywhere with him, except when there was a sung Mass, when I had to go and sing. For my services I received no pay but my food and clothing. I was taught music at the mission by an Indian teacher called Domingo.

The system which had been observed by the father ministers was continued by Señor Pico. There was a nunnery for the single girls and a department for the bachelors. The first was in the charge of a matron called Bernardina. I was in the department of bachelors during the administration of Pico. The same regime continued under Estudillo and Ortega. During the administration of Marron the Indians were living outside the mission.

When I was a boy the treatment given to the Indians at the mission was not (at) all good. They did not pay us anything, but merely gave us our food and a breechcloth and blanket, the last renewed every year, besides flogging for any fault, however slight. We were at the mercy of the administrator, who ordered us to be flogged whenever and however he took a notion. Pío Pico and those who followed him were despots, and in addition Señor Pico required us to carry our hats in our hands whenever we met him as long as we remained in sight.

To the question whether we were taught to read and write, I reply that we were only taught to pray and recite the Mass from memory. They did not teach me to read the church music. There were singers and instrumentalists, but everything was from memory. I never saw them give a paper with the music written on it to anyone. I recall hearing it said that at Alisal there was a school for teaching Indian children to read and write, and that two children were taken there from each mission; but that was before I was born. In my time it was not done.

When Padre Peyrí left Calfornia, he took two boys from San Luís Rey to Rome. One of them, named Diego, returned to California and I saw him at the pueblo of San José, where he died. The other, whose name I do not remember, rose to the point of singing the Mass. I heard it said that after he was ordained he came to Mexico and died there.

During the time of the missions, neophytes were prohibited from riding horseback; the only ones permitted to do this were the *alcaldes* [mayors], *corporales* [soldiers], and *vaqueros* [cowboys].

At the time of Padre Francisco's sudden death I found myself in San Diego, working in the *Barraca* [warehouse], in the old one — I took care of sending hides on the boat of Don José Antonio Aguirre. Señor Estudillo sent on that ship a string of mules of perhaps more than one hundred for the other bank/side (*banda*). Also the mules and lambs that I brought from San Luis Rey were loaded on.

When I returned to that mission Padre Francisco was already buried, and the minister in charge was Padre José María Zalvidea, who had been there with the *padre* for some time, having come here from San Juan Capistrano Mission to take Padre Francisco's place.

When Señor Marron took charge of the mission nearly all the cattle had disappeared. The Indians no longer served the mission, although some of them were there. Afterwards, in the time of the Americans, what was left of the cattle was (divided) among the Indians at Pala, but nothing came to me because I had left in 1849 for the gold placers in the north, and never returned to San Luís Rey Mission.

Julio César, "Recollections of My Youth at San Luís Rey Mission," trans. Nellie Van de Grift Sánchez, in Edward D. Castillo, ed. and trans., *Spanish Borderlands Sourcebook: Native American Perspectives on the Hispanic Colonization of Alta California* (New York: Garland, 1991), 13–15. Printed by permission.

Above: nineteenth-century sketch of Our Lady of Angels, the parish church in Los Angeles's "La Placita" (document 18), by noted western artist William Henry Jackson; below: photograph of the same parish church nearly a century and a half later. Courtesy National Park Service, Scott's Bluff National Monument and Cecilia González-Andrieu.

Part 2

ENDURING COMMUNITIES OF FAITH IN THE SOUTHWEST

A todo el mundo Luz nueva,	To all the world new Light,
¿adonde, cielos hallaré	but where, oh heaven, will I find
ese Mesías prometido?	the Messiah who has been promised to us?
Pues el camino he perdido	I have lost my way
me hallo en la breña —	and find myself in the wilderness,
¿que haré?	what will I do?
¿A quien le preguntaré	Who can I ask where the road is
por donde sale el camino para Belén?	to take me to Bethlehem?
Astros, sol, luna, y estrellas	Planets and sun, moon and stars,
muéstrenme sus luces bellas	show me your wondrous lights
para que pueda con ellas	that by their splendor I may find
hallar mi Redentor.	the way to my Redeemer.
Pues ya no tengo temor.	I am no longer fearful.
Porque me dejo admirado.	I am full of awe.
Una harmonía que ha sonado	A melodious harmony
por las regiones del viento	drifts through the wind
me saca de este cuidado.	and makes me unafraid.

Shepherd's speech from Los Pastores (see document 13). Trans. Cecilia González-Andrieu.

Introduction

The conquest of northern Mexico began with the war between Texas and Mexico (1835–1836), which resulted in the establishment of an independent Texas republic. Nine years later the United States annexed Texas and provoked another war by building Fort Brown (present-day Brownsville, Texas) in disputed territory across the Rio Grande from Matamoros. The war between the United States and Mexico (1846–1848) resulted in Mexico's loss of nearly half its territory: the present-day states of Texas, Nevada, California, Utah, and parts of New Mexico, Arizona, Colorado, and Wyoming. In 1848, the Treaty of Guadalupe Hidalgo brought an official end to this war and, in addition to establishing new borders between the two nations, purportedly guaranteed the citizenship, property, and religious rights of Mexican citizens who chose to remain in the conquered territories (Griswold del Castillo 1990). Six years later the Gadsden Purchase, or, as Mexicans call it, the Tratado de Mesilla (Treaty of Mesilla), completed the U.S. takeover of former Mexican territories. With

45

the threat of another U.S. invasion as the backdrop for negotiations, James Gadsden "purchased" the southern sections of present-day Arizona and New Mexico for $10 million. This land acquisition enabled U.S. entrepreneurs to expropriate the profits from this region's rich mine deposits and establish a route for expanding rail transportation networks (Acuña 84–86).

Anglo-American newcomers to the vast region from Texas to California frequently depicted the Spanish-speaking Catholics they encountered as superstitious and ignorant of their faith, culturally depraved, economically backward, and politically corrupt. Drawing on the "Black Legend" of anti-Spanish racist stereotypes inherited from England, as well as an intense disdain for any form of racial mixture, Anglo Americans went so far as to label Mexicans "an imbecile, pusillanimous race" and even "scarce more than apes" (Weber 1979). Some newcomers attempted to justify the U.S. conquest of what is now the Southwest with the claim that Anglo-American pioneers redeemed morally and intellectually impoverished Spanish-speaking communities. In an 1851 work, for example, Francis Baylies applauded the Franciscans who worked in the missions of San Antonio during the eighteenth century, although he incorrectly identified them as Jesuits. He then added:

> After the expulsion of the Jesuits [*sic*], everything went to decay. Agriculture, learning, the mechanic arts, shared the common fate; and when the banners of the United States were unfurled in these distant and desolate places, the descendants of the noble and chivalric Castilians had sunk to the level, perhaps beneath it, of the aboriginal savages; but it is to be hoped that the advent of the Saxo-Norman race may brighten, in some degree, the faded splendor of the race which has fallen. (11)

Significantly, in this passage Baylies implicitly divided the history of the Southwest into three major eras: the "golden age" of the missions, Mexican debauchery, and Anglo-American redemption. Like many of his Anglo-American contemporaries, Baylies acclaimed the work of the Spanish missionaries who lived among the Native Americans in northern New Spain. But he also contended that the eventual secularization and decline of the missions resulted in a spiritual void accompanied by the decay of economic, political, and social life. This depiction of Mexican debauchery allowed him to then claim that U.S. westward expansion redeemed culturally and spiritually desolate peoples and territories.

Besides providing a convenient rationale for conquest, the contention that the northern Mexican borderlands were culturally and spiritually desolate at the time of U.S. occupation ignores communities which endured a tumultuous period of political, economic, social, and ecclesial change during U.S. territorial expansion (Hinojosa 1990; Wright 1990, 1998). For example, despite the decline of the mission system, some missions did not fall into decay and disuse even after the U.S. occupation. In California, Mission Santa Barbara continued to serve as a worship center for local residents (document 14). Similarly, the mission at Ysleta, Texas, remained an important parochial center of Hispanic worship (document 22). Both of these former missions have continuously functioned as Catholic houses of worship to the present day. Moreover, parishes like Nuestra Señora de Los Angeles (or La Placita, as it is commonly known) in Los Angeles (documents 18a, 18b) and private shrines such as El Santuario de Chimayó in New Mexico (document 23) have had predominantly Hispanic congregations and devotees since their foundation during the Spanish colonial period. Such centers of communal life and worship are a visible reminder that advancing Anglo Americans did not fill a spiritual void among Spanish-speaking Catholics but brought the invaders in contact with enduring communities of faith.

Mexican Catholic residents adopted varying strategies of isolation, negotiation, and resistance as U.S. territorial expansion engulfed their lands. In the process of resisting the political and ecclesial changes that beset them, they frequently articulated an identity rooted in the Hispanic Catholic heritage that preceded the U.S. takeover of the region by more than two centuries. Furthermore, enduring communities of faith expressed their identity through Mexican Catholic rituals and devotions celebrated in parishes, shrines, private homes, and neighborhoods. Within the wider context of U.S. conquest and varied Hispanic responses to the resulting social upheaval, during this period enduring Mexican Catholic expressions of faith shaped Catholic identities in occupied territories.

U.S. Conquest

Military defeat merely initiated the process of U.S. conquest and expansion. As new territories changed hands through victory in battle and subsequent treaty negotiations, law enforcement personnel, judicial officials, and occupying troops imposed U.S. rule. Violence against Spanish-speaking residents at times reached epidemic proportions; the extensive lynching of Mexican residents in 1850s California even included the hanging of a woman. Without recourse to the official judicial system, a mob of Anglo Americans condemned a woman named Josefa to avenge the death of their fellow miner, Fred Cannon, whom Josefa had killed with a knife after he broke down her door in a drunken rage (Acuña 118–21). In this and numerous other instances, the judicial system afforded little if any protection for Spanish-speaking citizens. Moreover, while the increased military presence provided some civilian jobs, it was also a visible symbol of the new regime that now ruled the conquered lands.

Newcomers also consolidated the conquest by asserting their dominion over political and economic life (Hall 204–36; De León 23–112). In San Antonio, for example, Mayor Juan N. Seguín was run out of town in 1842 by enemies he described as "straggling American adventurers" who threatened and murdered Mexican families in order to steal their land (Seguín 113). No other Mexican-descent resident served as mayor until the election of Henry Cisneros nearly 140 years later. When Texas became a state in 1845, Mexican San Antonians lost control of the city council their ancestors had established and led for more than a century; over the following century they held less than 5 percent of city council posts. At the same time, after Texas statehood citizens of Mexican heritage increasingly became a working underclass and lost most of their land holdings (Matovina 1996: 10–18).

Demographic shifts facilitated the diminishment of Hispanic political and economic influence. Nowhere was this shift more dramatic than in California, where the Gold Rush altered the demographic profile almost overnight. Even southern California settlements relatively distant from the gold mines experienced a rapid influx of newcomers. Census figures for Los Angeles indicate Hispanics accounted for more than 75 percent of the population in 1850; with the accelerated growth of Anglo-American and other city residents, by 1880 this figure had dipped below 20 percent (Engh 1992: 188). In nearby Santa Barbara, Spanish-surnamed residents comprised two-thirds of the census count in 1860; by 1880 they scarcely numbered one-fourth of the town's population (Camarillo 117). Other communities experienced a more gradual demographic shift, such as Tucson, Arizona, where Mexican-descent residents remained the majority until the early twentieth century (Sheridan 3, 259–62). In Laredo, Texas, and various other towns and cities on the U.S.-Mexican border, residents of Mexican descent have continuously comprised the overwhelming majority of the local population to the present day.

Hispanic hegemony in religious life and public celebrations also dissipated as population growth among Anglo Americans and other groups facilitated the formation of new congregations and public festivities. By 1890 in Los Angeles, for example, there were seventy-eight religious organizations, including groups such as Congregationalists, Jews, Buddhists, Baptists, Unitarians, and an African Methodist Episcopal congregation (Engh 1992: 189–90). At San Antonio, Anglo Americans promoted the participation of Mexican-descent residents in the parades and ceremonies of newly organized "American holidays" like the Fourth of July. As one report of an 1851 celebration stated: "We have many foreigners among us who know nothing of our government, who have no national feeling in common with us. . . . Let us induce them to partake with us in our festivities, they will soon partake our feelings, and when so, they will be citizens indeed" (Matovina 1995: 53–54).

Parishes and other elements of Catholic life were not immune to change during the turbulent period of transition following the U.S. conquest. Dioceses were established at places like Galveston (1847), Santa Fe (1853), San Francisco (1853), Denver (1887), and Tucson (1897). European clergy served in many areas of the Southwest, with the French predominating in Texas, New Mexico, and Arizona and the Irish in California. During the second half of the nineteenth century, episcopal appointments in the region reflected this same pattern (with the exception of Thaddeus Amat and Joseph Alemany, two Spaniards who served as bishops in California). Scores of women religious also crossed the Atlantic and began schools, hospitals, orphanages, and other apostolates in the Southwest (Sandoval 1990: 30–36).

Frequently differences in culture and religious practice led newly arrived Catholic leaders to misunderstand and criticize their Hispanic co-religionists. One French priest claimed that, among the Mexican-descent Catholics he encountered in Texas during the 1840s and 1850s, "the religion of the great majority is very superficial, the great truths of the faith are overlooked, and the most essential duties of a Christian are neglected" (Matovina 1995: 67). Los Angeles's first resident bishop, Thaddeus Amat, oversaw an 1862 diocesan synod which forbade Hispanic faith expressions like Los Pastores (see document 13), a prohibition promulgated in order to avoid "the scandal which arises from such plays" (Engh 1994: 92). Despite his initial participation in rituals like an 1858 Corpus Christi procession (document 18b), Amat and the synod fathers also decreed that public processions, funeral customs, and religious feasts strictly adhere to the rubrics of the Roman Ritual. Thus they banned long-standing local practices like festive displays of devotion during public processions, interring corpses within church buildings, cannon salutes as a form of religious devotion, and the fiestas and entertainments which accompanied religious celebrations (Engh 1994: 94–95).

To be sure, in some instances foreign clergy acclaimed the religious practices of Spanish-speaking Catholics and worked in concert with Hispanic faithful. Bishop Jean Marie Odin, the first bishop of Texas, participated in Mexican religious feasts like local celebrations in honor of Our Lady of Guadalupe and spoke enthusiastically of the religious zeal demonstrated in these celebrations (Matovina 1995: 43–44). Unlike Bishop Amat, his contemporary in Los Angeles, San Francisco's first archbishop, Joseph Alemany, did not ban Hispanic religious feasts and practices and apparently enjoyed the confidence and respect of Spanish-speaking Catholics in his see (Burns 134–35; Engh 1994: 95–97). Nonetheless, criticism and conflict frequently marked the relations between established Hispanic Catholic communities and foreign clergy and religious who arrived in the wake of U.S. conquest.

While Catholic leaders were often harsh in their assessment of Hispanic Catholicism, a number of Protestant observers were utterly condemnatory. Observing the vibrant public devotion for the 1847 feast of Our Lady of Guadalupe at Monterey, California, Reverend Walter Colton, a navy chaplain and minister in the Congregationalist tradition, mockingly quipped, "I wonder if Guadalupe knows or cares much about these exhibitions of devotional glee" (224). Baptist minister Lewis Smith wrote from Santa Fe in 1853 that, along with various other rituals, on Good Friday "the farce of crucifying the Savior was enacted in the church" (Steele 94). Undoubtedly the most renowned of the attacks on Hispanic traditions was directed at the brotherhoods of Los Hermanos de Nuestro Padre Jesús Nazareno (Brothers of Our Father Jesus the Nazarene), or Penitentes (document 24), in northern New Mexico and southern Colorado. Local residents frequently deemed outside observers of their rites "Penitente hunters" because of their intrusive presence and the sensationalistic reports they wrote about the brotherhoods' religious practices. The most notorious of these sensationalistic and ethnocentric reports was that of journalist Charles Lummis, who wrote a widely read 1893 book that described in detail the "barbarous rites" he observed among New Mexican Penitentes (79–108).

Protestant leaders attributed U.S. expansion to divine providence and

adopted a view of religious "manifest destiny" which saw Hispanic Catholicism as inherently inferior and Protestantism as a force that would inevitably
conquer all of the Americas. For example, one Protestant minister wrote that
the Anglo-American takeover of Texas was "an indication of Providence in
relation to the propagation of divine truth in other parts of the Mexican
dominions[,]...Guatemala and all South America" as well as "the beginning
of the downfall of [the] Antichrist, and the spread of the Savior's power of the
gospel" (Matovina 1995: 41).

Mexican Responses to Conquest

Conquered Mexicans responded to the U.S. takeover in various ways. Some
offered military resistance to the foreign invaders. After the U.S. occupation
of New Mexico, the 1847 Taos Rebellion resulted in the killing of territorial
governor Charles Bent and at least fifteen other Anglo Americans before it
was suppressed (Romero 1998). California defenders during the war between
the United States and Mexico won battles in the Los Angeles area and at
the hamlet of San Pasqual, although subsequently they came to terms peace-
ably when the larger and well-armed invasion force overwhelmed them (Pitt
33–35). When New Mexican governor William Carr Lane sought to occupy
Mexican territory in 1853 (land later ceded to the United States through the
aforementioned Gadsden Purchase), Father Ramón Ortiz rode out from his
El Paso parish to confront the governor. The curate then returned to El Paso
and alerted local authorities, who mounted a force of eight hundred men to
defend their borders (Taylor 78–79).

Even after the U.S. conquest of northern Mexico, armed resistance erupted
in various locales. Contemporary Mexican Americans still acclaim Joaquín
Murieta for his vigorous defense of his people and his family honor in California after the U.S. war with Mexico (Vargas 143–46). In the decades following
the Civil War, guerrilla leaders like Tiburcio Vásquez in California and Juan
Cortina in Texas led retaliatory movements protesting the endemic violence
and injustice their people suffered at the hands of Anglo Americans (Acuña
43–47, 124–25). Although their adversaries labeled them outlaws and "bandi-
dos," to this day many Californians and Texans of Mexican heritage consider
them heroic defenders of a dominated people. Claiming the right of self-
defense against Anglo-American oppression, Hispanic residents also took up
arms during the 1877 El Paso Salt War and when Las Gorras Blancas (the
White Caps) sought to safeguard land claims in San Miguel County, New
Mexico, from 1889 to 1891 (Acuña 47–49, 70–74; Vargas 182).

In other instances, Spanish-speaking residents defended their rights in the
political arena. Native Texan José Antonio Navarro made various legislative
attempts to protect the ancestral lands of Mexican Texans. While his fellow
lawmakers did not enact any of his land claim proposals, at the 1845 Texas
Constitutional Convention Navarro was able to prevent passage of an "odious"
and "ridiculous" law that restricted suffrage to the "free white population"
(Navarro 19–20). Like Navarro, native Californian Pablo de la Guerra futilely

tried to protect the land claims of Mexican-descent residents in his state. In an often-quoted 1856 speech to fellow members of the state senate, he described Mexican Californians as "strangers in their own land" and testified that he had "seen seventy and sixty year olds cry like children because they had been uprooted from the lands of their fathers." He further claimed that their plight was caused in part by "a legislature hungry to take away from us our last penny simply because the [Anglo-American] squatters are more numerous than the native Californians" (de la Guerra 19–20).

Spanish-speaking residents also founded mutual aid societies and other organizations to protect their rights and promote their common concerns. One such organization was La Alianza Hispano-Americana (the Hispanic-American Alliance). Initially founded as a local group at Tucson, Arizona, in response to a nativist threat, within three years of its 1894 establishment the group expanded its vision and convened its first national convention. Like similar organizations created to promote change at the local, regional, and national levels, La Alianza is noteworthy for its advocacy of Hispanic causes such as political representation, participation in civic and economic life, labor organizing, and desegregation in schools and other public facilities (Acuña 96–97, 294–95).

Yet another arena for resistance was the issue of language. In 1858, elected officials at San Antonio instituted a program of teacher certification for public schools, decreeing that public funds would be available solely for the salaries of certified teachers in schools where the principal language was English. José Ramos de Zúñiga, the editor of a local newspaper called *El Correo*, contested this law. Ramos de Zúñiga contended that, when limited to speaking English in school, Spanish- (and German-) speaking children ended up speaking neither language fluently (Matovina 1995: 55). During the mid-1850s at Santa Barbara, California, where 60 percent of the twelve hundred residents spoke only Spanish, Hispanic leaders overcame Anglo-American Protestant opposition and succeeded in retaining Spanish as the *only* language for public school instruction (Pitt 226).

Catholic clergy's misunderstanding and criticism of Hispanic religion at times resulted in open conflict. In 1875, for example, Bishop Dominic Manucy of Brownsville, Texas, rejected a request that twenty-two exiled Mexican sisters reside in the area and serve Mexican-descent Catholics. Local Spanish-speaking Catholics were incensed at Manucy's decision, particularly since they offered to pay the sisters' living costs. On the day the women religious were to board the train and depart from Brownsville, an angry crowd removed their train from its tracks and refused to let authorities replace it. In the end the bishop's decision prevailed, undoubtedly alienating many Catholic faithful from their prelate (Juárez 230–32).

Some Catholic priests contested the policies and decisions of new bishops appointed to the region; the most notorious instance of such disagreement was the conflict in New Mexico between Father Antonio José Martínez and Bishop Jean Baptiste Lamy, which is treated below. In Santa Barbara, California, Franciscan priest José González Rubio respectfully but firmly contested some controversial directives of Bishop Thaddeus Amat. A native of Guadalajara, González Rubio came to Alta California in 1833 and was the most important Catholic leader in transitional California. He served as the secretary for Bishop Francisco García Diego y Moreno, the first bishop of California (1840–1846) and the only bishop who lived in what is now the Southwest before the U.S. takeover. After García Diego's death in 1846, González Rubio was the administrator of the diocese until the appointment of Bishop (later Archbishop) Joseph Alemany in 1850. He then served as a diocesan vicar general for Bishop Alemany and later Bishop Amat. Spanish-speaking Catholics held him in such high regard that, when his Franciscan superiors reappointed him to Zacatecas in 1856, some one thousand parishioners and other supporters "kidnapped" him by blocking his entrance to the boat on which he was to depart! They then enlisted the support of Archbishop Alemany in San Francisco and remained firm in their resolve to keep their priest until his superiors changed his appointment and allowed him to stay. Despite his outstanding service and reputation, however, in 1858 Bishop Amat removed him as his vicar general; the prelate also revoked the priestly faculties of González Rubio and his two fellow Franciscans at Santa Barbara, effectively suspending them from public ministry. During the ensuing controversy, Amat even called for the removal of González Rubio and his fellow Franciscans from California. Amat's accusations directed at the Franciscans included his claims that they permitted moral laxity, fostered superstitious devotions among their parishioners, and incited the people to rebel against his episcopal authority. As the leader of the local Franciscans, González Rubio diplomatically but resolutely protested Amat's decision on both canonical and moral grounds. The case went to Rome, where Archbishop Alemany and superiors of the Franciscan order emphatically denied all charges against the Santa Barbara Franciscans. Faced with formidable opposition, in 1861 Amat restored the Franciscans' faculties; subsequently González Rubio continued his priestly ministrations in California until his death in 1875 (Neri).

Native Spanish-speaking residents of the conquered territories further resisted Anglo-American hegemony by writing memoirs and historical accounts that reflected their perspective on U.S. expansion. Californian Antonio María Osio penned a lengthy 1851 memoir which included a description of forlorn residents in the capital of Mexican California, Monterey, as U.S. troops occupied their town, lowered the Mexican flag, and replaced it with their own national banner. He commented that the local populace "began to think about the loss of their nationality and of everything they had worked so hard to create. For experience has always shown that conquerors never have been able to maintain a brotherhood with those they have conquered" (Osio 232).

On at least one occasion another resident of the former Mexican territories defended the record of the priests in his region. On 12 December 1848, Bishop (later Archbishop) John Hughes of New York wrote José de la Guerra y Noriega of Santa Barbara seeking information about conditions in California for the Provincial Council of Baltimore to be held the following May. Hughes's inquiry included the assertion that all Mexican clergy had abandoned California, leaving Catholics there "destitute of all spiritual aid." In his response, de la Guerra stated that "with due respect to the Mexican priests, ... the information which has been given to Your Illustrious Lordship regarding their conduct [abandoning their parishioners] during these latter times does not correspond with the facts." He reported that there were still sixteen priests in Alta California (Thompson 219–25).

In many locales where Spanish-speaking residents remained the majority, Anglo Americans consolidated control by means of a "peace structure," a "post-war arrangement that allows the victors to maintain law and order without the constant use of force" (Montejano 34). The peace structure entailed an accommodation between Anglo-American newcomers and the defeated elites of Spanish-speaking communities, an arrangement that did not alter traditional authority structures but placed Anglo Americans atop the existing hierarchy. Often marriages between Anglo-American men and daughters from the elite families of a locale played a key role in this arrangement (Matovina 1995: 38). These marriages offered Anglo Americans the advantages of land, inherited wealth, and social status. At the same time, they offered Spanish-speaking residents allies to help protect familial interests and land holdings within the new political and economic structures. After the U.S. takeover, such allies were particularly useful as many of the conquered peoples did not speak English, were unfamiliar with the legal system, and were vulnerable to accusations of disloyalty against the new regime.

Despite intermarriages that enabled elite families to retain some of their former status after the U.S. takeover, the common plight of poverty and discrimination often united family members, especially those of working-class families, in the mutual struggle to sustain themselves and a sense of pride in their heritage. To be sure, gender and generational relations shifted within many Mexican households as families confronted the political, social, and economic changes that beset them (G. Gutiérrez). At the same time, the cultural ideal of solidarity among extended family members provided significant "strategies for survival during hard times" (Griswold del Castillo 1984: 55; see also Tijerina).

Some residents of the former Mexican territories survived their political takeover through isolation from their conquerors. In the small towns of northern New Mexico, for example, some degree of autonomy was possible because of the physical distance from U.S. institutions and influence. While this isolation was often the result of circumstance as much as design, Spanish-speaking communities embraced the opportunities for cultural continuity that their isolation afforded. Nonetheless, in the end, urbanization, shifts in local economies, and other changes influenced even the most isolated settlements.

In more urban areas, Spanish-speaking barrios resulted from forced segregation as well as the desire for separation from Anglo-American society. As an ethnic enclave, the barrio mediated a sense of split existence between the familiarity of Hispanic home and neighborhood and the alienation of the Anglo-American world where barrio residents often worked and sometimes went to school. At the same time, however, the barrio provided a strong base for group survival, cultural retention, and ethnic pride. In this way it was a structure which enabled Spanish-speaking communities to sustain themselves despite the conquest and rapid social changes they endured (Camarillo; Griswold del Castillo 1979; Matovina 1995: 49–82).

Resistance and Identity

In the process of defending their rights in both church and society, various residents of the former Mexican territories articulated an identity that accentuated their preconquest heritage. This expression of an identity rooted in established local customs and religious traditions is illustrated in the well-known conflict between Father Antonio José Martínez, a popular leader among native-born New Mexican Catholics, and Frenchman Jean Baptiste Lamy, the first bishop (and later first archbishop) of Santa Fe. Upon his arrival at New Mexico in 1851 Lamy encountered Catholic communities with long-standing traditions and the largest group of local clergy in any of the conquered territories. Two decades earlier Padre Martínez had advocated successfully for the abolition of tithing regulations in New Mexico, arguing that fiscal conditions in this frontier territory precluded the feasibility of this practice. Within three years of his arrival, Bishop Lamy suspended several New Mexican priests, reinstituted mandatory tithing, and decreed that heads of families who failed to tithe be denied the sacraments. Padre Martínez publicly protested the prelate's actions; the resulting controversy led to his eventual suspension and excommunication. In his response to Lamy after hearing of the bishop's decision to suspend him, Martínez protested that decision, as well as Lamy's lack of response to his previous missives and the suspensions of other New Mexican priests like José Manuel Gallegos and Juan Felipe Ortiz. He also called on Lamy to rescind his decree on mandatory tithing, arguing that this decree "goes against canon law," was at odds with Catholic practice in the region, and "harms the spiritual well-being of the faithful" (document 17). Implicit in Martínez's statements was the contention that Lamy was an outsider who did not understand or appreciate the Hispanic Catholic heritage that marked the territory now under his jurisdiction (Romero 1976).

Spanish-speaking residents also drew on their Hispanic Catholic heritage to defend themselves in the political arena. In 1855 citizens of Mexican descent at San Antonio opposed the anti-Catholic, anti-immigrant Know-Nothing Party. They accused Know-Nothings of condemning them to "political slavery" solely because they chose "to worship God according to the dictates of our conscience and the rituals of our ancestors." Claiming their status as native-born residents of Texas, they also contended that Know-Nothings were immigrant "strangers to this land, with four years, or less, of residence in our state" (document 16). Local leader José Antonio Navarro wrote an open letter to his fellow citizens of Mexican-Texan heritage that was read publicly and subsequently published in both the English and Spanish press. Navarro reminded his hearers that his people's Hispanic-Mexican ancestors founded their city and built the parish of San Fernando in which they worshiped God. Citing

Know-Nothing anti-Catholic attitudes, he also proclaimed that "the Mexico-Texans are Catholics, and should be proud of the faith of their ancestors, and defend it inch by inch against such infamous aggressors" (Navarro 21).

New Mexican Rafael Romero made a similarly spirited defense in 1878, when the territorial governor blocked Jesuit attempts to establish the tax-exempt and degree-granting status of their new school in Las Vegas, New Mexico. Romero's public address during festivities for the close of the school's first academic year acclaimed his hearers as native New Mexicans whose "ancestors penetrated into these deserted and dangerous regions many years before the Mayflower floated over the dancing waves that washed Plymouth Rock." He went on to remind his audience that Jesus was also "tormented by a provincial governor," claiming that the oppressive actions of their current territorial governor were worse than the misdeeds of Pontius Pilate, whose sin, according to Romero, was one of omission rather than direct persecution of the innocent. Defending himself against possible retorts that he spoke too harshly, he went on to ask rhetorically: "Am I not a Catholic citizen of a Catholic land, New Mexico? And have I not, as a New Mexican Catholic, been grossly insulted by a pathetic public official? What does it mean when a man sent to be the governor of a Catholic land, in an official message directed to Catholic legislators and to our Catholic people, piles insult upon insult against a religious order of the Catholic Church?" (document 20).

In these and other instances, Hispanic residents sought to defend their political rights by identifying themselves as the descendants of Spanish-speaking Catholic ancestors who founded and developed their communities. Drawing on their preconquest heritage, they expressed the heightened religious and ethnic consciousness of native-born residents who retained legitimate claims for respect within their homeland. By asserting that Anglo Americans and European clergy were immigrant newcomers to their region, they contrasted their own identity as the harbingers of Hispanic Catholic civilization with that of the newcomers who scorned their heritage and usurped their political rights. Thus rhetorically they reversed their antagonists' claims that Hispanic Catholics were "foreigners" and religiously and culturally depraved. In the process they expressed an identity as Catholics whose preconquest heritage merited their ethnic, religious, and political legitimation.

Enduring Communities of Faith

Many Hispanic Catholic communities in conquered territories celebrated and asserted their collective identity through their long-standing rituals and devotions. The persistence of established religious traditions is particularly striking in light of Catholic and Protestant leaders' attempts to ban, replace, and condemn these traditions. In the face of such efforts as well as military conquest and occupation, indiscriminate violence and lawlessness, political and economic displacement, rapid demographic change, the erosion of cultural hegemony, and the appointment of foreign clergy and religious, Spanish-speaking Catholic feasts and devotions provided an ongoing means of communal expression. Undoubtedly fear and anger at their subjugation intensified religious fervor among some devotees. Primary documents that describe enduring expressions of faith illuminate a significant element of Hispanic Catholic identities during the tumultuous historical period that followed the U.S. conquest of northern Mexico.

Not surprisingly, women frequently played a key role in worship and devotion and in transmitting communal identity to the next generation (Díaz-Stevens 1993b). Women themselves authored relatively few of the extant documents that narrate enduring expressions of faith, no doubt due in large part to the patriarchal structures and excessive workload that precluded many women from having the time and wherewithal to compose diaries, memoirs, and other written records. Nonetheless, several women who did record their recollections, along with various male observers, reveal in their writings women's roles in communal and private prayer. Several devotees attest that their mothers and other female relatives handed on their faith and cherished religious practices to them (documents 21a, 23). At Santa Rita, Texas, and Conejos, Colorado, young women served in public processions as the immediate attendants for the image of Our Lady of Guadalupe, the principal ritual object in annual Guadalupe feast-day celebrations (documents 15, 19). Young women occupied similar places of prominence in processions at Los Angeles for the feasts of the Assumption (document 18a) and Corpus Christi (document 18b), as well as the Our Lady of Mount Carmel procession at Ysleta, Texas (document 22). Even when male Penitentes provided significant leadership for communal worship, as in Arroyo Hondo, New Mexico, women played vital roles in local traditions like the annual procession for the feast of St. John the Baptist (document 24).

At the same time, however, the documents in this chapter reveal the leadership roles men played in communal ritual and devotion, evidence that contests the stereotypical view that the vast majority of Hispanic males were uninvolved in religion. The Penitentes are the most conspicuous example of this, but laymen exercised leadership in all the public processions mentioned in the preceding paragraph. Male devotion was also evident outside public ritual, as in the case of Manuel Castillo, a rancher in the Tucson area who held a special celebration every year on the feast of San Isidro to fulfill a *promesa* (solemn vow or promise) he had made (document 21b).

Activist laywomen and laymen organized and promoted their ethno-religious traditions with, without, or despite the clergy. When priests were not available in places like northern New Mexico (document 24) or for the annual San Isidro procession through the fields near Tucson (document 21b), lay leaders sustained the community's worship life and traditions. When newly arrived Catholic clergy and women religious accompanied the people in established feasts at places like Santa Rita, Texas (document 15), Los Angeles (documents 18a, 18b), and Conejos, Colorado (document 19), lay leaders welcomed them into celebrations that retained a pronounced Hispanic flavor. In some cases the clergy even introduced new feasts which were consistent with local religious sensibilities and met a fervent reception from their parishioners, as in Ysleta, Texas (document 22). When local clergy attempted to censure devotional practices at La Capilla de Nuestro Señor de los Milagros (the Chapel of Our Lord of Miracles) in San Antonio, however, devotees continued their traditions despite clerical objections (document 26). Similarly, after Bishop Amat curtailed public displays of devotion at Los Angeles, Hispanic worshipers enacted processions within church walls and continued domestic devotions like home altars and celebrations associated with El Día de los Muertos (the Day of the Dead) and other special feasts (Engh 1994: 103–5).

Significantly, in addition to Catholic clergy, Protestants, Anglo Americans, and other newcomers participated in the rituals and devotions of Spanish-speaking Catholics. In 1846, Mexican residents at Monterey, California, enacted Los Pastores in the home of Reverend Walter Colton, an ordained minister in the Congregationalist tradition (document 13). An 1861 Anglo-American visitor to Santa Barbara marveled that, during the Holy Week services he attended, the predominantly Mexican-descent congregation was joined by Native American, North American, Irish, German, French, and Italian worshipers. He concluded that "no place but California can produce such [diverse] groups" (Brewer 69–70). Both at Santa Barbara and at Tucson, even Chinese immigrants reportedly attended Hispanic communal celebrations (Brewer 70; document 21b). Anglo Americans participated in a 1902 confirmation rite at Las Cruces, New Mexico (document 25); non-Hispanics were also among the numerous visitors to San Antonio's La Capilla de Nuestro Señor de los Milagros (document 26). The presence of newcomers at Hispanic shrines and celebrations illustrates Hispanic attempts to prolong local traditions and even incorporate these newcomers into their expressions of religious and communal identity.

Once other groups were sufficient in number to form their own congregations and social circles, however, their participation in Hispanic faith expressions frequently abated. With the emergence of religious pluralism and the organization of diverse public celebrations, particularly U.S. holidays like the Fourth of July, the hegemony of Hispanic faith expressions and festivities ceased. While these faith expressions and festivities were an identifying mark of towns and local communities in the years prior to the U.S. takeover, afterward they increasingly differentiated Hispanics from other groups that settled in the occupied territories. Thus the rise of religious and cultural pluralism in conquered lands enhanced the perception that Hispanic faith expressions were a distinguishing characteristic of their ethnicity and group identity (Matovina 1995: 49–82).

To be sure, some communities struggled for their very survival; in the process their observance of long-standing traditions often abated or even ceased. At Santa Barbara, during the latter decades of the nineteenth century many "traditions and customs were necessarily modified in order to survive. Some cultural activities disappeared altogether" (Camarillo 65). During this same time period, San Antonio's annual feast-day celebration for Our Lady of Guadalupe, which for over a century had included public processions and festivities in the city streets and plazas, consisted solely of church services

(Matovina 1996: 13–16). Nonetheless, as Bishop Henry Granjon of Tucson noted in 1902 during his first pastoral visit to Las Cruces, New Mexico, many Mexican-descent Catholics in the Southwest "continue[d] to observe their own traditions and customs as they did before the annexation of their lands by the American Union." Among these traditions and customs was *compadrazgo* (literally "godparentage"), the network of relationships among families that is created through sponsorship in sacramental celebrations. According to Bishop Granjon, in the Southwest "these multiple attachments, mostly between families, maintain the unity of the Mexican population and permit them to resist, to a certain extent, the invasions of the Anglo-Saxon race" (document 25). Lay initiative enabled a number of local populations to adapt and continue their expressions of faith, assert their collective identity, and endure as ethnoreligious communities. In the wake of an expansionist U.S. takeover, Hispanic Catholics articulated an ethnoreligious identity that fortified their resistance to the effects of conquest and expressed their own ethnic legitimation.

13. Los Pastores, Monterey, California, 1846

Spanish subjects founded a presidio (garrison) at Monterey in 1770, and the presidio chapel became a cathedral after the 1840 designation of Monterey as a diocese. Under both Spanish and Mexican rule Monterey was the capital of Alta California and the site of the customshouse (Abrahamson). Reverend Walter Colton (1797–1851), an ordained minister in the Congregationalist tradition, was a navy chaplain whom U.S. military commanders named mayor of Monterey after U.S. troops occupied the town. Five months after the U.S. takeover, Colton wrote the following diary entry describing Los Pastores, a festive proclamation of the shepherds who worshiped the newborn infant Jesus. He also commented on the bell ringing, bonfires, and skyrockets that marked the local celebration of Christmas Eve.

Thursday, December 24. As soon as the sun had gone down and twilight had spread its sable shadows over the hills and habitations of Monterey, the festivities of Christmas Eve commenced. The bells rang out a merry chime, the windows were filled with streaming light, bonfires on plain and steep sent up their pyramids of flame, and the skyrockets burst high over all in showering fire. Children shouted, the young were filled with smiles and gladness, and the aged looked as if some dark cloud had been lifted from the world.

While the bonfires still blazed high, the crowd moved towards the church; the ample nave was soon filled. Before the high altar bent the Virgin Mother, in wonder and love, over her newborn babe; a company of shepherds entered in flowing robes, with high wands garnished with silken streamers, in which floated all the colors of the rainbow, and surmounted with coronals of flowers. In their wake followed a hermit, with his long white beard, tattered missal, and his sin-chastising lash. Near him figured a wild hunter, in the skins of the forest, bearing a huge truncheon surmounted by an iron rim, from which hung in jingling chime fragments of all sonorous metals. Then came, last of all, the Evil One, with horned frontlet, disguised hoof, and rove of crimson flame. The shepherds were led on by the angel Gabriel in purple wings and garments of light. They approached the manger and, kneeling, hymned their wonder and worship in a sweet chant, which was sustained by the rich tones of exulting harps. The hermit and the hunter were not among them; they had been beguiled by the Tempter, and were lingering at a game of dice. The hermit seemed to suspect that all was not right, and read his missal vehemently in the pauses of the game; but the hunter was troubled by none of these scruples, staked his soul, and lost! Emboldened by his success, the Tempter shoved himself among the shepherds; but there he encountered Gabriel, who knew him of old. He quailed under the eye of that invincible angel, and fled his presence. The hermit and hunter, once more disenthralled, paid their penitential homage. The shepherds departed, singing their hosannas, while the voices of the whole assembly rose in the choral strain....

Saturday, December 26. It is an old custom here for the shepherds, when they have performed their sacred drama in the church, to repeat it, during the holydays, in the residences of some of the citizens. One of the first personages to whom they pay their respects is the chief magistrate of the jurisdiction; I was accordingly saluted this evening with their festive compliment.

The large hall, occupying the centre of the building, was sufficiently ample to accommodate them, and some fifty gentlemen and ladies as spectators. They brought their own orchestral accompaniment, which consisted entirely of violins and guitars. Their prelude had so many sweet harmonies that the listener determined to listen on. The dialogue and chant of the shepherds would have awakened their appropriate associations, but for the obtrusions of the hermit, hunter, and devil, who now gave much freer scope to their characteristic peculiarities than they did in church....

Sunday, December 27. The dramatic shepherds have just passed my door on their way to the mansion of Gen. Castro, where they are to perform their pastorals.

Walter Colton, *Three Years in California,* with an introduction by Marguerite Eyer Wilbur (Stanford, Calif.: Stanford University Press, 1949), 129–30, 132, 134.

14. Holy Week at Santa Barbara, California, 1851

The presidio (garrison) of Santa Barbara was founded in 1782; four years later Franciscans established Mission Santa Barbara about three miles northwest of the presidio. Although the two institutions were just a short distance apart, settlers completed the presidio chapel in 1797 to help keep the Franciscans' missionizing efforts distinct from the worship life of Spanish subjects connected to the garrison. Soldiers, their families, and other civilians began to develop a pueblo (town) near the presidio shortly after its foundation; by 1826 residents had elected their first town council. The presidio chapel served as the house of worship for both pueblo and presidio until town residents established Nuestra Señora de Dolores (Our Lady of Sorrows) parish in 1856 (Camarillo; Hawley). Native Santa Barbara resident Pablo de la Guerra (1819–1874), a leading Californio political figure under both Mexican and U.S. rule, recorded his impressions of Holy Week at Mission Santa Barbara in 1851. He describes the

*color, pageantry, and sensory appeal of Mexican Catholic worship and mentions
ritual traditions like the Tenebrae or "earthquake" service which recalls the cos-
mological disruptions after Jesus' death (see document 24), the Siete Palabras
(Seven Last Words of Christ), and Los Judeaos, a mock "execution" of Judas
Iscariot.*

Holy Thursday

Day has dawned. It continues serene and beautiful. The countryside — an
inclined plain between the town and the mission — in the garb of spring-
time, is entirely covered with the freshest green intertwined with thousands
of variegated and fragrant flowers. Already at about 7:30 in the morning the
various roads crossing this flowery countryside leading to the mission were
crowded with people walking, the greater part of whom were women dressed
in their best colorful dresses which competed with the variety of colors and
the capricious forms of the flowers of the field. All were making for the mission scattering over the fields at times to pick flowers. Of these they fashioned
colorful and cleverly contrived bouquets with which to adorn the sepulcher.

The young people generally very elegantly fitted out traveled on fine horses
greeting the girls they passed with those pleasant remarks of gallantry so peculiar to our race. Somewhat later the main road was filled with a great number
of all types of carriages from the elegant and light *carretela* to the heavy and
simple coach. Thus this interesting column of people continued to advance
until 9 o'clock. From time to time, the sonorous and harmonious tones of the
mission bells resounded as they swung to and fro in the high majestic tow-
ers filling the expanse and calling the faithful, their sounds echoing from the
high mountains which almost encircle the town. It was indeed a scene of great
movement, a continuous march of people so that the plain presented a most
beautiful panorama.

When the hour for Mass was at hand the great concourse of people entered
the church. I, because unaccompanied and because I wanted better to enjoy
the scene in one general view of the interior of the church, preferred to go
up into the choir loft, and purposely was one of the last to enter the church
precisely to view the entire scene at a single glance. I entered after the Introit
[opening prayer] had begun and I cannot refrain from acknowledging that the
impact of the sudden view of everything I beheld, moved me. That view was
indeed, reverently majestic and imposingly grandiose. Wherefore, I am going
to describe for you, however poorly, the things I saw.

The spacious church was decorated very tastefully and with a noble simplicity. The twelve pilasters reaching to the ceiling were draped from their
capitals to their bases with purple damask in cylindrical form. The collaterals
from roof to floor were similarly covered with the same purple damask dot-
ted with stars. From the ceiling hung twelve large chandeliers, some of glass
hung with hanging prisms, others of gilded wood and of bronze. A beautiful
rich canopy also of purple damask adorned with orphries and fringes of gold
covered the altar prepared for Mass. This reached to about two thirds of the

distance to the ceiling. The spacious floor was so covered with people that it was impossible to see the carpets that covered it. From the choir loft, this mass of people, the variety and colors of their clothing, the whimsical diversity of the decorations, the graceful variety of their feathered and flowered hats, etc., all presented a most interesting scene that was both picturesque and pleasing.

It remains for me now to describe what is most difficult because it was more grand, the most pleasing and finely decorated of all, the sepulcher. This beautiful structure occupied the entire space of the sanctuary and reached almost to the ceiling. It consisted of six Ionic columns placed at the exterior end of the sanctuary. These supported arches that reached to a height of two thirds of the sanctuary area. Upon these there rested a covering that reached across to the opposite wall where it was sustained by other arches on an equal number of columns also in the Ionic style. In the center of this covering there was a cupola that reached to the ceiling of the church. The cupola, arches and columns were done in imitation jasper stone. A little distance within these columns there arose a spacious staircase with twelve or more steps that led to a sort of platform surrounded by a graceful balustrade. This together with the steps and cupola was adorned with a multitude of lights, urns, and flower pots full of fragrant bouquets and an infinity of whimsical greens and various other adornments. From this large platform another large staircase smaller than the other led away in a semicircular form upon which led to another platform or small table about three *varas* [yards] long and upon which had been erected in the center a beautiful pedestal or frame where the urn or tabernacle rested which was to receive the Blessed Sacrament and [is] called the depository.

This little table was in the center of a circular colonnade in beautiful Corinthian style which in the form of a small temple sustained a light and pleasing cupola. This and the colonnade appeared to be of alabaster. Abutting all this was a "sun" about a *vara* in diameter whose center was of a transparent red which had behind it very ingeniously placed a small lamp whose oscillating and at times vibrating light showed through the red of the "sun." It seemed really to emit or throw some rays from a weak light and somewhat melancholically against the place of repository. This latter was a curious work of the Indians. All of it (except the door which is of glass) is adorned with precious mother of pearl from sea shells and has in relief the instruments of the Passion from the cross to the very cock that crowed to St. Peter.

Around the large cupola there hung twelve very thin vines which were not seen from below and from these hung twelve very beautiful angels with feathered wings in the act of flying. These with candles in their hands surrounded the temple where the urn was placed. They moved with the slightest breeze and thus seemed to fly around the tabernacle. Now just imagine seeing all these great furnishings with their staircases, arches, cornices, balustrades, columns, cupolas, generously covered bouquets, with a diversity of greens, a great number of small tables with curious plants and a thousand other curious adornments and you will have some idea of the beautiful view that the sepulcher presented today.

Now that I have described for you, though imperfectly, the interior of the church, it remains for me to depict the religious function of this day which was very solemn. I will not omit describing the procession. When this began, the sepulcher which till then had not been illuminated began to lighten up into a brilliant burning blaze. The large concourse of people opened up a path between them (because in this church there are no benches) in order to allow the King of Kings to pass through their midst. The procession was led by twelve young boys dressed in white crowned with flowers, who in the afternoon were to participate in the Washing of Feet, like the apostles. Then followed the religious who formed a choir during the procession and sang the tender hymn, *Pange Lingua* [a traditional song of praise sung before the Blessed Sacrament]. In this order they marched majestically through the entire length of the church, the people remaining on their knees facing from both sides the Blessed Sacrament. All that varied multitude with their faces turned toward the floor in reverent and humble prostration before the Holy of Holies at the same time rendered the deepest, most fervent and profound adoration deep in their souls. Oh, from the choir loft in one quick view, all this was a most tender and moving sight.

I was so overcome by feeling and so tenderly was I moved that I could not refrain from making in that instant the following entreaty: "Lord, deign to accept propitiously the humble and profound adoration which we here today offer you and which the whole Catholic world offers you around the world in reparation for the humiliation and ridicule which you suffered when you were led in an ignominious procession through the streets of Jerusalem." When I was still thinking along these lines, an English priest from Oregon who is temporarily staying here and who was kneeling by me, touched me slightly at the elbow and with his eyes full of tears, said to me: "Sir this is very solemn, it is too imposing, too affecting, sir."

When the procession arrived at the sepulcher, amidst the clouds of aromatic smoke born aloft by various censers, the Blessed Sacrament was deposited with all reverence while the multitude remained prostrate for a long time offering its act of adoration and raising its fervent prayers to the Divine Prisoner. When the function was over and it was still forenoon, the atrium, the corridors, the neighboring houses were full with people deciding how they were to spend the day there for nearly all the families were present, as was the custom, for this purpose.

Wherefore they went prepared with everything necessary to spend the day in the open. Soon they began to move toward the Arroyo Pedregoso which was about 300 *varas* from the church. This arroyo was running high because of the recent heavy rains. The water wended its way noisily and crystalline through many rocks that are within it and which pleases the sight and gratifies the ear. In this area, for this torrent whose banks hold a multitude of tufted oak, alders, willows and other shady trees, the people formed into a reunion and while some prepared food, others spread carpets and mats about the place in order to enjoy themselves. Others began to put out plates, tablecloths, napkins, while others still (the majority) played, ran about the rocks, talked, flirted, or went visiting and walking with companions.

Now you will suppose that I was among the latter but however beautiful and alluring it all was, despite many invitations and urgings, I preferred to abandon such a lovely spot, such pleasing companions and such varied and delectable entertainment, and return to my house for duty called me there. Another reason was that deep within me I had a little something that made me sad and the spirit to join in the joy left me. For this reason I returned home on foot both to do some work and to enjoy the fresh breeze from the sea which came to me laden with the aroma of the many flowers. In the afternoon I did not feel very well so I did not return to the mission for the ceremony of the Washing of the Feet, the Tenebrae, etc. As a result I say nothing about them. Good-by until tomorrow.

Good Friday

Although the countryside between this town and the mission is the same as I described it yesterday, nevertheless the aspect which it presents today is very different because the multitude which now cover it going to the mission had divested itself of its showy and rich clothing and in its place it had substituted the rigorous weeds of mourning. Nor is the sonorous ringing of the bells heard resounding through the valley. The very sky itself as if it desired to show sadness and mourning is somewhat cloudy, the sun withholding its resplendent rays. The church itself presents the aspect of deep sorrow.

Its windows are covered with dark curtains that allow hardly more than a weak, tenuous light to penetrate. Its pilasters now hold a black crepe as if they realize that this is a day of sorrow. From the ceiling there no longer hang the many lights that were there yesterday. The altars are bare. The organ is silent. The sonorous bells are substituted for by the harsh sounding *matraca* (wooden rattle). The sepulcher itself is entirely without lights except for the twelve that the angels carried which, as I have said, appeared to fly around the tabernacle keeping company with the Creator. Everything had put off the appearance that irresistibly called for rejoicing and contemplation of the Most High and August Mystery which was about to be recalled — the death of the God-Man. Even now when I am writing this at eight o'clock in the evening, I still feel moved by today's solemnities and by the grandiose reverence with which I convey all of them to you. The Passion, so beautifully and tenderly described by St. John, was sung with such harmony and majesty that at certain portions of it, I saw more than one contrite tear fall.

The veneration of the cross, a thing truly excellent, was done with such dignity and reverence that there occurred not even one of those commotions or disorders that unfortunately always take place in this most reverent act. Thereupon the sumptuous sepulcher having been lighted, the Blessed Sacrament was removed with the same solemnity with which it was placed there the day before. After the procession arrived at the altar, the *Pater Noster* [Our Father] and the oration to the Eternal Father having been intoned, bestowing peace on us and delivering us from evils, past, present, and to come, the Blessed Sacrament was consumed and the function was concluded. In a short time, but wearing no vestments, all the community was on its knees, sang alternately the psalm, *Miserere* [Psalm 51], and the morning function came to an end. I did not attend the afternoon function but I am told that Father [Francisco] Sánchez gave a brilliant sermon on the Seven Words, he weeping as much if not more than the congregation which it appears was quite large. Good-bye until tomorrow.

Holy Saturday

The atrium of the church is adorned with various crossed arches covered with wild flowers for under them will be celebrated the blessing of the new fire and the Easter candle. The interior of the church still retains its dark and impressive obscurity of yesterday. Even more so because even the twelve lights which were about the tabernacle have disappeared. Also gone is the structure of the great sepulcher and in its place there is only a heavy black veil which covers the whole front of the church from ceiling to floor. In the midst of this impressive and solemn darkness all the many ceremonies which on this day precede the Mass were sung. The number of people was as great or greater than on Holy Thursday or Good Friday. When the Litanies were over, which were sung very well chorally, it was noticed that various persons and students of the college gathered at different places in the church so that it happened when the Gloria was sung, each one did what he was supposed to do which I will describe later [Line missing].

At last the Mass began, celebrated by Father [José] González [Rubio] accompanied by four assistants in their rich vestments and dalmatics. The singing of the antiphon was done by the choir in very moving harmony and after the *Kyrie* [Lord have mercy], but all without musical accompaniment, the celebrant intoned with prolonged chant the *Gloria in Excelsis Deo* [Glory to God in the highest]. When he commenced to sing it, as if in one magic stroke, all the black hangings of the windows, pilasters, and collaterals disappeared and then they appeared dressed in rich curtains and hangings of rose color spread with stars. The altar was illuminated with a profusion of lights forming two pleasing figures intertwined with various bouquets placed with most proper taste and symmetry.

From the ceiling of the church which was also illuminated hung a multitude of flags and pennants of all colors which when unfolded were allowed to fall filling the ambient of the church with thousands of curious figures made of wafers of all colors. At the side of the altar there appeared on a small, elevated table something similar to an open cave representing the sepulcher and on both sides of it, sleeping, four Roman soldiers very well fashioned. On the other side and on a similar table there was seen a large stone and a boy sitting on it dressed as an angel. High above all the lights was seen a great, very white cloud as if composed of pinewood bundles of snow. The change of scenes was executed in a very fine manner. The great and sudden contrast was so powerful and beautiful that I saw some people brought to tears. Added to this the sonorous echo of all the bells which, carried on the wings of the wind, filled the space proclaiming the resurrection. The band of music from the choir loft filled the church with proper melodies. With all this you will derive but an imperfect idea of the effect which the intoning of the *Gloria* produced in the congregation which filled the precious temple.

But there still remains for me to tell the most tender, the most impressive part of the august and moving ceremony. It occurred when the celebrant had prayed the *Gloria* at the altar and when he was about to be seated at the scamnum; the bells stopped ringing and the music ceased at the same time, only an imposing silence remaining. At that moment there came from behind the curtain or veil which covered the wall behind the altar two young girls dressed in mourning who approached the angel and who represented the two Marys. They made a very natural show of fear and then the angel in a very sweet voice which was accompanied by a violin and two flutes hidden behind the curtain, sang the words: "Fear not; whom do you seek?" and the young girls singing in unison replied: "We seek Jesus, he who was crucified." Then the angel with a strong and melodious clear voice answered in song: "He is not here for he has risen as he said." Then the cloud was broken in two remaining as in the form of a pleasing curtain and in the center shone with splendor a magnificent statue of the Savior with the standard of the cross. The angel fell on his knees and adored the Lord and the entire congregation as if moved in one electrifying instant prostrated itself also. Then the choir in full orchestra broke out with the singing of the *Gloria in Excelsis Deo*, etc. etc., which lasted almost half an hour. Thus continued the *Misa de Gloria* until the end with which ended the celebration of Holy [Saturday].

I would like to say something about the various Judases who appeared hung in effigy in various locales and of their testaments but I shall let this go so that when Guillermo Carrillo sees you he can give an account of it for he knows almost by heart some of them and he can recount them with charm which I cannot do.

> Pablo de la Guerra, "Holy Week in Santa Barbara" (1851), De la Guerra Family Papers, folder 1093b, Santa Barbara Mission Archive Library, Santa Barbara, California. Trans. Maynard Geiger (original document misplaced in archive, Geiger's transcript cited here). Printed by permission.

15. Our Lady of Guadalupe Celebration at Santa Rita, Texas, 1851

Before the U.S. takeover of south Texas, Catholics in the area of present-day Brownsville were served from the parish of Nuestra Señora del Refugio, which was across the Rio Grande at Matamoros. Once under U.S. control, south Texas became part of the Galveston diocese. Subsequently priests stationed at Brownsville visited the south Texas ranchos periodically to administer the sacraments, give religious instruction, and participate in feast-day celebrations. One rancho particularly noted for its Guadalupan devotion was Santa Rita, located about eight miles north of Brownsville. Residents of this rancho built a small wooden chapel to honor their patroness. When priests from Brownsville began making pastoral visitations at Santa Rita, this chapel was already a pilgrimage site for residents from both sides of the Rio Grande. The local Catholic community, which numbered close to eight hundred in 1850, organized annual Guadalupan festivities. Father Emanuel Domenech, a diocesan priest from France assigned to the Brownsville area, wrote the following observations after attending their Guadalupe celebration in 1851 (Matovina 1994: 116–18).

We celebrated at Santa Rita the feast of Our Lady of Guadalupe, the patron saint of the Mexicans. The principal proprietor at Santa Rita, intending to go live at Bahía [present-day Goliad], wished, for the last time, to impart to this feast all possible solemnity. For this end he invited singers and several others from Brownsville. On the eve of the feast, about twenty five of us went on horseback, conducted by this rich *ranchero*, who started off at a gallop, all following through clouds of dust, raised by the horses' hoofs.

On our arrival at Santa Rita, we found seven or eight hundred *rancheros*, assembled from the surrounding country. As this crowd could find no cabins to sleep in, it divided itself into groups, which encamped in the gardens, in the courtyards, and even in the streets and squares of the *rancho*. The chapel, situated to the north of the place, was made with stakes sunk in the earth, potter's clay, and a thatched roof. The belfry, which was completely separated from the body of the church, was of the shape of a gibbet and mounted two old Mexican clocks.

Shortly after nightfall, we repaired to the chapel. The litany of the Blessed Virgin was sung in chorus, as also vespers, and then we formed a procession by torchlight. Young girls in white bore on a pole, ornamented with streamers, flowers, and draperies, an image of the patroness of the Mexicans. They were followed by musicians playing the violin and mandolin, while I walked alone after them, and the people followed close behind. All bore lighted torches or lanterns in their hands and recited the rosary aloud. As we passed in front of a cabin, the procession was saluted by the discharge of a gun, a rocket, or a musket.

I rarely witnessed a more interesting spectacle. These white gowns, that portable altar, covered with lights and flowers, these torches, this singing in the midst of silence and darkness, made a deep impression. After the ceremony came the amusements. For an hour the men assailed one another with harmless rockets, which were thrown and exploded amidst bursts of laughter; and as no feast, even religious, terminates without a *fandango* [dance], the dancing saloon was fixed in a spot where the grass was shorter and more sparse. Coffee was kept boiling in a huge kettle and distributed gratuitously, and the dance opened. The crowd assembled for the celebration of the feast being greater than had been expected, provisions soon became scarce, and coffee alone remained. Experience had taught me what noise is made on such occasions; I therefore went to spend the night beneath a fig tree, away from the ball. Next morning I offered the holy sacrifice in the chapel and preached for the last time.

After Mass, the greater part of the guests was half starved and loath enough to return home fasting. I was of the number and therefore proposed to go and have breakfast at the *rancho* of Doña Stefanita, situated three miles from Santa Rita. We set off on horseback, to the number of thirty. Doña Stefanita, a small, shriveled old woman, placed at our disposal, with patriarchal generosity, her poultry yard and her provisions. A goat, some hens, and melons supplied us with an abundant breakfast. Barring the Irish, I know of no people who exercise such cordial hospitality as the Mexicans.

Abbe [Emanuel] Domenech, *Missionary Adventures in Texas and Mexico: A Personal Narrative of Six Years' Sojourn in Those Regions,* trans. from French (London: Longman, Brown, Green, Longmans, and Roberts, 1858), 357–59.

16. Response to Know-Nothing Attacks, San Antonio, 1855

The anti-immigrant, anti-Catholic Know-Nothing Party achieved its first Texas victory in the San Antonio municipal elections of 1854, gaining control of the mayoral office and the city council. During the Know-Nothings' first weeks in office they repealed a law requiring the city secretary to translate ordinances and other matters into Spanish and banned the long-standing practice of Mexican fandangos (dances). In response to the Know-Nothing threat, San Antonians of Mexican descent joined with the Democratic Party in a vigorous organizing effort for statewide elections the following year. On June 28, Mexican-descent leaders convened the first in a series of "Democratic Meetings of Mexican-Texan Citizens of Bexar County." They promulgated formal resolutions, declaring their opposition to the Know-Nothings and identifying themselves as staunch Catholics who were not immigrants (as the Know-Nothings had alleged) but the true native citizens of Texas. Democrats won the 1855 state elections, besting their Know-Nothing opponents by almost three to one among Bexar County voters (Matovina 1995: 70–74).

Whereas: Of late a certain faction has fomented a spirit of intolerance against all those who profess the Catholic faith, denying them even minimal participation in the affairs and administration of this city, and,

Whereas: That certain group, which aspires to rule our county and our state, is a branch of a secret society with political objectives, whose influence extends throughout this entire Union, and whose principal goal, by means of a variety of intolerant measures, is to exclude the native Catholic population of this Union from their inalienable rights,

1. *Be it resolved:* That as sons of Texas, members of the Catholic Church, and citizens of the United States, we will always oppose any form of secret political association.

2. *Be it resolved:* That although we as Catholic citizens do not expect, nor even desire, privileges greater than those enjoyed by every other citizen, we cannot allow our rights to be dismissed nor denied. Therefore, we oppose and will always oppose all insidious attacks against equal rights and freedom of thought.

3. *Be it resolved:* That as sons of Texas, citizens of the United States, and zealous advocates of institutions that promote freedom, it is impossible for us not to feel indignation and contempt toward the secret political association which casually calls itself "Know-Nothings" and which organized in our city in clandestine and mysterious meetings, with the

main objective, among others, to reduce to a condition of political slavery those of us who dare to worship God according to the dictates of our conscience and the rituals of our ancestors.

4. *Be it resolved:* That our only wish is to stand by the honor, glory, and prosperity of this country in which we were born, in the land which we love. At the same time, we pit our obedience to the law and our interest in the well-being of Texas against those who dare to deny us our inalienable rights and who are, in the main, strangers to this land, with four years, or less, of residence in our state.

5. *Be it resolved:* That we unite ourselves with the Democratic Party of our county and state in opposition to any and all secret political associations, and most particularly to the insidious and treacherous "Order of the Know-Nothings."

> *Bejareño* [San Antonio], 7 July 1855, copy in Newspaper Collection, the Center for American History, the University of Texas at Austin. Trans. Dora Elizondo Guerra.

17. Padre Martínez Protests the Actions of Bishop Lamy, New Mexico, 1857

Padre Antonio José Martínez (1793–1867) was the leading figure among nineteenth-century New Mexican priests. His numerous accomplishments include a distinguished academic career as a seminarian in Durango, the establishment of a primary school and seminary preparatory school in his hometown of Taos (from which some thirty students went on to be ordained for the priesthood), the operation of the first printing press in what is now the western United States, authorship of numerous books and pamphlets, formal certification as an attorney, and extensive service as an elected New Mexican representative in legislative bodies under the Mexican and later the U.S. governments. In 1854, Frenchman Jean Baptiste Lamy (1814–1888), the newly arrived first bishop (and later first archbishop) of Santa Fe, reinstituted mandatory tithing and decreed that heads of families who failed to comply be denied the sacraments. Martínez publicly contested the prelate's action in a newspaper article and a series of letters that included the following selection. This letter was part of Martínez's response to Lamy after hearing of the bishop's decision to suspend him; besides contesting the prelate's tithing decree he also protested Lamy's lack of response to earlier correspondence as well as the bishop's suspension of several other New Mexican priests. Subsequently the conflict between the two churchmen led to Lamy's excommunication of Martínez and to a schism between Martínez's supporters and the official leaders of the Santa Fe diocese (Romero 1976).

Taos, 13 April 1857

Most Illustrious Sir:

Given my present situation, I feel it is my right to bring a few observations to your excellency's attention. At issue is your lack of response to the several letters that I sent you last year between November and December, as well as to the one I sent you this past March. In the interim, Father Damasio Taladrid [whom Bishop Lamy had assigned as Padre Martínez's assistant pastor with the right of succession] has maligned me with slanderous statements directed at me in person, in writing, and frequently even in his Sunday sermons. His most recent outburst was made in your excellency's name.

On October 1 of last year, I sent your excellency a letter listing a variety of issues, not the least of which was Father Taladrid's repeated attacks on my integrity. As our superior it was just to expect that, as part of your duty, your excellency would give my complaint your immediate attention. Instead, your excellency chose to remain silent, refusing to address the issues outlined in my letter until October 24, when I received your letter sentencing me in the following terms: "Be advised that, because you chose to mock my authority by offering Mass in your home without my approval, you are hereby suspended. From this date forward you will refrain from celebrating and administering the sacraments, until such time that you retract all of the scandalous statements you published in the *Santa Fe Gazette*...."

Does your excellency propose to treat me as he has other defenseless clergymen whom he accused without recourse, and who have chosen to bear their plight without complaint, perhaps in hope of eventually finding redress? Such was your excellency's behavior toward the pastor of Albuquerque, Father José Manuel Gallegos. In 1852, Father Gallegos had received written permission from the vicar general himself to be away. Your excellency, upon your return from the United States, saw fit to suspend Father Gallegos and to remove him from his pastoral post, appointing instead your vicar, Father José Machebeuf. To this day that situation remains unchanged. In 1853, your excellency exercised the same prerogative with the *vicario foraneo* [district vicar] and pastor of Santa Fe, Father Juan Felipe Ortiz. First you broke up his parish, completely ignoring church law as regards the division of parochial boundaries. Then you removed Father Ortiz from his parish and took it as your own. Finally, you suspended him, a penalty that he continues to suffer despite his innocence and meritorious service. I omit making mention of other discredited clergymen. I do, however, wish to call your excellency's attention to his circular letter dated 14 January 1854, about which I will make a few brief comments regarding your second and fifth rules, since it is my right to express my opinion, as I did in the articles I published in the *Santa Fe Gazette*....

As regards the fifth rule, I challenge the validity of the following clause: "To the faithful of this Territory...Be aware that we have forbidden priests to administer the sacraments and officiate at religious burials for heads of families who refuse to comply with mandatory tithing." As it stands, this clause suspends pastors in perpetuity and excommunicates the heads of families who do not comply with mandatory tithing. The clause goes against canon law, which places only temporary censures as a remedial measure, as well as the Catholic Church's laws of property ownership. What is more, this Territory belongs to the Republic of the United States of North America, and your diocese falls under the jurisdiction of the metropolitan of Saint Louis, where mandatory tithing is not enforced. Its ministers derive income from honoraria and free will donations.

Your excellency, all of the above demonstrates my rights as already explained in my letter of 12 November. Although information did filter down to me via Joaquín Sandoval, my envoy, it was mostly my own conscience and my own knowledge of church law that told me that I could not possibly have been suspended nor censured under any other ecclesiastical rules, since it was your excellency's duty to have informed me of such penalties in writing, as it was your excellency's duty to discuss with me personally his views about the articles I published in the *Santa Fe Gazette* expressing my opinion to the public. Your excellency is well aware that in our republican form of government citizens have the freedom to express their opinions and even to publish them in the newspaper, especially when it involves issues that threaten the common good.

In light of all that I have stated, I propose the following to your excellency: First, that your excellency withdraw his circular of 14 January 1854, since it harms the spiritual well-being of the faithful. Second, that you openly acknowledge as valid my convictions presented in my aforementioned letter of 12 November, stating that I was not then nor am I now suspended nor censured by any other ecclesiastical rules. Third and last, that I be acknowledged as the rightful pastor of Taos, that Father Damasio Taladrid be reassigned, and that you appoint a different assistant pastor who will be in harmony with my authority. With regard to the question of my resignation, I would do so only after serious thought and only if it was for the benefit of my parishioners.

I look forward to seeing justice done and to having all of these issues resolved in compliance with church law, as it is in your excellency's power to do so.

I remain your faithful and respectful servant.

Antonio José Martínez

Antonio José Martínez, letter to Jean Baptiste Lamy, 13 April 1857, Archive Collection AASF Loose Documents, Diocesan, 1857, no. 16, Archives of the Archdiocese of Santa Fe. Trans. Dora Elizondo Guerra. Used by permission of the Catholic Archdiocese of Santa Fe.

18. Feast-Day Processions in Los Angeles

Spanish subjects founded El Pueblo de Nuestra Señora de los Angeles del Río Porciúncula in 1781. Initially they worshiped at Mission San Gabriel twelve miles to the east, which Franciscans led by Junípero Serra (1713–1784) had established in 1771. In 1822, however, they completed construction of their parish church, Nuestra Señora de los Angeles, or La Placita (literally "the Little Plaza"), as it came to be known in common parlance. Subsequently public ritual and feast days became more prominent in the community. Franciscans from Mission San Gabriel continued to serve the Los Angeles community until 1851; a succession of French, Italian, and then Spanish clergy assumed pastoral duties at La Placita for the remainder of the nineteenth century (Engh 1992, 1994).

18a. Feast of the Assumption, 1857

Newcomers to Los Angeles during the 1850s noted the Mexican Catholic tradi-
tions of the local populace in their diaries and in the town's first newspapers.
Prominent among these traditions were Marian feast days like the Assumption,
which is described below in an 1857 newspaper report.

Saturday last, being the anniversary of the *Asunción,* translation, and ascension
of the Virgin Mary, was celebrated with religious and secular festivities.

The Spanish baptismal name of this city is *La Ciudad de Nuestra Señora de*
Los Angeles, and the 15th of August is celebrated as the anniversary of the patron saint of our vineyard city. According to the Catholic doctrine, the mother
of Christ did not die but was taken up into heaven without the separation of
the spirit from the body and is continually adored by all the heavenly throng
of angels and archangels as their queen.

After the conclusion of the early Mass, and at about 9:00 a.m., High Mass
was celebrated in the Catholic church. The California Lancers, on foot and
armed with rifles, assisted in the celebration of the Mass. The firing of this
company (composed entirely of natives of the country) and with but little
or no previous drilling, was most admirable. At the conclusion of Mass, the
pupils of the female school, headed by their instructresses, the Sisters of Charity, came out of church in procession, bearing the image of our Lady under
a canopy; they were joined by the Lancers and, passing around the public
square, re-entered the church.

The appearance of this procession as it left the church, and during its
march, was imposing. The canopy covering the representation of the angelic
queen, [which was] tastefully ornamented, was born by four girls dressed in
white. The girls of the school, with their heads uncovered, and in uniform
white dresses, followed; then came the Lancers, the rear of the company being
brought up by a mounted division which, armed with lances, had been on
duty during the morning.

In the afternoon, at prayers, the Lancers again attended church and joined
the evening procession. Their appearance and deportment throughout the day
was highly commendable.

Los Angeles Star, 22 August 1857, copy in Los Angeles Public Library.

18b. Feast of Corpus Christi, 1858

Although Marian feast days like the Assumption and Nuestra Señora de los
Remedios were prominent among Mexican Catholics in Los Angeles during
the mid–nineteenth century, the most conspicuous and frequently reported
public ritual among Los Angeles devotees was the Corpus Christi feast. The fol-
lowing newspaper report illuminates the vibrant Corpus Christi procession of
1858, which included Vincentian priest Blas Raho (1806–1862), the pastor of
La Placita. Despite his subsequent attempts to ban or curtail public processions
and other local Mexican Catholic customs (see p. 49), Bishop Thaddeus Amat
(1810–1878), a Vincentian confrere of Raho and the first resident bishop in Los
Angeles, also participated in this celebration.

Immediately after Pontifical Vespers, which were held in the church at 4 p.m., a solemn procession was formed which made the circuit of the Plaza, stopping at the various altars which with great cost, elegance, and taste had been erected in front of the houses where the sacred offices of the church were solemnly performed. The order of the procession was as follows: Music — Young Ladies of the Sisters' School bearing the banner of the school, followed by the children of the school to the number of 120 in two ranks. They were elegantly dressed in white, wearing white veils and carrying baskets filled with flowers which during the procession were scattered before the bishop and the clergy. Next came the boys of the church choir. Then twelve men bearing candles; these represented the twelve apostles. Then came Father [Blas] Raho and Bishop [Thaddeus] Amat, bearing the Blessed Sacrament, supported on each side by the clergy, marching under a gorgeous canopy carried by four prominent citizens. These were followed by a long procession of men, women, and children marching two by two. The procession was escorted by the California Lancers, Captain Juan Sepúlveda commanding and the Southern Rifles, Captain W. W. Twist in command.

Very elaborate and costly preparations had been made by the citizens resident on the Plaza for the reception of the Holy Eucharist; among the most prominent of which we noticed the residence of Don Jesús Dominguez, Don Ignacio Del Valle, Don Vicente Lugo and Don Augustín Olvera. These altars were elegantly designed and tastefully decorated being ornamented with laces, silks, satins, and diamonds. In front of each the procession stopped whilst sacred offices appropriate to the occasion were performed.

Having made the circuit of the Plaza, the procession returned to the church, where the services were concluded. After which the immense assemblage dispersed, and the military escorted the Young Ladies of the Sisters' School on the return home.

> Los Angeles Weekly Star, 5 June 1858, copy in Anaheim Public Library, Anaheim, California.

19. Our Lady of Guadalupe Celebration at Conejos, Colorado, 1874

Spanish-speaking residents engaged in agricultural and ranching pursuits in the San Luis Valley of south-central Colorado during the Mexican period (1821– 1848), but they did not establish permanent settlements until the 1850s. The Catholic populace constructed small chapels but did not build the first parish church in the valley (and in present-day Colorado) until 1857, when the founders of the newly formed Conejos settlement constructed a house of worship dedicated to Our Lady of Guadalupe. At first diocesan priests served the parish; in 1871 exiled Neapolitan Jesuits assumed the pastoral responsibilities for this congregation (Stoller and Steele xvii–xxxiv). While the Jesuits sought to shape the Conejos parish's religious life according to their own theological vision, they also celebrated local traditions like the feast of Our Lady of Guadalupe, as is evident in the following letter of Jesuit priest Salvatore Personè (1833–1922).

The twelfth of December, 1874, was one of the most joyous and delightful days ever seen in Guadalupe, Conejos County, Colorado Territory, on account of the celebration of the fiesta of Our Lady of Guadalupe, general patroness of all Mexicans and special patroness of the Conejos parish. The function was well planned and organized, the crowd in attendance was large, and the people came not only from Conejos County but from neighboring counties as well. The weather was good and the sun bright, seemingly striving to make the fiesta the more stately and solemn and thus to pay due honor to the Queen of Heaven. To increase the brilliance of the festivities, there was a new altar screen of wood above the altar, and a new statue of Our Lady received its blessing just before the procession. The pastor had invited two of the leading gentlewomen of the county to assist as godmothers at the solemn blessing of the statue, Doña María Cornelia Salazar, wife of Major Manuel S. Salazar, and Señora Juana Epifanía de Jesús Valdéz, wife of Don José Simon García, merchant of the same city. The blessing took place at noon and the procession set out just afterwards. Don Crescencio Valdéz led off the sacred cortege, mounted and with banner flying, and there followed about 320 persons either on horseback or marching two by two, led by Brigadier General José Victor García and Don Pablo Ortega. Following the men on horseback came a man carrying a processional cross flanked by two acolytes, and after them came a great concourse of gentlemen and ladies forming two columns, with two young ladies carrying banners, and then a great number of girls in uniform carrying pennants in their hands. Then came the choir of singers and the image of Mary Most Holy borne by eight ladies dressed in white and surrounded by various gentlemen, four of whom carried a canopy and six of whom surrounded the Virgin carrying lighted torches in their hands. Those who bore the canopy were Señores Celedonio Valdéz, M[anuel] S. Salazar, Gabriel Martínez, and Captain Julian Espinosa; carrying lights were Señores Manuel Archuleta, Bonifacio Romero, Gabriel Lucero, Juan Francisco Chacón, Damasio Lucero, and Flavio Trujillo. A priest in cope walking between two acolytes came next, followed by a great number of the faithful. When the procession returned to the church the Rev. Father [Raffaele Luigi] Baldassarre, SJ, celebrated Holy Mass and Father [Lorenzo M.] Fede delivered an eloquent sermon. The enthusiasm and devotion of the faithful were great throughout the day, and they say much for the religious spirit of the people of this locale.

Salvatore Personè, letter of March 1875, trans. Thomas J. Steele, SJ, in Marianne L. Stoller and Thomas J. Steele, SJ, eds., *Diary of the Jesuit Residence of Our Lady of Guadalupe Parish, Conejos, Colorado: December 1871 – December 1875* (Colorado Springs: Colorado College Press, 1982), 185–86. Printed by permission.

20. Speech at Colegio de Las Vegas, New Mexico, 1878

Rafael Romero (1850–1919) was a politician, superintendent of schools, and rancher from a prominent New Mexican family. His distinguished educational background included studies at Princeton University. In 1878 he gave an address during festivities for the close of the first academic year at the Colegio de Las

*Vegas, a Jesuit school that later became Regis University and Regis Jesuit High
School in Denver. During the preceding year the Jesuits had attempted to establish the school's tax-exempt and degree-granting status. Although their request
copied language from a similar petition approved for the Sisters of Loretto four
years earlier, a new territorial governor vetoed the Jesuit bill and publicly insulted
the Jesuits and the Catholic Church. When the territorial legislature overrode his
veto, he convinced the U.S. Congress, which regulated all territorial legislation,
to annul the passed bill. Romero's speech on this occasion was published in*
La Revista Católica, *a Jesuit-operated newspaper based in Las Vegas (and later
El Paso, Texas) and the first Spanish Catholic newspaper in the United States
(Steele 148–49).*

Ladies and Gentlemen:

I have been honored by being asked to offer some remarks on the present
occasion. I am aware of and appreciate the great honor conferred upon me by
such an invitation on such a propitious occasion. . . .

A great number of those who are here present are the descendants of those
valiant and daring men of the proud blood of Spain, the oldest settlers of the
United States. Our settlements not very far from here are the most ancient
over which the grand American flag flies [*sic,* St. Augustine, Florida, is actually the oldest permanent settlement in the continental United States]. Our
ancestors penetrated into these deserted and dangerous regions many years
before the Mayflower floated over the dancing waves that washed Plymouth
Rock. Some of the settlers came here resplendent in the gorgeous rich clothing of sixteenth-century *hidalgos* [nobles], soldiers of the crown, while certain
other persons arrived quite simply dressed. [They were] the noble and intrepid
[Franciscan] soldiers of the Cross, whose more recent colleagues [the Jesuits]
give us in our own day proof of their commitment to and solicitude for the
education of youth. The emigrants who disembarked at Plymouth Rock came
under the flag of England. Our forebears arrived under the royal pennon of
heroic Spain. New England was colonized by men of a daring, valiant, energetic, unbending spirit — but in imitation of the false "standard-bearer of
enlightenment," they committed the sin of pride and were cursed with the loss
of their faith. New Spain, or what we call today New Mexico, was settled by
equally fearless and forceful men who joined their pride to a wonderful court-
liness. They were noble, friendly, and loyal, but they were at the same time
endowed with a loftier concept of the Creator and possessed of a more refined
love of their fellow men, and they rejoiced to acknowledge the supreme authority of God (*Applause*). Catholics settled New Mexico, people filled with
respect for any group concerned with the culture and growth of Catholic faith
and doctrine (*Applause*). And it is the most pleasant recompense for being
true descendants of the ancient explorers of New Mexico that in the midst
of all the troubles and changes of this world they have preserved the faith
and doctrines of their ancestors, holding them all in the greatest reverence and
considering them the object of their most sincere and obsequious submission.
Besides the doctrines of the Catholic faith and on a human level, they honor
the teachers of these sublime lessons by means of which man comes to disdain

the delights of this earth and aspire to the glories of heaven. And among the expositors of these doctrines, as you are surely aware, the Jesuit Fathers do not occupy the last place. [Here the Jesuit editors of *La Revista Católica* omitted some of Romero's laudatory remarks about the Jesuit order.] From the classical classrooms of Coimbra to the remote regions through which the Oregon River flows, ignorant till our own days "of all sound except that of its own waves"; from the Tibetan plains to the mountains of Peru, the black-robed sons of Loyola have raised the cross of the Redeemer, have kindled the only light that conducts man from earth to heaven. In their efforts with barbaric and inhuman tribes as well as in their battles against the passions and vices of the overly sophisticated, they have met with what they anticipated — suspicion, enmity, opposition, and oppression. Those adversities have fulfilled the prayer of their illustrious founder Ignatius, at one time a gallant Spanish soldier. He knew human nature with a superhuman intelligence, and he prayed that his sons would never lack persecution, the genuine wellspring of steadfastness, of indifference to the world, and of reliance on heaven. Here in our ancient land of New Mexico, you know how this prayer of Saint Ignatius has been fulfilled.

The Savior God was tormented by a provincial governor, and we are not without a governor who has been playing a worse part even than Pilate (*Applause*). The Pilate of old failed by not protecting the innocent; our new one devotes himself to persecution (*Thunderous Applause*). And should I then put a muzzle over my mouth? Why should I fail to speak the truth? Am I not the master of my own home? And am I not so to speak in my own home? Am I not a Catholic citizen of a Catholic land, New Mexico? And have I not, as a New Mexican Catholic, been grossly insulted by a pathetic public official? What does it mean when a man sent to be the governor of a Catholic land, in an official message directed to Catholic legislators and to our Catholic people, piles insult upon insult against a religious order of the Catholic Church? That man does this, and am I supposed to refrain from stigmatizing his language, or on an appropriate occasion, attacking it as it deserves? Does he suppose that the sons of Spanish *hidalgos* need lectures on morality from those who style themselves "ex-Mormon bishops" and official vagabonds from "Western Reserve" [University]? I care nothing about the vociferations of the gang whose mouthpiece our present Pilate is, nor would I care to reply to them. All that I want is to let our foreign brethren [the Jesuits] know that we do not forget who we are and that as long as we keep our eyes on the enemy, we laugh at their attacks (*Applause*).

It is a beautiful cardinal principle of our creed that we distinguish between the individual and his deeds. We can reprove and totally execrate a man's bad deeds without asserting that the man himself is bad. In my ears always echo those terrible words "Judge not lest you be judged." So I denounce the evil deeds, but to the man himself I extend the cloak of charity and apply to him the consoling prayer of the Divine Master, "Father forgive him, for he knows not what he does" (*Prolonged Applause*).

The misguided governor is merely the mouthpiece of a deviant element of a small minority of the people of the United States. And perhaps he believes he is doing right. Out of charity let us say that he does. But I reply to those evangelists of "reason": why not listen to the teachings of our God, the warnings of plain logic, of reason clear and simple? They say that governments ought to see to their own continuation. How can you enable them to survive unless you teach the youth of the nation that God is Lord of this little planet of ours, which He on a certain occasion deigned to fetch out of nothingness? How can you inculcate this effectively in children if you do not do so daily in the place where they are taught, where their minds grow? If you exclude religion from the schools where the youth are instructed, does not common sense tell us that those children will have no religious instruction? The child is father to the man; they will become what they were in their infancy and adolescence. Schools without religion produce irreligious adults. They will obey laws as long as it pleases them or so long as the laws are enforced with sufficient physical force. Men without religion become bandits, desperadoes, Communists, destroyers of the social order, rebels against all political power. Secular schools produce secular men who rob banks and cut throats if they think they can do so while getting something and getting away with it. And why not? By virtue of their theory, they would be stupid if they did not.

Is that the sort of society you want? That is what you will have if you abolish religious instruction. The motto of our new Pontius Pilate and his followers is "Down with religious education." The motto of the Jesuit Fathers is "Religion and Knowledge...."

> Rafael Romero, speech at Colegio de Las Vegas, *Revista Católica*, 31 August 1878, University of Texas at El Paso Library, in Thomas J., Steele, SJ, ed. and trans., *New Mexican Spanish Religious Oratory, 1800–1900* (Albuquerque: University of New Mexico Press, 1997), 151–59. Printed by permission.

21. Religious Devotion in Tucson, Arizona

Spanish subjects founded the presidio *(garrison) of San Agustín de Tucson in 1775. Located ten miles north of Mission San Xavier del Bac, which Jesuit Eusebio Kino (1645–1711) had established in 1692, under Spanish and Mexican rule the settlement was a frontier outpost of the Sonora province. Mission San Xavier was the center of worship for Tucson residents until 1863, when they founded San Agustín parish in Tucson itself. Bishop Jean Baptiste Salpointe (1825–1898) was appointed vicar apostolic of Arizona in 1868 and centered his ministry at San Agustín parish; residents constructed a new San Agustín church in the mid-1890s, and it was named a cathedral when Tucson became a diocese in 1897 (Sheridan).*

21a. Private and Public Devotion, 1882

This passage is from the memoirs of Federico José María Ronstadt (1868–1954). He was born in Las Delicias, Sonora, Mexico, and in 1882 moved to Tucson, where he and his family became influential citizens. Largely composed in the last decade of his life, Ronstadt's reminiscences include a description of his devotional practices during his first years in Tucson. They also recall his participation

in the month-long festivities for the community's patronal feast of San Agustín;
these festivities began on August 28 (the saint's feast day) and encompassed
Mexican Independence Day on September 16.

My first year in Tucson, Tía Chona saw to it that I made my first communion
and was confirmed. I was confirmed by Bishop [Jean Baptiste] Salpointe at
the old St. Agustín Cathedral on Church Plaza. Part of the old building and
the main cut stone entrance still stand. It is now used for a garage. This is a
historical landmark that should be preserved.

The prayers that my mother taught me I have always remembered. Morning and night I have always said besides the Lord's Prayer and my Hail Marys
[the following prayers]: *Gracias y alabanzas te doy gran Señor y alabo tu gran*
poder pues con el alma en el cuerpo me has dejado amanecer. Yo te pido creador
mío por tu caridad y amor, me dejas anochecer en gracia y servicio tuyo por siem-
pre jamás, Amén. Angel de mi guardia, amable compañía. No me desampares de
noche ni de día. Con Dios me acuesto, con Dios me levanto. Dios conmigo, yo con
El, Dios adelante y yo tras de El. [I give you praise and thanks, great Lord, and
I praise your great power, for you have allowed me to awaken with my soul
still in my body. I ask you, my Creator, in your charity and love, to allow me
to reach the evening in Your grace and service forevermore. Amen. Guardian
angel, amiable companion, do not abandon me this night or during the day. I
lay me down with God and I get up with God. God with me and I with God;
God before me and I behind God.]

Then to end I have always said one more short prayer that my father
taught me: "*Virgen Purísima cúbreme con tu manto celestial* [Most pure Virgin, cover me with your heavenly mantle]," and in the morning, "*Virgen*
Purísima no me dejes caer en tentación [Most pure Virgin, do not let me fall
into temptation]. . . . "

My first 16th of September (Mexican Independence Day) 1882 in Tucson
was celebrated with a great public feast. They had a number of fine floats in
the parade, and a troupe of boys had been uniformed and drilled to act as a
guard of honor to the queen and her court. I was a private in that troupe. The
parade marched to Levin's Park where the annual fiesta of St. Agustín was in
full sway. This feast (honoring the patron saint of Tucson) started on the 28th
of August and lasted for a month.

Federico José María Ronstadt, *Borderman: Memoirs of Federico José María*
Ronstadt, ed. Edward F. Ronstadt with a foreword by Bernard L. Fontana
(Albuquerque: University of New Mexico Press, 1993), 80–81, 92. Printed by
permission.

21b. San Isidro Feast Day, 1894

This newspaper report illuminates the devotion in the Tucson area on the
May 15 feast of San Isidro. The practice of promesas, *or offering promises in ex-*
change for the granting of a petition, is also evident in this account, as rancher
Manuel Castillo offered a grand supper each year on this feast to fulfill a promise
made years before.

All honor was shown today to San Ysidro Labrador. San Ysidro is the rural saint, the patron of the fields and crops. The image was carried today about the fields below town, with a gay procession following. They went through every field. The custom is to take a single field at a time and march around it with songs, an occasional firing of guns when the participants become particularly enthusiastic, and then return to the house. A new start is made for each field.

At every house refreshments are on hand and are served. A feature is usually an olla filled with teswin, a light wine made from corn. No other intoxicants are permitted. The procession through the fields today lasted much of the day. The first of the crop of each field was promised to the patron saint. The Chinese gardeners have come to have due regard for this annual festival and were among the heavy contributors, some of them giving money.

One rancher, Manuel Castillo, made a promise years ago to give a special celebration to this festival each 15th of May. Tonight, as usual, he will serve a grand spread, and all members of the procession will be there to partake. After that the special prayers, presumably for good crops in the coming year, will follow and last the whole night through. At midnight another big supper will be served.

Tucson Citizen, 15 May 1894, copy in Tucson-Pima Public Library.

22. Our Lady of Mount Carmel Feast Day, Ysleta, Texas, 1882

New Mexican settlers and some Native American groups fled to the area of El Paso del Norte after the Pueblo Revolt of 1680 in northern New Mexico (document 2). In October of that year, they celebrated the first Catholic Mass near present-day Ysleta, just east of El Paso. Shortly thereafter Franciscan friars and Tigua Indians established Mission San Antonio de la Ysleta. The mission was originally located on what today is the Mexican side of the Rio Grande, but an 1829 flood destroyed the mission, shifted the river's flow, and placed the mission site on the opposite side of what later became the international border between Mexico and the United States. Ysleta parishioners completed a new church in 1851. Diocesan priests served as pastors of the church until 1881, when Jesuits assumed the pastorate. Under the Jesuits the church was rededicated to Nuestra Señora del Monte Carmelo (Our Lady of Mount Carmel), although to this day many parishioners of Tigua ancestry still refer to it as the church of San Antonio (Timmons). Despite ongoing Tigua allegiance to their indigenous heritage, Mexican Catholic parishioners and traditions were clearly evident by the time of the following 1882 newspaper report. The account illuminates the animated feast-day celebrations which Mexican-descent Catholics organized for local patron saints, in this case the Ysleta parish's new patroness, Our Lady of Mount Carmel.

Of all celebrations of the Mexicans in the United States, none are entered into so heartily as those in honor of some patron saint. Other *fete* days, local or national, are considered of minor importance. Therefore, when it is announced that a celebration in honor of a patron saint is to take place, the usual calm serenity of Mexican life is agitated by a ripple of excitement that manifests itself in decorations, elaborate church ceremonies, processions, fireworks, etc.

The celebration of Our Lady of Mount Carmel, the patron saint of Ysleta, was no exception to the rule. Saturday evening last the old church was brilliantly illuminated, within by candles and without by lanterns, bonfires burned in the plaza, and hundreds of little red lanterns lined the tops of many houses along the principal streets. An immense throng of people crowded the church during the services inside, then poured out upon the plaza to see the fireworks. A band of musicians having two or three brass pieces, a bass drum, clarinet, and a violin, alternated with a choir of young ladies, and sometimes accompanied them. A file of men then marched up with rifles and opened the pyrotechnic display by a volley from their guns, scores of rockets pierced the gloom above. This was the climax, but not the finale. A "fire-tree" was next lighted. This "tree" was about fifteen feet high and constructed so as to reveal, when consuming, many brilliant balls and circles of fire. The torch was applied to a fuse at the bottom, and the fire ascended by stages; when it reached the last stage but one, the little balls of fire formed a shield of red, green, and yellow bars extending lengthwise, and at the top a conical frame was set revolving. In the apex of the cone was a quantity of powder which exploded with a terrific report and clothed the charred tree in a beautiful shower of sparks. This wound up the display for the evening, and the band playing a Mexican national air, marched down to a saloon for refreshments.

Sunday forenoon services were again held in the church, which was profusely decorated for the occasion. This building, as most old Mexican churches, is built in the shape of a cross. In each arm of the church was a statue, and back of the altar was a statute of the Virgin Mary and the infant Christ, with some saint kneeling before them. The band that performed the evening before was now in the gallery at the rear of the church, and an organ stood near the altar. A choir of little girls sang with an organ accompaniment by a priest, and a choir of young ladies, assisted by the band, also sang several tunes, while the riflemen outside the door occasionally fired a salute to enliven the entertainment and make the priests and congregation jump. One is reminded of the old mountaineer who said New Mexico is where they worship God with drums and shot guns.

About 6 p.m. the grand procession was formed. About sixty horsemen wearing broad, red sashes were in the lead; men on foot and wearing blue sashes followed next in order; then came a number of women in ordinary costume, followed by a large number of young women dressed in white — in this part of the procession the image of Our Lady of Mount Carmel was borne. Following these were the little girls also dressed in white, and in the midst of them, under a canopy supported by men, walked the parish priest. The whole number in line must have been nearly a thousand. The procession passed around the plaza and up to the church again, as the wind blew so hard the march had to be discontinued. Fireworks were again in order and the display this evening was more brilliant than that of the night before. Two fire-trees, hundreds of rockets, circles, shooting of guns, music, etc., completed the program.

A priest from Albuquerque, and one from San Elizario, assisted the Ysleta priests in the church services. Benito Gonzales engineered the pyrotechnic display. The fireworks were made at Ysleta by a Mexican. Many people from El Paso, Socorro, and San Elizario, participated in the celebration.

El Paso Herald, 19 July 1882, copy in University of Texas at El Paso Library.

23. Pilgrimage to Chimayó, New Mexico, 1890

Tewa Indians acclaimed the healing properties of Chimayó's sacred earth centuries before Catholic settlers arrived at this locale on the western side of the Sangre de Cristo Mountains. Spanish subjects completed the first chapel at the site in 1816 and dedicated the Santuario de Chimayó to Nuestro Señor de Esquipulas (Our Lord of Esquipulas), a Guatemalan representation of the crucifixion associated with a Mayan sacred place of healing earth. During the 1850s, however, devotees of the Santuario de Chimayó added a statue of the Santo Niño de Atocha (Holy Child of Atocha) in response to a new local shrine dedicated to the Santo Niño. Subsequently the Santo Niño and the miraculous dirt became the focal points for santuario devotees. They remain so today for the thousands of pilgrims who continue to visit Chimayó (R. Gutiérrez). María Montoya Martínez (b. 1881?) lived in the pueblo of San Ildefonso, New Mexico, near Santa Fe and was a renowned potter who led the revival of Pueblo pottery-making during the first decades of the twentieth century. Ethnologist Alice Marriott (b. 1910) interviewed Maria extensively from 1945 to 1946 and subsequently wrote about her interviewee's life and experiences. The following passage is based on those conversations and records María's recollections of her childhood pilgrimage to Chimayó after she recovered from smallpox (Marriott).

She [María's mother] took a bundle from the back of the wagon, and she and María went towards the carved doors of the old church. A small bell hung on a wire there, and Mother put out her hand and set the bell to ringing gently. It hardly rang, but the soft tap was enough. A Spanish man, so old that he was bent, came around the corner of the building.

"Do you want to go in?" he asked, and when Mother nodded, he took a bunch of keys that hung from his belt, selected one of them, and unlocked the door. Slowly one leaf of the door swung inward, and they went inside.

There were votive lights blooming like yellow yucca flowers on an iron stand before the altar, as the old man led María and her mother down the aisle. Then the man turned to his left and unlocked a grilled iron door beside the altar. There was darkness behind the door — darkness and a sense of depth. Mother drew María towards it. The child smelled an earthen dampness, like the darkness of the storeroom at home, and it surprised her. Most churches smelled of dry dust, not wet.

"There are steps going down," said Mother. "You must go down them. When you get to the bottom, take off all your clothes. Don't be afraid, because nobody can see you. Then take this holy medal and scrape off the earth on the sides of the hole. Rub the earth all over your body. That's what makes you well."

"Will you go with me?" María asked.

"Just you can go. This is your pilgrimage. After you have rubbed yourself with the sacred earth and dressed again, take the medal and dig out enough earth to fill your water bottle. That much you can take home with you, to drink there to make you well. While you are doing this, you should say your 'Our Father.' Don't think about any thing but your prayers and the *Santo Niño*."

So this was what you did at the end of a pilgrimage! María did not mean to think of other things or to disobey her mother and possibly be rude to the *Santo Niño,* but she was too surprised to stop thinking. She had not expected a hole in the ground or that she would have to go down into it alone. Carefully, feeling her way with her toes, she went down the four steps behind the grill. She knew she must be staining her white moccasins, but perhaps the stains of the sacred earth would not show when she came out.

"Say your prayers aloud so I can hear them," María heard her mother's voice say above her.

María never knew how long she stayed in the hole under the church. She undressed and rubbed herself with earth and dressed again. She filled the water bottle, cautiously feeling along the wall with the medal to loosen the earth. Many people must have been there before her, for she could feel with the tips of her fingers the deep scratches they had left in the walls of the pit.

Her mother was waiting, kneeling just outside the grill when the child came out. The bundle lay on the ground beside the woman, and a dark shawl covered her head. When she saw María, Mother reached out, without rising, and opened the bundle.

"These things are your offerings," she said. "You can take them to the altar and leave them there."

The old Spanish man stood at the head of the church aisle. He nodded without speaking when he saw María coming towards him and led the way to the altar and its wreaths of blooming lights.

"You can put the things down here," he said in Spanish.

There was cloth in the bundle, purple cloth, like María's own best dress. There were a little black rosary and a big piece of buckskin, and there were three ten-cent pieces. . . .

She left the offerings and crossed herself in front of the carved and painted figure of the *Santo Niño* that stood on the great altar. Then she turned and walked back to her mother, who was kneeling now in the aisle of the church. From the side aisle on the left of the church, Father and Tío Tilano also rose. Together they all four went out into the sunset.

"Give me the bottle of earth, please," Mother said, and María handed it to her.

"What will you do with it?" she asked.

"You will have to mix it in water and drink it before breakfast every morning for the next four days," her mother answered. "This is good earth. The Indians knew about it and how to use it a long time ago. Then the *padres* came and learned about its power, and the *Santo Niño* came and told them what to do, so they built the church here. Everybody knows that the earth is good. It makes everyone well who drinks it, for the rest of his life."

Alice Marriott, *María: The Potter of San Ildefonso,* with drawings by Margaret Lefranc (Norman: University of Oklahoma Press, 1948), 36–37. Copyright 1948 by the University of Oklahoma Press. Printed by permission.

24. Holy Week and Feast Days, Arroyo Hondo, New Mexico, ca. 1890s

The following description from Cleofas Martínez de Jaramillo (1878–1956) is based on her recollections as a native-born resident of Arroyo Hondo, a village twelve miles north of Taos. Martínez de Jaramillo founded La Sociedad Folklórica at Santa Fe in 1935 and promoted the Hispano heritage of Taos County through her writing, speaking, and efforts to organize events that enhanced cultural awareness and appreciation (Weigle and White 444). Her recollections illuminate the leadership of women in various feasts and devotions. They also illustrate the leadership role of Los Hermanos de Nuestro Padre Jesús Nazareno (Brothers of Our Father Jesus the Nazarene), or Penitentes. The Penitentes evolved as brotherhoods in the towns and villages of northern New Mexico and southern Colorado well before the U.S. takeover of the area. Their most conspicuous function was to commemorate Christ's passion and death during Lent and, in particular, during Holy Week, although they also provided community leadership and fostered social integration. Organized as separate local entities, Penitente brotherhoods consisted of two major groups, the Hermanos de Luz (Brothers of Light), who were responsible for administrative functions, and the Hermanos de Sangre (Brothers of Blood), who performed penitential acts during the brotherhood's Lent and Holy Week rituals. Additionally, brotherhoods had a leader named the hermano mayor (older brother) and a morada (literally "habitation"), or chapter house, where they held meetings and religious devotions (Espinosa).

During Lent every year [the local people] reenacted with sincere religious fervor the Sorrows of the Passion Play. The Penitente brotherhood took charge of the religious ceremonies, inasmuch as there was no resident priest in the town in my time....

The Tenebrae. On Wednesday evening, *Las Tinieblas* were held at the *morada.* The name *Tinieblas* was given this office because towards its close all the lights were extinguished to represent the darkness that shrouded the face of the earth at the time Christ expired on the cross, as well as to express the profound mourning of the Church at that time.

Fifteen candles were placed on a triangular wooden stand. Those at the sides were snuffed out successively, beginning with the lowest one, at the end of each of the eleven Penitential Psalms, representing the flight of the eleven apostles; the other three candles represented the three Marys. When the central light, representing Christ, was the only one left, it was removed by the *rezador* [prayer leader] to the back of the altar, where they continued their chant. Between chants, one of the *rezadores* stepped out to the front of the altar, and striking a match he whirled it around saying, "*Salgan vivos y difuntos, que aquí estamos todos juntos*" [Come out living and dead, for here we are all together]. The flash of light from the match represented the lightning. In the dim light the bent, huddled figures of the Penitentes, their bodies bare to the waist, filed in through the low door. With their masked faces and long white trousers they looked ghostly. The air in the small oratorio room, already packed with men and women kneeling on the floor, became stifling.

Above the roar of the wooden *matraca* [rattle], the rumbling of chains, the wail of the reed *pito* [pipe], groans and prayers, was heard the thud-thud of the Penitentes' blood-matted whips.

The removal of the central light and its sudden reappearance represented Christ's death and resurrection....

On Maundy Thursday at two o'clock in the afternoon, the *Emprendimiento* (Seizure of Christ) took place. The men carrying the statue of *Nuestro Padre Jesus,* a life-sized statue of Jesus of Nazareth, crowned with thorns and dressed in a long red tunic, led the procession out of the Church. The *rezador,* reading the seizure and trial of Christ, walked behind the statue, followed by the throng of women.

From *la morada* on the opposite side of the town two files of brethren of light, representing the Jews, started out. These men had red handkerchiefs tied over their heads with a knot on top representing a helmet. They were preceded by a man dressed like a centurion. The Jews carried long, iron chains and *matracas,* or rattlers. On meeting the procession coming from the church, they stopped before the statue and asked, "Who art Thou?" The men carrying the statue answered, "*Jesús de Nazareno.* (Jesus of Nazareth.)" The Jews then seized the statue, tied the statue's hands with a white cord, while their leader read the arrest sentence. The other Jews stood, loudly clanging the chains and rattling the *matracas.* They led the procession back to the *morada,* carrying with them the statue.

El Encuentro. The next morning — Good Friday — the same two groups took part in the ceremony. This time the group that left the church carried the statue of *Nuestra Señora de la Soledad* (Our Lady of Sorrows), dressed in black, a black mantle covering her head, over which a silver halo shone. The procession of men representing the Jews came from the *morada* carrying the statue of Christ. The two groups met half way around the town, representing the meeting of Christ and His mother. One of the women took a white cloth from her head and, approaching on her knees, wiped the face of the statue, while the grieving Marys wept real tears aloud. The *rezador* read the passage of the meeting of Christ and His mother as the procession walked back to the church.

About half an hour later, *La Procesión de Sangre* (literally "the procession of blood") of all the Penitentes combined, in the long double file of flagellants, was seen winding its way up the rocky trail to the *calvario,* then back again to the *morada.* Special self-imposed penances were practiced between one and three o'clock in the afternoon. A lone Penitente sometimes staggered up the trail surrounded by brethren of light. He dragged his feet tied with a heavy iron chain. On his back a bunch of sharp cactus needles pricked his flesh at every step.

Good Friday. Las Tres Caidas (Three Falls). The largest and heaviest cross was picked out and laid upon the shoulder of the *hermano* who chose to represent the crucified Christ. A crown of thorns was placed on his head, and a bunch of prickly cactus was hung on his back. Laboriously, the Penitente dragged the scraping cross up the rocky trail. Two brethren of light walked on each side of him, one reading the three falls in the Stations of the Cross from an open book in his hand. The other, acting the part of Simon Cyrene, helped the *hermano* lift the weighty cross when he stumbled and fell under its weight. A group of brethren of light had already dug a pit and gathered a pile of rocks by Calvary Cross. They stood around the *calvario*, awaiting the arrival of the *Cristo* brother, who on reaching the hill was stretched upon his cross and tied with ropes. The cross was raised and placed in the pit surrounded by the pile of rocks to hold it upright.

The *hermanos* knelt with bowed heads around the cross, praying and reciting the Seven Last Words of the crucified Savior. The voice of the man upon the cross grew more and more faint, as he repeated the words, until his body hung limp, and he was taken down and carried on a blanket, too weak to carry his cross back to the *morada*.

Las Estaciones. At three o'clock the people gathered at the church for the Stations of the Cross. The procession of Penitentes, some carrying crosses and others switching their lacerated backs, came first. Between the two files walked a masked Penitente pulling a small cart in which stood the statue of Death. "Comadre Sebastiana" death was called. The *acompañador* [attendant], walking behind the cart, now and then picked up a large stone and dropped it into the cart to make it heavier to pull. The men carrying the statue of *Nuestro Padre Jesús*, another man with a crucifix, and the reader walked in the center of the procession. As the *rezador* read each Station of the Cross, the people knelt on the ground, then arose and walked singing a verse of the *alabado de las columnas*.

Én una columna atádo,	Onto a pillar,
Estaba El Réy del Cíelo.	The King of Heaven was tied.

Chorus

Herído y ensangrentádo	Wounded and bloody,
Y arratrádo por los suelos.	He was dragged on the ground....

Sabado de Gloria [Holy Saturday] closed the Holy Week with joy and cheer, for Lent ended at noon on Holy Saturday, and a big *baile* [dance] was given that night....

•

[Although I attended a boarding school, each year] I arrived home in time for the feast of the beloved disciple St. John. The women of the village were up early on the twenty-fourth of June. At six o'clock they were bathing in the river or in the *acequias* [canals]. Later in the morning the small children were seen also in the river and ditches, splashing cold water at each other, for on this day the waters in the streams were believed to be holy. Better health awaited those who rose early to bathe at least their faces and feet in the holy water. For was it not St. John who baptized Jesus in the river Jordan and blessed the waters?

The day was kept at Arroyo Hondo as a Rogation Day [day of prayer for abundant harvests]. By eight o'clock in the morning a procession started from the church in the upper town. Standing on a wooden platform, the statue of Nuestra Señora del Rosario, dressed in a gala blue silk dress, and the statue of San Juan, carried in the arms of one of his devotees, were taken on a tour through the fields, along the foot of the second ridge of hills to the lower village — a distance of three miles. On arriving at the village, the procession visited each house. A boy beating a drum went ahead announcing the approach of the procession, which halted about ten feet from the door of the house. The lady of the house came out to meet the *santos,* with an *escudilla* [shallow bowl] full of live coals, over which aromatic incense had been sprinkled. She incensed the statues and helped carry them into the *sala* [room], where they were placed on an improvised altar decorated with wild flowers and tree branches.

Around the altar the crowd of people knelt while the lady of the house recited prayers, sang a hymn, and pinned a flower or jewel on Our Lady's veil or dress. Then the people arose and proceeded to the next house. Having visited every house in the lower village, the procession walked to the middle town, then up the *cordillera* [row of houses] to the upper town, reaching the church at dusk, where a wake in honor of the saints was held. Sometimes the wake was held at the house in which the procession stopped before dusk.

On the Fourth [Third?] of May was celebrated *El Dia de la Santa Cruz* (Feast of the Holy Cross). At the chapel or at the home of a devotee an altar was erected in tiers. On the top tier a wooden, decorated cross was placed. From here it was brought down and rested on each step, while a prayer or hymn was sung or recited. Then the cross was taken out in procession to the next village, where a wake was held in honor of the Holy Cross.

Día de Santiago. The feast of *Santiago,* the national patron saint of Spain, was and still is celebrated in some of the northern towns, on the twenty-fifth of July. After the morning services at the church, the statue of Saint James, the patron saint of *los caballeros* (horsemen), was carried in procession through the town. Two files of gallant horsemen, *socios de Santiago,* with their horses' bridles decorated with flowers and flags, rode ahead of the procession. A few yards from the procession they halted, turned, and rode back through the center of the procession in pairs to meet the statue. The two files crossed and galloped ahead. Again they whirled and galloped back to the statue, repeating this during the whole procession. . . .

Dia de Santa Ana. The next day was *Santa Ana*'s day. Every woman fortunate enough to own a riding horse and side saddle brought them out. And with a white sheet thrown over the saddle and tied underneath to keep the long flowing skirts from soiling, she rode off, dressed in all her finery, to join the other lady riders. When tired of riding, they dismounted at the dance, which continued through the hot afternoon into the night.

These holy days were always gala occasions eagerly awaited and long remembered.

Cleofas M. Jaramillo, *Shadows of the Past (Sombras del pasado)* (Santa Fe, N.Mex.: Seton Village Press, 1941), 67–72, 85–87.

25. Confirmation at Las Cruces, New Mexico, 1902

*Although Spanish-speaking residents lived in the El Paso area from the late six-
teenth century, they did not establish nearby Las Cruces until 1849. Significant
population growth followed upon the construction of railroad lines through
the town in 1881. In May 1902, Bishop Henry Granjon (1863–1922) of Tucson visited his flock in southwest New Mexico, administering confirmation at
Las Cruces and various other settlements (Granjon 126–27). Bishop Granjon's
account of his pastoral visit to Las Cruces noted the enduring practice of confirming children as infants among local Mexican Catholics as well as the practice
of* compadrazgo *(literally "co-parentage"), an honored Mexican tradition that
entails the extension of familial ties to a child's godparents.*

The confirmation ceremony was to take place following High Mass. The
church, too narrow for the occasion, overflowed with people. Four-fifths
were Mexicans or *mestizos* [a mix of Spanish and Native American ancestry].
This was apparent from the tanned complexions, the shining black eyes, the
abundant ebony hair, and the brightly colored outfits. A small number were
Americans from all parts of the Union....

Since the audience was mixed, it was a matter of my addressing them in two
languages, English and Spanish. I began with Spanish. The short speech was
given without incident before an attentive audience, but I had scarcely begun
my discourse in English, for those who did not understand Spanish, when I
perceived among the Mexican ranks some kind of growing agitation. Men and
women were rising, leaving their benches, going from here to there, passing by
each other. Uncooperative babies soon began to scream their heads off and fill
the church with a deafening commotion. In these former Spanish colonies, it is
the custom to confirm the children at a young age. When all is said and done,
confirmation of adults is rare and generally is limited to Americans. The Mexicans treat confirmation like baptism and have it administered to young babies.
Moreover, each child is furnished with a godfather or godmother according to
its sex. To be invited to serve as godfather is considered a great honor and a sign
of deep friendship. It establishes, from that moment, between the godparents
and parents of the child tight, strong bonds which cause the godfather to be
considered as a member of the family, and he is treated as such until death. The
institution of *compadres* and *comadres* is universal among the Mexicans; it fills
their lives with an important role, and they value it like the pupils of their eyes.

You can ask any service whatsoever of your *compadre;* it will not be denied. Your house is his; your belongings are at his disposition. These multiple
attachments, mostly between families, maintain the unity of the Mexican population and permit them to resist, to a certain extent, the invasions of the
Anglo-Saxon race. The Mexicans who live in the United States do not bother
to learn the language of the country, which is English, and continue to observe their own traditions and customs as they did before the annexation of
their lands by the American Union.

Henry Granjon, *Along the Rio Grande: A Pastoral Visit to Southwest New Mexico
in 1902,* ed. Michael Romero Taylor, trans. Mary W. de López (Albuquerque:
University of New Mexico Press, 1986), 37–39. Printed by permission.

26. La Capilla de Los Milagros, San Antonio, 1907

La Capilla de Nuestro Señor de los Milagros (the Chapel of Our Lord of Mira-
cles), or La Capilla de los Milagros, as it is commonly known, is a sacred place
of prayer and healing. Members of a family named Jiménez reportedly rescued
a crucifix from a fire at San Fernando parish (see document 4), probably in
1828, and, despite the clergy's refusal to recognize their efforts, enshrined it
in a private chapel for devotees from far and near. Veteran San Antonio Ex-
press reporter Charles Merritt Barnes (d. 1927) wrote the following newspaper
feature on the chapel in 1907. Barnes's report reflected his perspective as an
outside observer of the chapel and its devotions, but also recorded local tradi-
tions about the origins of the chapel and its famous statue, both of which are
still popular among contemporary devotees (Matovina 1996: 15).

In the triangle formed by Laredo, Ruiz and Salado streets and on Ruiz Street is
a quaint structure that, although famous, attracts but little attention from the
ordinary passerby. It is in such an isolated neighborhood that very few ever
visit it, and yet there are many who make long pilgrimages to do so.

The place is a small private Catholic chapel. Its name is "Our Lord of Miracles" or *"Nuestro Señor de los Milagros,"* as the inscription on the cross above
it indicates. On the other side of the cross is the inscription [which] indicates that it was built in 1813, but this is likely to be an error as the history
of the chapel which is authentic, and its main feature, differ in dates [?]. The
chapel was erected to shelter a statue that is much more famous than any other
feature and forms the main object of the shrine.

This statue itself has a very interesting history. It was brought to this country from Spain by the Franciscan friars about 1716 [?] and placed originally
in San Fernando Cathedral. There it remained for some years until a fire consumed a considerable portion of this edifice. It was rescued from this fire and
carried to one of a row of adobe huts that stood on the north side of the Main
Plaza about where the present Bexar County courthouse is. This was the first
fire which occurred in the Old Cathedral of San Fernando....

The family whose members saved this sacred relic from the flames of the
first fire was named Jiménez. After they rescued it, they retained it and built a
shrine for its reception. They had heard of its miraculous efficacy. It had been
famous in Spain before being brought hither. The Franciscans had brought it
here for the purpose of converting the Indians and for use in teaching them
the lessons of Catholicism. The savages [*sic*] saw the statue, heard the words
of the friars, and were converted in large numbers. Not a few became devout
members of the church.

Then came the fire that encompassed the partial destruction of the cathedral and some of the statues placed there. This one was saved and carried to
the first place mentioned. After it was set up there, the priests would not recognize the shrine nor say Masses there, and for a long time placed it under the
ban. Later on the Jiménez family removed it. Old Don Juan Jiménez, who
died here about five years ago almost a centenarian, received it from his elder
brother, who built the chapel at 113 Ruiz Street where it is now enshrined. He
bequeathed it as his most precious possession to his daughter, Candelaria, who

is now the wife of Clemente Rodríguez. The chapel is on the same premises as her house. A large double gate admits to both. The chapel has a broad portal. Above this is painted a pair of outstretched wings and the cross is above them.

There are always devotees with it whenever it is open. These are ever to be found kneeling and reciting some orison. They invariably kneel before this statue, which is suspended in the center of the eastern end of the edifice. The statue itself is the object that engages and commands continuous attention. It was an ancient object at the time it was brought hither from Spain. The statue is a representation of Our Savior on the cross. About it is a pale blue tunic. This tunic is a garment that is greatly venerated. The chapel, the statue, and the tunic are much more famous elsewhere than here. Their fame is extant over Mexico and many have come all the way from there to offer orisons before the statue and within the chapel.

Those who come there to pray invariably make an offering, promising if their supplications are heeded and their prayers granted to give some valuable object. Most of the supplicants are those who are afflicted with some mal-ady. The offerings they give are generally representative of the part afflicted. The votive offerings are invariably of either silver or of gold according to the means of the afflicted supplicants. Most of these offerings, which are miniature hands, arms, or various limbs, are pinned to the tunic about the statue. Their prayers do not always relate to the supplicants themselves, but sometimes to their possessions. For this reason several miniature horses and dogs or other animals are to be seen there.

One of the supplicants who gave a votive offering was a wealthy widow residing in Mexico. She suffered from some painful malady of the head and her offering was a crown of thorns. The thorns were of gold and their base or support was silver. This offering was very expensive. She spent some time in prayer before this statue, after which she returned to her Mexican home from whence she came all the way here to make her devotions at this shrine. On her return she had the offering made by a jeweler there and sent it here by express.

Most of those who go there to pray carry a candle with them and kneel and pray as long as the candle burns. They carry a fresh candle with them each time they visit the place. Sometimes there are several supplicants there. All of them are earnest and devout. They never interfere with each other or notice one another.

This chapel is one of the places where the famous play of the *Pastores* [see document 13] is held. This is usually during Advent [*sic*, traditionally during the Christmas season] and up to Christmas Eve. Sometimes the play is pro-longed until after the New Year begins. These productions of the *Pastores* do not seem to interrupt the devotions of those [who] supplicate before it. They either join the players or resume their orisons after the players have finished their performances.

When the *Pastores* are being produced there the chapel is decorated espe-cially for the latter occasion. On general occasions it has other decorations besides the statue mentioned. These decorations consist principally of pictures of members of the Holy Family, but there are also flowers and other ornaments about the place. At each side of the chapel are wooden settees placed there to seat those who are not kneeling in supplication. The latter kneel on the hard, bare floor. They also are true to their promises. They invariably keep them and present the gift they offer at the commencement of their supplications. No one is ever known to have failed to keep faith.

Many miracles are alleged to have been the result of the prayers offered at this shrine and by those kneeling before this statue. Some evidence of them has been left in the chapel as mute witnesses. These evidences are rude crutches of the halt and lame who, having been cured, left their crutches behind to attest their cures.

Many tourists, actuated by no other impulse than curiosity, visit this chapel. They allude to it as the "Wonder Chapel." Some of them find it interesting and fee the people who own it. Others merely glance at it and go on. . . .

I have never heard of any of the other statues being venerated as that in the little chapel on Ruiz Street. This latter seems to be the most famous statue in San Antonio. It is likely that it is older than any of those even now in San Fernando Cathedral. It appears to be about 3 ½ feet tall. Although apparently fragile, it has stood through several centuries the strains of time but has received great care which doubtless accounts for its almost miraculous preservation. The fabric about it seems frail also, but it continues to hold the objects suspended from it and doubtless contains strength with its ornamentality.

Until very recently the old chapel on Ruiz Street was in a very dilapidated condition. Its walls showed evidences of decay and it otherwise gave visible evidence of the carking tooth of time. But recently some mysterious and anonymous friend, probably one of the supplicants, supplied funds for its repair, and its appearance has considerably changed. The old walls have been painted up, their crevices filled and a new coat of whitewash has been given the outside. Inside new woodwork has been placed to form the interior walls, fresh paint enlivens the chapel and the ornaments have been brightened so that the place has not the same aged appearance it had a few years ago, but the statue still appears as of old, but bearing little evidence of the great age it has attained.

San Antonio Express, 28 April 1907, copy in San Antonio Public Library.

Children share in the joyful anticipation of receiving candies and other surprises from a *piñata* in the Chicago archdiocese's Fiesta de San Juan (document 34a), the patron of Puerto Rico, ca. 1955. Courtesy Claretian Publications, 205 W. Monroe, Chicago, IL 60641.

Part 3

CROSSING BORDERS: THE IMMIGRANT EXPERIENCE

Pero recordamos que llamaste a Abrahán de su patria,
que conduciste a Moisés en el Exodo
y a Juan Bautista en el desierto.
Como Cristo suspendido entre cielo y suelo,
estamos crucificado en un Limbo
y ni somos de aquí ni de allá,
porque nos has dado servirte
como un espíritu solitario en larga espera.

But we recall that you summoned Abraham from his homeland,
that you led Moses in the Exodus,
and John the Baptist in the desert.
As Christ hung on the cross between earth and sky,
we are crucified in a Limbo,
belonging neither here nor there
because you have given us the lot of serving you
as a solitary spirit in great expectation.

Antonio M. Stevens-Arroyo, "Plegaria de añoranza puertorriqueña (Canon of Puerto Rican Nostalgia)," in Antonio M. Stevens-Arroyo, *Prophets Denied Honor: An Anthology on the Hispano Church in the United States* (Maryknoll, N.Y.: Orbis Books), 112–14. Printed by permission.

Introduction

The incorporation into the United States of Latino communities in Florida, Louisiana, Texas, New Mexico, Arizona, and California during the first half of the nineteenth century marked the beginning of a significant Hispanic Catholic presence in the country, a presence that has continued to grow to the present through immigration. In the late nineteenth century and first half of the twentieth century Latinos arrived mostly from Mexico, Puerto Rico, and Cuba. Since the 1950s, immigrants from the Dominican Republic, Central America, and South America have added their numbers to the mix of Latino communities. The documents in this chapter explore the complex interplay between the Hispanic immigrant experience and evolving expressions of Latino Catholic identities in the United States, with particular attention given to the migratory experience of Puerto Ricans, the second largest Hispanic group in the United States (after Mexican-descent residents).

Latin American Immigration to the United States

As with most immigrants, Latinos came to the United States to escape forces of instability and displacement they had little control over. They came for a number of reasons, including difficult conditions in their countries of origin and forces created by North American economic and political expansionism that intimately linked Latin America to the United States.

The nations that emerged from Spain's imperial experience in the Americas had to contend with a colonial legacy with specific characteristics that impeded Latin America's insertion into the world economic system. These characteristics included political systems that empowered elites at the expense of the larger society, economic systems of privilege that ensured the domination of the few over the many, and social systems based on debilitating racial and ethnic distinctions. After independence from Spain in the 1820s, the emergent Latin American nations found themselves facing internal division and conflict as a result of this legacy. National consensus was difficult to build in the various countries and traditional structures persisted despite the dismantling of Spain's political and centralized bureaucratic system, the replacement of mercantile economic thought with liberalism and capitalism, and some changes in social forms. The Latin American wars of independence, constant revolts and civil wars in the emerging countries during the first half of the nineteenth century, the Cuban struggles for independence beginning in 1868, the Mexican Revolution of the early twentieth century, Puerto Rico's efforts to industrialize in the 1950s, the Cuban Revolution in 1959, and the chaos in Central America during the 1970s and 1980s illustrate the results of some Latin American efforts to break with the structures of privilege and inequality inherited from the colonial era.

Significantly, these tensions in Latin America that caused disruptions and displacements did not occur in isolation or independently of outside forces. United States territorial and economic expansionism into Mexico, Cuba, Puerto Rico, and other Latin American nations during the nineteenth and twentieth centuries often aggravated political tensions in the region and created economic linkages that facilitated the movement of people north, strengthening migration particularly after 1900. In general, then, economic and political difficulties in Latin America combined with employment possibilities in the United States led to the growth of U.S. Latino communities.

Following the end of the U.S. Civil War, railroad construction, mining, and agriculture in the regions from Texas to California, and then in Mexico itself, linked the regions economically, creating migration flows of Mexican labor north. The Porfirio Díaz regime (1876–1911) in Mexico promoted economic growth linked to foreign interests, leading to prosperity for some but displacement and migration for others who went to the United States looking for work. United States interests in Caribbean products, particularly sugar and tobacco, also encouraged the movement of Cubans, Puerto Ricans, and Dominicans to the United States. Beginning in the 1870s thousands of Cuban and Puerto Rican workers arrived in Florida and New York to labor in the cigar industry, which remained prosperous into the 1920s (Cardoso 18–37; Pérez 1994: 158–73; Sánchez-Korrol 12–13).

In the early twentieth century, the most significant Latin American migrations continued to come from Mexico, Puerto Rico, and Cuba. Mexican immigration accelerated substantially after the outbreak of the Mexican Revolution in 1910. During the depression era of the 1930s Mexican migration all but came to a halt (and in fact deportations created a significant return migration), but the northward flow of Mexicans resumed in increased numbers after World War II (Cardoso).

The Puerto Rican case illustrates the underlying economic dynamics that caused Latin Americans to move north. Following the U.S. occupation of the island in 1898, Puerto Rico's subsistence farming and primarily agricultural economy increasingly became a single, cash crop enterprise. During the last decade of Spanish rule, the island produced fifty-seven thousand tons of sugar a year. Five years after the U.S. takeover that rate had increased to two hundred thousand tons per year; by 1930 it was nine hundred thousand tons a year. This transition to a single export commodity subject to price fluctuations on international markets placed a great deal of pressure on the traditional subsistence economy. As landowners concentrated their landholdings to facilitate productivity and growth, Puerto Rican farmers were displaced. Also problematic was the nature of sugar production, which provided work only part of the year during the harvests, leaving workers unemployed or underemployed the rest of the year. Puerto Ricans left home in increasing numbers, searching for a more stable livelihood in New York and other U.S. cities. The number of Puerto Ricans living on the mainland increased from 1,513 in 1910 to nearly 53,000 in 1930. Migratory pressures became even more dramatic after World War II when policymakers introduced incentives to create a manufacturing base, a program known as Operation Bootstrap. Industrialization initiated a new era in the island's economic history, producing a nascent middle class. At the same time, the urbanization of a primarily rural people and the uneven participation in the economic benefits of industrialization caused many more to leave home in an unprecedented migration to the mainland (Fitzpatrick 17, 33–36).

Besides the kinds of economic dynamics revealed in the Puerto Rican case, other factors have contributed to a general increase in migration from Latin America since World War II. These include generalized urbanization, increases in birth rates and life expectancies, growing expectations for better lives among the people, improved transportation, ties with family members already in the United States, and the communications revolution. These factors brought people from all over Latin America to the United States (Reimers 121–32).

A factor that strongly influenced the resumption of massive Mexican immigration after the depression was the infamous guest-worker or Bracero
Program (1942-1964), which brought some five million contracted workers north from Mexico, a number of whom stayed or eventually returned
to establish homes in the United States. Perhaps even more significant
were the undocumented migrants who crossed the Mexican border into the
United States. Most stayed permanently. After the Bracero Program ended
the number of undocumented workers increased dramatically, a trend that
has continued to the present (Reimers 37–60). This increase in Mexican migration was accompanied by increases from across Latin America and the
Caribbean. The Cuban Revolution in 1959 initiated an exodus from the island that eventually resulted in over a million Cubans arriving in the United
States. From the mid-1960s through the early 1980s, immigrants from the Dominican Republic averaged about 12,500 a year. This increased to an average of
22,000 immigrants a year in the late 1980s. South American immigrants also
increased, the largest groups arriving from Colombia and Ecuador (187,560
and 101,452, respectively, between 1966 and 1987), but also significant numbers from Argentina, Chile, Brazil, and Peru. The other major influx was from
Central America, with the largest contingent coming from El Salvador, about
106,390 from 1966 to 1987. None of these figures include undocumented en-
trants (Reimers 139–46). By the 1990s, then, virtually all of Latin America
was represented in the immigration flows to the United States, making the
U.S. Latino community much more complex and diverse.

Hispanic Immigrants and the U.S. Catholic Church

A continuing flow of immigrants, along with the relative proximity of their
native countries, has enabled many Latinos in the United States to maintain
ties with their homeland and its traditions. This is particularly true of groups
like Mexicans in the Southwest, who have reinforced their language, culture,
and religious practices through ongoing contact with their native land. For example, although he moved from his native Sonora to Tucson in 1882, Federico
José María Ronstadt returned home regularly to visit family members and celebrate traditional religious feasts like Christmas and Holy Week (document
28a). Similarly, Catholics who live in borderland cities like El Paso–Juárez
have testified that Catholic life, ministry, and devotion transcend the political border which "divides" Mexico and the United States (document 28b). In
the case of Puerto Ricans, who are U.S. citizens by birth, their unique status
as "citizen immigrants" enables them to visit their homeland more frequently
than other Latino immigrants, a phenomenon often referred to as "revolving
door immigration" or "commuter immigration." Of course, not all Hispanics reside in the borderlands, nor can all Latino immigrants return home at
regular intervals. Mexicans and other Hispanic immigrants have established
numerous communities in the Midwest and other northern locales since the
first decades of the twentieth century (documents 29a, 29b; Badillo). Even

today some immigrants who lack documentation refrain from visiting their homeland because they fear they will not be able to return; others go home rarely (if at all) because of limited financial resources and/or the political situation in their native country. Nonetheless, many contemporary immigrants remain in contact with their country of origin (and other countries where Spanish is spoken) through Spanish television programs and improved communication technologies. As one contemporary Colombian observer notes, "the majority [of South Americans] are still sentimentally attached to their country of origin and maintain communication with it by telephone, videos, and letters" (document 39).

Immigrants themselves have facilitated homeland ties and fostered group solidarity through efforts such as founding Spanish-language newspapers and *mutualistas* (mutual aid societies), commemorating their national heroes and patriotic holidays, and establishing a variety of local community networks and associations (J. García; Sánchez-Korrol). As in society at large, in the Catholic fold Hispanics' initiatives are significantly influenced by their interactions with other U.S. residents, particularly Euro-Americans. At times these interactions have been cordial and cooperative, but often they have resulted in disagreement and even painful conflict. On the official ecclesial level, this diversity of interrelations is illustrated by Hispanic attempts to establish national or "ethnic" parishes. Like other Catholic immigrants to the United States, Hispanics have advocated for these parishes as a means to retain their language, cultural practices, sense of group identity, and Catholic faith. For example, in the early 1870s a coalition of Spanish-speaking Catholics at San Francisco successfully promoted the establishment of a national parish. The consuls of Chile, Peru, Nicaragua, Colombia, Bolivia, Costa Rica, and Spain, as well as various other Hispanic residents, comprised this coalition. They contended that a national parish was necessary both for monolingual Spanish speakers and for bilingual Catholics who longed to pray in "the sublime language and in the same prayers their tender mother taught them" (document 27). When church leaders established national parishes, like Bishop Michael James Gallagher did in founding Detroit's Our Lady of Guadalupe parish with Mexican immigrants in 1920, Hispanic Catholics extolled these leaders for "the zeal and love that you have shown to us" (document 29b). The widespread policy of establishing national parishes for various European immigrant groups began to change by the 1920s, when Cardinal George Mundelein of Chicago became the first major U.S. prelate to reverse this policy. Mundelein contended that these parishes increased nativist anti-Catholic sentiment and that the rise of the second generation among many immigrant groups warranted a greater use of English and a more integrationist approach. Soon other bishops followed Mundelein's lead in seeking both to prohibit new national parishes and to "Americanize" existing parishes (Gleason 48–49).

Contemporary scholars contend that the prelate who most influenced the abolition of Spanish-speaking national parishes was Cardinal Francis J. Spellman (Díaz-Stevens 1987; 1993a: 99, 115; Vidal 1990: 129–30; 1994: 70–87). Shortly after his 1939 appointment as New York's archbishop, Spellman reversed a national parish policy that had been extant in his see for nearly a century. Although he did not state the reasons for his ban on national parishes directly, the official report of the first Conference on the Spiritual Care of Puerto Rican Migrants illuminates his approach to this issue. Held in April 1955 at San Juan, Puerto Rico, this conference brought together some of the leading thinkers and pastoral agents involved with Puerto Ricans, both from the island and from the mainland. Spellman wrote an introductory dedication for the conference report, extolling "integration" as the goal of Catholic ministry among Puerto Ricans on the mainland (Ferrée, Illich, and Fitzpatrick 7). The final summary of the conference proceedings stated that national parishes were no longer a viable pastoral strategy because the third generation of an immigrant group frequently moves out of these parishes, leaving the congregation depleted and the church building in disrepair. Furthermore, the children of immigrants too often abandon their ancestral religion because they identify the Catholic faith with the archaic practices of their national parish community. The summary also cautioned that some one-third of baptized Catholics in New York would belong to national parishes, a number presumably prohibitive given available resources and personnel. Finally, conference participants concluded that, "since the people [Puerto Ricans] will eventually become integrated with the established population, it would be wiser to begin the process of integration from the very beginning" (Ferrée, Illich, and Fitzpatrick, sec. 1).

The abandonment of the national parish strategy with regard to Puerto Ricans in New York reflects a similar shift in the policy of other dioceses. For example, the aforementioned 1870s effort to create a Hispanic national parish at San Francisco was successful, while a 1950 attempt to establish another such parish at San Jose (at the time still part of the San Francisco archdiocese) was not. In this instance the attitude of archdiocesan authorities had clearly shifted from the approach of their predecessors some eight decades earlier; these authorities denied the 1950 petitioners' request because they perceived national parishes as segregationist (Burns 167–68, 226).

Contemporary thinkers like the late Jesuit sociologist Joseph Fitzpatrick contend that the decline of the national parish has left a vacuum among Hispanic groups like the Hondurans in New York which only "enormous creativity and effort" can remedy (document 37). Despite the consistent refusal to establish national parishes for Latinos, however, today many Latinos comprise territorial parishes that in effect are national parishes since their congregations are overwhelmingly Hispanic. One such parish is San Juan Bosco in the Little Havana district of Miami, which has served as "a cathedral of Cuban traditions" since Father Emilio Vallina and other Cuban exiles founded it at an abandoned car dealership in 1963 (document 36).

Despite policies against national parishes and official prescriptions for "integrated" church structures, Puerto Ricans and other Hispanic Catholics frequently have found ways to continue celebrating their treasured expressions of faith. For example, two presentations given at the 1955 Conference on the Spiritual Care of Puerto Rican Migrants confirmed (perhaps inadvertently) the resilience of Puerto Rican Catholicism on the mainland. Father Phillip Bardeck, the Redemptorist pastor of St. Cecilia parish in New York, defended the practice of fostering integrated parishes like St. Cecilia, where English- and Spanish-speaking congregants worshiped under the same roof. To the pastor's surprise, however, Puerto Rican parishioners objected when he sought to move a Spanish Mass from its original site in the basement to the church itself. He then put the matter to a secret ballot, and an "overwhelming" number of Puerto Ricans voted to retain the Spanish Mass in the basement. According to Bardeck, this vote reflected the Puerto Rican perception that, in the tight schedule of the upper church, "they would have to give up some of the customs that they had brought up with them from Puerto Rico" (Ferrée, Illich, and Fitzpatrick, sec. 2, p. 10). Similarly, Father Vincent Cooke reported that the Archdiocese of Chicago promoted the Caballeros de San Juan Bautista (Knights of St. John the Baptist) as a temporary Puerto Rican pious association that would foster "integration" and "assimilation" (document 31). Many Puerto Ricans, however, saw the Caballeros as on organization that would help them maintain their religious practices, ethnic identity, and group cohesion on the mainland (Padilla 126–66; Vidal 1994: 129–33).

Puerto Ricans on the mainland also reinforced their collective identity through feast-day celebrations like their patronal feast of St. John the Baptist (June 24). In New York during the 1950s, Puerto Ricans numbering in the tens of thousands celebrated the Fiesta de San Juan with an annual Mass, colorful procession, and daylong festivities that included a civic and cultural program of events. According to one observer, this vibrant celebration "offered an opportunity for a public demonstration of the religious and cultural values of the Puerto Rican community.... It was the first citywide event that gave presence to the Puerto Ricans" (document 34a).

Renewal movements like the Cursillo de Cristiandad (Brief Course in Christianity) were yet another means for Puerto Ricans to express and reinforce their identity. The Cursillo weekends began on a regular basis in the New York archdiocese in September 1960. These weekends were immensely popular and influential among Puerto Ricans and other Hispanics, in large part because they "provided a framework and community to the individual Hispanic immigrant otherwise submerged in New York's dominant non-Hispanic culture and in danger of losing his identity as Hispanic and Catholic" (document 34b). For Puerto Rican couples like Tomás and Ana (document 33), who had brief experiences with the Pentecostals and Baptists, the Cursillo was instrumental in their "return to the church of [their] youth" and "[finding] an identity in their local parish." In these and many other instances, Puerto Ricans and other Latinos have established, supported, and refashioned organizations, feast days, devotional practices, predominantly Hispanic parishes, and other church structures that enable them to formulate and express their Latino Catholic identities on their own terms.

Immigration and Latino Catholic Identities

Given their ongoing migration and contact with the wider Spanish-speaking world, as well as their considerable efforts to practice Catholicism in a way that reinforces their ethnoreligious traditions, it is not surprising that the identity of many Puerto Ricans remains rooted in their island homeland and heritage. To be sure, some Puerto Ricans decry the loss of cultural identity among their compatriots on the mainland, as Sylvia Quiñones Martínez did in a 1955 address to the National Conference of Catholic Charities. Quiñones observed that "in their attempts to be accepted and considered as equals, Puerto Ricans tend to imitate mainlanders and discard their customary manner of living." She also contended that "by discarding long-established customs and traditions and adopting an entirely new way of living, Puerto Ricans are depriving others of something that is simple and beautiful which could contribute tremendously to Catholic life here [on the mainland]" (document 32). Despite such complaints that Puerto Ricans are losing their treasured heritage, even Puerto Ricans born in the United States continue to articulate an identity that is intimately tied to their ancestral place of origin. For example, upon hearing of his appointment as archbishop of San Juan, Puerto Rico, in 1999, New Jersey–born Roberto González stated: "It is true that I was not born on Puerto Rican soil, but I will make bold to say that I was, in spite of this, born in Puerto Rico. One's national identity does not depend exclusively on the place where one was born." He went on to add: "In the case of Puerto Rico, our history has led us to find this reality also beyond our shores. And it was in that 'other Puerto Rico,' that 'Puerto Rico beyond the sea,' where I was born, and I have always recognized it as a single people with that of the island, and a single spiritual reality" (document 40). Although Archbishop González clearly was attempting to announce his solidarity and connectedness with his new flock, his statement reflects a common perception of Puerto Ricans on the mainland about the retention of their culture and national identity.

The Puerto Rican experience illustrates the tendency of many Latino immigrants to retain significant elements of their ethnoreligious heritage. A number of Hispanic émigrés have actively promoted cultural retention among their fellow immigrants. In many instances they push for increased Catholic ministries to Latinos in their own language and cultural style, often attempting to persuade Catholic officials by arguing that such ministries fortify Latino resistance to Protestantism (documents 27, 29b). For example, in a 1951 report on the religious conditions of Puerto Ricans in New York, Encarnación Padilla de Armas and other Puerto Rican women opined that "the most striking aspect of the Puerto Rican situation is the constant and energetic activity of Protestants." Their report emphasized that Protestants offered extensive min-

istries in Spanish and that some eight hundred Puerto Rican ministers served
in New York, where at that time there was "not a single Catholic priest of
Puerto Rican origin." Furthermore, Protestant ministers attracted Puerto Rican congregants by "follow[ing] the same external rites and customs that are
characteristic of the Catholic Church in Puerto Rico." These Puerto Rican
Catholic women took it upon themselves to prepare a report that would incite
archdiocesan authorities to establish "a more organized, coordinated effort" of
Catholic outreach among Puerto Ricans (document 30).

Often expressions of an ongoing link to the homeland are even more intense among those who fled persecution and violence in their native country.
Such is the case of one Salvadoran with the pseudonym "Ramiro," who escaped to the United States in 1986 as a civil war raged in his homeland.
Subsequently Ramiro offered public testimony on numerous occasions about
the repression that U.S. foreign aid helped support in El Salvador. In his view,
Salvadorans in the United States retain a deep, almost mystical bond with their
compatriots at home because "refugees are a *pueblo* (people) of El Salvador
who have had to leave their country to ask for peace" (document 38).

In addition to illustrating the Latino immigrant tendency for cultural retention, the Puerto Rican experience also reflects the complexity and, in
the final analysis, the unpredictability of how individual Hispanic Catholic
immigrants will adapt to the U.S. milieu and formulate their sense of identity. In the case of Gloria, who emigrated from the Dominican Republic
around 1965 at the age of ten, the difference in adaptation after arrival in
the United States was quite distinct even among members of the same family. While insisting that she will always be Dominicana, Gloria also describes
herself as "assimilated" and "the most integrated into U.S. society" among
her eight siblings and other family members. Her brothers and sisters agree
with her assessment; one brother even "caused her great pain by saying that
she was no longer Dominicana." Like some other Hispanics who "assimi-
late," Gloria became "disillusioned with the church" and Catholic teachings
due to the "cultural conflict" she encountered after leaving her homeland
(document 35).

Not surprisingly, a higher degree of contact with non-Hispanics is a frequent commonalty among immigrants who accommodate themselves more
readily to the U.S. milieu. Gloria, for example, contends that she adopted U.S.
ways more rapidly than other family members because she so consistently in-
teracted with non-Hispanics during her university studies, in her profession,
and in her social circle. Similarly, a Mexican immigrant who resettled at Chicago in 1920 attested that, after arriving in the United States, she attended
a mixed-nationality parochial school where her best friend was Italian and
another friend was "American." Although she came to the United States at
age ten and had already received her first communion in Mexico, eight years
later she stated that "I nearly always make my confession ... in English" (document 29a). Undoubtedly her frequent contact with English-speaking friends
(a level of contact facilitated by the distance between Chicago and the nu-

merous Spanish-speaking communities closer to the Mexican border) accounts in part for her preference of using her second language in celebrating this sacrament. Unlike Gloria, however, she retained a relatively strong Catholic allegiance. In fact, her participation in an integrated Catholic parish facilitated her adaptation to the U.S. milieu.

Assimilation and cultural retention are not the only options that Hispanic immigrants choose as they adapt to life in the United States. Colombian pastoral minister Fanny Tabares points out that most South American immigrants teach their children the Spanish language and encourage their children to have a healthy pride in "their culture, their ancestors, their social and religious customs." However, she also notes that South Americans in the United States are "a minority group within the Hispanic community" who make great sacrifices to "accept as their own customs which, though Hispanic, originated in countries not their own." Within Catholicism, she observes, South Americans often participate in the devotions and religious traditions of other Hispanic groups. But they also celebrate Catholic feasts that reinforce their national identities, such as the Peruvian feasts of San Martín de Porres and El Señor de los Milagros, the Colombian feast of Our Lady of Chiquinquira, the Venezuelan feast of Our Lady of Coromoto, and the Argentinian feast of Our Lady of Lujan (document 39). The South American penchant for integrating into existing Hispanic faith communities while retaining a strong affinity to their specific ethnoreligious heritage reveals that "Latino" (or "Hispanic") and national identities can coexist as immigrants adapt both to a new land and to an increasingly diverse Latino population.

At the same time, Tabares calls for "the birth of a new culture" which "harmoniously incorporates various older ones." She claims that "South Americans, in concert with others, have particular gifts and strengths needed to create this kind of church" (document 39). While difficult to realize in concrete situations, this vision of creating a new culture entails an identity rooted in one's Hispanic Catholic background but also an openness to the possibilities that the U.S. pluralistic milieu offers for cultural synthesis and transformation.

Clearly, Hispanic Catholic immigrants do not conform to a rigid pattern in their process of identity formation, nor in their process of adaptation to life in the United States. The documents in this part illustrate some of the varied ways Latino immigrants understand what it means to be Hispanic, what it means to be Catholic, and how these two markers of identity interrelate with each other. Several of these documents show that Catholicism has been a resource for some Hispanic immigrants during a time of upheaval and excruciating transition to life in a new land. Collectively, the documents reveal that, in instances of both collaboration and painful conflict, the influential encounter with the Catholic Church in the United States has shaped the ways Hispanic immigrants formulate and express their evolving identities.

27. Circular Letter Promoting a National Parish at San Francisco, 1871

Like other ethnic groups, Hispanics have promoted national parishes in the United States as safe havens that reinforce their language, culture, and Catholic faith in a strange new land. As early as 1871, Catholics at San Francisco proposed a national parish to serve the Spanish-speaking population in their growing city. Significantly, although most Spanish-speaking residents were of Mexican descent, representatives from the consulates of Spain and various Central and South American nations were among the leaders in this effort. Four years later, Archbishop Joseph Alemany (1814–1888) established the national parish of Our Lady of Guadalupe. A predominantly Hispanic congregation comprised this parish until 1992, when the shift of the Spanish-speaking population to other parishes and sections of the city led to its closure (Burns 134).

Circular

The Spanish and Hispanic Americans of San Francisco in assembly unanimously issue this proposal.

To the Spanish and Hispanic Americans of San Francisco.

Gentlemen:

We believe that the happy idea of building a parish church exclusively for the Hispanic American residents and visitors to this ever growing city is not only consistent with evangelical doctrine, which commands us to propagate the faith by means of persuasion and the practice of virtue, but also reestablishes, in this great city, the splendor, brilliance, and influence of our race. Even if at present it finds itself in the backwaters of society, our culture's greatness, dignity, and humanism are not diminished.

Religion, it has been appropriately said, is "the soul of Spanish honor." Society could not begin to function effectively without the virtues that religion teaches and promotes, as they destroy vice and deter criminals. Whether in a large city or the smallest village, religion is humanity's greatest strength and resource. When faith is absent, the soul suffers, flounders, and loses its kindness and sensibility, those qualities that manifest its higher origin. Without faith, morality dwindles, passions unleash, and societies decay and churn with anarchy and discord, as we have recently witnessed in the beautiful capital of France.

Unity engenders strength, and strength begets respect.

In this city, those of us whose origin is Spanish will never achieve strength or respectability if we do not unite. Unity cannot exist in a vacuum, it must have a core, and its core must be religious, otherwise it cannot become the powerful instrument that is so essential.

In order to achieve a significant impact, there needs to be a cause so powerful that it can stand up to all opposition.

In vain have political and philanthropic societies tried to present a united front. Perfect harmony will be impossible to achieve as long as their efforts continue to be blocked and thwarted by other disuniting causes such as nationalism, political opinion, and personal ambition.

Only the one true religion we have professed from our birth; only the one Sovereign God, impartial and just, who owes nothing to anyone, but who gives us all; only the one faith without which salvation is impossible; only divine law, eternal and immutable, from which no one is exempt; only these things can bring us together, and only in the shelter and shade of religion can we develop our plans on sure footing. Our plans are inspired by charity, brotherhood, and a solid education based on the tenets of our religion, which is the basis for humanity's joy and well-being.

Let us give praise and glory to the Supreme Being who has inspired the project that we propose. We hope the day will come when the persons who oppose us will be convinced that their fears are unfounded, and will help us to move forward.

We address this proposal to all persons of Spanish origin who reside in this city and its environs. We hope their efforts will create a powerful and energetic movement that animates the timid and persuades those who are yet unconvinced. And to those who are already prepared to endorse our cause, may our enthusiastic spirit sustain and support them in this most arduous enterprise.

We have calmly listened to the objections made by some, and with due respect to each one we shall attempt to respond to the insurmountable obstacles that, according to those persons who oppose it, stand in the way of building this proposed parish church. There are four main objections:

1. That our race is invisible, both in numbers and financially.

2. That poverty impedes the construction of this church we so zealously espouse.

3. That as we adapt and adopt this country's traits and customs, we are losing the distinctiveness of our own heritage, will soon become indistinguishable from North Americans, and, in the end, will lose our native tongue and speak only English.

4. That in a large city like this with numerous Catholic churches and with our people scattered throughout various parts of the city, a central church isn't necessary, since it would only serve those who live near it.

We will try to dissuade these misgivings, giving them due consideration, but proving that they are mere shadows and are not to be feared. Yes, there are problems, but they can be overcome, and the idea of a church is not only possible but also logical.

Let us address the issue that our race is not visible. Do you know why?

It is not visible because it is a race that is sensitive, generous, noble, and able to live in limitless abnegation. It is not filled with the savage greed that pits man's higher self against the pursuit of fortune. If you want to witness charity personified, look at the poor and humble day laborers, who barely earn their daily bread but will share their scarce food with a compatriot or with anyone in need. Take note of the compassionate manner with which they encourage others to have patience, how they help them find work, and even care for the sick as if they were members of their own family.

What member of our race would abandon the victim of a horrible epidemic or, for cowardice, leave him in pain and desperation? None. None of us has a heart of stone, and if one of us should falter, giving in to poor example, he soon tries to assuage the voice of his conscience and atones by means of private offerings. Our race is invisible because it is the precious stone buried in the soil of this populous city. Are we to turn our back on it because it is not visible? No! A thousand times no! Our energy, virtues, and perseverance will make up for our relatively limited numbers; our self-sacrifice and endurance will overcome our lack of money and material goods.

Not even poverty can prevent the construction of the new church that is so ardently desired. Every day we are witnessing the formation of industrial and charitable societies that, sustained only by seemingly insignificant donations, nonetheless bear abundant fruit. Do our detractors really believe that, if *all* our people contribute, some from their excess and others with a slight sacrifice, there will not be enough for a work that costs not in the millions of dollars, but only several thousand?

These detractors will agree with us, then, that if *all* Hispanic Americans give according to their means, we could collect enough not only to build a church but also a school and whatever else we want. Organize small group meetings, involve the fair sex, since they are more pious than we are, and we will have abundant funds, with each one offering their donation, whether privately or publicly.

Who could possibly resist a request from an innocent little girl asking for donations to support the church whose doctrine shapes her into the pure and unsullied being that she is? Faced with such innocence, even the miser trembles with emotion and opens his purse, while the poor who have little or nothing to give, bless her and admire her pious faith and self-sacrifice. Let us now address the third objection. We believe that those who pose it haven't considered the opprobrium and censure they incur from people of good judgment.

After all, is it not a crime to lose our culture's distinctiveness because of our apathy and indifference? Our detractors themselves criticize the aloofness and absence of love in other cultures, whose relationships seem based not on moral qualities and evangelical virtues, but on self-interest and personal gain. Nonetheless, they abandon our brethren whom they encourage to adapt or even lose themselves among a people whose character and beliefs these detractors condemn. It is not civil to abandon our brothers. The greater or more imminent the threat, the larger should our efforts be; the closer our culture is to being eroded and perverted, the more resources we should offer, the more means we should seek, the greater sacrifices we should make to uplift, unite, and sustain it. Saving someone from perishing is a heroic and sublime act, but if a man turns away from a dying person, he is vile, debased, and despicable. This is why we say that those who have posed this third objection have not really thought through their statements or weighed their words.

In one way or another, San Francisco will always be a place of encounter between North Americans and the peoples of our race. Those who return to their native land, as well as many who remain here, will never know more English than they do now. *Californios* [Californians of Mexican descent] are a prime example, as are others, who no matter how long they have lived here still manage to preserve their native tongue. Let us suppose for a moment that they do become fluent in the dominant language of this country, will they then cease to cultivate the language of their birth? Although necessity obliges them to use English, they will still preserve their native tongue all their lives, not only because of its literary beauty and glory, but also because it nourishes their soul. Suppose they wish to express their affection, open their conscience, and lift their prayers to the Lord of mercy — their hearts would never feel fulfilled or unburdened unless they pray in the sublime language and in the same prayers their tender mother taught them.

Most immigrants prefer to speak in our language rather than English. It might even do well to offer classes on our language. This would not only preserve its purity and spread its use; it would also help induce many others to adopt our religious beliefs. Which other language can praise our omnipotent God more exquisitely, and lift the cares of the soul more aptly, than the Spanish language? More than any other language, Spanish expresses sweetness alongside grandeur, mysticism alongside gentleness, characteristic nobility alongside versatility of style. Our language is one of prodigious beauty. And how will we hear this beauty? Let us build a pulpit around which we can all gather to hear the divine maxims of the Gospel spoken in the grand and sublime language of our lineage of heroes.

Having already shown how a Hispanic American church will serve the members of our race who already know English, we will now demonstrate how absolutely essential it is for those who haven't learned English.

In the words of the apostle of the masses [St. Paul], "How can they believe (or have faith) if they don't hear? How can they hear if there is no one to preach?" [Romans 10:14]. And how can someone preach to them (we ask) if they don't understand? Even with all the Catholic churches in San Francisco, a church with preaching and teaching in Spanish is as essential to many members of our race as faith itself is essential for salvation.

Furthermore, let us suppose someone is on their deathbed and requests the ministrations of a priest. A confused messenger runs from church to church and from priest to priest until he finds one that speaks Spanish, while our compatriot, our friend, or perhaps even our loved one dies without the comfort of our holy religion and without a word of consolation. Gentlemen, this has happened, continues to happen, and could happen to each of us if we don't prevent it by building a designated church with a priest who dedicates himself solely to the spiritual needs of our race.

The fourth objection is that building a new church is counterproductive because our race is scattered all over the city. But isn't some sacrifice expected in finding a way to attend church? Or are we suggesting that, when necessary, attending a nearby church be forbidden? No! Nothing of the sort is suggested. Those who for some reason cannot attend every Sunday or feast day will perhaps attend once a month or even once a year; if others find it is absolutely impossible to attend at all, this should not stop them from supporting the construction of more Catholic churches for the honor and glory of God and the spiritual comfort of the suffering. It is precisely because we are so scattered that there should be more churches. Do those of us who attend churches nearer to us not find comfort and assurance in the proverb that tells us we should "love our neighbors as we do ourselves"? Should we not feel bolstered by the knowledge that our alms and prayers are saving other kindred souls in churches across the city from ours?

We will not take the time to enumerate all the graces and blessings that the Holy Fathers in the chair of St. Peter bestow on those who build or contribute to the building of a new church. If we consider as a generous and humanitarian benefactor a man who contributes from his personal wealth to charitable causes that alleviate only poverty, misery, and physical infirmity, what do we call the man who contributes to uplifting our spirit to our Creator and who, directly or indirectly, might save us from eternal damnation? In the first case, our body is saved although one day it will perish; in the second case, it is our immortal soul that is saved. What should those of us who believe in an afterlife prefer? Do we prefer passing glory or pleasure to the eternal joy that we hope for in the Lord? All who believe will rejoice in our project of building a church.

"Feed the hungry and clothe the naked" [Matthew 25:35–36]. What hunger can compare with the hunger of a soul lost in the whirlwind of a dissolute life and imprisoned by vice? How much more naked can a man be than to be divested of all virtue? How many of our race are spiritually destitute because they seldom, or perhaps even never, hear the word of God? Let us contribute to their conversion by building a church. Initially they might attend out of curiosity or out of national pride. But later they will hear the sublime truth of the Gospel and, once struck by Christ's love, a single sentence might, like a ray of sunlight, dispel the darkness of their indifference and, like St. Augustine, they too will come to be saints who will pray for us and praise God throughout all eternity.

Let us unite our wills, then, and energetically support our project, continuing the fund drive already begun. Let us ask our friends, relatives, and neighbors to contribute. And let us be assured that the next time we contact our fellow Catholics, it will be to invite their attendance at the imposing ceremony for the cornerstone laying of our parish church, in which our posterity will praise God and bless our memory.

We the undersigned execute this circular at San Francisco on 2 August 1871.

Henrique Barroilhet, Consul, Chile
Federico de la Fuente, Consul General, Peru
F. Herrera, Consul, Nicaragua, Colombia, Bolivia, and Costa Rica
Camilo Martín, Consul, Spain
29 other signees

> Spaniards and Hispanic Americans of San Francisco, "Lo que puede y necesita la raza española en San Francisco" (circular letter printed in San Francisco), 1871, copy in Bancroft Library, University of California, Berkeley. Trans. Dora Elizondo Guerra.

28. Borderlands Catholicism

Mexican Catholics who migrate to the United States frequently shape and re-inforce their religious and ethnic identity by maintaining ties with families, friends, and parish communities in their homeland. As the following two documents show, these ties are particularly strong among those who settle in areas proximate to the U.S.-Mexican border.

28a. Arizona-Sonora, ca. 1880s

This passage is from the memoirs of Federico José María Ronstadt (see document 21a). After he moved to Tucson in 1882, Ronstadt frequently visited family members at Altar, Sonora, for important occasions like Christmas and Holy Week.

I can never forget the religious celebrations that Father Suastegui and the good people of Altar used to have in those days. Around Christmas time they would have a pageant to show some of the historical events before the coming of the Savior: A young girl representing Mary, a young girl dressed as an angel announcing to Mary the conception of the Christ Child, then the trek of Joseph and Mary to Bethlehem, the Nativity, the coming of the three wise kings following the star of Bethlehem. The star looked real, traveling along a wire. All of these, to me, very beautiful and impressive tableaux remain fresh in my memory.

During Holy Week they also had tableaux and a pageant showing the Way of the Cross. In the courtyard of the church there would be a forest of olive [trees] where the soldiers of Pilate would arrest Christ; while all this was going on, no church bells would be heard. The calls were made by *matracas* (a board with two iron rings that boys would always carry along the streets of the town, shaking them and making a noise like drumming on a board with metal paddles). This pageant would end on Saturday at the resurrection when all the bells would resume their pealing. The church choir would sing *Gloria in Excelsis* [Glory in the highest] and the children would empty baskets of flowers into the air. The Judas would be burned in effigy and the whole town would rejoice.

Federico José María Ronstadt, *Borderman: Memoirs of Federico José María Ronstadt,* ed. Edward F. Ronstadt with a foreword by Bernard L. Fontana (Albuquerque: University of New Mexico Press, 1993), 108–9. Printed by permission.

28b. El Paso–Juárez, ca. 1910s

This testimonial letter was written by Mrs. Samuel Torigoe (née Maese) about Father Carlos M. Pinto (1841–1919), an Italian Jesuit who served in the El Paso–Juárez area from 1892 to 1919. Besides acclaiming Pinto's apostolic zeal, her letter shows that Catholic life, ministry, and devotion transcended the international border between Juárez and El Paso (Owens; Fernández 1998).

I am the daughter of Concepción Maese, who was a longtime faithful helper of Father Pinto. I was married in 1908 at Clifton, Arizona, and after about two years in that city moved to Juárez to live with my parents in a religious article store annexed to Father Pinto's church.

We lived in Juárez until 1910 when Pancho Villa's Revolution broke out. I was present when Father Pinto was thrown out of his church by ten Mexican soldiers who came with an ex-Catholic priest named Vicente Pimentel. Everyone in the building was taken upstairs and questioned. Included among them were my parents and Father Pinto.

I remember well how the soldiers took everything of value besides a trunk of money, gold coins, etc., destined for the new chapel, which was dedicated to the Sacred Heart and which had been built by Father Pinto. This money had been entrusted to my father for safe keeping, as was all the money in the church. So faithful and honest was he, and so devoted to his dear friend, Father Pinto, that no record was ever kept of the money. In fact, Father Pinto did not even know that my father had hidden a large pot full of coins in a coal bin outside the church. This was all the money that was saved from the hands of the soldiers.

I knew of the hidden pot because I had accidentally chanced upon it when searching for fresh-laid eggs one day. A chicken had jumped from the coal bin so I went in to investigate.

The soldiers had left me alone when they herded everyone upstairs, evidently not knowing that I was one of the family. I ran out immediately, dug out the pot from among the coals, and ran with it to the president of the *Hermanos de Mapimi,* a religious sodality of *Santo Cristo de Mapimi.* The treasure pot was later returned intact to Father Pinto.

Father Pinto was escorted by the revolutionaries to the bridge. When he tried to return to Juárez later in the day he was stopped at the very bridge and forbidden to return. This was the last time that Father Pinto saw Juárez.

Far from being discouraged, Father Pinto consoled his faithful Don Concho with these words: "Don't worry, Don 'Chonito,' I am going to build a new church in El Paso and we will live in peace here." (This was the Holy Family church.)

During the Revolution many Mexicans, mostly from the state of Chihuahua, had fled to El Paso. Father Pinto had the keen desire to build the Holy Family church for them. The refugees responded enthusiastically and were very helpful. One of them, Don Luis Terrazas, a rich cattleman, became a great benefactor. In fact he contributed most of the money for the new Holy Family church. Father Pinto now brought Don Concho and his family to the new church and gave them living quarters in a room behind the church.

Father Pinto loved the Mexican people. He lived among them, worked among them, and died among them. He should be called Apostle of the Mexican people as well as the Apostle of El Paso. Even when cast out of Mexico by the Revolution, Father Pinto had the determination to continue to work among his own. Three or four years after the Revolution he started to beautify the Sacred Heart church in Juárez. Mrs. Samaniego gave the land where the Sacred Heart church in Juárez is built.

Father Pinto's illness was a very painful one and Don Concho or Concepción Maese asked to serve him during this time, out of gratitude for what Father Pinto had done for him and his people.

When the news of Father Pinto's death reached the people of El Paso and Juárez numerous men, women, and children came to the Sacred Heart church to view his remains and to pray for his soul.

Mrs. Samuel Torigoe (née Maese), testimonial letter, ca. 1940, as translated and cited in Lilliana Owens, *Reverend Carlos M. Pinto, SJ, Apostle of El Paso, 1892–1919* (El Paso: Revista Católica, 1951), 178–79. Printed with the permission of the New Orleans Province of the Society of Jesus.

29. Mexican Immigrants in the Midwest

Early in the twentieth century, Mexican immigrants began to form communities outside the Southwest in regions as disparate as the central plains of Kansas and Nebraska, central Michigan, and in industrial areas along the steel belt running from northwestern Indiana to Milwaukee. The following two documents reveal that conditions in the Midwest necessitated considerable initiative for the formation and sustenance of national parishes and Mexican Catholic life, while also posing the possibility of adapting homeland language and traditions within heterogeneous Catholic parishes (Badillo).
                                                        — *This section contributed by David A. Badillo*

29a. Statement of a Chicago Resident, 1928

Mexican Catholics in the Midwest learned the ropes of residential succession, mixing with other national groups in churches, as elsewhere in cities. This interview shows distinctions made by Mexicans between ethnic "Italians" and "Americans," as well as some of the effects of language differences on parish life, in this case the hearing of confessions.

Yes I went to the Dore, Dante, and Goodrich Schools. I finished eighth grade, then I married. I could have still been in school if I hadn't been so foolish. My baby is nice and my husband is a good man but I think that I should have gone to school more. We have been living in Chicago eight years. My mother was a widow and I am the only child. I went to the Guardian Angel School the last two years. My mother wanted me to learn to pray. I had made my first communion in Mexico. I did not go to school in Mexico so that I had to start in first grade when I came here at the age of ten. I am eighteen now. At school the teachers and everyone treated all nationalities alike. The girls did not fight among themselves. My best friend was an Italian girl. I used to go to her house and eat with her and she used to come to see me. I also had an American girl friend but I thought more of the Italian. We still visit and I often go to see her mother.

I had my baby christened at the Guardian Angel church. I know the priests over there better than I do the one at St. Francis, although we go to St. Francis regularly on Sunday. My husband's mother lives with us. She keeps the baby while my husband and I go to church, then she goes to another Mass. I nearly always make my confessions at Guardian Angel because I like it better. The priests there are Italians but they hear confessions in English. Most of the school children make their confessions in English. We learned English in the Guardian Angel. There is one of the sisters at the Guardian Angel that I just love; she is so nice.

Anita Jones interview with Mrs. Mesa, 25 July 1928, Chicago and Calumet areas, field notes, Paul Schuster Taylor Papers, BANC MSS 84/38c, carton 11, folder 34, page 262, the Bancroft Library, University of California, Berkeley. Printed by permission.

29b. Letter to the Bishop of Detroit, 1932

Mexican immigrants at Detroit took an active role in congregational life at the national parish of Our Lady of Guadalupe, which the immigrants established in 1920 with the backing of Bishop Michael James Gallagher (1866–1937). Nonetheless, competition from Protestant ministers, not to mention "nonbelievers," posed a threat to many Mexican lay leaders, as did conflicts among the laity or between them and the local pastor. The following letter to Bishop Gallagher illuminates the growth of disparate religious, political, and personal loyalties among Detroit's Mexican Catholic population. It also reveals the distress produced in the difficult struggle for the preservation of Mexican Catholic identity and practice in the United States (Badillo 262–65, 273–76).

18 October 1932

Most Illustrious and Reverend Lord Bishop
of the Catholic Diocese of Detroit, Michigan

Most Illustrious Lord:

We, the undersigned, members of our Holy Mother, the Catholic Church, with broken hearts appear before your illustrious person to inform you of the sad events which are taking place in the midst of the poor Mexican colony in this city. The majority of our colony used to be good Catholics until a few months ago when a disastrous propaganda against our Faith started; first, by a strong propaganda to make Mexicans embrace the Baptist Church, and they have succeeded in a good measure especially by a recent revival, and we were witnesses from outside of their meeting hall, and were very sad to see so many that used to be good Catholics until some months ago join the Baptists. Secondly, by a society of Mexican working men which meets every Saturday and carries out every doctrine against our Holy Mother the Church, inducing Mexicans to become Communists. One of the leaders is that great Mexican painter, Diego Rivera, of whom you have perhaps read in the papers. He talks against the existence of God, and consequently denying everything pertaining to religion. Many other private societies are working against our Holy Mother the Church.

We wish that your Lordship would investigate what is the cause of our Faith being lost by so many of our colony. We are thankful to your Lordship for your efforts in our behalf in the past by giving us a parish church dedicated to Our Lady of Guadalupe, but we are afraid that the zeal and love that you have shown to us has not been taken up by Father Castillo, who is criticized and accused by many of a lack of priestly interest in our behalf. We feel abandoned and without any leader in this serious matter.

Begging you, Most Illustrious Lord Bishop, to remedy our situation, and assuring you of our respect and sincerity in this letter as a duty of conscience, we beg to remain

Your most humble subjects in Christ,

Simón Muñoz
Reyes Padilla
Antonio Macias
Emil Rodriguez
Carlos Saborío

Simón Muñoz et al., petition to Bishop Michael J. Gallagher, 18 October 1932, Our Lady of Guadalupe parish file, Archives of the Archdiocese of Detroit. Reprinted with permission of the Archives, Archdiocese of Detroit.

30. Report on the Religious Conditions of Puerto Ricans in New York, 1951

A native of Arecibo, Puerto Rico, as a young woman Encarnación Padilla de Armas went to Havana, where she married a Cuban and acquired a doctorate in law at that city's university. In 1945 she arrived in New York, a young widow with a small boy and $150 in her pocket. One year later a classmate of hers became the head of the newly founded Puerto Rican government office in New York; he offered her employment and got her involved in New York's Liberal Party, of which she eventually became vice president. In 1951 Padilla de Armas met Jesuit priest Joseph Fitzpatrick (1913–1995), to whom she spoke bit-

terly about the New York archdiocese's neglect of the Puerto Rican community. Fitzpatrick asked her if she would be willing to write a report on the situation and promised that he would deliver it personally to Cardinal Francis Spellman (1889–1967). Prepared by a group of Puerto Rican women that Padilla de Armas led, this report was one of the factors in the founding of the archdiocese's Spanish Catholic Action Office two years later. While not directly challenging the archdiocesan policy of integrated parishes, the report protested the complacency and inadequate efforts in the existing apostolate among Puerto Ricans. Subsequently Mrs. Padilla de Armas exercised distinguished leadership in Hispanic ministry, including a position with the Division for the Spanish-Speaking (later the Secretariat for Hispanic Affairs) of the National Conference of Catholic Bishops, where she was instrumental in the calling and preparation of the 1972 First National Hispanic Pastoral Encuentro (see document 69).

As a group of Catholic women, we have been deeply concerned, as many other Catholics have been, about the religious condition of the many Spanish-speaking people who are coming into the city of New York. Most of these are Puerto Ricans. We are aware of the wonderful efforts that are being made by a number of pastors in the city to provide these people with adequate religious care, and to enable their children to attend parochial schools. However, like everyone familiar with the situation, we are amazed at the immensity of this problem, and we realize how inadequate are the existing efforts of Catholics to meet this task. At the same time, Protestant groups seem to have no end of energy and resources to do the work that we as Catholics should be doing.

In order to bring to the attention of our Catholic authorities some of the facts of this situation which they may not be aware of, we have compiled the following information gathered in our ordinary, everyday lives, about the Spanish-speaking people. It is not a scientific survey; it is a record of the situation as we see it every day. It may serve as a help to a more organized, coordinated effort to bring these people the religious help they desperately need.

Lower East Side: We can start with lower Manhattan as a sample district. The boundaries of this district are the East River to Broadway, Battery to Fourteenth Street. This had been a predominantly Jewish and Italian neighborhood and is probably still considered such by most people in the city. However, the Puerto Ricans have been crowding into the area, some of them newly arrived from the island, others forced to leave their homes in other sections where new housing projects are being built. It is estimated that in the area from South Street up to East Houston, there are 80,000 Puerto Ricans. There are more than 8,000 families, many of which have more than 5 children. In this entire area there is only one Catholic church that provides spiritual care by Spanish-speaking people for the Puerto Ricans. This church is on 6th Street and Houston. Actually it is a mission of Nativity parish, is staffed during the week by a Spanish-speaking sister, and has the services of a Spanish-speaking priest on Saturdays and Sundays. This church, actually a little chapel, accommodates 75 persons, although the sister says she knows 246 families in the immediate vicinity alone. Recently the parish held a mission in Spanish for the Puerto Ricans. Unfortunately, there is no parochial school in the area for any of these children.

At the same time in the area there are twelve (12) Puerto Rican Protestant churches with fourteen Puerto Rican Protestant ministers. Each minister has at least his wife helping him to do community and house-to-house work. In that same area the community centers, Manhattan House, Livingstone House, and the New Era Club are doing tremendous community work with after school programs for the Spanish-speaking people of the area. The Puerto Rican children attend these clubs and are influenced by the Protestant religion and views.

There is also a hospital in the area, Governor's Hospital, where it is estimated that 75% of the patients are Puerto Rican. There seem to be no Spanish-speaking priests who visit the Catholic patients here. However, a Protestant minister is available every single day in this area and Puerto Rican ladies serve in the hospital as volunteer interpreters.

A similar situation can be found in the area around the Italian church at Rutgers and Henry Streets. On Rutgers Street the five blocks from South to Henry Street on both sides are occupied largely by Puerto Ricans, particularly the section from Cherry to Madison. It is estimated that 85% of the families in these blocks are Puerto Rican. Unfortunately the Italian church has no facilities for community work, but two Protestant churches with Spanish-speaking ministers attract the Puerto Ricans.

A similar situation is developing in the area from Broome to Grand Street and from Mulberry to Mott Street. This was considered a predominantly Italian neighborhood. But today the large majority of the families are Puerto Rican. The Protestant church at 387 Broome Street has a Protestant Reverend of Puerto Rican origin who works in the area.

Hell's Kitchen District: 13th–48th St., 7th–10th Avenue: In this area a large percentage of the population is now Puerto Rican. There is a Catholic church on 14th Street, between 7th & 8th Avenue, the oldest Spanish Roman Catholic church in Manhattan. However, although the priests here speak Spanish, they are of French nationality. They are not as well prepared to understand the psychology of the Spanish-speaking people as other priests would be. The church of Saint Francis Xavier, on West 16th Street, has a large number in their parish, but has not succeeded yet in providing services in Spanish for these people. The parochial school has a number of Puerto Rican children and operates as a youth center some nights of the week....

Summary: In summary it may be well to add a few general comments about the situation.

Activity of Protestants: Undoubtedly the most striking aspect of the Puerto Rican situation is the constant and energetic activity of Protestants among these people.

This is the mainland counterpart to the situation on the island itself. Since the American occupation of Puerto Rico and the departure of the Spanish clergy, there were never sufficient priests to provide spiritual care for the people. The American influence was followed by a large influx of Protestant missionaries. For instance, at present there are only 800 priests on the island as compared to 3,200 Protestant missionaries, many of whom are of Puerto Rican origin. In New York, there are about 800 Puerto Rican Protestant ministers but not a single Catholic priest of Puerto Rican origin.

The number of Protestant churches is enormous. In an appendix at the end of this report is a list of [more than 100] Protestant churches for Puerto Ricans in New York. What is more, these Puerto Rican ministers follow the same external rites and customs that are characteristic of the Catholic Church in Puerto Rico. Thus the people are confused, believing that they are practicing their religion even when they attend the Protestant church.

Perhaps not a little of the success of the Protestant ministers is the fact that they come from the Spanish tradition, understand the psychology of the people, and can work effectively with them. This may indicate that, in the transition to American ways, it will not be sufficient to depend entirely on the zeal of English-speaking priests. Rather, a blend of spiritual care given both by English-speaking priests together with assistance from priests of Spanish or Puerto Rican background may be most effective.

However, the important thing is zealous concern for these people on the part of any priest who can reach them. If this could equal the zeal and effort of the Protestants, the difficulties would soon begin to be met.

The fact that much of the response of the Puerto Ricans to the Protestant approach is the result of real zeal may be illustrated by the case of the Protestant minister in the Bronx named Mr. Tunon. When Reverend Tunon began his work in the Bronx, he worked with a very poor community. He opened his church in a little store 10 by 12 feet at 1064 Interval Ave. After five years work he had built the first Spanish-speaking church by rebuilding on the same land with the cooperation of his people. It was his zeal and concern that convinced the Puerto Ricans to help him do this work. The new building cost $68,000 and every cent was contributed by Puerto Ricans. This seems to indicate that, if the Puerto Ricans have the proper leadership, they will respond to it generously; that if they see the same zeal on the part of the priests, they will be responsive to their obligation to support their church.

Community centers: The importance of community centers as a means of helping the Puerto Ricans and of influencing them cannot be stressed enough. It is through this medium that Protestant influence is often strongest. In view of this, it was doubly unfortunate that the community center on 106th Street opposite Saint Cecilia's was allowed to fall into Protestant hands.

Material assistance: The Catholic people are apparently not aware of the great material assistance that the Puerto Ricans need, and which could be relieved by a little organization. Many Puerto Rican children do not have winter clothing, some of them do not even have shoes. This interferes sometimes with attendance at school and also at church. Were this brought to the attention of Catholic people, they would probably respond as generously as they respond to the appeals for clothing for Korea, etc. In this case, Spanish-speaking people should take the lead in informing other Catholics about this.

Mixed congregations: It has apparently been the policy of the New York Archdiocese not to set up separate "national" parishes for the Puerto Ricans. In view of the speed with which they are moving through the city, this seems to be a wise policy. But it must be accompanied by clear instructions to all churches that the Puerto Ricans must be received as regular parishioners. There are doubts about this on the minds of some pastors who do not know whether they would be encroaching on specialized jurisdictions if they went all out to attract the Puerto Ricans to their parish. Similarly, Catholics already in the parish should be instructed of this policy and should be instructed also of their obligation of receiving these new people as brothers in Christ. Unfortunately, this last has not always been so, since there are a number of parishes where the Puerto Ricans are given to understand that they are not wanted, that they should go to some "Spanish" church.

Marriage: The difficulties of Puerto Rican family life are rather well known. Thousands of these families exist only through common law arrangement. This is a carry over from a practice on the island, where priests reach them too seldom, and where they begin to live together as husband and wife. This leads to serious problems when they come to the mainland. Thousands cannot get into public housing projects because they cannot prove the legality of their marriage. Some of them are common law marriages because they have never been taught differently, others because they did not have the money for a civil or religious marriage. There is a vast field for zealous work here, since with a little attention and kindness many of these marriages could be validated in the church.

Protestants are able to handle this much more easily than Catholics because they avoid most of the complicating details of Catholic marriage. Similarly in burials. Thus some attention must be given to facilitating both these rites in order to make the return of the Puerto Rican to the church that much easier.

Rural missions: Every year thousands of Puerto Ricans come to the mainland for temporary work as farm laborers. It is doubtful whether any priest ever visits them while they are on these farms. Nevertheless, Protestants have been very zealous in their pursuit of these people. They provide much needed assistance, guidance, and spiritual care. It is important to work out some coordinated means of information about the location of these farm colonies and to have someone who can provide the proper care for them.

Similarly, during the summer, Protestants send Puerto Ricans to camp or arrange with Protestant families to take them for 3 or 4 weeks during the summer. In this environment the young Puerto Ricans fall under a strong Protestant influence.

In view of all this, it appears that much information is needed about the spread of Puerto Ricans throughout the city, of the care they need, the care they actually receive. This would have to be followed by some coordinated approach to the entire problem. It cannot be solved by a single parish nor a single pastor. It requires the coordinated effort and understanding of the entire Catholic population.

Encarnación Padilla de Armas et al., "Report of Some Catholic Women on the Religious Condition of Puerto Rican Immigrants in New York City," 1951, photocopy from personal archives of Jaime R. Vidal. Printed by permission.

31. Report on Ministry among Puerto Ricans in Chicago, 1955

In April 1955 thirty-five priests from mainland dioceses and another thirty-five from the island met at San Juan, Puerto Rico, for the first Conference on the Spiritual Care of Puerto Rican Migrants. While most Puerto Ricans on the mainland have settled in New York City, fifteen other dioceses also were represented at the conference. Father Vincent W. Cooke (1906–1997) presented the report on the Chicago archdiocese's efforts to serve its growing Puerto Rican population – the second largest on the mainland. Chicago archdiocesan officials imitated their New York counterparts in the decision to serve Puerto Ricans on an integrated basis; consequently they established the Caballeros de San Juan Bautista (Knights of St. John the Baptist) as a primary means to engage and organize Puerto Rican Catholics. Church leaders saw the Caballeros as a transitional organization that would help integrate Puerto Ricans into the North American church and then disappear in favor of existing societies such as the Knights of Columbus. Many Caballeros members, however, perceived the organization as a vehicle for preserving Puerto Rican religious practices, ethnic identity, and group cohesion on the mainland. These divergent organizational visions were an important factor in the eventual decline of the organization during the 1960s (Padilla 126–66; Vidal 1994: 129–33).

Parishes — Some 20,000 Puerto Ricans now live in the Chicago Archdiocese and are widely scattered throughout the city. Fifty-three parishes report some Puerto Ricans living within their boundaries or attending their Masses on Sunday. Almost all of these parishes are making some attempt to incorporate these people into their parish life. Of the twenty-five parishes which have any sizable number of permanent Puerto Rican residents, twenty have already started some kind of special program in Spanish and the others are making arrangements to do so. These special programs usually include confessions in Spanish, one Mass with sermon in Spanish, or one or more missions in Spanish during the year. In about ten parishes Puerto Ricans have become members of such parish societies as the Holy Name Society, Legion of Mary, etc....

The Knights of Saint John — The Knights of Saint John is a Catholic Men's Club consisting for the most part, although not exclusively, of Puerto Rican migrants. The purposes of organizing it are: (a) to encourage regular attendance at Mass and reception of the sacraments — easier to encourage through an organized group than on an individual basis — because all members of the organization must receive Holy Communion in a group once a month; (b) to develop some social organization among the Puerto Rican migrants and to break down their isolation from one another. This is helped by establishing club houses where the members may spend their leisure time in various social activities — pool, dancing, dominoes — and the development of women's and children's groups along with the men's. This also provides a feeling of group security which we feel is a prerequisite to eventual integration both into the local parish and the community; (c) to provide an opportunity for civic and educational activities — English classes, instruction classes, women's sewing classes, open forums, political discussions, etc.; (d) to develop "self help" consciousness among the members and give the Puerto Ricans an opportunity to discover what their own problems are and how to deal with them. When the group decides on a plan and requests help, it receives whatever help is available from [Catholic] Charities. Although Charities gives some financial aid to the groups, e.g., the first two or three months rent on a clubhouse, and some of the furnishings which are too expensive for the club to buy, the groups are encouraged to become self-supporting as soon as possible. Two of the three councils now existing have become self-supporting in less than six months; (e) to develop some leadership among the migrants by the experience of leading and directing a group and by close association with the organizer who meets often with the officers for this purpose; (f) to develop training and experience in democratic procedures by regular meetings which are run in a democratic manner; (g) to develop community contacts for the organization whenever possible and to encourage common activities with non–Puerto Rican groups. It is hoped by stressing this assimilation that this purely Puerto Rican organization can eventually disappear.

The organization is a simple one consisting of semi-independent councils in the various areas where Puerto Ricans live. Usually one "area parish" — one parish within a given area which may have a Spanish-speaking priest on the staff who takes a special interest in the migrants — is the center of the organization and the monthly communions and other special religious services are held there. One of the priests from this parish is elected chaplain of the organization, which gives it a personal tie to the local parish. Charities employs one full-time organizer who does the initial organization, usually with the help of some members from one of the other councils. The organizing is done on a strictly "grassroots" basis by visiting as many of the Puerto Rican homes in the area as possible. Before a council is fully organized by some of the members of the group, a personal invitation to join is extended. No attempt is made to give any special attention to certain groups within the Puerto Rican community such as businessmen, lawyers, or politicians. They are contacted along with everybody else and in the same manner.

Several more councils will be organized within the coming year.

Vincent W. Cooke, Archdiocese of Chicago [Report], in "Report on the First Conference on the Spiritual Care of Puerto Rican Migrants," April 1955, photocopy from personal archives of Jaime R. Vidal. Printed by permission.

32. **Plea for Retaining Puerto Rican Faith Traditions, 1955**

Sylvia María Quiñones Martínez was born in San Germán, Puerto Rico, raised and educated in New York, and then worked in that city as a bilingual secretary. At the time of the presentation that follows she was also a parishioner at Incarnation parish, where she worked among Puerto Rican families as a member of the Legion of Mary. In April 1955 she served as secretary for the first Conference on the Spiritual Care of Puerto Rican Migrants (see document 31). She delivered the following address to the forty-first National Conference of Catholic Charities held at Grand Rapids, Michigan, in November 1955. Her idealized depiction of Puerto Rican culture and her claim that Puerto Ricans too easily discard their ethnoreligious traditions in order to be accepted reflect common sentiments among various other Latino immigrants.

Although the development of new industries in Puerto Rico has raised the standard of living and has created more jobs, there has also been a marked increase in the growth of population on the island. During the last ten years, about one fourth of the population has come to the mainland and established residence. Most of those who have come here are the *campesinos.* These are the country people who earn a living from the soil and whose livelihood has been affected by the introduction of mechanized methods of cultivation.

In order to understand the psychology of the Puerto Ricans who live here, it is important to understand the psychology of the *campesinos.* One of the most remarkable things about them is that, despite their poverty, they show an abundance of charity toward each other.

When campaigns are launched in the States for the placing of homeless children, I cannot help but think of the simple practice which my people in Puerto Rico have of solving this problem. Whenever a child is left without a home, a relative, friend, or neighbor will automatically assume responsibility for the child. They will give to him the love and affection he has suddenly been deprived of. This is not done to impress anyone, since in all probability the family already has enough mouths to feed and is struggling to make ends meet. It stems from the Puerto Ricans' deep sense of love for the family and from a desire to preserve family life. Loyalty and dedication to the family are natural instincts in the Puerto Rican.

On a recent visit to my aunt's home in Puerto Rico, I was introduced to a new member of the family, a small, rather shy boy of twelve. Several years before he had come to their door asking for a plate of food, for which he was willing to work. His mother was dead and his father was very ill. When his father was sent to the hospital with tuberculosis, it was taken for granted that he would make his home with my relatives. Due to the effects of malnutrition, he started suffering from a serious disease. My aunt nursed him, although she realized that she was exposing her own family to his illness. She did not think of consequences; her only thought was that the child needed care and affection. She believed, with the Puerto Rican's simple faith, that Divine Providence had sent this child to her. She knew that God would help her to take care of him. Today the boy is healthy and strong and a source of joy and comfort to them. He is as much at home with them as though he had been born into the family.

Puerto Ricans love big families and the companionship of those who are dear to them. Houses are usually small because they can be built cheaper. Lack of money and the constant danger that their homes will be washed away in the event of a hurricane discourage people from planning to build larger houses. Children usually live with their parents after they are married. They are accustomed to being surrounded by people and miss the warmth and activity of a big family. It is customary and taken for granted that the older folks will live there too. Add to this widowed aunts and uncles, sons and daughters who remain single, and anyone else who has no other place to live, and you can understand why their homes are crowded. This overcrowding is generally misinterpreted and is attributed to lack of dignity on the part of Puerto Ricans, and to complete disregard for the importance and need for privacy. Actually it is a result of the great charity and deep feeling for family ties which is so typical of them. They are accustomed to inconveniences and prefer to live in crowded quarters, rather than be separated from each other.

Puerto Ricans are predominantly Catholic and religion plays a very important part in their lives. They will drop into church at any time of day. While religion is very sacred to them, it is practiced simply and informally. They believe that God is their Father and the church is His home. A common sight on the island is to see people in church walking from one saint's statue to another, talking to them as though they were personal friends. In their prayers, a special or favorite saint is asked to intercede for them. If the wish is fulfilled, flowers are placed at the foot of the statue of the saint, out of gratitude for his intercession. Our Lady is their mother, and they turn to her in times of joy and sorrow. She is asked for very special favors and promises are made to her and, if granted, mortifications are practiced and penitential habits worn in her honor.

Pastors and priests are friends and they are called by their first name, i.e., Father Tom, etc. They are accustomed to having priests drop in at their home occasionally to inquire about them, not just when someone is sick or dying.

Religious holidays are a time for public demonstrations of faith. During Holy Week, all unnecessary activity stops, and the Passion is reenacted in churches throughout the island, followed by processions depicting the death and resurrection of Christ. On All Souls Day, after the evening recitation of the rosary, the people walk in procession to the cemetery, led by the priest, reciting the rosary. They pray at the graves of their loved ones and return home in silence. At Christmas time, public demonstrations are also held, but of a happy nature. Everyone goes to Midnight Mass and afterwards the plazas swarm with people in a festive mood. Then comes the traditional "cena," or feast, and the endless rounds of parties.

Love of gaiety, music, companionship, and of life itself, are things which are imbedded in Puerto Ricans from the crib, and the means through which they give expression to their feelings. These things are not acquired, but are rather a very part of their existence.

Many traditions are theirs from childhood. Asking the blessing of parents before leaving the house — no matter how many times a day nor how old they may be — or before going to bed. There is the custom of calling godparents "madrina" and "padrino," rather than by given names. The walls of homes are often covered with religious pictures and there is great faith in the use of sacramentals.

Puerto Ricans are easygoing by nature, but they are also very sensitive and extremely sentimental. The death of a friend, no matter how casual, can bring tears to the eyes of the most hardened. When a member of a family dies, relatives go into deep mourning and social activities cease. These are only a few of the things which are characteristic of Puerto Ricans.

Because of the criticism to which Puerto Ricans are exposed on the mainland, for trying to live as they did on the island, there is a tendency — particularly among the younger people — to lose the sentimentality for those things that have been a part of their culture and upbringing. In their attempts to be accepted and considered as equals, Puerto Ricans tend to imitate mainlanders and discard their customary manner of living.

They no longer attach importance to large families and refuse to take in anyone else's children, for fear of lowering their standard of living. On the contrary, women usually go to work and place their own children in nurseries. The additional income is used to keep up appearances before their neighbors.

Old people are considered a burden and are either sent to institutions or are forced to live by themselves. Lonely or unmarried relatives must find other homes. The housing shortage, or a desire to live in the suburbs by the young people, forces members of a family to live at great distances from each other. This causes them to drift apart and breaks up the family unit.

It is considered old-fashioned to cover walls with religious pictures and the practice of religion becomes cold and formal. Instead of giving expression to their deep faith, religious emotion is hidden by false pretenses.

By discarding long-established customs and traditions and adopting an entirely new way of living, Puerto Ricans are depriving others of something that is simple and beautiful which could contribute tremendously to Catholic life here, as well as to a better understanding and closer relations with others on the mainland.

Sylvia Quiñones Martínez, presentation (untitled), in *Proceedings of the Forty-First Meeting of the National Conference of Catholic Charities* (Washington, D.C.: National Conference of Catholic Charities, 1956), 74–77. Reprinted with permission of Catholic Charities USA.

33. Recollections of Life in Puerto Rico and New York, 1982

The Office of Pastoral Research for the Archdiocese of New York conducted an extensive study of Hispanics in New York from 1979 to 1982. Led by project director Ruth T. Doyle and field director Olga Scarpetta (1938–1992), this land-

mark study resulted in a two-volume publication that focused on four primary research areas: an analysis of demographic and parish data, critical essays that synthesized previous investigations of Hispanics, a survey of twelve hundred Hispanics, and twelve in-depth case studies. The following selection is taken from one of these case studies; it reflects the tentative ties many Puerto Ricans have with institutional Catholicism as well as the evangelizing influence of the Cursillo (document 34b) among Puerto Ricans and other Latinos (Doyle).

Tomás was born in Puerto Rico in 1940. He spent the first 12 years of his life *"en un barrio"* ["in a neighborhood," with the connotation of a poor or working-class neighborhood]. He had two sisters and one brother. His father was a heavy drinker. His mother worked very hard to support the family. When Tomás was 10 years old his mother left and took the two sisters with her; the two boys remained with the father.

Soon after the mother left his father became attached to another woman. They would visit her but it was not until the following year, when his father moved to New York, that she joined the household. The father came to New York with his new common-law wife and the children were left in Puerto Rico until the following year.

Tomás was a very sick child. Most of his childhood he suffered from rickets. He had an unattended ear infection that left him with a speech and hearing impediment. It was hard for him to communicate. He became shy, somewhat of a recluse and very much attached to his mother.

As a result of his ear problem he only attended school for one year; then he was asked to leave and has never gone to school since then. As he puts it, "All that I know I have learned by myself." And this includes reading and writing. After he left school he worked as a shoe shine boy in the streets and sometimes he would help out in a cardboard factory. When he came to New York he was placed in a special speech program until he was 17.

His mother learned of their move to New York and followed them. She contacted the father and made attempts to see the two boys but his father rejected it. Finally, when Tomás was sixteen, his aunt contacted the two children and told them where to find the mother. From that moment on Tomás would find any excuse to stay with her. At seventeen, he found a job, left his father, and moved permanently with his mother. At this same time he indicates that it became easier for him to communicate.

Tomás is now married. He has three children plus a foster child. They often have foster children in their home. They want to raise children *"que les falta amor"* (that lack the love they need).

He was out of work three months at the time of the interview and somewhat anxious about the present economic state of the country because many of his neighbors are unemployed as well.

He speaks English well but timidly and he prefers Spanish. He was shy in speaking about his personal life but extremely vocal in describing his religious life and experiences.

Tomás was raised a Catholic but received little instruction. His mother was a devoted Catholic and went to church every day. He would go with her but never knew what religion was about. His father often changed religions but in reality had none. It was when Tomás returned to live with his mother in New York at 17 that he was confirmed and received first holy communion.

At the age of 20 he dated a girl whose family was deeply involved in the Pentecostal Church. "She told me if I wanted to be her boyfriend I'd have to become Pentecostal, so I did." He became a nominal Pentecostal.

When he married Ana, a Catholic, he returned to the Catholic faith for the sake of a unified family.

At the age of 30 he was told he needed an ear operation, the fifth since childhood. He became depressed and was visited by a local Pentecostal pastor who prayed over him and cured Tomás without the operation. Tomás became an avid Pentecostal with crusading, missionary zeal: "That night I went to bed early. The brother came with the minister about 7 p.m. They told me to relax and pray with them. The minister put his hand on my ear and began to read the Bible. I repeated the words softly. After a half hour he said, 'Now you are okay.' The next day I went to the doctor and he told me I no longer needed the operation. After this miracle I returned to church."

Now Tomás became a dedicated Pentecostal. He asked his wife to join him in his church, but she refused. This caused problems in his married life. When their son became ill and was hospitalized, no Pentecostal visited him and Tomás became disillusioned with his co-religionists. He left the congregation. His wife had become a Baptist the year before at the invitation of a friend. Eventually he followed his wife to the Baptist Church but was never convinced by their teachings.

The following year they both left the Baptist Church. He disliked the negative preaching and the attacks on the religion of his parents and his childhood. He developed a strong sense that he was wandering without direction. Shortly afterwards his wife returned to Catholicism; he felt confused and alone without religious attitudes. In 1975 he had a dream about the Sacred Heart and felt this was a call to return to the church of his youth. He contacted a local priest, made the Cursillo, and found peace. Ana then made the Cursillo as well and both have found an identity in their local parish.

Recently they both have been attending Charismatic prayer meetings and Masses and studying the Bible in classes held by the local charismatic leadership. They speak glowingly of their church, their prayer life, and of the place of Jesus in their family life.

Ruth T. Doyle et al., *Hispanics in New York: Religious, Cultural, and Social Experiences* (New York: Archdiocese of New York Office of Pastoral Research, 1982), 1:166–68. Printed by permission.

34. Reflections on the Evolution of Hispanic Ministry in New York, 1982

Monsignor Robert Stern was director of the Spanish-Speaking Apostolate (a successor to the Spanish Catholic Action Office; see document 30) for the New York archdiocese from 1969 to 1972; currently he is director of the Catholic Near East Welfare Association. The following two passages come from a history of Hispanic ministry in New York that Stern wrote for the archdiocese's study of Hispanics (document 33).

34a. Fiesta de San Juan, 1950s

At the suggestion of Father Ivan Illich, a leading figure in ministry among Puerto Ricans, in 1953 the archdiocese initiated an annual festival in honor of St. John the Baptist, patron of Puerto Rico. In the following selection Monsignor Stern narrates the early development of the Fiesta de San Juan, which became the principal annual event for New York Puerto Ricans by the late 1950s. Subsequently, archdiocesan officials led by Monsignor Robert Fox, the coordinator of Spanish Catholic Action from 1963 to 1969, altered the fiesta's format and activities in an effort to make it more congruous with their perceptions of contemporary ecclesial and social needs. Many Puerto Ricans did not respond favorably to these changes; by the end of the 1960s the secular Puerto Rican Day parade had displaced the fiesta as the primary expression of New York Puerto Ricans' solidarity and collective identity (Díaz-Stevens 1990; 1993: 126–34, 159–64, 195–96; Vidal 1994: 94–97, 101, 107–8).

On June 24, 1953, forty-five hundred people participated in a Solemn Pontifical Mass at St. Patrick's Cathedral in the presence of His Eminence, Cardinal Francis Spellman. The sermon was in Spanish. This celebration marked the beginning of a New York tradition and an important one in the development of the Puerto Rican community. At that time there were not yet any large public manifestations of Puerto Rican presence, culture, or religiosity. According to Msgr. [Joseph F.] Connolly, the special Mass for the feast of the patron saint of Puerto Rico's capital was consciously meant to be "the Spanish American equivalent of a 'St. Patrick's Day.' "

The celebration of the feast was repeated in the cathedral again in 1954 and 1955. Bishops from Puerto Rico attended, Spanish songs and hymns were sung, all the seminarians studying Spanish were urged to attend, and dignitaries from the Puerto Rican community in New York were in attendance. The cathedral was filled to excess again in 1954 when the Spanish sermon was preached by one of the first two New York priests trained in Puerto Rico, who had just returned from a year on the island.

After the third celebration of the fiesta in the cathedral in 1955, at the suggestion and urging of Father Ivan Illich a whole new style of celebration was planned for 1956. With the help of Father Joseph Fitzpatrick [of Fordham University] and Mrs. Encarnación Padilla de Armas [see document 30], an outdoor celebration was arranged at Fordham University's Rose Hill campus in the Bronx. The idea was to create something of the ambiance of a typical Puerto Rican "Fiesta Patronal" [feast-day celebration for the patron saint of a locale] with elements of religious, civic, and popular celebration. Besides the field Mass to open the fiesta, there was a Puerto Rican style barbecue, speech making, songs and entertainments, and children's games. When a horde of children and adults scrambled for the sweets and gifts that fell from the piñata [container of sweets that children break open in a festive game], the Irish-American police rushed to cover Cardinal Spellman, fearing he might be in danger of being assaulted!

The Fordham celebration of the fiesta was a great popular success. However, the thirty thousand people who attended proved to be too much for Fordham's campus. For the next year, the rapidly growing event needed even more space and accessibility — it was decided to put it into a public stadium on Randall's Island!...

For 1957, Father [James] Wilson [the new coordinator for the Spanish Catholic Action Office] hired a city stadium on Randall's Island and announced the fiesta there. As stadiums go, it was out of the way. Although it's near Manhattan, especially Spanish Harlem, it's on the Triboro Bridge approach and hard to get to. Even so, about thirty or forty thousand people turned out for the fiesta. It was a great Catholic spectacle: hundreds and thousands of *Hijas de María* [Daughters of Mary] marched in their white dresses, the rosary was recited, great floats with tableaux of the mysteries of the rosary passed, people marched with their parish society banners. A Pontifical Mass was celebrated at a great altar especially erected in the center of the stadium's field. Cardinal Spellman was escorted into the stadium by a huge procession of laity, altar servers, and clergy. He was greeted with shouts of "¡Viva el Cardenal!," "¡Viva la Iglesia!," and great roars of applause.

An elaborate civic and cultural program followed the Mass. Special dignitaries were introduced, long and short speeches were given, congratulations were offered on all sides, and a distinguished assemblage of artists, musicians, and other entertainers, Puerto Rican and Latino in general, professional and amateur, entertained the crowds. It was meant to be a typical Puerto Rican fiesta patronal. As the formalities of the liturgy concluded, the great crowd gradually dissolved into clusters of family picnics, games, and song. The stadium is in the center of a vast public park on Randall's Island, and the area was carpeted with Puerto Rican families intermixed with the clergy and religious who spoke their language.

The new pattern of the San Juan Fiesta was set. From year to year under Father Wilson's guidance it became bigger and better. The spectacle varied, there were ever-new dignitaries present, but the combination of religious-civic-cultural events was held. As the fiesta became an institution, people vied to become associated with it. Father Wilson organized a Citizens' Committee for the fiesta that met regularly during the year to plan and promote it and which became in its day one of the most prestigious of Puerto Rican Catholic organizations. A high honor was the naming of the new president of the fiesta at the conclusion of each year's ceremonies. A distinguished roster of Puerto Rican lay leaders tell the tale of this office.

In its day, the San Juan Fiesta was a very important thing. It corresponded to a deeply held Puerto Rican value: *respeto.* . . . The fiesta offered an opportunity for a public demonstration of the religious and cultural values of the Puerto Rican community, for until then they had no special expression of their culture or language or dignity. It was the first citywide event that gave presence to the Puerto Ricans; there was nothing else. For several years it remained the main Puerto Rican event in New York.

Robert L. Stern, "Evolution of Hispanic Ministry in the New York Archdiocese," in Ruth T. Doyle et al., *Hispanics in New York: Religious, Cultural, and Social Experiences* (New York: Archdiocese of New York Office of Pastoral Research, 1982), 2:300, 308–9. Printed by permission.

34b. The Cursillo, 1960s

The importance of the Cursillo de Cristiandad (Brief Course in Christianity) among Puerto Ricans and other Hispanic groups throughout the United States is impossible to exaggerate. As a lay-run movement that trained participants to actively live and spread their Catholic faith, the Cursillo offered numerous Hispanics a rare opportunity to exercise ecclesial leadership. One major goal of the Spanish clergy who founded the Cursillo in their homeland was to provide a retreat experience that would correct the deficiencies they perceived in Hispanic popular Catholicism. In practice, however, the Cursillo almost always gave U.S. Hispanic Catholics a "turf" of their own where they could express themselves in their own language, customs, and devotional style. As Monsignor Stern points out in the following reflection on the Cursillo's development in New York, the popularity and significance of the Cursillo among Puerto Ricans and other New York Hispanics stemmed in large part from the movement's significance as a means of collective self-expression (Davis 1999; Díaz-Stevens 1993a: 109–11; Vidal 1994: 109–11, 139–41).

A very long range goal [for the New York archdiocese] was the development of indigenous leadership in New York's Hispanic community, first a well formed lay leadership and then, hopefully, religious vocations from strongly church-affiliated Hispanic families. Father Wilson [see document 34a] was very interested in the importation of a new and widely successful instrument of evangelization and conversion developed in Ciudad Real, Spain, that was producing electrifying results in Spain, Mexico, and other parts of Hispanic America, the Cursillo de Cristiandad or Brief Course in Christianity. After an earlier, first, and unsuccessful experiment, the Cursillos began to be given on a regular basis in the archdiocese in September 1960. At that time a team of Mexican American laymen from Laredo, Texas, came to give the first Cursillo. Although it was enthusiastically received and extremely effective, it was the original Spanish pastoral design twice removed. In December, at the archdiocese's invitation, an expert pair of Spanish laymen came from the mother diocese of the Cursillo movement in Spain to give New York's second and third Cursillos.

The Cursillo is actually a highly and tightly organized, three-day, study-retreat weekend with a strong emphasis on community experience. In content it addresses itself, especially in its original form, to the distortions and inadequacies of traditional popular Hispano American Catholicism and to a theological understanding of the sacramental life, Christian maturity, and the responsibilities of the lay person in the church. After attending a Cursillo, the average participant is enthused, highly motivated, and disposed to active involvement in the apostolate in his or her local parish.

At first the Cursillos were given at Tagaste Seminary of the Augustinian Recollects. By December 1961 the archdiocese established Saint Joseph's Center on West 142nd Street in Manhattan for the Cursillo movement and other works of formation under the direction of the Coordinator of Spanish Catholic Action. The Augustinian Recollects undertook to staff it. In March 1962 the Cursillo movement had grown to such an extent that it was deemed appropriate to set up the recommended diocesan structure of governance for it, the Secretariat, the members of which are named by the bishop.

During the past two decades and more the Cursillo movement has been the chief instrument of Hispanic lay leadership formation within the archdiocese. Several thousand lay men and women have "made" a Cursillo, and thousands of them have received further and specialized formation for the apostolate in the associated programs of the Cursillo movement at Saint Joseph's Center. The "cursillistas" have provided the nucleus of Hispanic lay leadership in almost every Hispanic parish of the archdiocese. Perhaps one reason for the rapid spread, great popularity, and considerable impact of the Cursillo among New York's Hispanics is that this diocesan-wide, citywide movement provided a framework and community to the individual Hispanic immigrant otherwise submerged in New York's dominant non-Hispanic culture and in danger of losing his identity as Hispanic and Catholic. Its religious celebrations and great rallies and assemblages both made each Hispanic cursillista very aware that he was not alone in New York and gave him great opportunities for self-expression, recognition, and leadership.

Robert L. Stern, "Evolution of Hispanic Ministry in the New York Archdiocese," in Ruth T. Doyle et al., *Hispanics in New York: Religious, Cultural, and Social Experiences* (New York: Archdiocese of New York Office of Pastoral Research, 1982), 2:312–13. Printed by permission.

35. Narrative of an Immigrant from the Dominican Republic, New York, 1982

The Dominican presence in the United States was fairly limited until the last years of dictator General Rafael Leónidas Trujillo, who ruled the Dominican Republic from 1930 to 1961 and severely restricted international migration. After Trujillo's 1961 assassination the migrant flow accelerated; the majority of these émigrés settled in New York and its environs. By 1990, Dominicans in New York numbered some seven hundred thousand and rivaled the local Puerto Rican

and Cuban populations in size (Torres-Saillant and Hernández). The following
case study is from an investigation of Hispanics in New York (document 33).

Gloria is 27 years old and single. She was born and raised in San José de las
Matas, a small town in the south of the Dominican Republic. She came to the
United States with her family at the age of ten. She went to high school and
college in New York. Now she has an M.A. in social work and is currently
employed as a psychiatric social worker in a large hospital in New York City.

Her recollections of childhood are pleasant. San José de las Matas is a small
town, isolated by mountains from the rest of the country. The closest city
is Santiago, but the road is long so there is very little traveling to and from
the city. It is a dry, arid area, with little rainfall. At the time Gloria lived
there the town had only one industry, a sawmill. Most people worked the
land, many their own plots. Others owned small stores in town or worked in
construction. Only a few houses had running water, electricity, or telephones.

There was little traffic so the children played on the street. There were
many children in the town and all played together. Most of the games were improvised. At times some older person would walk by and gather the children
to tell them anecdotes from the past.

Families were large and close-knit. People of all ages participated in family
activities. The men would go to the bar, drink beer, and stand on the corner
watching the women go by. Women's place was in the home. For a woman to
work outside the home was rare in the town.

Everyone in town knew each other. The favorite pastime was visiting
others. There was one movie house, but centers of recreation and social life
were the house and the river.

While in the Dominican Republic Gloria's family was often separated. Gloria's parents owned a "bodega" (small store) but they were often away. Gloria
does not know why. The two oldest children spent most of the time with the
grandmother who lived closer to the school. The parents would generally pay
an aunt or some other woman to take care of the other seven children while
they were away.

The separation from the parents was hard on the family. As she states:
"[The separation] had a strong impact that affects the communication we
now have. Although we had this experience together I don't remember talking
much about the fact that my parents were not there."

The whole family was poor in the Dominican Republic. Since coming to
the United States seven of the nine children have attended university: two are
social workers, one a nurse, one a teacher, another works in a family agency,
only two work in factories. Her parents, on the other hand, went from having
their own family business — a market or *bodega* — to her father working as a
dishwasher in a restaurant and her mother in a sweatshop as a sewing machine
operator in the garment industry. Yet, the parents could never have afforded
the education for the children in the Dominican Republic.

Gloria herself had wanted to be a university graduate, a professional, and as she said she has acquired that. She is contemplating going back to school to specialize as a clinical social worker to do individual therapy.

Gloria wants a family but a small one — only one or two children. For her children she wants a good education, a profession, for them to have a firm identity, beliefs, traditions, and an intimate family. She wants them to have a solid basis or foundation for their lives. She desires that they learn Spanish and, if she were to marry a non-Hispanic, that they learn something of her heritage.

In New York City she feels that she lives in a depressed area and that aspects such as the subways dehumanize her and others. Too many people do not care about how their neighborhoods are kept.

Gloria feels that of all her family she is the most integrated into U.S. society — she specifically used the term "assimilated." Her brothers and sisters also feel that way about her. The reasons were given as follows: the university she attended and the classes she took, her college friends, her present group of friends, and the professionals she relates to in the job who are primarily non-Hispanic. Gloria commented that when she was here in the United States the most important impact on her life were her boyfriends — Jews, Italians, and Puerto Ricans, all of whom helped her to learn how to live in this society.

She considered the most tragic part of her life to be an attempt to integrate the values of her native land with those she had to learn here. She spoke of "las dos culturas" (the two cultures) and the conflict created by a fear that she was losing her values and with her values her past, her childhood. "I am no longer the person I used to be as a child." She was puzzled as to how easily people could lose values that were developed over such a long period of time. She was not really too successful in integrating the two. Even her brother caused her great pain by saying that she was no longer Dominicana. Gloria's ambivalence toward her background is further brought out by her willingness to marry a non-Dominicano and to have many non-Hispanic friends. Throughout the interview she slipped back into English and made mistakes in Spanish that embarrassed her and she asked the interviewer to correct her several times. Still, she insisted that she would always be Dominicana, "There are beliefs and traditions that I feel."

Gloria was raised a Catholic. She was baptized, attended Mass on Sunday, and received the sacraments. Religious activities like the sacraments, novenas, frequent confession, and the rosary were routine during her childhood.

Both parents were Catholic although the mother practiced more frequently than the father. Almost everyone in town was Catholic. When Gloria lived in San José de las Matas there were no churches of other denominations.

When the family arrived in the United States the mother continued enforcing the same religious practices. Recently both parents became Evangelical. Now Gloria no longer practices, although she still considers herself Catholic. She became disillusioned with the church. Mass had no meaning; people showed no respect. Mass was more a social gathering than a religious event.

Her disenchantment was not only with the people who participate in church. Changes that have occurred in recent years have led her to question the validity of the teachings of the Catholic Church. For example, for years she liked to pray in front of the saints, but then the church took out the statues of the saints.

In college she became more disillusioned with the church. She studied philosophy and theology and began noticing contradictions in the Bible. This reinforced her doubts.

Priests and nuns changed their behavior, they became more worldly. Gloria began to lose respect for them. She said: "After the Catholic Church removed the saints, the priests and nuns became very modern. They changed not only their dress but also their actions. The image that I had of them has changed radically. There was no longer anything especially holy about them." Her parents, although no longer Catholic, still would like her to practice. People she knew from church ask her what is wrong with her that she no longer participates in church activities. All are concerned with her actions. Gloria thinks this change is probably linked with the cultural conflict she has encountered in terms of values. She tries to integrate Dominican values with those in the United States. At times this is impossible. She deals with the conflict by retaining the Dominican values that she feels "are good for me and are not outdated. This type of conflict is not easy to resolve, however; it takes a long time to decide that a value is no longer as important as it was before."

Ruth T. Doyle et al., *Hispanics in New York: Religious, Cultural, and Social Experiences* (New York: Archdiocese of New York Office of Pastoral Research, 1982), 1:153–56. Printed by permission.

36. Report on San Juan Bosco Parish, Miami, 1983

Today few U.S. bishops allow for the official establishment and recognition of national parishes in their dioceses. Nonetheless, many contemporary Latino congregations function as de facto national parishes. Led by their compatriot Father Emilio Vallina, in 1963 Cuban exiles at Miami founded one such parish, San Juan Bosco. Nicaraguan refugees later joined their Cuban co-religionists at the parish. To this day Father Vallina continues as pastor, and San Juan Bosco remains a vibrant center of Cuban and Nicaraguan Catholicism.

Every Sunday morning, a cheerful woman pouring tiny cups of *cafe cubano* from a tall thermos greets parishioners at the door of St. John Bosco Catholic Church.

The treat is a very Cuban welcome to the Little Havana church named after the nineteenth-century Italian priest who devoted his life to the care of homeless children.

Inside the box-like, beige building on West Flagler Street at 13th Avenue, statues line the walls, small mountains of red votive candles at their feet.

Among them is Cuba's patron saint Our Lady of Charity, a Cuban flag draped by her side along with yellow and white mums and gladioli, St. Barbara and St. Lazarus, popular among Cubans, and the Virgin of Regla, named after the Cuban port town where she is said to have appeared long ago.

Today — 20 years after homesick Cuban refugees pooled their pennies and their devotion to turn the old car dealership into the place they call San Juan Bosco — this is more than a neighborhood church.

It is a cathedral of Cuban traditions — a sanctuary for the poor East Little Havana neighborhood of overcrowded rooming houses and unemployed refugees and its latest wave of Spanish-speaking exiles.

"We have established a refuge here for people with material as well as spiritual problems," says the Rev. Emilio Vallina, a Cuban exile himself who officiated the church's first Mass May 30, 1963, before 57 Cuban refugees.

Vallina likes to recall how the inaugural Mass was celebrated at a theater seven blocks away because the two-story building at 1301 W. Flagler St. was not ready until December.

Now, San Juan Bosco boasts an attendance of about 3,500 devotees on Sundays and hosts an array of community programs that offer more than religious guidance: Children learn about their Spanish roots in their parents' language; lonely seniors eat healthy meals, learn crafts and even get free manicures; political exile leaders gather to ask of God what men have not been able to do — liberate their homelands.

In Cuba, Vallina celebrated Mass at Jesús del Nazareno, a sanctuary in Arroyo Arenas, an old working-class neighborhood in suburban Havana. The parish was known for its devotion to a statue of Christ (dressed in a dark gown, to signify penitence) which the people believed to be miraculous. It was often the site of pilgrimages from the capital.

"In 1961, [Fidel] Castro began persecuting the Church," Vallina said. "Religious schools were closed. Mobs came into the churches and beat up people and priests. My time came to leave."

He left the island that same year. Jesús del Nazareno remains one of two national sanctuaries on the island.

At San Juan Bosco, a similar statue of Christ wearing a deep purple robe stands tall in a corner of the temple. During the Lent period before Holy Week, a huge cross is fixed on its shoulders.

The statue, a copy of the one in Cuba, was donated to the church by an exiled family from Arroyo Arenas....

In a congregation of exiles — 91 per cent of the parishioners are Latin and most of those are Cuban, according to Vallina — the word Communist is blasphemy. The latest group of exiles are Nicaraguans, who say their situation is similar to that of the Cubans 20 years ago.

Last March [1982], when Pope John Paul II visited Nicaragua and was treated with irreverence by the country's Marxist leaders, San Juan Bosco church offered a Mass to express its respect for the Pope.

As hundreds of Nicaraguan exiles prayed at the pews, leaders of the anti-Sandinista movement passed out political flyers in the back. Other counterrevolutionaries left their combat posts in Costa Rica and flew to Miami for the Mass. Msgr. Manuel Salazar Espinosa, the former bishop of León, Nicaragua, now exiled in Costa Rica, blessed the people in the Indian Miskito dialect.

"Sons of my country, ardent as our volcanoes, placid as our plains, we can think of nothing else than to return," the bishop said.

On a late Wednesday afternoon recently, airplanes coming in for a landing and cars tooting their horns outside broke the stillness surrounding the altar being readied for Mass.

A well-dressed woman clutching a Tupperware lunchbox and a small shopping bag lit a candle to the Virgin Mary, prayed, and left. A handful of men and women with cotton-white hair sat solemnly waiting for the ceremony to begin.

"Most of the people who come during the weekdays have requested the Mass for a deceased loved one," Vallina said. "Or they are the most fervent devotees."

Others just need a place to be.

An old vagrant, his tan shirt and pants black and gray with mud and his breath smelling of liquor, strolled in mumbling to himself and sat on the front row.

Once Mass began, the old man tried to follow the customary rigors of standing, kneeling, and sitting, but he became confused and often did the opposite. Sometimes, his whispers could be heard when the others were not praying.

He sat through three Masses. Then he left a little before 9 p.m., just as the door was closed for the evening.

Outside, a handmade sign, nailed high on a palm tree and facing the westbound, one-way traffic, seemed to turn the San Juan Bosco tradition into a promise: *"El Que A Mi Viene, No le Echo Afuera."*

He Who Comes To Me, Will Not Be Turned Away.

Miami Herald, 7 August 1983, 1G, 6G. Reproduced with the permission of the Miami Herald.

37. A Honduran Tragedy in New York, 1990

On 25 March 1990, Honduran immigrants and other New York residents were shocked to learn that a fire at a social club in the South Bronx had left eighty-seven people dead, most of them Hondurans. In the wake of this tragedy, renowned Jesuit sociologist Joseph P. Fitzpatrick (1913–1995) observed that the isolation of Honduran immigrants compounded their agony. He concluded that the official policy against national parishes in New York and elsewhere left a vacuum in the Catholic outreach to Latinos which only "enormous creativity and effort" could remedy.

In the early hours of Sunday morning, March 25, 1990, a large number of Honduran immigrants were enjoying a weekend of fun together at the Happy Land social club, a hangout for Honduran soccer players, high school students, and young folk in the Bronx. A Cuban who had been rejected from the club torched the main entrance. In the ensuing fire, 87 persons died, most of them Hondurans. It was a tragedy that shocked not only the nation of Honduras, where a day of national mourning was proclaimed; it shocked New Yorkers of all social levels who are hardened by the crime and the trials of life in the South Bronx.

But the ones on whom the tragedy fell like an unbearable burden were the Honduran immigrants themselves. To compound their grief was their isolation from one another. As the *New York Times* reported it, one of their greatest pains was that they had no place to grieve; no place to gather where they could feel *en su casa* (at home), a familiar spot where relatives and friends would meet, a tiny bit of turf in a large and complicated city that would be a little bit of home, of Tegucigalpa, or San Pedro Sula or La Ceiba; a place where they would know, without distraction, that they were still Hondurans, *El Pueblo de Honduras*. There was no political club, no large community center, no parish that would proclaim their identity, would tell the world who they were, most of all keep them aware of who they themselves were. They were scattered; they had to face the tragedy alone. Many generous priests, religious, and lay people, especially at the local parish of St. Thomas Aquinas, were impressive in their support of religious faith and human compassion. But the care was as scattered as the Honduran people themselves.

This raises again, very sharply, the problem of the old national or language parish for newcomers to the city or nation. It raises again the importance of the close-knit, supporting system of the immigrant community that enabled earlier immigrants to New York to make it against impossible odds. The established citizens generally criticized the ghettos, the immigrant neighborhoods, the parishes where a foreign language was heard, where fiestas, celebrations, the important moments of baptism, marriage, and burial moved with the same rhythms and the same style as in the old country. It was the immigrant community, bound together by the corner store, the hometown club, the newspaper, the burial society, most of all the parish, the synagogue, the religious congregation. This was the source of stability and security, of mutual support and help — and sometimes exploitation of the immigrants by their own. But it was "theirs," and it was this network of relatives and friends that gave the immigrants the strength to move with confidence and assurance into the mainstream of American life....

[Today's] parish, the heart of the community, has its own difficulties. The Germans, Italians, Poles, and others have moved to the suburbs; and the [New York] Archdiocese finds itself with large churches on its hands; German parishes with no Germans, Italian parishes with no Italians, Irish parishes with no Irish. When Hispanics arrive to take their place, the archdiocese is not likely to start a Hispanic parish across the street from an almost empty German or Polish parish church. And there may be just enough of the old-timers around to make a fuss if their church is given to Hispanics or others. Where large concentrations of Puerto Ricans or Dominicans exist, this tends to take care of itself. But for people as scattered as the Hondurans, this is not so easy. Furthermore, there are few native Hispanic priests to accompany their people. For religious ministry, Hondurans, like other Hispanics, must often look to American priests who have learned Spanish and have studied the culture of the Hispanic people. Many of these priests are beloved by their Hispanic people, but it is not quite the same as the Irish with their Irish priest or the Germans with their German priest. And when the Hondurans find themselves in a Bronx, Manhattan, or Brooklyn parish, they are most likely sharing the parish with Puerto Ricans, Dominicans, Cubans, Americans, or Caribbean blacks. Thus the lament of the Hondurans: "We are all scattered; we have no place to grieve, where we can gather together and be at home."

Therefore, the central problem remains: How can the church minister to Hispanic people in the difficult circumstances described above, and fulfill the same function that the national parish fulfilled a century ago? This requires enormous creativity and effort. In some cases, a determined effort to create a sense of unity among the disparate groups of parishioners has been successful. I have seen some excellent examples of parishes where the efforts of a pastor or parish ministers or dedicated lay people have achieved a wonderful level of unity and collaboration. A sensitivity to the problem is essential to the deeply rooted need of immigrants to be able to create a satisfying community of their own, to whatever extent that is possible. Ministry in their own language and meaningfully related to their own culture is essential. Urging them to learn English and adapt quickly to American ways is understandable among established residents, but this is not meeting the challenge. Hondurans, for example, will eventually learn English and adapt to American ways. All the immigrants have done so. But the immediate problem is to enable them to create a situation in which they have a sense of security among their own, the continuity of their way of life, a confidence in the sense of who they are. To achieve this in the turbulent variety of contemporary parishes, in the face of convulsive change, requires extraordinary effort. It is a challenge the church has never faced before. It must meet it now. It requires the courage to face the reality of the situation, the imaginativeness to innovate within older and out-of-date structures, and the willingness to face change. God gave the vision and courage to our predecessors of the last century. If we are responsive to God's call, we also may be blessed with the vision we need today to enable newcomers to create, in new and difficult situations, a satisfying sense of community, a basis of solidarity among their own, and a place, not only to grieve when tragedy occurs, but to grow as well as citizens of a new land.

Joseph P. Fitzpatrick, "No Place to Grieve: A Honduran Tragedy," *America* 163 (21 July 1990): 37–38. Printed by permission.

38. Testimony of a Salvadoran Refugee, 1991

A civil war ravaged El Salvador between 1979 and 1992, claiming the lives of over seventy-five thousand victims until a 1992 peace accord brought some al-

leviation to hostilities. Refugees numbering in the hundreds of thousands fled the country, many of them to the United States. In 1986, one refugee with the pseudonym "Ramiro" crossed into the United States with the assistance of leaders from the Sanctuary Movement, which granted shelter to Salvadoran and Guatemalan refugees as a form of protest against the U.S. government's sup-port of their nations' military regimes. A former seminary student and protégé of slain Salvadoran archbishop Oscar Romero (1917–1980), Ramiro, once in the United States, quickly became a strong public advocate for his people and homeland, first through a Jesuit-run house in Los Angeles and later with various organizations in Washington, D.C. The following selection is an excerpt from an interview with Ramiro that Harold Recinos conducted as part of his research on Salvadorans in the United States (Recinos).

In early 1987, I came [from Los Angeles] to Washington, D.C., as a par-ticipant in the second refugee caravan that was organized by the Central American Refugee Center (CARECEN), Ayuda ("Help"), and Casa del Pueblo ("House of the People"). The Methodist, Catholic, Baptist, Episcopalian, and any church connected with sanctuary were incorporated into the caravan. I had to give testimony in twenty-seven states. I gave the testimony of a refugee intended to let people know what was going on in my country. Well, this is how I came to Washington. My open participation in the caravan spiritually moved the North American *pueblo* (people). When I shared with them that a leader died, they took him away, but his name will never be taken. I said some-day you will find his photo and his name, Monseñor [Oscar] Romero. During this caravan, I was given the homilies and photo of Monseñor Romero to re-member our leader who watched over human rights in our country and in the whole world. This is how I came to Washington, D.C.

University people always asked, "Why did you leave El Salvador?" I like to be asked this question. I always informed them that for me this was a very big question, but a good one. I would respond, "You who are in this supposedly powerful country, but whose power is in money; how would you feel living under bullets that you had no idea where they were coming from or going? What would you have to do to get out of that country that was in war, espe-cially after being threatened with death? How would it be to leave and have to live on the streets with nothing to eat? What would it be like to go out into the street afraid that you would not return alive at the end of a day? Fearing that you would become disappeared or return home dead?" Thus, I told them that because of the war I had to emigrate to this country. I did not want to become a criminal either in military service or in the guerrilla [movement], as they call it. However, in our country the guerrillas do not exist. What does exist is the rebellion of a *pueblo pobre* (poor people) against the rich and against a military regime. In my own flesh, I suffered the bullets that afflict the people. I absorbed the air of bombs, not pure air. I gave them this testimony and showed them the bullet wounds. I shared with them [North Americans] what I studied. I urged them to form base communities to go to our republic to see the consequences and to experience in their own flesh the noise of bullets and bombs. They would then say, "You are right. I would have left as well to save my life." Of all the questions, I liked this one the most when it was asked by university and church people alike....

I think the role of refugees is the most important in a war. If refugees did not come out of the country, people would simply say that in El Salvador there is war but only words would be heard, just news would be heard. But the countries of the world have become aware that El Salvador is at war because people have left with physical damage, given testimony of that war, and shown the injuries they have received. All of this has caused the United Nations to take notice of the refugees. Refugees are a *pueblo* of El Salvador who have had to leave their country to ask for peace.

Harold J. Recinos, transcript of "Ramiro" interview, 13 November 1991, Washington, D.C. Trans. Harold J. Recinos. Printed by permission.

39. Reflections on South American Catholics in the United States, 1997

South Americans number more than one-fourth of the Roman Catholics in the world, but comprise only a small minority of U.S. Hispanics. Nonetheless, in recent decades the number of South Americans in the United States has increased dramatically, with Colombians, Ecuadorians, and Peruvians predominating. In comparison to other Latino groups in the United States, South Americans tend to have a higher income and level of education. They are also more geographically dispersed. The following selection is taken from an article by Fanny Tabares, who has extensive pastoral experience in the United States, Peru, and her native Colombia. Currently she is the director of Hispanic ministry in the Diocese of Kalamazoo, Michigan.

In general, Hispanics live a traditional, nostalgic, and conservative faith in order to preserve their identity and cultural roots and pass them on to their children. At times they are more conservative here than in their native country because they do not have as many possibilities to express and live their popular religiosity. Even though South Americans have been able to adapt to this country and settle in relatively well, the majority are still sentimentally attached to their country of origin and maintain communication with it by telephone, videos, and letters. Their experience at the core is that of a stranger in a strange land. For the most part, the church does not meet them in their exile. They have to integrate themselves the best they can into local parishes that generally are ill equipped to receive them.

Some churches have tried to respond to the special characteristics of South Americans within their parishes. We have, for example, celebrations of the Peruvian feasts of Señor de Los Milagros, Saint Martín de Porres, and Saint Rose of Lima; the Venezuelan feast of Our Lady of Coromoto; the Colombian feast of Our Lady of Chiquinquira; and the Argentinian feast of Our Lady of Lujan.

Priests and religious have rarely been able to immigrate here with their respective parishioners. However, many parishes and dioceses have contacted different Spanish-speaking countries blessed with vocations to ask for priests to serve the South American communities in the United States.

A significant number of South Americans find themselves in leadership positions within their parishes, dioceses, and on a national level within the church. With their Christian values of solidarity, hope, family unity, and almost a blind faith, they have responded admirably to the church here. With great sacrifice they have learned to accept as their own customs which, though Hispanic, originated in countries not their own.

The United States bishops see the Hispanic people as a prophetic voice and hope for the church. They encourage the faithful to defend life and to speak out for justice and solidarity. This posture of the church has helped many South Americans who have worked in base communities in their native countries. They follow a theology of liberation and commit themselves to the poor, the immigrant, and the refugee. They strive to discover in history and in the present moment the call of God to develop a theology and spirituality from the perspective of the poor, the immigrant, and the Hispanic.

What can South Americans offer the church here in the United States? Their very presence calls the whole church to remember its universality, to work together for a church, indeed, a world where there are no barriers of race, culture, or language, but rather bridges uniting common hopes and dreams.

It is not easy to separate the gifts and the needs of South Americans from their culturally related Hispanic brothers and sisters. However, I will attempt to do so. Among the ministry proposals I would make are the following:

• Recognize and celebrate in the parish religious feasts special to different nationalities in such a way that no one feels excluded, and celebrate universal characteristics of different nationalities.

• Be conscious of the fact that many South Americans, though not yet able to communicate well in English, may be well prepared academically to understand the complexity of all that happens around them. They desire to continue forming themselves and deepening their integration into this society including the political, social, and religious aspects. They also have a deep thirst for God and wish to feel welcomed and recognized for who they are. They long to serve and to participate in their new church community.

• Generally, South Americans have high self-esteem and prefer to give rather than receive. For this reason, even though they have needs, they prefer to keep them to themselves rather than to ask for help. They feel humiliated if treated as the underprivileged poor. They are very proud of themselves, and the best way to relate to them is to ask for their help with some project or ministry.

• Many people from South America bring with them a highly developed social consciousness and can be of great help in parish programs that attend to social needs and welcome new persons in the community. Many previously put their lives at risk for others back home and have much experience of social and Christian commitment born of a serious study of a theology of liberation that reflects their experience of exodus and exile. The church must find ways to use to its best advantage this prophetic dimension.

• Statistics show that South Americans who come to this country are well prepared academically in ways that qualify them to serve as a bridge between the Hispanic community in general and the communities of other cultures, especially the European American. The parish should recognize and use this valuable gift in building up the whole church community.

• In general, South Americans come from cities where communication technology and life structures are more or less comparable to those of the United States. For this reason, it is easier for them to adapt to the world of technology in the United States than for those Hispanics who come from rural backgrounds. *Campesinos* who emigrate to the city from rural areas in their native lands find it difficult to adapt to an urban set of values and lifestyle. Their way of life, and how they relate to their families and to their neighbors, changes. People from South America can be of great service in helping others adjust to new urban environments.

• To be able to speak someone's language does not necessarily mean that one speaks from the same reality. It is important for people, particularly for South Americans, to understand the situation of those Hispanics who have come to this country not well educated, nor well adapted, nor with proper documentation. Some middle- and upper-class South Americans may not understand the discrimination and racism that some Hispanics have experienced in the United States because of their color or national origin. Parishes have a great responsibility to form their pastoral leaders so that their service in the community may be that of missionaries grounded in evangelical values. This involves sensitizing others, particularly middle- and upper-class South Americans and Latinos in general, to the plight of the disadvantaged.

• Parishes have to take into account that not all South Americans in the United States find themselves in privileged positions. Many South Americans suffer alone due to economic and social marginalization. As a minority group within the Hispanic community, and because of their reluctance in soliciting help, many suffer alone. By promoting social gatherings parishes can gain a better understanding of the specific needs and gifts of individuals and groups within the Hispanic community and help them interact and come to know each other.

• Parishes at times put all Hispanics in the same mold, as if they all had the same education, same interests, and the same life experience. Sometimes adult religious education for Hispanics has little content, fails to challenge, and is better suited for children. In these instances valuable leaders can be lost, including professional people who have skills in organizing and building community. The challenge is to develop adult-centered ministry which responds to different social and economic groups and to different pastoral needs, and to do ministry with a universal vision in which each person finds a place, feels welcome, and responds to the call to put one's gifts at the service of the church community.

• South Americans who have legal residence in the United States can be of great help to those who struggle in obtaining citizenship. They can speak in defense of the rights of immigrants and be a voice for those who cannot speak publicly for fear of being deported. The church, for its part, must make its voice heard more strongly in defending the rights of immigrants, taking to heart the gospel obligation: "I came as a stranger and you received me in your home" (Matthew 25:35). The church must be prophetic, announcing the good news of the kingdom of God today and denouncing the ever-greater injustices and inequalities among different ethnic groups and even among white minorities. How can the United States church, in a world of consumerism and competition, make its preferential option for the poor? At times we think that the poor are only in other countries (*Economic Justice for All*, 170). But here in the United States many millions are poor, and many, by virtue of their undocumented status, find their rights severely limited. Only in walking together, sharing our gifts and our dreams, can we become the leaven of the kingdom of God in this young church of the United States.

• In general, South Americans speak Spanish at home and teach their children this language. They speak with pride to their children about their culture, their ancestors, their social and religious customs. This has helped young people feel proud of their ancestry and, though at times within social or educational settings they are singled out and made fun of, they are better equipped to feel secure in their identity. This high level of self-esteem nourished in the home provides a firm foundation for doing well professionally and academically in this country. Mastery of two languages has also contributed to their success on the university level. History teaches us that the way to destroy or diminish a culture from within is to forbid use of its language and religion.

In conclusion, the church must offer a bilingual ministry, integrating children, youth, and adults in an open dialogue across generations, maintaining itself free of politics regarding language. Let us remember the words of Pope John Paul II when he came to the United States: "The Catholic church also speaks Spanish." Hispanic youth ministry ought to proclaim the birth of a new culture. By recognizing the great potential of Hispanic youth as a symbol of hope and new life, the church of the United States will grow in number, quality, and Christian commitment.

This rich and marvelous new culture harmoniously incorporates various older ones. Like a symphony played by a variety of instruments, each appreciated for its unique sound, together they create a masterpiece. South Americans, in concert with others, have particular gifts and strengths needed to create this kind of church.

Fanny Tabares, "Pastoral Care of Catholic South Americans Living in the United States," *Chicago Studies* 36, no. 3 (December 1997): 275–81. © 1997 Civitas Dei Foundation. Used with permission by the publisher, Liturgy Training Publications.

40. Bishop González's Message upon His Election as Archbishop of San Juan, Puerto Rico, 1999

Roberto González was born of Puerto Rican immigrant parents in Elizabeth, New Jersey. However, as is typical of Puerto Ricans' "revolving door immigration," he spent a significant part of his childhood in Puerto Rico. He joined the Franciscan order in New York and after ordination earned a doctorate in sociology from Fordham University. González participated in a number of important sociological studies on the Hispanic Catholic community before being named auxiliary bishop of Boston in 1988 and then coadjutor (1995) and eventually bishop (1997) of Corpus Christi, Texas. In March 1999 he was appointed to succeed Cardinal Luis Aponte Martínez as archbishop of San Juan, on which occasion he released the following message to the people of Puerto Rico.

A little more than half a millennium ago the church first sank her roots into this new and marvelous continent called America. And it was here, precisely in this very city, in this Archdiocese of San Juan, that the miracle of the apostolic succession was accomplished with the arrival to this land of Puerto Rico of the first successor of the Apostles in the whole of the New World, from Alaska to Tierra del Fuego, the first Bishop of Puerto Rico, Don Alonso Manso, who arrived here on December 25, 1512. Today this miracle is repeated anew.

The apostolic succession is a miracle, since it is totally a gift from God, a work of his Grace. It does not depend at all on one's human merits or talents, although it does ask from us the cooperation of our freely given obedience. This obedience is the only thing of my own which I can offer in order to respond to the mission that has been commended to me. I fully acknowledge my sinfulness and the poverty of my personal talents, and I commend myself entirely to the prayers of each of you, so that I may be enabled to be faithful to my mission. I make my own the words of my Spiritual Father, Saint Francis of Assisi, whose charism set my feet on the road which has brought me to this place: "Lord, make me an instrument of your peace!"

How awesome and mysterious are the ways of Divine Providence! Back in 1964, when I graduated from the eighth grade in the Academia Santa Mónica here in Santurce, who could have told me that I would be the next archbishop of San Juan; the successor of that very archbishop who in that very year was beginning his faithful ministry! (By the way, I can only hope that as my teachers of that year — the sisters of St. Joseph, Sister Maura Patricia and Sister Grace, their principal Sister María Reparatrice, now enjoying her 99th year of youth, and my lay teacher Señora Josefina Soto — think back on those days, they must surmise that my behavior must have improved a lot since I was a boy!)

It is true that I was not born on Puerto Rican soil, but I will make bold to say that I was, in spite of this, born in Puerto Rico. One's national identity does not depend exclusively on the place where one is born, for this could be a mere accident of chance. The identity of a Puerto Rican is found in the heart and runs through the veins; it is what we profoundly and affectionately call *la mancha del plátano* [literally, "the plantain stain," which is almost impossible to eradicate, and is colloquially used as a symbol of Puerto Rican identity which cannot be eradicated even by years of willful efforts at assimilation]. It is a spiritual reality which affects the way a person perceives, evaluates, and cultivates his or her life — hence the concept of "culture" — in solidarity with a people who live out their humanity according to a unique and particular tradition, a tradition which projects itself toward a common destiny which is congruent with its historical roots.

In the case of Puerto Rico, our history has led us to find this reality also beyond our shores. And it was in that "other Puerto Rico," that "Puerto Rico beyond the sea," where I was born, and I have always recognized it as a single people with that of the island, and a single spiritual reality. And because of this I want to send from here, from this dear piece of land from which springs our shared identity, a warm *abrazo* [embrace] to our brothers and sisters who live far from the island, and especially to those with whom I shared one Faith and one Hope, and whom I had the privilege of serving as a priest in New York and as an auxiliary bishop in Boston.

Our Puerto Rican identity is part of the Latin American world, and I have had many opportunities of experiencing this, especially with my brother bishops of Latin America, with whom I have been privileged to share the drama that our peoples are living in this age. Although I never served as a priest in this island, I have always made an effort to stay in touch with the realities of Puerto Rican life. As the years ran their course, I have done everything in my power to deepen my bonds with the members of my family who live in Puerto Rico, with my friends, and with the bishops and priests of this island. However, I acknowledge that I have a lot to learn in order to serve you effectively....

My heart finally turns to the mother of our Christian family, our patron, Our Lady of Divine Providence. To her I entirely commend my ministry as archbishop of San Juan de Puerto Rico, and I dare to make my own the words of our Holy Father: "*Totus tuus:* I am wholly yours, my mother"; we are wholly yours! That is what we want to be.

Message of Archbishop-Elect Roberto González, OFM, 26 March 1999. Trans. Jaime R. Vidal. Printed by permission.

Cuban rafters off the coast of Florida, 1994. Courtesy *The Miami Herald*/Charles Trainor.

Part 4

EXILES, FAITH, AND THE HOMELAND

VIRGEN DE LA CARIDAD

Virgencita Santísima del Cobre	Oh! Blessed Lady of El Cobre
desde el destierro en tu capilla santa,	in exile I come to your chapel,
yo te pido la fé, te pido tanta	asking for faith in abundance
que para todos mis hermanos sobre.	enough for all my brothers.
En columnas de fuego tu capilla	In pillars of fire your chapel
es santuario del triste peregrino,	is the weary pilgrim's sanctuary.
es remanso de amor, es luz que brilla	It is love's retreat, it is a light that shines
como sembrado de estrellas un camino.	like a pathway seeded with stars.
Hoy que sangra el cubano sin consuelo,	Suffering, inconsolable Cubans,
a tus pies de rodillas	before you on their knees,
pedimos piedad,	seeking your mercy ask you
que le digas al Dios de nuestro Cielo.	to intercede with our Heavenly Father.
Con tu gracia, tu amor y tu bondad,	Through your grace, love, and goodness,
que redima por siempre a tu pueblo,	ask that He redeem your land forever.
Anda, Madre!	Make haste Mother!
Virgen Santa de la Caridad.	Oh, Blessed Lady of Charity.

Sergio Becerra, "Un ramillete Cubano a la Virgen de la Caridad," in Florinda Alzaga and Ana Rosa Nuñez, eds., *Cuba Diaspora* (annual of the Unión de Cubanos en el Exilio published at Caracas, 1981), 110. Trans. Dora Elizondo Guerra. Courtesy of the Cuban Heritage Collection, Otto G. Richter Library, University of Miami.

Introduction

Latino exiles have sought asylum in the United States since the time of Latin America's independence wars against Spain beginning in 1810. Most of these exiles were at least nominally Catholic, and they came as a result of the pe-

---

Illustration above: Virgen de la Caridad del Cobre (document 48) by contemporary Cuban artist Alfredo G. Cardentey. Courtesy Alfredo G. Cardentey.

riodic political and social upheavals that have characterized Latin America's historical development during the last two centuries. These upheavals were about change, Latin Americans' efforts to free themselves from the legacy of Spain's colonial structures. Since achieving political independence from Spain, the region has struggled to construct a series of nations from highly fractured societies, socioeconomically and racially, a process that has caused revolution, war, disruption, displacement, migration, and exile.

This journey toward nationhood and nationality in Latin America inevitably included the Catholic Church, a central force in Latin American societies since its arrival with Christopher Columbus in 1492. Catholicism played a foundational role in Spain's American colonies during the sixteenth and seventeenth centuries, forming a critical component of an emergent Latin American identity. Nevertheless, competing visions regarding what role the church should play in society at certain historical moments created tensions, conflicts, violence, and the displacement of Catholics. During the eighteenth century a "modernizing" Spanish Crown influenced by the Enlightenment and rationalism attempted to curb the power and influence of the church. In the late nineteenth century, liberalism and positivism further undermined church authority throughout Latin America, and during the twentieth century reformist and Marxist revolutionary movements sought political and socioeconomic change that included the absolute separation of church and state. Nineteenth-century liberals and twentieth-century revolutionaries viewed the church as aligned with the conservative elites, representing the status quo. In response to deepening social problems during the latter half of the twentieth century, the Latin American church, with the encouragement of the momentum from the Second Vatican Council (1962–1965), gave more attention to the plight of the poor and vulnerable. A gathering of Latin American bishops (CELAM) at Medellín, Colombia, in 1968 explored the church's past failures in the region and called for reform, including social justice, political participation, and grassroots evangelization (Mainwaring and Wilde 10–15). In time, an important segment of the church identified itself with the region's poor and oppressed, leading to outright confrontation with Latin America's elites who feared grassroots organizing for change in a period of the global Cold War.

Throughout the nineteenth and twentieth centuries, then, the Latin American church found itself having to contend with forces of change that required redefinitions of the church's role in society. The documents in this chapter focus on Cuban and Mexican Catholic exiles who left their countries in the midst of the turbulence that accompanied the struggles to formulate these redefinitions.

Cuban Catholic Exiles

Cubans have been seeking political refuge in the United States for two centuries. During the nineteenth century Cubans commenced their struggle for independence from Spain, and, among the thousands of exiles who went to the United States, many became disillusioned with the church's pro-Spanish position. On the other hand, the 1959 Communist revolution in Cuba led to the exodus of Cubans by the hundreds of thousands; these exiles became more supportive of a church that strongly condemned the Communist path.

Cuba remained a Spanish colony when the rest of Latin America (except Puerto Rico) became independent by 1825. A prosperous sugar boom kept the Cuban elites loyal to their traditional relationships with Spain. Nevertheless, within a few years many Cubans became restless and sought reforms, including political representation, the abolition of the slave trade, and a more open economic system. Cuban challenges to the colonial system led to Spanish repression and the exile of dissidents. Many went to the United States and formed expatriate communities that organized active opposition to Spain (often in support of Cuba's annexation to the United States) throughout the late 1840s and early 1850s. In 1868 an insurrection broke out on the island.

This first independence war lasted until 1880, leading to the further growth and consolidation of sizable exile centers in New York and Florida. These communities continued their anti-Spanish activism throughout the 1880s and 1890s, culminating in a second insurrectionary war for independence in 1895. This war led eventually to the Cuba-Spanish-American War in 1898, U.S. occupation of Cuba from 1899 to 1903, and the establishment of a Cuban republic as a U.S. protectorate (Pérez 1988; Poyo).

For the most part, during the nineteenth century Cuban exiles in the United States were skeptical if not outright antagonistic toward the Catholic Church. The church in Cuba, headed mostly by Spaniards, had generally supported Spanish rule on the island, alienating many of the thousands of Cubans who left the island during the century. Many abandoned Catholicism in exile and turned to other ideas, religions, and philosophies of life, including freemasonry, Protestantism, anarchism, and socialism. For the heavily working-class and multiracial communities in New York and Florida, socialism and anarchism spoke more strongly than did Catholicism, as did the African-based religious tradition of Santería. Many of the prominent middle-class exile leaders in Key West tended to be Masons or Protestants, especially Episcopalians, Methodists, and Baptists. A generally anticlerical attitude prevailed among Cubans, and only a relatively few Cubans in this exile community identified themselves as practicing Catholics (document 42; Deulofeu).

During the twentieth century, the exile experience continued to play an important role in Cuban political life, especially with the successful revolution of 1959 led by Fidel Castro. Unlike the nineteenth century, practicing Catholics and church activists were heavily represented in the exodus from Cuba's Communist revolution. A quickly radicalizing revolution led to almost immediate confrontations between the revolutionary government and the church. Catholic concerns about Communism culminated in a National Catholic Congress on 28 November 1959 held in Havana at the Plaza Civica, or Plaza de la Revolución, as it later became known. Approximately one million people gathered at the plaza to reaffirm their Catholic allegiance or at least to register their concern about the country's political direction (Kirk 78–80).

In August of the following year a message from the Cuban Catholic hierarchy acknowledged the need for reforms to advance the economic, social, and cultural welfare of the poor, but also called for procedures that recognized the rights of all citizens. Of more concern to church leaders, however, was the government's deepening commercial, cultural, and diplomatic relations with the Communist bloc nations. They declared that "the great majority of the Cuban people, who are Catholic, are against materialistic communism and atheism, and can only be led to communism through deceit and coercion" (*Voz de la Iglesia en Cuba* 115–18). As the government consolidated its position throughout 1960, thousands of Catholics fled the island. Many joined exile counterrevolutionary groups and participated in the failed Bay of Pigs invasion on 17 April 1961. The role of Catholics in this effort to overthrow the Cuban government was not lost on Castro, who initiated a strong repression against the church. By the end of the year the church was silenced and virtually all vocal Catholic activists left Cuba.

While many Cuban Catholic exiles continued their active armed opposition to the Castro government, throughout the 1960s others initiated the process of building communities to promote faith, identity, and an exile consciousness. Cubans initially established themselves mostly in the Miami area, but the federally run Cuban Refugee Program settled Cubans in countless cities across the country, including New York, Union City (N.J.), Chicago, and Los Angeles. By 1963, some two hundred thousand Cubans had arrived in the United States, including the core of Cuba's Catholic militant laity and leadership. All foreign priests and a significant portion of Cuban priests also left or were deported, including the auxiliary bishop of Havana, Monsignor Eduardo Boza Masvidal. These priests played an important role in serving the exile community especially in Miami. Drawn heavily from Cuba's middle and upper classes, perhaps 80 percent of the early arrivals identified with the church, and these exiles took a leading role in organizing Catholics in political, social, educational, and church institutions (M. C. Garcia 1997).

In exile, Catholic militants reestablished familiar organizations from the island that served to reconnect networks of people who had worked in common cause at home. Miami Catholics wasted little time creating a formal presence. By 1963 a predominantly Cuban parish church, St. John Bosco (document 36), already operated in Little Havana. Over the next decade additional parishes with strong if not majority Cuban congregations appeared, many of them served by native Spanish-speaking priests (Walsh). Numerous Catholic schools opened to accommodate the demand among Cubans, including schools from Cuba that had been intervened by the Castro government. Perhaps the most well known were Belén and Lasalle schools. These *colegios* offered an English-language Catholic education within a Cuban cultural environment that promoted the Spanish language, Cuban identity, and an exile consciousness (Pérez 1994). The Cuban lay organizations Acción Católica (Catholic Action) and Agrupación Católica Universitaria (Catholic University Group) reestablished themselves in exile, utilizing well-established networks from Cuba to promote Catholicism in the exile communities. Perhaps the most important symbol of Cuban exile Catholicism was Nuestra Señora de la Caridad del Cobre (Our Lady of Charity). In 1961 an image of the Cuban patroness arrived in Miami from Cuba on her feast day, September 8, drawing thousands of Cubans to a worship service. Impressed by the depth of the devotion, Archbishop Coleman Carroll announced the need for a sanctuary dedicated to the Virgin. In 1973, La Ermita de la Caridad del Cobre was consecrated and quickly became a place of pilgrimage for Cubans who linked the Virgin and their religious traditions to their sense of Cuban nationality (Tweed).

Though the Cuban exile experience reflected a heterogeneous patchwork of ideologies, groups, and interests, Catholics played a particularly important role in forming community, especially during the early years, creating a political and ideological response to Communism in their homeland, and strengthening faith and an exile identity. From paramilitary activity to participating in the early political organizations of support for the Bay of Pigs invasion, to espousing formal Christian-based political agendas, to initiating intellectual discussions and debates about the various exile strategies for dealing with the revolution, Catholic activists were in the forefront and gained considerable support and legitimacy from the other sectors of Cuban communities in exile.

Mexican Catholic Exiles

Church-state conflicts leading to Catholic exile experiences also affected Mexican society, where church power and influence were very strong, even more dramatic than in the Cuban case. Liberal and revolutionary movements seeking change in Mexico engendered fierce opposition from the church, often leading to considerable violence. Though Padre Miguel Hidalgo raised the cry of revolution against Spain in 1810 under the banner of Our Lady of Guadalupe, the liberal struggle for change in Mexico during the nineteenth century, culminating with the Mexican Revolution beginning in 1910, contained deeply rooted anticlerical attitudes. Liberal leaders who emerged after Mexico's independence from Spain embraced the Enlightenment and advocated a significantly diminished role for the church in political and civic affairs. Despite efforts by conservatives to maintain the strong colonial tradition of inseparability of church and state, liberals advanced their ideas in the Reform Laws of 1859 and 1860, which, among other things, separated church and state, outlawed the monastic orders, and nationalized church properties.

These reforms and others were eventually incorporated into the Mexican Constitution during the 1870s despite considerable church opposition and open resistance to the measures. Anticlerical attitudes appeared in their strongest form in the Constitution of 1917, a document that emerged after seven years of civil war initiated by Francisco Madero's movement against President Porfirio Díaz. The Constitution mandated the expulsion of foreign priests and women religious, banned religious education in the schools, forbade public displays of worship, nationalized church property, and required the registration of priests with the state (Burns 138).

Though successive Mexican governments approached confrontation with the church cautiously, beginning in early 1926 President Plutarco Elías Calles took concrete steps to implement the Constitution of 1917. Resistance led to the closing of churches and the arrest of priests. State governments followed the lead, enacting further curbs on church activities. By the middle of 1926, Catholic armed resistance known as the Cristero Rebellion began. Violence on both sides eventually forced an accommodation between the Mexican government and the Vatican in 1929. Sporadic conflict continued and resurgent anti-Catholic policies under President Lázaro Cardenas in 1934 aggravated the tensions. In time, Cárdenas relaxed the government's zealous anticlericalism and a tenuous peaceful coexistence emerged between the church and state (Quirk 145–247).

The Mexican Revolution (1910–1917) and subsequent direct conflicts resulting from the Cristero Rebellion (1926–1929) led to a large migration of Mexicans to the United States, especially California and Texas. Among those arriving in the United States were Catholic priests targeted by anticlerical revolutionaries such as Pancho Villa, who operated in northern Mexico. One estimate is that twenty-five thousand political refugees had arrived in San Antonio by 1913; they were joined by thousands more during the next two decades (Hinojosa 1994: 33). By August 1914, the archbishops of México, Michoacán, Oaxaca, Durango, and Linares and the bishops of Sinoloa, Saltillo, Aguacalientes, Zacatecas, Guadalupe, Tulacingo, Chiapas, and Campeche resided in exile at San Antonio. Even more Mexicans went to Los Angeles. Over 150,000 migrants arrived in that city by 1925; that number nearly doubled when the Cristero Rebellion erupted (Burns 184). By 1928 some one thousand Mexican priests lived in Los Angeles. These exiled priests, along with lay leaders and women religious, played an important role in the creation of new Mexican parishes and missions and in revitalizing local Mexican worship traditions. In Los Angeles, twelve Mexican parishes were founded between 1923 and 1928. By 1936 there were sixty-four Mexican parishes in the Archdiocese of Los Angeles alone, many started or staffed by exiled priests from Mexico (Burns 162–63). The Mexican church hierarchy and priests in the United States managed to keep the issue of the Mexican government's "socialistic" and anti-Catholic leanings highly visible, raising consciousness about the fate of the church among Mexican (and other) Catholics in the United States during the 1920s and 1930s (G. Sánchez 167–70).

At San Antonio's San Fernando Cathedral parish societies and associations doubled during the first thirty years of the century. Feast-day celebrations increased dramatically by the early 1930s. Mexican exiles played an important role in reviving public rituals at San Fernando, especially processions through the plazas and streets, which had languished under Anglo-American influence. The most influential voice for shaping Mexican national consciousness in San Antonio was the newspaper *La Prensa*. Founded by exile Ignacio E. Lozano, *La Prensa* developed and propagated the exile's ideology of "el México de afuera" (literally "Mexico abroad"). This mentality did not depict Mexicans in the United States primarily as immigrants seeking economic opportunities or other personal gain. Rather, it portrayed the newcomers as exiles who fled repressive conditions at home in order to preserve their national patrimony and await the opportune moment to return and initiate national reconstruction. "El Mexico de afuera" convictions included an unyielding dedication to nationalism, Mexican national symbols, the Spanish language, Mexican citizenship, and the Catholic faith rooted in devotion to Mexico's national patroness, Nuestra Señora de Guadalupe (Our Lady of Guadalupe). *La Prensa*'s view of the exiles and their world resonated with many readers; its circulation extended well beyond San Antonio's city limits and, significantly, peaked at over thirty-two thousand in 1930, just after many exiles had left Mexico during the Cristero Rebellion. The exiles' response to President Calles's suppression of the Mexican church was strong and reflected their Catholic devotion and commitment to patriotic and cultural traditions. Indeed, Our Lady of Guadalupe became the very symbol of this opposition to the Mexican government's repression of the church (Matovina 1997b: 43–45).

Mexican Catholics in Los Angeles, exiles and immigrants alike, also became a strong source of support for the Cristero Rebellion. Several parishes in southern California took the name Cristo Rey in solidarity with the revolt. In 1930 forty chapters of the Santo Nombre (Holy Name Society) existed in southern California; they were dedicated to promoting Mexicans' consciousness of their culture, heritage, and faith. Most telling, the Our Lady of Guadalupe procession, begun in 1928 by the Hijas de Maria (Daughters of Mary), served in 1934 as an important tool for rallying opposition to the Mexican government's policies toward the church. That year the procession was advertised as "a memorial service for those who had suffered persecution in Mexico" (Burns 185–86). This event, attended by some forty thousand people, was supported by U.S. church officials and led to a vigorous protest by the Mexican consul. He charged the parade was organized by "a group of persons...already well known as the traditional enemies of the economic, social, and cultural progress of Mexico" (G. Sánchez 168).

Cuban and Mexican Catholic Exile Identity

While Latin American Catholic exiles in the United States have come from many different countries at different historical moments bringing radically diverse experiences and perspectives, the documents in this chapter illustrate exile themes from the particular cases of Cuban and Mexican exile Catholics. By definition exiles maintain their focus on the homeland; they yearn to bring change to their lands of origin so they may return. Though many, perhaps most, never physically return home, they build communities that reflect their commitment of daily homage to their heritage. Scholars tend to make distinctions between economic immigrants and political exiles, and to some extent this is valid. People who intentionally and with strategic deliberation leave their homes in search of work, to survive economically, engage the country they enter with a somewhat different psychological perspective than those who are unexpectedly torn from their homes as a result of political disruption, violence, and civil war. Exiles are often people who have coped in their homeland and never had any intention of leaving, but, finding themselves in foreign lands, they do what they can to maintain a connection. Their daily activities involve thinking about going home. This may mean becoming activists in attempting to change conditions in their nations of origin or dedicating their lives to some other activity that accommodates this yearning to return. While this dichotomy of economic and political migrants offers a useful way to speak about why people leave their homes, it is necessary to acknowledge that both economic and political motivations may often coexist in a single person and that economic migrants may adopt an exile perspective once out of their country, while political migrants may thoroughly engage their new country of residence and become immigrants. How then do we identify exiles? Regardless of the circumstances that cause people to leave home, it is their daily expressions in the country they move to that defines an "exile" state of mind. Communities with a strong exile identity, for example, establish organizations and publish newspapers that focus primarily on their country of origin. Local community activities maintain a strong focus on the homeland, from organizing exile armies to "liberate" the homeland to funding activities that support some homeland related movement. Daily conversations such as those at the family dinner table often focus on the homeland.

The following documents encompass different periods and offer concrete illustrations of what exile has meant for Cuban and Mexican Catholics in the United States. One of the most traumatizing experiences, beyond the actual violence and disruption in the homeland, has always been the process of leaving. Arrest and deportation are common experiences among exiles, who suffer the pain of being forcibly removed from their country, or are forced to flee on their own. In 1927, for example, the archbishop of Puebla, Monseñor Pedro Vera y Zuria, suffered expulsion from Mexico. On his forced train trip to Laredo he meditated on his situation and, hoping to make the best of it, determined that "I shall wear a kindly smile and speak words of consolation; I shall maintain an unbroken correspondence with the faithful of my diocese, no matter their station or state in life; I shall not allow a single letter to go unanswered" (document 45). In his first interview after his 1961 arrest and deportation from Cuba, Bishop Boza Masvidal emphasized that "I left Cuba against my will" (document 49). As a Cuban and as a priest he fully intended to remain in Cuba and attend to his duties, but he was expelled by a regime he felt was attempting to destroy the church. Faced with this reality, Boza Masvidal created an organization with his fellow expatriates that encouraged Cubans to embrace their new lives in exile but not to forget who they were; he called on Cubans to remain faithful and committed to their Cuban identity (document 50).

Once in the United States, exiles faced the inevitable yearning for the homeland so characteristic of people displaced from their homes, family, and community. "We are always with the desire of returning and we see that the day never comes, God knows how long we will remain here," wrote Mexican exile Dolores Dávalos de Venegas to her father-in-law in 1932. "The boys have days when the moment they remember something over there, they would like to go back," she went on. "They remember very well many things, especially when we would go to the ranch and they want to know if the little donkey is still there and the little dog" (document 46). This yearning could last a lifetime, as in the case of Father Felix Varela, a Cuban exile who lived in the United States for some thirty years (1823–1853). In a visit to Varela in his last years, a fellow exile was surprised about how Varela yearned for contact with friends and teachers in the Havana he had not seen in years. "That man told me, among other things," noted Varela's visitor, "that my visit had brought him great joy because during our conversation he felt like he had been in Havana, from where no one has written him in years, and from where he hadn't had any news." Varela also told him that "I used to receive a few examples of exams given in classes, and I took pleasure in reading them, but it has been many years since I've had that pleasure" (document 41). Generations later, in 1962, other Cuban exiles wrote, "We haven't left Cuba in order to live more comfortably or to earn more money.... We have come here prepared to fight, to organize a crusade, to struggle for God and for Cuba" (document 51). In 1992, Cubans in the United States who viewed their experience as a "Babylonian exile" wrote, "The spiritual climate of the Babylonian exile is the yearning for the fatherland, both bitter and sweet at once; together with it, as the years go by, the urgency of preparing for return is part of that climate" (document 56).

This personal, familial, and communal yearning also revealed itself through explicit religious expressions that emphasized loyalty and commitment to nationalist definitions — for example, in the veneration of Nuestra Señora de Guadalupe and Nuestra Señora de la Caridad del Cobre among Mexicans and Cubans, respectively. The 1934 Guadalupe celebration in East Los Angeles (document 47) revealed a strong relationship between national identity and the Virgin as did a celebration of La Caridad's feast day in 1961 (document 48).

Catholics also created organizations aimed at directly influencing their country of origin in different ways. In 1925, the Asociación Nacional de los Vasallos de Cristo Rey (National Association of the Vassals of Christ the King) in San Antonio raised funds for a national monument to the Sacred Heart of Jesus at Cubilete in Mexico so Mexicans could become more aware of the "true" ruler of Mexico (document 43). In the early 1960s, Cuban organizations of various kinds formed paramilitary units to infiltrate the island and support armed opposition to the government. On the other hand, convinced that violence did not offer a solution to Cuba's problems and their exile condition, other Cuban exiles created the Instituto de Estudios Cubanos (Institute for Cuban Studies) to study and analyze the Cuban revolutionary process instead of promoting paramilitary activities (document 52). In time others came to the same conclusion. The Christian Democratic Movement, which had created a military wing in the 1960s, decided in 1990 to change strategies in the wake of the collapse of the Soviet Union and became the Christian Democratic Party. Sensing the fall of the Castro government, the party initiated preparations for a return to the island to participate in multiparty politics and guarantee an explicitly Christian voice within the new political system (document 55). All of these organizations provided exiles with a sense of community and a way of keeping engaged with their country of origin.

Catholic exiles also worked to influence national and international public opinion, denouncing existing governments in their homelands. In 1926, El Paso's *Revista Católica* accused Mexican diplomats in the United States of falsely characterizing Mexican Catholics as opposed to the interests of the Mexican people. It cited another El Paso newspaper's viewpoint: "He [Mexican diplomat] states that the Mexican clergy follow 'obstructionist tactics against all government programs.' That is a lie. The truth is that Mexico's government has developed politics of aggression against church rights and the clergy are exercising their right and commitment to fulfill their sacred duty by condemning the government's programs because they go against justice, God's plan, and that of the nation" (document 44). Half a century later, Cuban Catholics in exile denounced human rights abuses in Cuba. On the occasion of the thirtieth anniversary of the United Nation's Declaration on Human Rights, for example, Cuban exile Catholics declared, "We want our words, replete with compassion, pain, and hope, to affirm to the world that we are not imploring nor requesting, we are demanding that human rights become a tangible reality for a silent people, who suffer and struggle for their freedom: the people of Cuba, a people in silence" (document 53).

After years in exile, many Cuban Catholics reflected on the meaning of their condition and how it affected their identities. Though they remained outside the country of birth that defined their identity, they remained connected, an extension of their country within the United States. Like their Mexican counterparts earlier in the century who spoke about "el Mexico de afuera," Cubans pointed to their history, customs, and religion as central features of identity that allowed them to retain a claim to their nationality despite years in exile. As exile bishops Eduardo Boza Masvidal and Agustín Román wrote, "*We are one people.* Geographically we see Cuba divided in two: the Cuba inside and the Cuba outside — on the island and in exile." They noted that Cubans on and off the island shared faith, culture, history, and suffering, but also optimism and hope for a future that would unite them (document 54).

Finally, exiles also considered their long-term obligations to their homelands and pondered the possibility of return. Cubans reflected on what role their Christian faith would play in their return home. "Although the hoped-for hour has not yet rung for the Cuban exile to return to the fatherland, we would be remiss in our duty if we did not begin, right now, to prepare with prayer and concrete plans. These plans have a name in the present vocabulary of the church: The New Evangelization." The exiles perceived this "new evangelization" as a way of seeking reconciliation and unity for Cubans on the island and abroad through the church (document 56). While the Cuban and other exile experiences are each unique with regard to concerns like perceived obligations to the homeland, the documents that follow reveal various key issues Latino Catholics confronted as they coped with the reality of exile.

41. Description of a Visit with Padre Félix Varela, 1852

On 25 February 1853, Father Félix Varela (1788–1853) died in St. Augustine, Florida. An exile from Cuba, Varela arrived at New York in 1823 after being condemned to death by the restored Spanish absolutist regime he opposed while serving as a Cuban delegate to the Spanish Cortes (parliament). In exile, Varela worked as a parish priest, advocating Cuban independence from Spain, calling for the abolition of the slave trade, and writing and thinking about politics, philosophy, and religion. He published an important exile newspaper, El Habanero, where he advocated Cuba's independence from Spain, and maintained active correspondence and intellectual exchange with his compatriots on the island. Although pardoned by the Spanish government in 1833, Varela refused to acknowledge that his support for constitutional rule represented criminal activity. He remained in exile and never returned to Cuba. In 1847, severe asthma forced Varela to relocate in St. Augustine, where he died several years later. Recognized as a precursor of Cuban pro-independence thought, Varela is often described by Cubans as "the one who first taught us to think" (Hernandez Travieso). The following document, by an exile of the next generation, Lorenzo de Alló, describes his visit with Varela shortly before the priest's death; it reveals Varela's unrelenting emotional and intellectual attachment to his homeland even after thirty years of exile.

St. Augustine, Florida
25 December 1852

Reverend Don Francisco Ruíz, Havana

My dearest friend:

I arrived in this city today and among the first things I wanted was to pay a visit to our mutual friend and noble teacher, Father Varela. Around 10:00 a.m. I set out for St. Augustine Church. A High Mass was about to begin and I assumed he would be officiating, but it wasn't so. As soon as the Mass was over, I went to the church courtyard, where I ran into a Black woman who guided me to our teacher's quarters.

Soon, in a wood frame building, I found a room similar, or perhaps a bit larger, than a college dormitory room. It was sparsely furnished. There was a table with a tablecloth, a fireplace, two wooden chairs, and a common sofa with a mattress for a seat. I did not see a bed, nor were there books, nor maps, nor any writing accouterments, nor anything except what I already mentioned. There were only two pictures of saints on the wall, and on the mantelpiece over the fireplace there was a poor excuse for a bell. A man was lying on the sofa. He was old, thin, distinguished, and with a look about him that spoke of mysticism and wisdom. That man was Father Varela.

I told him who I was and asked to kiss his hand. For an instant he didn't recognize me, but soon he remembered me perfectly. He asked about you, Casal, Bermudez, about Luz, and practically about all of the students and faculty of his day, and also about a few of the secular students. I was impressed with how, even after thirty-one years, he was still able to think so clearly, and remember even the most mundane things.

When I first entered his room, Father was stretched out on the sofa, slightly propped up by three large pillows. I insisted that he remain that way. He explained that due to three or four ailments he had to stay in that position most of the time. He said he could no longer read nor write, not only because of his infirmities, but also because he could no longer see well. He talked about how he lived in that room courtesy of Father Aubril, a French priest and pastor of the parish, who had taken him under his care and without whose kindness he would have certainly already perished.

When he would reminisce about the college and his friends and students, his enthusiasm seemed to banish illness. As he described his condition, his entire demeanor, his face, his gestures, his words were of total acceptance. One could not help but to admire him as a most fortunate man.

Father Varela still has his hair, he still has his own teeth, and he hasn't lost his Cuban gestures and mannerisms. Only when he speaks in English, a language that he speaks as fluently as his own, does his physiognomy take on an anglicized air. Whereas everyone enjoys his presence and loves him, only Father Aubril offers him a helping hand. How unfathomable is this mound of dirt we call a world! . . .

We have an obligation in the name of all that is good, and to avoid the stigma of being ingrates, to look with compassion at this man who has been our benefactor and our professor who loves us. That man told me, among other things, that my visit had brought him great joy because during our conversation he felt like he had been in Havana, from where no one has written him in years, and from where he hadn't had any news. He also said, "I used to receive a few examples of exams given in classes, and I took pleasure in reading them, but it has been many years since I've had that pleasure."

Poor, priest! His life is one of pain, in which he simply vegetates. His words are of peace, love and faith; if they were written and published they would enhance the sphere of wisdom and morality. His head is clear as ever, but if his virtues and religion were not as strong and steadfast, his gigantic talent would only serve to make his situation seem unbearable.

Lorenzo Alló

Letter of Lorenzo de Alló to Francisco Ruíz, St. Augustine, Florida, 25 December 1852, cited in José Ignacio Rodríguez, *Vida del presbítero don Félix Varela* (New York: Imprenta de "O Novo Mundo," 1878), 361–64. Trans. Dora Elizondo Guerra.

42. Description of Cuban Catholics in Key West, 1892–1900

Cubans began arriving at Key West in significant numbers after 10 October 1868, when insurgents declared Cuban independence and launched a violent and bloody war against Spanish colonialism on the island. Though Spain pacified the island in 1880, Cubans continued to leave Cuba for political reasons and to work in an emergent Cuban cigar industry in Key West, and later in Tampa. Key West's cigar worker community continued to conspire against Spain and helped launch the final independence war in 1895 (Poyo). Given the Catholic Church's support for continued Spanish rule in Cuba and opposition to the insurgents, a significant number of Cuban exiles became alienated from the church during this era. Many became Masons and others joined Protestant denominations, particularly the Episcopalians, Methodists, and Baptists (Deulofeu). Still others, especially those of the working classes, were attracted to socialism and anarchism. Despite this alienation of Cubans from their church, priests and the Sisters of the Holy Names of Jesus and Mary worked among them, first under the authority of the bishop of Savannah and later as part of the diocese of St. Augustine. Key West's first Catholic church, Saint Mary Star of the Sea, was dedicated in 1852. The Sisters of the Holy Names arrived from Canada in 1868 and opened schools for girls and boys. They also established the Convent of Mary Immaculate in 1875. By 1879 so many Cubans had arrived in Key West that church officials supported the establishment of a Cuban chapel, Nuestra Señora de la Caridad del Cobre (A History of St. Mary Star of the Sea Catholic Church 8–20). The following select chronicles by the Sisters of the Holy Names reveal the challenges they faced in creating a viable Cuban parish in Key West.

December 8, 1892

Opening of the Cuban church. After the Cuban revolt against Spanish domination, many Cubans emigrated with their families to Key West, as much to gain a livelihood (which their country could not give them) as to flee from the theater of war. In leaving their country, the greater number of these unfortunate exiles also abandoned the practice of all religious duties. A great many, not understanding the English language in which the religious instructions were given, left the church, and no longer practiced the faith. After many pressing appeals and explanations, His Excellency sent the Rev. Father Domingo Bottolaccio to aid these poor Cubans and to try to form a parish. A little chapel was built and dedicated to Our Lady of the Nativity, and on the feast of the Immaculate Conception the first Mass was celebrated before a congregation of some thirty people. We offer our prayers that this little congregation will grow and that its members will be worthy of the beautiful title of Catholic Christians.

January 15, 1893

Reception of the Children of Mary [Hijas de María] *in the Cuban chapel.* Today we have the consolation of seeing six of our Cuban children enrolling under Mary's banner and promising her their love and fidelity. The reception took place in the modest Cuban chapel that was decorated with flowers and ferns. May our Immaculate Mother bless these dear children and keep them pure, in order that they may always bear with honor the sweet title of "Child of Mary."

May 1, 1893

Even though the number of Catholics among our pupils is limited, and that in many families religion is almost unknown, we have the happiness of knowing that we do some good in rekindling the torch of faith so often in danger of extinction. Today, twenty American pupils and thirteen Cubans received their first holy communion. May these young children keep the delicate perfume of faith and the innocence that today seems to fill their young hearts!

End of the Month of May, 1894

For the first time in Key West the exercises for the month of Mary were solemnly held in the Cuban church. The Sisters went every evening to supervise the children as well as to conduct the singing. Copies of the litanies and Spanish hymns were distributed to the faithful who joined their voices with those of the children to praise the Mother of God. The Rosary was said in common; the Rev. Father Bottolaccio read for a time from a pious book. The singing of the "laudate" ended the service. Every night the little chapel was filled with women and children; some men, attracted by the music, came in and listened attentively to the reading, then, no doubt moved by some secret grace obtained by the Mother of Mercy, they returned again. Several were converted after having attended the devotions proper to this blessed month. It is with joy that we already perceive the fruits of grace abundantly produced among the poor Cubans by the prayers and hymns addressed to Mary that they might return to the practice of their religious duties.

December 25, 1894

The beautiful feast of Christmas fills our souls with happiness and also, we hope, with precious blessings. Who could offer to the Christ Child the homage of her heart's adoration without receiving His blessing in return? We had the consolation of having the first Mass of the day said in our Chapel and the blessing of receiving Holy Communion. At ten-thirty in the Cuban chapel, Holy Mass was celebrated with all possible pomp. Elaborate decorations, an orchestra, a Christmas pageant representing angels adoring the Messiah — in short — everything at Holy Mass was done in Cuban style. We hope that it attracted these poor exiles to the church by awakening in their memories the religious customs of their childhood, and brings them back to the religion of their ancestors.

May 1, 1895

May devotions begin in the Cuban church. By our fervor and sacrifices, and above all by the intercession of our Blessed Mother, we wish to do violence to Heaven in order to obtain the conversion of our poor Cubans who, in spite of their deplorable indifference toward all religious duties, are still attached to the devotion to the Blessed Virgin. The crowd that fills the chapel tonight makes us hope for the fulfillment of our prayers.

June 10, 1895

The death of a young Cuban child, Horatio Calderón, is a great loss to the Chapel of Our Lady of Charity and is one that all regret; for, for more than two years this child was a most faithful acolyte. Of a difficult and stubborn character, he was, however, at home in the sanctuary where everything interested him. His devotion, while not showy, was solidly pious — much more so than that of most children of his age — and he often astonished the priest by the questions he would ask and also by the seriousness and depth of his answers. God, satisfied with the promise showed by this child, spared him the struggle of life by taking him from this world after an illness lasting several weeks. While he was sick, the boy edified both his parents and his visitors by his patience and piety. One of his greatest consolations before he died was the promise made to him by Father Bottolaccio to have him laid out in his acolyte's cassock. Father promised, too, that he would take charge of the funeral, and that all the altar boys would form a procession to the cemetery.

The last words of the young child were those of an apostle. He used all the zeal at his command to convert his parents and his death was that of a saint.

March 1, 1896

Confirmation. His Excellency, Bishop [John] Moore, confirmed forty [*sic*] of our American and Cuban children this morning in St. Mary, Star of the Sea Church. Here are their names: Joseph Ashe, Andrew Whalton, Joshua Smith, Joaquín Gato, Eddie Gato, Aloysius Lowe, Leo English, Victor Díaz, José Chocon [Chacón?], José Lang, Agatha Seville, Irene Wiggins, Teresa Lang, Christina Baker, Clara Delgado, Gracie de Cárdenas, Mercedes de Cárdenas, Beatrice Valiz, Norma Hayman, Angela Hayman, Violet Johnson, Camille Johnson, María Torres, Catalina Ascensio, Rafaela Pérez, Carmen Martínez, Marcelina Martínez, Mercedes Lima, Ana M. Navarro, Isabel Ebra, Mercedes Ebra, Amanda Gutiérrez, María del Carmen Dubrocq, María L. Tajle [Tagle?], Rosa María Garbez [Galvez?], Aydee Mendoza, Ramona Rivera, Ana M. Barrero, Virginia Pérez, Petrona Mendoza, Manuela Mendoza.

March 19, 1897

Feast of St. Joseph. To give more solemnity to the celebration of the patronal feast of the pupils of St. Joseph's College, the Reverend Father Bottolaccio celebrates Holy Mass at the Cuban church. We have the consolation of seeing a large number of children present. During the celebration of the Mass their childish voices rose in two hymns: "O the Priceless Love of Jesus" and "Holy Joseph." After Mass everyone went home to enjoy the holiday granted them.

May 9, 1897

First Communion. The Cuban chapel is completely decorated with greenery and flowers. The altar of the Queen of Heaven scintillates with light, and the Blessed Virgin seems to smile on us. The pious faithful in deep recollection crowd the church for the coming event. All of a sudden there is a murmur, then children's voices begin to sing the angelic salutation, then a procession of thirty-nine children — Cuban, American, and Colored — file down the aisle of the little church and take their places in the center. All are dressed in their best, and prepare by fervent aspirations to receive Jesus for the first time in their hearts. May our sweet Jesus take possession of those hearts, and keep them always for Himself. In the afternoon at the Benediction of the Blessed Sacrament (which was given for the first time in the Cuban chapel) the children renewed their baptismal vows and recited an act of consecration to the Blessed Virgin (both in English and in Spanish).

December 1, 1898

Sister Marie Tharsile is anointed. Opening of classes. Sister Marie Tharsile, whose weak health was giving cause for anxiety, seems to be rapidly approaching the grave. Reverend Father Faget, SJ, believes it his duty to give her Extreme Unction this morning. At half past eight this morning, the bell assembled us all at the bedside of our sick Sister. Nothing could be more touching than the scene taking place in our dormitory. (Due to the fact that all the other rooms are still in the hands of the government, we did not even have a room for our dying Sister.) But our Good Master always knows where to find His faithful servants in order to strengthen and console them. Peace and happiness radiated from the face of our sick Sister who seems to have recovered her faculties in order to enjoy the presence of our Lord to the full. At nine o'clock the voice of duty forces us to leave the bedside of our Sister to go to our respective classes, because today is the date assigned for the return of our pupils. One hundred twenty answered the call. We open both our hearts and doors as wide as possible to receive them. The Cubans, ordinarily so numerous, are hardly represented this year. The freedom of their nation, won by the Americans, has inspired the majority to return to their native land, and this has greatly decreased our classes.

July 17, 1899

Visit of Monsignor Francis de Paul Barnada. His Excellency, recently consecrated archbishop of Santiago, Cuba, honors us with a visit. The Right Reverend Archbishop is en route to his see that he recommends to our prayers several times. He inquires with a paternal interest into our work with the Cuban children, whose character he seems to understand perfectly. We firmly believe that his benediction will bring us success, for it is of a holy missionary.

"Chronicles of the Sisters of the Holy Names of Jesus and Mary – Key West, Florida" (typescript), n.d., records of the Sisters of the Holy Names of Jesus and Mary, Albany, N.Y. Reproduced with the permission of the Sisters of the Holy Names of Jesus and Mary, Albany, N.Y.

43. Establishment of a Pious Association at San Antonio, 1925

Mexican exiles established men's and women's sections of the Asociación Nacional de los Vasallos de Cristo Rey (National Association of the Vassals of Christ the King) at various San Antonio parishes, starting with San Fernando Cathedral in 1925. Vasallo initiates dedicated themselves to the Sacred Heart of Jesus

and Our Lady of Guadalupe as the true rulers of Mexico, asserting their con-
viction that religious devotion was the best way to save their native land from
violence, religious persecution, and political corruption. Besides promoting de-
votion, Catholic allegiance, and the defense of the Catholic Church, the Vasallos
raised funds for a national monument to the Sacred Heart of Jesus at Cubilete, a
mountain at the geographic center of Mexico which devotees named for Cristo
Rey. The following document is the minutes of the Vasallos' founding meeting
at San Fernando (Matovina 1996: 19–20).

In San Antonio, Texas, County of Bexar, United States of North America, on August 30, 1925, a meeting composed of invited guests was assembled in the meeting room of San Fernando Cathedral, official seat of the San Antonio Diocese, at four in the afternoon. Proceedings were opened by the president, Félix V. García, who represented his excellency, Emeterio Valverde Tellez, Bishop of León, Guanajuato, Mexico.

Having opened the meeting, the president proceeded to welcome everyone in the name of his excellency the bishop of León, who by his apostolic courage and great enthusiasm has succeeded at establishing in Mexico two admirable initiatives. First, to raise a national monument to the Sacred Heart of Jesus on the mountain of Christ the King, previously known as El Cubilete. Second, to initiate a vigorous campaign in defense of Catholic religious interests that would encourage each Mexican to be more diligent in his religious practices as the most effective means for restructuring the country nationally, a task which will be achieved through the auspices of the Mexican National Association of the Vassals of Christ the King, whose seat is in the city of León, in the diocese by the same name.

Immediately, the president proceeded to present the actions already taken and the projects proposed for the construction of the monument to Christ the King, a project directly supported by the Diocese of León and unanimously and enthusiastically seconded by the Mexican bishops. The project only awaits the general cooperation of Catholic Mexicans living in and outside of Mexico in order to achieve this marvelous initiative to raise, at the peak of Christ the King Mountain, the symbolic monument that is to manifest that Christ the King reigns as sovereign of Mexico in the hearts and homes of every Mexican; since Cubilete Mountain has been recognized as the geographic center of the Republic of Mexico, it is indeed the heart of the entire nation.

During the course of his presentation, Mr. García talked about the myriad tribulations suffered by the Catholic Church at the hands of the religious persecution as well as the calamitous injustices, and he invited all present, in the name of his excellency, the prelate of León, to participate in the goals and efforts of both of these remarkable initiatives. The invitation to participate was particularly issued to those men whose faith seems lukewarm, who when confronted by the many challenges that pit them against their religion, end up by renouncing it, and even by joining those who persecute it. The president condemned cowardice and timidity, saying that neither can begin to exist in the hearts of those Mexicans who are true Catholics and who are defenders of the religion that is historically and traditionally the very soul of the Mexican people.

He then went on to explain the procedures for organizing the local San Antonio chapter; whose numbers would include Mexican expatriates and San Antonians of Mexican origin. Because of its rich religious traditions, San Antonio, County of Bexar, will be the first place to establish such a parochial chapter. All persons, male and female, children not excluded, will be able to acquire the necessary articles and symbols of their membership. These will consist of a medal and colors, plus whatever additional instructions are necessary for fulfillment of their commitments as Vassals of Christ the King.

To that end and in agreement with the schedule set by the rector of the cathedral who will also be director of this local chapter, Sunday, September 6 is the date for the ceremony of the blessing of the medals and colors and for their distribution among each of the Vassals of Christ the King. The cost of the silver and aluminum medals to be made available will be determined by the treasurer; funds for the construction of the monument to Christ the King, on the other hand, will be obtained strictly from voluntary and discretionary donations. These donations are not to be considered part of the membership fees and are to be used exclusively for the building of the monument and to cover the costs of promoting this cause in the United States. It is recommended that men and women form individual groups consisting of eleven persons with one among them acting as leader.

Subsequently the president proceeded to read from the documents authorizing Mr. García as the organizer of the association and as representative of the campaign to build the monument to Christ the King. His excellency the bishop of León signed one of the accrediting documents. Monsignor Arthur J. Drossaerts, bishop of San Antonio, Texas, signed the other two. The latter prelate gave his full approval and blessings to the initiative and to Mr. García.

The president concluded his formal presentation with a patriotic and exciting affirmation that, now unified and duly organized, the association can move forward with both of the remarkable initiatives proposed by the bishop of León.

Mr. Macario Guzmán took the floor to thank all of those present, including the bishop of León and Mr. García, for the extraordinary project which will work toward unifying those Mexicans who live away from Mexico, as well as for the magnificent ideal which will place Christ the King in the heart of every Mexican. Other persons took the floor to affirm what had just been said. There followed the appointment of the various committees that will be in charge of the women's and the men's groups.

"Actos de la Sociedad de Vasallos de Cristo Rey de la Catedral de San Fernando," libro primero (1925–1934), Catholic Archives at San Antonio, Chancery Office, Archdiocese of San Antonio. Trans. Dora Elizondo Guerra. Courtesy of the Catholic Archives at San Antonio. Not to be reproduced without the proper authorization of the Archives.

44. Editorial regarding Religious Persecution in Mexico, 1926

The Jesuit magazine Revista Católica, *first published in Albuquerque (1873–1874) and Las Vegas, New Mexico (1874–1918), and then in El Paso (1918–1962), followed events in Mexico very closely during the 1920s and 1930s, particularly with regard to church-state relations and the increasing confrontations and violence associated with the Cristero Rebellion (see documents 45, 46). Editors of the magazine in 1924 included several Latin American Jesuits. In one of its editorials,* Revista *reprinted the editorial comments from the 7 March 1926 issue of* El Pueblo, *a Mexican newspaper published at El Paso.* Revista *editors responded to claims by Mexican diplomats in the United States that the Catholic Church in Mexico opposed the government's progressive and popular measures aimed at advancing the welfare of the Mexican people.*

Mr. Arturo Elías, consul general of Mexico in New York, also had the shamelessness to send a letter to the *New York Times* in which he describes the religious persecution, such as it is. In that letter, he attempts to justify his government's actions and to discredit the Mexican Catholic clergy. The following statement is among the letter's ridiculous and false accusations, which epitomize a lack of common sense, a fact subsequently confirmed by a local newspaper.

"The Mexican clergy aren't like that of the United States, because the latter firmly supports its civil authorities, whereas the Mexican clergy are in constant opposition with its civil authorities. They completely ignore their spiritual, political, and social mission."

In its edition of March 7, *El Pueblo*, the Spanish language newspaper from El Paso, replied to this string of Jacobin accusations, which are full of insincerity and bad faith. And after it refuted the ridiculous statements in the aforementioned letter, it made the following observations in the paragraph transcribed below.

In the belief that the American nation is made up of morons, Mr. Elías proceeds to lie with unabashed boldness.

He states that the Mexican clergy follow "obstructionist tactics against all government programs." That is a lie. The truth is that Mexico's government has developed politics of aggression against church rights and the clergy are exercising their right and commitment to fulfill their sacred duty by condemning the government's programs because they go against justice, God's plan, and that of the nation.

He states that the clergy follow the same "tactics" against *public* schools. That is a lie. The truth is that the clergy defend and try to protect the faithful from the dangers and harm produced by sectarian schools, which the state converts into tools of "anti-fanaticism" (as they blatantly describe it) and instruments to combat the Catholic faith of the Mexican nation.

He states that the clergy use the same tactics against the government's efforts to improve the lot of the rural and urban workers. That is a lie. The truth is that the clergy are the best friend both rural and urban workers have. The clergy were the first to attempt to better the conditions of the working classes long before the Revolution, which brought into power the most recent government, showed its face. The truth is that the clergy condemn the expropriation of private property and all the other excesses perpetrated by the government. It is a government that uses popular improvements as a ploy and, while under the same pretext the government continues an immoral and anti-religion propaganda, the clergy are working to counteract it.

He states that the Mexican clergy are not the same as the clergy of the United States, "because the latter firmly support their civil authorities, while the Mexican clergy are constantly at odds with their civil authorities." That is a lie. The truth is that, as members of one universal church that is the same everywhere, the clergy of both nations are the same. The truth is that it is the "government" that is at odds with the Mexican clergy. The Mexican clergy have been dispossessed of their citizenship, have been literally reduced to the condition of a pariah, have been assaulted and will continue to be assaulted with all manner of aggression and abuse. The clergy are the same, the difference is in their governments.

The government of the United States respects the rights and liberty of its clergy. The Mexican government is a rabid aggressor without scruples for the clergy's freedom or ecclesiastical rights. If the government of the United States were to prohibit religious education, even in private schools; if it were to snatch away from its clergy their right to have schools; if it were to dictate to the religious orders, usurp all church property, and unleash the barbarism and infamy of which the Mexican government is guilty, the North American clergy would cease to be the "firm supporters" referred to by Mr. Elías and would become the abused pariah, the defenseless victim that the Mexican clergy are due to the lack of decency of the "constituted authorities."

Mr. Elías claims that the Mexican clergy are "the enemy of all spiritual, political, and social progress." That is a monumental lie. A lie that Mr. Elías doesn't dare to propose, were it not that he thinks the American nation is made up of fools.

"Falsas afirmaciones del embajador Mexicano en Washington," *Revista Católica* 52 (28 March 1926): 201–2. Trans. Dora Elizondo Guerra. Printed with the permission of the New Orleans Province of the Society of Jesus.

45. Journey into Exile from Puebla, 1927

During late 1925 and 1926, tensions between the Catholic Church and the Mexican government led to direct confrontations and violence. Opposed to the implementation of anticlerical measures from the Constitution of 1917, church officials defiantly challenged the state's authority to reduce the church's role in Mexican life. In early 1926, President Plutarco Elías Calles (1877–1945) launched a massive assault on the church after leading Mexican prelates openly spoke against the Constitution and the Calles government. Church properties were confiscated, non-Mexican priests were arrested and deported, and clergy were required to register with the Mexican government. The hierarchy reacted by ordering priests not only to resist government intrusions but to cease all church activities until the offending decrees were rescinded. This led to violence, and during April 1927 the government began deporting Mexican priests and bishops (Quirk 205–8). Among those exiled was the archbishop of Puebla, Monseñor Pedro Vera y Zuria, whose exile memoir tells of his deportation experience.

22 April 1927 — On the Road to Laredo. Things have happened so fast that I don't know if I'm dreaming or awake. I'm going to try to reconstruct the events in the stillness of the Pullman, with only the sound of the clickety-clack of the train and the steady breathing of my courageous and blessed brother — martyr of Pachuca and bishop of Huejutla, who is sleeping soundly.

I was feeling satisfaction at having given a special blessing in the bishopric to the women members of the Society of Sanctuaries of Calvary, for whom I officiated after their hour of prayer and meditation between 9:00 and 10:00 a.m. When I had just begun to dictate to my secretary, Jorge Mendizabal, a short work I am presently writing called "Visit to the Blessed Sacrament," three men from the military headquarters showed up and said they were looking for me. I stepped out to meet them and they informed me that their commander wanted to talk to me in his office. Since he had previously offered to warn me of any danger without taking me into custody, I grabbed my coat and hat and followed the men. Father Alfredo Freyría and my visitors came along with me. We arrived at the house on Victoria Street (this had previously been a Catholic school, founded by my predecessor the Reverend Perfecto Amézquita), only to discover when we got there that we had been deceived. The chief of operations was in Mexico City. After making us wait half an hour, Colonel Escobedo, the chief of staff, said to me, "I have orders from high command to send you to Mexico City on the train that is about to leave." I asked if I could be allowed to go home to pack a few things for the trip. He replied that his orders were not to allow me to go anywhere.

I got into the car that took us to the railroad station without another word. Two military agents in plain clothes took me while Father Freyría went home to gather our luggage. During the wait for the train, surrounded by the somber faces of the railroad workers who were on their way to lunch, I saw three of my priests, a handful of seminarians, and two nuns coming toward me.

At 12:20 p.m. the train pulled away, taking with it my body but not my spirit, which remained with my beloved Puebla. My companions were two agents, two of my priests, Father A. Freyría and Father Aniceto Trujillo, and also Father Eduardo Alcalá.

In San Martín Texmelucan I had my first meal in exile. It was a piece of chicken leg and a tortilla, and it bothered me to not be able to share it with my companions. Later that afternoon, Father Trujillo was able to obtain, by an act of charity, a pot of rice pudding and some tamales that were our lunch and dinner.

We arrived at the San Lázaro Station in Mexico City, where we awaited yet other agents to take me to the government office. Once there, around 8:00, I ran into his excellency, Manríquez Zárate, whom I embraced. He had just been brought upstairs from the office of interrogation in the basement. He was wearing his episcopal vestments as if ready to officiate in his cathedral and had a serious expression proper to his rank and station.

I recall the coldness of the words, which were the only words Delgado, the office manager, uttered: "Do you have your luggage? You will board the train to Laredo, on orders from headquarters." (He said it by rote, as if dictated directly from high command; it rang familiar, like the water with which Pontius Pilate washed his hands.)

A group of Catholic women led by their president, Mrs. Elena Lascurian de Silva, arrived and gave me $150.00, presenting it as a gift from the Orbañanos family who had been so loved by my father. They also brought an infantry cape and a chest packed with clothes for his excellency Manríquez. God bless their kindness.

We were taken to the Colonia Railroad Station in an official car. There were hundreds of people waiting to give us a tearful farewell. Delgado allowed us to give the second-class fare that we received from the government to the two policemen, who were to guard us all the way to Laredo, so that they could join us in first class. That allowed all of us to travel in Pullman.

Moments before our departure, Canon Miguel M. Márquez showed up to receive instructions for the vicar general and gave us money, an act of divine providence. At 9:00 p.m. on our way to Laredo I blessed my companions and my archdiocese (entrusting it to Our Blessed Lady of Good Refuge, St. Michael the Archangel, St. Sebastian, and St. Christopher with a plea to defend her) and blessed all those responsible for the immense privilege to suffer for Christ.

No one can say to me: "Et non dixerunt qui praeteribant: Benedictio Domini super vos" ("Those who marched didn't even say, 'May God's blessing be with you'" — Psalm 128). If I were not so tired I would have recited at our departure that whole piece of the poet's: "I spoke to them falteringly, unable to hold back my tears. Live happily for your good fortune is secure; our misfortune, on the other hand, is about to get worse."

Our group is made up of Father Alfredo Freyría, who has chosen to go into exile with me, as well as Enrique Mora, Jorge Nuñez, and two policemen who are traveling with us. The policemen don't look too menacing; I think we shall soon tame them.

April 23. Sleep finally overtook me, unfortunately, because I missed seeing Querétaro, my beloved refuge. Maybe there were friends awaiting me there. But, we must hasten the bitter chalice. *Calicem salutaris accipiam* [I will accept the cup of salvation]!

His excellency Manríquez has shared his joys and disappointments with me; God has just granted him the consolation of having absolved a sinner.

The arid, lonely road between San Luis and Saltillo induces one to either meditate or doze. I am determined not to burden or show my suffering to those who will surround me in exile. I shall keep in mind the words of

St. Teresa, who in reference to pain and suffering said, "What an imperfection it is to listen to all that groaning and whining in a quivering voice as if you were sick; if at all possible, even if you are sick, for the love of God don't whine!" I shall wear a kindly smile and speak words of consolation; I shall maintain an unbroken correspondence with the faithful of my diocese, no matter their station or state in life; I shall not allow a single letter to go unanswered.

Sunday, 24 April. We arrived in Laredo at 6:00 a.m. The American consul, Mr. Harry Leo Walsh, could not have been nicer to us. He acted very much in the tradition of a Knight of Columbus. He took us to the immigration office in his car and took us to breakfast at his home. He also picked up our luggage, assisted us with all the burdensome aspects of getting our pictures taken, getting measured, and being interviewed. After two hours of these lengthy and tedious requirements he helped us cross the international bridge.

Thanks to God we have left behind us the jurisdiction of the master of philosophies and convictions who forbids the leaves in the trees and the voices of men to move or speak without his consent or permission.

Thanks to God, the bridge doesn't have a sign that says, "Depart forever": We shall return to sing the *Te Deum* [a religious chant of praise for God's wondrous deeds] in the cathedrals of Mexico City and Puebla.

Pedro Vera y Zuria, *Diario de mi destierro* (El Paso, Tex.: Editorial Revista Católica, 1927), 3–5. Trans. Dora Elizondo Guerra. Printed with the permission of the New Orleans Province of the Society of Jesus.

46. Correspondence of an Exiled Cristero Supporter, Los Angeles, 1932

Spontaneous violence erupted in central and western Mexico when President Plutarco Elías Calles (1877–1945) enforced anticlerical articles from the Mexican Constitution of 1917 (see document 45). The resulting guerrilla war, known as the Cristero Rebellion (1926–1929), drove numerous exiles north to the United States. According to official census figures, the Mexican population at Los Angeles more than tripled during the 1920s, approaching one hundred thousand by the end of the revolt (Meyer; G. Sánchez 90). Dolores Dávalos de Venegas (1900–1991) and her husband, Miguel (1897–1994), supported the Cristero movement early in its formation. After the family fled Jalisco in 1927, the Mexican government froze the assets from their general store; in Los Angeles they bought and operated a small grocery shop. Dolores's letter to Miguel's parents, still in Jalisco, illuminate her longing for home and her family's struggles in their land of exile.

Los Angeles, 11 February 1932
Juan Venegas
Guadalajara, Jalisco

My esteemed compadre:

We are very pleased to know that all is well with you. We also have nothing to complain about, thanks be to God.

It appears that illnesses have let up on my comadre, she must have recovered; in the photograph she looks good in spite of the fact that she had been so sick. May God grant that she continue in good health so that when I return I will find her in better health than when I left her.

It's a good thing Pancho is taking medicine and God grant that it will be sufficient and he will not be in need of an operation, since I am very fearful of operations although sometimes they are indispensable.

We hear that Orozco y Jiménez [the exiled archbishop of Guadalajara] is here; we have not seen him, it is through the newspaper that we know he is here. We would like very much to greet him; if we know where he is we will go see him.

We are always with the desire of returning and we see that the day never comes, God knows how long we will remain here. The boys have days when the moment they remember something from over there, they wish they could go back. They remember very well many things, especially when we would go to the ranch, and they want to know if the little donkey is still there and the little dog; don't think they have forgotten anything, even Lalo says that he remembers and this at the age of one year, just to show you what good memories my children have. The baby girl already walks, she is very chubby and has rosy cheeks, she is just a doll and we are crazy about her, it must be because she is the only girl; you will see her, soon we will photograph her and when you see her you can tell me what you think of her, she is very homely only very cute.

If Chayo [Dolores's sister-in-law] were to come over here, it would give us much pleasure to go see her. When you go see her please give her our regards, and tell her when she has time to write to us, it would give us much pleasure, and to please always remember us in her prayers.

Our compadre José, the baby's godfather, already left for Mexico with all his family. He is in the capital, and he wrote to us, and tells us not to even think of returning because things get worse by the day. We also received a letter from Jesús Ruiz and he tells us to go so we can all be under the protection of Our Lady of Guadalupe, that over there there are many things one can do, he even gives Miguel the idea of starting a bakery, that it would give him very good results, or a pasta factory, that it also gives results. I believe the best thing is for us to wait and see how things will continue and not move before then.

I don't remember if in my last letter I sent you some pictures of the boys; if I didn't do so, then I can send you some photos that were taken at school.

It is a very good idea to close Sundays even if late. That's what we do on Sundays. We close around one or two and we open again at six.

I've been writing this letter for a long time and on top of this I ended up being sick for five days in bed. I had a very bad cold and for that reason I am just now finishing it.

Miguel must have told you by now what happened to us. It's not enough that business has been so bad, we were robbed. Don't think that it bothered me, I see it as a natural thing, ever since over there everything was taken from us, I have not been attached to anything. My only illusion is my husband and my children; as long as God grants us health, what else can I desire, for food will not be lacking.

Tell Agustín to write us, we have not seen his handwriting for a long time, and to tell us everything, since he loves to talk so much. . . .

I wrote to my comadre and she has not answered me, is it because she did not receive it or she doesn't have time? Tell her to have Lupita write it for her and to tell me everything, she writes very well, I have seen her letters that she sends to the boys and they are well-written.

I will write no more because I am very boring, I write a lot but say nothing, and cannot be understood, for even I cannot understand my own writing.

Receive my greetings from Miguel and each one of the children.

My regards to each one of the children and for you and my comadre the most sincere affection from the last of your daughters.

> Dolores Dávalos de Venegas to Juan Venegas, 11 February 1932, document provided by and trans. María Teresa Venegas. Printed by permission.

47. Report of Guadalupe Celebration in East Los Angeles, 1934

Despite the peace accord between government and church officials that ended the Cristero Rebellion (1926–1929), religious persecution in Mexico reintensified after the 1934 election of President Lázaro Cárdenas (1895–1970). The vibrant Our Lady of Guadalupe celebration in East Los Angeles that year reflected religious devotion as well as political protest against the Mexican government's antichurch policies. While Mexican exiles had organized a public Guadalupe procession annually since 1928, the 1934 event attracted over forty thousand participants, including Los Angeles bishop (later archbishop) John J. Cantwell (1874–1947), other English-speaking Catholics, and groups of Italian, Japanese, and Polish Catholics. In a newspaper article, published in Los Angeles's La Opinion, *G. L. Arce described that year's Guadalupe celebration and assessed its significance for the Mexican exile community. Arce was a member of the Asociación Católica Juventud Mexicana (Mexican Catholic Youth Association), which at the time had some thirty groups and thirteen hundred members in the Los Angeles area (Engh 1997: 43; G. Sánchez 167–70).*

It is a gratifying consolation for Mexicans to see how on this side of the line that divides us, Catholics of this hospitable country and the Mexicans who care about the welfare of the nation have launched a true spiritual campaign to move God's mercy with its prayers and its pleas, and to ask Christ the King to put an end to the anarchy and persecution that prevail in the martyred Mexican nation.

Many noble achievements of this spiritual campaign merit being recognized by the whole world; they show how the children of Christ, regardless of race and because they are free of prejudice, are of one mind and will spill the balm of compassion on the heart of our nation that for a quarter of a century has been suffering the most overwhelming trial because of its profession of faith.

Among those achievements are some of the following:

General Communion on the 12th — Yesterday, 12 December 1934, courtesy of Bishop Cantwell, diocesan prelate, all the faithful from the huge diocese of

Los Angeles and San Diego approached the altar to take Holy Communion. The celebration of the sacrament was offered for relief from the religious persecution in Mexico. We saw how in all the churches of the diocese, the faithful received the sacrament with the same fervor and devotion typical of the compassionate faithful of this country. Thousands of the faithful received it with one thought in mind — Mexico. The prelate himself, assisted by several priests, spent a long time distributing Holy Communion. We saw the faithful leave the holy banquet to pray from the bottom of their hearts, through the intercession of Our Lady of Guadalupe, asking the God within to solve Mexico's grave problems.

A Demonstration by Catholics: Another impressive event, which took place in the streets of East Los Angeles, was the awesome manifestation that took place last Sunday in the home of the Exalted Patroness of Latin America and Queen of Mexico.

Participants: Five divisions formed in a column made up the procession, with religious and secular clergy at the head of each column. The Holy Name Society organized the whole event; the procession marched in columns for several city blocks and it included a few floats. It proceeded along the route the organizers had previously designated.

Members of the Spanish-speaking chapters of various pious societies such as the Catholic Action Society and the Holy Name Society led the procession, followed by their English-speaking counterparts and other societies of this hospitable country. The procession proceeded without a single setback, in perfect order and in all seriousness and composure with people conscious of their role as Catholics, setting aside their feelings of rancor against the tyranny that unfortunately prevails in Mexico.

Music bands from the Loyola School, the Boy Scouts, and other groups were positioned between the columns of marchers. The procession began at 2:30 in the afternoon, like a gigantic troop off to battle, when in fact they were only prepared to launch their prayers for a martyred people.

At four in the afternoon, the procession reached an orphanage run by nuns, which is on Boyle Street, where an altar had been raised on its porch for the veneration of the Blessed Sacrament.

The Speeches: The cumbersome task of finding room for everyone was carried out with the extraordinary ease and efficiency that only the Americans know how to achieve. When the entire multitude of people found their places on the grounds of the orphanage, there was perfect silence, and from the porch his excellency, Bishop Cantwell, rose to survey the crowd.

This dignified American prelate then spoke to the multitude with a microphone set up for the occasion. His calm, peaceful, and candid voice poured over the hearts of the crowd like dew of benevolence and love for the beleaguered. He pointed out the contrast between what is happening in Mexico, where not even in the remotest corner God can be praised, and the freedom enjoyed in this nation whose salient virtues are liberty and tolerance. He spoke of Christian brotherhood toward the oppressed and pointed out how under the Stars and Stripes there is ample room for the oppressed and the disenfranchised. He talked about how in this free nation that is aware of its role in the world even its outcasts can worship the God of their fathers and find protection guaranteed them under the laws of this Republic. He closed by exhorting everyone to pray so that someday Mexico too will enjoy the same freedom, which is the greatest prize of civilization and culture. This dignitary, the prince of the church in Los Angeles, was interrupted several times by applause from the crowd.

The Speech in Spanish: Immediately following, a Paulist priest in exile from Mexico took the microphone. He was the Reverend Father Isidoro, a missionary priest in Mexico. With his missionary zeal and assertive vigor he moved the crowd to a pitch that matched his own enthusiasm and energy. In searing phrases he condemned Mexico's tyrannical government. He described vividly some of the atrocities carried out by the authorities of the Republic of Allende el Bravo [a reference to the Calles regime]; his words like a hot iron condemned the cowardly actions of the persecutors. It is impossible to quote him word for word; suffice it to say that his discourse vehemently denounced the Calles regime. His speech was rewarded with resounding applause. Cheers went up for Christ the King and Our Lady of Guadalupe and they arose from the crowd in a sincere protest against the persecution.

Patriotic Songs: Thousands of voices sang the beautiful hymn to Our Lady of Guadalupe, followed by other hymns. Then the American and Mexican national anthems were sung by all present, with hats off and everyone standing. Finally the hymn to the Blessed Sacrament was intoned and Bishop Cantwell led the Benediction of the Blessed Sacrament.

A Most Solemn Moment: When the *Tantum Ergo* [a Benediction hymn] was sung and the beloved pastor of the people of Los Angeles raised the monstrance containing the Sacred Host in which God becomes Man, all brows were lowered, all knees bent in genuflection, all hearts focused on only one thought, one wish, one hope — freedom for the church in Mexico! What an unforgettable, sublime, and solemn moment. It can be said that all those hearts were bound in the love of God and that they raised a fervent prayer to Him for all of those who do not have the freedom to pray openly to God in the land that cradles them. Meanwhile, the Knights of Columbus presented arms and the bishop rendered the triple benediction. In that instant, as if by magic, not a single sound could be heard. It was as if those fifty thousand people had suddenly gone mute.

Other Observations: It would take too long to describe all the additional participants included in this breathtaking manifestation. Native American tribes participated, as did the Huehuenche tribal dancers. There were floats depicting the Virgin's four apparitions, there were portraits, standards, and flags that swayed over the heads of the participants in a sea of colors. There isn't enough space here to describe it all.

Agents for President Calles in this city went to great lengths to prevent this event from taking place. They tried to diminish its splendor but they did not succeed. Even the weather seemed to cooperate with Catholicism on the march. The morning started out drizzly and it seemed to promise a cold and wet day, but by 1:00 in the afternoon the sky had cleared, if not completely, sufficiently to make for a comfortable and pleasant day.

Let us give thanks to God for these gifts and let us be ever grateful for this noble country that is so charitable toward Mexicans. We greatly appreciate the Christian brotherhood that brought together people of all stripes to help plead for a hurting, bleeding country. To all, may God bless your kindness and brotherly love in Christ.

G. L. Arce, "La campaña espiritual en favor de la Iglesia Católica en México," *La Opinión* (Los Angeles), 13 December 1934, Los Angeles Public Library. Trans. Dora Elizondo Guerra. Printed by permission.

48. Arrival of the Virgen de la Caridad del Cobre in Miami, 1961

By 1961, thousands of Cuban Catholics from all over the island had resettled in Miami, where they initiated the work of building communities and organizing against the Cuban government. Cuba's patroness, Nuestra Señora de la Caridad del Cobre, became one of the exile community's most powerful symbols of national redemption, a symbol in which politics and faith met. Cubans had venerated the Virgin since the seventeenth century, and she became the official patroness of Cuba in 1916. Though the original image of the patroness resides in the church of Cobre in eastern Cuba, a replica from a parish church in Guanabo Beach just east of Havana arrived in time for the Virgin's feast-day celebration on 8 September 1961 (Tweed 15–26). Subsequently, Cuban exiles continued to celebrate the annual feast of their patroness with great solemnity; their 1966 celebration inspired Miami archbishop Coleman Carroll (1905–1977) to call for the construction of a sanctuary dedicated to La Caridad del Cobre. He named Monsignor Agustín Román to head the effort, and during the next seven years exiles funded the construction of the sanctuary that was consecrated on 2 December 1973. The following document describes the 1961 celebration in Miami and reveals the religious fervor and political intent of Cuban exiles.

The Struggle Has Been Defined

While the faithful in the homeland were being persecuted and shot for gathering to celebrate the feast of the Virgen de la Caridad del Cobre, the Cuban exiles in Miami congregated in the city's stadium in a gigantic ceremony in honor of the Patroness of Cuba.

Tens of thousands of exiled Cubans swelled the stadium's bleachers and filled part of the greens that surrounded the makeshift altar where the image of the Virgen de la Caridad del Cobre had been placed. Just hours before, the statue had been secretly brought into Miami in a boat. People waved white handkerchiefs in greeting, a gesture reminiscent of that grand Catholic congress of two years earlier in Havana, when one million Cubans gathered in the Civic Plaza to manifest their Christian spirit and their rejection of the atheistic and materialistic doctrines of oppression and usurpation that were beginning to emerge.

With the same gesture of waving white handkerchiefs, Cubans who had managed to escape the red menace now gathered to pray to the Virgin for all those who remained in their homeland, and who were being persecuted, humiliated, jailed, and perhaps even executed for defending their ideals.

Bishop of Miami Coleman T. Carroll celebrated a mass that started at 8:00 p.m. Father Francisco Villaverde, a young Cuban priest, gave the sermon. A rosary offered for the salvation of Cuba followed in a most impressive ceremony in which young ladies, exiles from Cuba, carried lighted torches and formed an enormous human rosary.

When the rosary ended, the thousands of Cubans gathered at the stadium waved their white handkerchiefs in the darkness of the night and began to acclaim Christ the King and a free Cuba. They sang to the Virgin and concluded by singing the national anthem.

Father Villaverde's Prayer

Father Francisco Villaverde, O.P., began by reminding us of the indisputable biological nature of motherhood. [He said:] Where there is a new life, there is always a mother to give it birth. Christianity, the beginning of a new life for humankind, also had a mother that gave it life and breath, and in the process gave the world the author of life itself — Jesus Christ. This mother, selected by God from all eternity, was the Virgin Mary: "full of grace"; "your Son will be called the Son of the Most High"; "She shall reign in the house of Jacob, and her kingdom shall have no end"; "all generations shall call her blessed."

Mary, who is Jesus' physical mother, is also our adopted mother. In Nazareth she accepted us as her children, and at Calvary she accepted us officially when she chose to accept the exchange of Christ for humanity. The history of humanity proves the concern for happiness that a mother has for her children.

She chose to reign in Cuba. She wanted to be the mother of all Cubans, so on a misty morning in 1625 her image was seen floating over the waters of the Bay of Nipe. She made her home in Oriente, and from the peaks of El Cobre she entered into the hearts and life of a people who would be born Christian, and who would have Mary as their queen and mother. She forged our Cuban nationality because she was there for the native Indians, for the Blacks, for the sons of Spain, for the peasants and for the Mambí [nineteenth-century fighters for Cuban independence].

She was at the side of the freedom fighters, of the combatants of [18]68, of [18]95, of [19]52 and of [19]59. On the 24th of September of 1915 the veterans of the War for Independence gathered at El Cobre and officially petitioned the Vicar of Christ, in the name of the Army of Liberation, that Mary, in her role as Our Lady of Charity, be declared the Patroness of Cuba. His Holiness, Benedict XV, approved, and on the 10th of May 1916, with great jubilation it was announced to the country.

Like good children we have gathered today around our mother's throne. We are but a small part of the larger Cuban family, though we are well represented. We are only your exile children. Here present are your children from that indomitable Oriente, which you selected as your home. From the summit of the mountain chain you look down with love on the misfortune of your children. Present also are your children from Camaguey, that Christian and noble province from which you gave heroes for Cuba's freedom, and from where you witnessed with pain how, like nowhere else in the country, your churches were desecrated and your priests brutally mistreated. Your children from Las Villas are also present. Las Villas is the heart of the island, where the country stood up to defend the rights of God and the rights of your children. Your children from Matanzas are here. Matanzas, the Athens of Cuba, where the Yumurí [Valley] speaks to us of peace and where the bread of life lifts our eyes and hearts toward heaven in order to encounter your Son. Havana's children are also here. Havana has been the most beleaguered in this unstoppable persecution, where so many of your young Christian children have given up their lives to murderous firing squads. Here also are your children from Pinar del Rio, farmers of pure heart who exude the scent of tobacco.

All of us, mother, all of us have come here on this night of your feast day to honor you as our mother and to plead for Cuba's salvation.

Blessed Mother of Charity, for the first time you are being challenged, and your power placed in the balance. The fight between hate and love has been put in motion. You are still our queen and mother, we beg you to use your power to intercede, before the throne of your Son, King of heaven and earth, to save Cuba from the yoke of terrible and atheistic communism.

Today is a day of commitment and of faith. It is a day of commitment and of faith to the homeland and to Mary. We must show commitment to our besieged homeland, where its children hate each other, where betrayal is the order of the day, and where brother turns against brother, converting the country into another Golgotha. We must commit to our homeland, so that together we can rebuild her from the roots up, setting aside our egos, distrust, ambitions, passions, jealousies, hate, and vengeance. Let us create a just and more humane future.

This day of faith in the destiny of the nation will be forged on the shoulders and hearts of the brave renewed men who will shape the new Cuba we long for.

It is a day for commitment to Mary, to reform our Christian life, and from our hearts to tear sin, the root of all evil; a day to gain a greater understanding and love for our faith, the only solution to the formidable problems confronting those who live without God in their lives; a day to open for Mary the doors to our homeland, our homes, our schools, our factories and fields, but we must begin by first opening the doors of our hearts; a day of commitment to live in accordance with the laws of her Son, the only foundation for happiness and peace.

It is a day to have faith in Mary; we trust in her power to grant us a renewed homeland. She will help us to become the renewed men that Cuba needs. Our Lady of Charity will teach us unconditional love.

Father Villaverde concluded with a remembrance and a plea. A remembrance for all those in Cuba who suffer: the church, our bishops, our priests, the prisoners, the persecuted, the children, the insurgents who each day face death in the mountains, those seeking asylum, families, and all those who have perished in defense of their faith and liberty. He asked us to pray that Mary unite Cubans in a shared community of ideals and love and bring peace to Cuba, praying to Mary, Our Lady of Charity, to save Cuba.

"La pelea esta planteada," *El Avance Criollo* (Miami), 22 September 1961, 8–11, 49–50. Trans. Dora Elizondo Guerra. Courtesy of the Cuban Heritage Collection, Otto G. Richter Library, University of Miami.

49. A Cuban Deportation Experience, 1961

Fidel Castro's radical political and socioeconomic transformations in Cuba beginning in 1959 led to almost immediate confrontations with the church. This conflict and political rupture with the Catholic Church during the first three years of the revolution culminated in the expulsion of hundreds of priests and religious. The most dramatic incident involved the arrest and deportation of Havana's auxiliary bishop, Eduardo Boza Masvidal, who became the most important clerical personality among the Cuban exile communities. On 8 September 1961, on the feast day of Cuba's patroness, Nuestra Señora de la Caridad del Cobre, some four thousand people gathered in Havana to protest the government's decision not to allow a procession. A confrontation followed, leaving a young boy dead. Two days later, the government detained Boza Masvidal and many other priests. On 17 September, 130 priests and religious were sent into exile on the Spanish steamer Covadonga *(Kirk 102–3).*

"I left Cuba against my will." These were the words of Monsignor Boza Masvidal to our correspondent in Spain. The Cuban disembarked at the port at La Coruña and received an extraordinary welcome.

Even on board the "Covadonga," it was difficult to approach the auxiliary bishop of Havana, Dr. Eduardo T. Boza Masvidal. He was being greeted by the bishop of the La Coruña Diocese, Monsignor Novo Puente, the president of the provincial delegation, the mayor, and a number of other officials who had come to receive him.

We welcomed him as representatives of *Avance* and, after graciously acknowledging his appreciation for our newspaper, whose patriotic editorials he praised, the prelate eschewed an interview.

"I must be cautious," he apologized. "Circumstances are difficult. Mine are particularly difficult being that I find myself in a country which, although it has many ties with my own, is still not my country. Also, though unfortunately not many are left, I hesitate to put at risk those religious who are still in Cuba. Please understand." We did understand but persisted nonetheless. We had no other choice but to pursue an interview. We too have a duty to fulfill, and so we asked him:

"Could your excellency, for example, tell us about your experience and problems on leaving Cuba?"

"They are already known. I was imprisoned for five days, and on the sixth I was taken to the ship in a G-2 vehicle guarded by seven men armed with machine guns. Naturally I was taken by force. I left Cuba against my will because in the face of everything it was my duty and obligation to remain in Cuba to tend to the spiritual interests of the church, and I was determined to fulfill my duty."

The Antireligious Terrorism

The interview became more and more difficult to conduct due to the constant interruptions from a flow of visitors boarding the ship to greet him. Bishop Boza received his guests with the utmost courtesy, despite his fatigue and anxiety, which were beginning to show. Nonetheless, we felt obliged to continue the interview, even if it might seem intrusive.

"Was your expulsion allegedly due to political reasons?" He managed to weave his reply through the jumble of conversations in the room.

"No, they never felt compelled to give me a single explanation. Besides, neither the other religious from Cuba nor I ever involved ourselves in politics but, obviously, precisely because of our priestly vocation, we do have the obligation to defend justice."

"Your excellency, do you believe that the antireligious terror will continue?" There is an expression of pain.

"Unfortunately it will continue. It is my impression that the Cuban government will not stop until every single religious is off the island."

"How many are presently left?"

"Less than one hundred and fifty to serve the 520 parishes in Cuba, in addition to the twelve in Havana alone. As for the nuns, some two thousand have been deported and they have kept only the Sisters of Charity who attend the lepers, the elderly who are sick, and the handicapped; only they can do this with total abnegation, compassion, and great heroism.

Fidel: Yesterday and Today

Since we were able, despite everything else, to coordinate an interview with Bishop Boza, other journalists began to gather round to take advantage of it. Welcome colleagues!

"Bishop Boza, do you think it might be convenient to make it clear, for the benefit of public opinion, when and why you supported Fidel Castro?"

"It is perfectly clear. I supported him when he launched his opposition against Batista, and even for a short while after he took power. Everyone believed that he was going to restore and establish a government with clear Christian directions. We were wrong! Everyone was fooled, even the good people who are always wary. We believed that Fidel's Revolution was going to bring about Christian Socialism. Later ... "

He left the paragraph suspended. Everyone understood what he wanted to say without actually having to say it. It is not an accident that this gifted, eminent man is capable of expressing that which is truly eloquent without uttering a single word.

A Civil War?

After responding to a question from a colleague of the local press (there are also journalists here from the United States) about the persecution of Spanish clergy, stating that it began with the false pretext of politics, and adding that there was a very large number of Cuban religious who had been deported, we asked him:

"Do you suspect, your excellency, that the situation in Cuba is going to culminate in a civil war?"

He responded quickly.

"That is a political issue on which I absolutely have no desire to comment. Our intention is not, as it has been maliciously suggested, to incite a campaign around that idea. It is the farthest thought from our minds."

We then asked him the same question in different words.

"However, don't you fear that this civil war business will be the only outcome?"

"I'm afraid so. Given that Cuba's issues have ceased to be Cuba's alone, and with direct communist involvement, I fear the crisis is going to became a very grave international issue."

Status of Worship in Cuba

Circumstances demanded that we force ourselves to wind down the interview and focus our questions on the more special issues. In a most cordial way, his excellency, the auxiliary bishop of Havana, also requested it of us.

"What is the actual situation for Catholics in Cuba? Are they allowed to worship?"

"As long as worship is not manifested publicly, they are allowed to worship in church...apparently."

"What do you mean, apparently?"

"Obviously, when Cuba is finally left without a single priest (and that's where things are headed), there will no longer be religious services."

"What has become of Cardinal Arteaga?"

"He is very old and very sick. That is why he has taken refuge in the Argentine Embassy."

"For that reason only, excellency?"

"Well, for that reason, and because of everything else."

"Is there an explanation for why some are not allowed to leave, while others, like yourself and others of this group who were forcibly detained, are allowed or rather are forced to leave?"

"It speaks for itself."

He smiled a big smile, the first since the interview began, and said for all to hear, which by then was a large group:

"You may interpret my silence, Mr. Journalist from *Avance*."

Stolen Pectoral Cross

There was an account circulating among all the passengers on the ship that when he boarded ship, in a final insult, his pectoral cross and wristwatch were yanked off of him. And it was quite obvious that he was not wearing either item proper to his prelate's rank and position. When we asked him about it, he said:

"Look. We are not in the business of promoting hatred. Not even against our greatest enemies! Once their deed was done, I simply blessed my attackers."

There was a barrage of questions. The circle of journalists had grown. But since the topics such as the seizure of cemeteries, religious schools, and the prohibition of Catholic teachings, etc., are already known by the *Avance* readership, we need not report the answers.

The final question — that final question that is asked in all good interviews — falls to us:

"Will you be, as the saying goes, going immediately to Rome?"

"I am always willing to be at the disposition of the hierarchy."

It now becomes impossible to move in the vicinity of Bishop Boza Masvidal. He is surrounded by dignitaries and by the people, who are now uncontrollable. They broke through the cordon set up by the naval police and invaded the ship. The auxiliary bishop of La Coruña and other authorities prepare to leave with Bishop Boza, who is granted the well-deserved honor of being the first to disembark.

The moment he appeared at the steps in his white vestments, young and unassuming, the crowd broke into cheers. A group of Cuban seminarians that came to receive him were beyond themselves with genuine joy. Despite his apparent fatigue the public recognized in Bishop Boza an ecclesiastic imbued with humanism, intelligence, and energy. Minutes later, when he addressed a few words to the faithful at the church of Saint George, during a solemn *Te Deum* [a religious chant of praise for God's wondrous deeds] that had been organized in honor of the newly arrived, the Cuban bishop was once again the recipient of the crowd's ovations.

While the public applauded him, Bishop Boza Masvidal, another victim of the tyrannical repression, blessed the crowd with no greater love than what he had shown his enemies.

One must be a true believer, a person with unconditional devotion, almost a mystic, to conduct himself as he did.

> "Salí de Cuba contra mi voluntad," *El Avance Criollo* (Miami), 13 October 1961, 8, 25, 41, 49. Trans. Dora Elizondo Guerra. Courtesy of the Cuban Heritage Collection, Otto G. Richter Library, University of Miami.

50. Organizing Charter of the Unión de Cubanos en el Exilio, 1961

As part of their exile activism, religious and lay leaders established formal organizations to bring exiled Catholics together, reflect on their situation, struggle against Communism in Cuba, and maintain national identity among exiles. In 1961, Monseñor Boza Masvidal, the exiled auxiliary bishop of Havana who lived in Venezuela, founded the Unión de Cubanos en el Exilio, which became an important organization among Cubans in the United States. Serving as a vehicle for mobilizing Cubans, UCE chapters appeared in many cities including Miami, New York, Atlanta, Dallas, and Orlando. The chapters sponsored cultural and political events in their communities and published newsletters that helped UCE mem-

bers remain connected and informed on religious and political matters ("UCE" 16–18). The following selection is the organization's founding charter.

General Rules of the U.C.E: This is a summary of the general rules created for our organization, the U.C.E. They are a minimum requirement to make the organization useful and productive and to create a united front in exile. Due to the differences in the cultures and customs of all the countries where exiled Cubans are scattered, we are presenting only a few general guidelines to serve as a framework for everyone. Groups from each place and region can then organize within the parameters of their respective situations.

We do not wish to discourage or inhibit the initiative, creativity, or spontaneity that each group can bring, for in this way we enrich each other. With that aim, it is *essential* that we be in constant communication with each other, sharing individual experiences. We pray that our common effort brings us the aid and protection of Christ our Lord and of our mother, Our Lady of Charity.

Let us get to the task at hand. For Christ and for Cuba! Onward!

1. *The U.C.E.* (Union of Cubans Exiles): It is a movement of spiritual union among Cubans who find themselves exiled from their country. It is composed of Cuban groups living in different countries or cities gathered together under the auspices of the international leadership with headquarters in Caracas, Venezuela. We hope to achieve coordination and unity among everyone, without detriment to the autonomy of the rules adopted by each chapter.

2. *The goals of the U.C.E. are the following:*

a). Reaffirm our Christian faith, making it a living and dynamic practice, and cooperate with the local religious authorities on all the issues that concern spiritual support for Cubans.

b). Strengthen our civic conscience, maintaining all those values that make up our national soul, encouraging and fulfilling our civic duties and keeping alive the flame of faith in the destiny of our homeland.

c). Sow fundamental, profound, and inspired ideas that can serve as a solid base in our fight for a better country and a better world; and create within our nation a mystique of commitment and action as a common denominator for true unity, which in reality is not unity but the convergence of fundamental points.

d). Create a social, Christian conscience based on "love, justice, truth, and liberty," that will free us from a purely negative anti-communism and will prepare us to create a just, fraternal, and free country.

e). Propitiate a healthy integration of exiles into the host country, participating and contributing, but without falling into an assimilation that would mean losing our native cultural values and personal identity. We can integrate into our host country and continue being Cuban.

f). Tend and help as much as possible the most needy, as a way of being charitable, which bonds us as brothers.

3. *A movement open to all:* As can be seen from the above objectives,

U.C.E. is not a revolutionary movement for liberating Cuba, nor is it a movement with future political goals. U.C.E. respects all organizations that work nobly for maintaining the ideals of justice; its objectives are not in opposition to theirs, on the contrary, they are complementary, deemphasizing ideological battles and instead promoting principles, education, and ideals for all. It is also not a Catholic religious organization, but a "movement open to everyone."

4. *The U.C.E. Organization:* It consists of the most essential steps for creating channels capable of fulfilling the goals:

a). In each locality an executive team will be created, composed of a small and varying number of persons, depending on each locality's possibilities. This team will promote the formation of small Christian communities that will meet periodically to deepen their faith and to encourage civic involvement and responsibility, as well as to hold meetings and general events that promote their goals. (*Note:* The celebration of a monthly Mass to pray for Cuba is recommended, as is the celebration of patriotic holidays and other special occasions. It is recommended that the monthly meetings and the Mass be held in the private homes of the small groups in order to promote shared experience, fraternity, and trust.)

b). The international leadership in Caracas will coordinate the work and all the local groups will maintain contact and receive instructions and orientation.

c). In Miami, site of the greatest concentration of Cuban exiles, will reside the international team responsible for ideological dissemination with the goal of sowing positive ideas and orientations for the exile community through publications, radio programs, and educational seminars.

5. *Members of the U.C.E.:* Any Cuban who wishes to participate may join, as well as friends from other countries that share our ideals. In general members can be broken down into two types:

a). Active, militant members who hold regular and organized meetings to promote and carry out the objectives of the U.C.E.

b). Members who sympathize and share the ideals of the U.C.E. and are in touch with it, participate in its organized events, and subscribe to and read its publications. Persons interested in joining the U.C.E. but living in places without chapters can write directly to the international chapter in Caracas.

6. *"Unión," the Bulletin:* The official U.C.E. publication whose efficient distribution is the responsibility of the local groups.

"Normas generales de la U.C.E.," *Cuba Diaspora, 1978: Anuario de la Iglesia Católica* (Caracas, 1978), 17. Trans. Dora Elizondo Guerra. Courtesy of the Cuban Heritage Collection, Otto G. Richter Library, University of Miami.

51. Obligations of an Exiled Agrupado, 1962

Hundreds and perhaps thousands of members of the Agrupación Católica Universitaria (ACU; Catholic University Group), known as Agrupados, fled Cuba after the establishment of Communism on the island. Founded in 1927, the ACU provided religious and spiritual guidance to Catholic youth who attended the secular state universities in Cuba through a structured program inspired by the spiritual exercises of St. Ignatius. The organization also worked to advance Christian values in Cuba by inspiring and training a select and motivated group of lay leaders among the professional classes; together these leaders were capable of influencing public and business affairs. As Catholic activists ACU members were encouraged to become involved in the nation's political and civic matters and in any movements not directly opposed to the church or religion. By the 1950s the ACU's presence at the universities was considerable (Pérez 1994: 201–2). The ACU was one of many activist lay organizations that were reinvigorating Catholicism in Cuba during the 1940s and 1950s. This editorial from ACU's newsletter in exile illustrates the deep frustration Catholics felt about the Communist revolution in Cuba, as well as the commitment of the Agrupados to faith and nationality. It calls for Catholics to set an example of militancy for the rest of the exile community.

There isn't a single Cuban who can become accustomed to or be passive or indifferent to the tragedy that our country is living.

It is true, one can become accustomed to everything. Even the pain caused by the death of a loved one can vanish with time. But that can't and should not occur in the case of Cuba.

The pain of our country's persecution and destruction is not a pain like others that sadden us at a given moment but eventually take their place in the past. This pain is death and torture committed every day, even every minute. It is the anguish of knowing that our brothers and families are imprisoned in that vast jail that was formerly "the pearl of the Antilles." Therein lies the bitterness of exile: to see our country physically and morally destroyed by the blows of the hammer and sickle; dispersed, misunderstood, errant, and even looked down upon.

We are all navigating on that same ocean of tears, pain, and blood, and we refuse to be mere spectators of the drama. We are and feel a part of it. There isn't a single Agrupado, in or out of Cuba, who doesn't personally feel, in his flesh, the destruction caused by this immense tragedy, these terrible moments.

We haven't left Cuba in order to live more comfortably or to earn more money. We haven't come to reconstruct in a foreign land what communism usurped from us in our country. We haven't come even looking for the peace and tranquillity that is our right and that we should have in our homes. We have not been prepared or trained for that. We have come here prepared to fight, to organize a crusade, to struggle for God and for Cuba for as long as we have the slightest breath in our bodies.

We are on campaign. Our King, Christ the King, beckons us to His flag "so that in following Him in strife, we can then enter with Him into the definitive triumph." We have meditated on this many times during our spiritual exercises. And when we are on campaign, we don't think about putting down roots, or about enjoyment.

There lurks the danger that we might not be in touch with our pain and responsibility. Life's concerns envelop and consume us daily; they jade us and sink us into a routine of daily obligations. We need to shake off the dust we gather on this road and be what we should be — apostles of good example.

Good example is perhaps the most appropriate apostolic teaching for Agrupados to adopt, but the example of today should not be that of a prominent, intellectual professional who, through his Christianity and from the peace and quiet of his place of work, influences those around him, encouraging them to follow his lead. Today our Christianity is the Christianity of the days of the catacombs, ruled by persecution and martyrdom.

Let it not be said in the future that there are second- and third-class participants in this fight. Every one of us, absolutely every one, must be on the front line, facing the enemy, willing to sacrifice all rather than abandon ground or flag.

> "Los profesionales," *Esto Vir* (Hoja intima de la Agrupación Católica Universitario en el Exilio) 31 (March-April 1962): 1, 8. Trans. Dora Elizondo Guerra. Courtesy of the Cuban Heritage Collection, Otto G. Richter Library, University of Miami.

52. First Cuban Studies Meeting, 1969

From 1965 to 1969, Cuban Catholic activists, frustrated with the continuing consolidation of the Revolution and the exiles' politics of violence, began talking of the need for a more systematic analysis of the Cuban reality. Groups in Miami, New York, Washington, D.C., Caracas, Madrid, San Juan, Puerto Rico, and other places organized a meeting of leading Catholic thinkers in exile. Held at Washington, D.C., in April 1969, the meeting launched what became the Instituto de Estudios Cubanos (IEC; Institute of Cuban Studies), an organization that promotes the scholarly study of the Cuban reality among people of varying academic and political backgrounds. Though the IEC is not a religious organization, its origins were Catholic, as is clear in the following prologue to the published proceedings of the first meeting, written by María Cristina Herrera, the organization's leader and most passionate advocate since the founding meeting. The members of the exile group associated with IEC were among the first to reject violence as an appropriate response to the Cuban Revolution and were leading advocates of establishing a dialogue between the exile communities and the Cuban government, which occurred formally in 1978 (M. C. García 204-6; Herrera).

In the course of ten years of traumatic experiences, we Cubans living in exile are valiantly and tenaciously working toward overcoming a mindset colored by pessimism and impotence. Cuban exile has been plagued and characterized by division, dispersion, and a critical absence of responsible leadership. There isn't a single more or less intelligent, capable Cuban who has not, in the course of this painful ordeal, felt the irrepressible need to "do something" to help alleviate, even if for just a moment, that mindset that erodes our hope.

It was on one of those Miami dawns, during one of those personal epiphanies, that a desire for intellectual and emotional survival gave birth to the idea of bringing about the Primer Reunión de Estudios Cubanos (PREC, the First Cuban Studies Meeting) as a vehicle for gathering together a handful of intelligent men and women capable of reestablishing communication among themselves, creating a mutual and positive exchange of ideas and experiences about the situation in Cuba.

It took several years between the time the idea for PREC first emerged to the time when it actually became a reality. Those years of trying to coordinate the idea of PREC were filled with untiring effort and energy on the part of persons involved in the project on three continents. From 1965 through April 1969, when PREC met in the city of Washington, D.C., the work progressed because of faith in the basic value of realizing this Christian Cuban reflection. Slowly small groups formed locally in different cities — New York, Washington, Miami, Caracas, San Juan, Lovaina, Madrid, Rome — and their reflections and concerns provided ideas and guidance for the final project. Communication between these groups was warm and, although they were geographically separated, they united in the common goal of creating something that would benefit everyone.

Keeping in mind the many frustrations of living in exile, especially as regards to politics, from the very beginning we insisted on focusing the meetings on intellectual and patriotic themes, keeping political objectives marginal and staying focused on the universal problems. As an apolitical effort, its chances of success were greater. We succeeded in conducting intelligent and honest discussion about the Cuban phenomenon that could offer some sense of direction for Cuba's present and future. That a group of compatriots could actually succeed in talking, thinking, and seriously discussing the "Cuban question" for four days; that the most diverse opinions were actually heard; that several generations and genuine ideological pluralism were present; and, that all of this developed in an atmosphere of mutual respect and camaraderie seems like an illusion. Yet that is exactly how it happened during Holy Week of 1969, when PREC was born in a meeting untouched by arrogance or a monopoly of opinion that could have overtaken it.

Among the number of cohesive factors at work in this first Christian Cuban meeting was representation from the world of academe and from secular members of different apostolic organizations within the Cuban Church, as well as the close bond of friendship among the majority of participants. There was a desire to gather a representative group of what could be deemed "a thinking and militant Cuban Christianity." Christian values and serious analysis permeated the spirit of the meeting, though Catholic activism was not a requirement for participation — present were Christians of other faiths and even an agnostic.

The definition and subsequent defense of the meeting's objectives were no small task. Those of us who have been working with this cause have had to face and defuse a variety of pressures bent on influencing our purpose.

Many doubted the feasibility and productiveness of such a meeting. Others expressed wishes to have this meeting address only political issues, or to have it serve as a catalyst for planning outright war, or to create programs of an apostolic and social nature throughout Latin America. The meeting was none of these things. The meeting was a first experience of dialogue between intelligent, caring, and capable Cubans, who spent a few intense days and agreed, with a certain happy amazement, that we had matured despite our trauma and despite our apparent inertia. Above all we left Washington satisfied with the idea of publishing and disseminating the results of our work.

María Cristina Herrera, "Prólogo," *Exilio* (spring 1970): 11–14. Trans. Dora Elizondo Guerra. Courtesy of the Cuban Heritage Collection, Otto G. Richter Library, University of Miami and María Cristina Herrera.

53. Exiles Denounce Human Rights Violations in Cuba, 1978

On the occasion of the thirtieth anniversary of the U.N. Declaration on Human Rights, the Unión de Cubanos en el Exilio (UCE; see document 50) organized an ecumenical prayer service entitled, "An Hour with God: For Human Rights, for Political Prisoners, for Cuba." Attending the service were Archbishop Edward McCarthy of Miami; Eduardo Boza Masvidal, the exiled former auxiliary bishop of Havana and founder of UCE, who traveled from Caracas for the occasion; and a number of evangelical ministers of various denominations. At the close of the service, the following Declaration of Miami was read. The document illustrates the concerns of Cuban Catholics, and others, regarding the state of human rights in Cuba.

One hundred and twenty-five years ago Félix Varela y Morales, patriot, Renaissance man, and priest, whose wisdom and ideals taught us to think, was dying in Florida. That exemplary Cuban saw that the ruling government was incompatible with the needs and character of the Creoles; he denounced, without fear, what he saw and he came to die close to Cuba, as close to Cuba as he could. Later, José Martí visited his graveside in St. Augustine to drink in the spirit of liberty that it emanated. Varela and Martí, a historic conjunction: two exiles whose commitment to Cuba grew deeper the further away they found themselves from her. We, the inheritors of their spirit and ideals, keeping alive the tradition of struggle for rights and liberty, want to make the following affirmation....

The Declaration of Human Rights promulgated by the United Nations on December 10, 1948, which we commemorate today, reminds us of the following fundamental ideals: the right of equality before the law; the right to work and be fairly compensated; freedom of religion, to establish a family, to participate in public life, to speak; the right, in short, to fulfill the human vocation of a full and just life in all of its dimensions. Any authority or government that deprives humanity of all or some of these rights assaults human integrity. We particularly feel solidarity with all the peoples of the Americas in their struggle to achieve justice and liberty.

We are the voice of nine million from one country — Cuba, a country that lives in silence, which has suffered and continues to suffer the violation of each and every one of those human rights.

We denounce that in Cuba freedom of speech in all its forms is denied and tyranny reigns, both privately and publicly.

We denounce that Cuba's government arbitrarily arrests and inflicts physical and psychological torture and uses brainwashing against those who oppose it.

We denounce that in Cuba there are political prisoners, not labeled as such, who, because of their political opposition, are sent to concentration camps and forced labor farms where they are subjected to what is called rehabilitation.

We denounce that the ruling government of Cuba denies freedom of education, especially of higher education, to all those who are not fully aligned with the revolutionary process; we have evidence that the regime removes children from their homes and places them in schools where they are indoctrinated in Marxism.

We denounce that Cuba's government denies the right to democratic election of officials, to form political parties, and to participate in public life at all levels.

We denounce that in Cuba the government imposes Marxist labor unions as agents of oppression and denies the possibility of promotion to all those not aligned with the regime, especially as a result of their religious convictions and practice.

We denounce that the government of Cuba denies the freedom to obtain food, clothing, shoes, household items, and other goods; that since 1962 those articles have been strictly rationed, even those domestic goods that the country produces in abundance; that the government punishes the acquisition of food and any other goods if obtained through unofficial means. This restriction, however, does not affect the new privileged class, government and foreign officials who have easy access to all of these products in sharp contrast with the hardships and humiliation suffered by the people who try to acquire rationed goods.

We denounce the Cuban government for violating the right to move freely within the country and out of it, imposing humiliating restrictions that are at times insurmountable.

We denounce that in Cuba all those who manifest their religious convictions without aligning themselves unconditionally to the regime suffer official ostracism at all levels — educational, professional, judicial, and in the workplace. The government has restricted all religious practices to the confines of the church and imposes humiliating situations and conditions that discriminate, especially toward the youth that attend church.

We, Cuba's people, also wish to speak up in praise, even if posthumously, of those Cubans who have been silenced already, either in their sacred struggle in defense of human rights, or in their search for a land where those rights are respected. We want our words, replete with compassion, pain, and hope, to affirm to the world that we are not imploring nor requesting, we are demanding that human rights become a tangible reality for a silent people, who suffer and struggle for their freedom: the people of Cuba, a people in silence.

El Pueblo de Cuba, "Declaración de Miami," *Ideal* 8 (January 1979): 18–19. Trans. Dora Elizondo Guerra. Courtesy of the Cuban Heritage Collection, Otto G. Richter Library, University of Miami.

54. From Cuban Exile Document, "Cuba, ayer, hoy y siempre," 1982

On the occasion of the eightieth anniversary of the establishment of the Cuban republic (20 May 1902), exile bishops Eduardo Boza Masvidal and Agustín A. Román issued a reflection entitled "Cuba, ayer, hoy y siempre" (Cuba, Yesterday, Today, and Always). A statement of commitment to the homeland that emphasized exiles had not forgotten their origins, the bishops' document invited Cubans to reflect, through the filter of faith, on Cuba's past and present. The following excerpt declares that though divided between los de dentro *(those on the island) and* los de fuera *(those in exile), Cubans are one people who seek similar goals: liberty and unity. Published two years after some 125,000 Cubans flooded into south Florida in a matter of months from the port of Mariel, the message reflects the bishops' conviction that Communism had been decidedly rejected by the Cuban people (Boza Masvidal and Román 2–3).*

Perhaps we are living the hardest, most difficult moment of our history, but this should not discourage us; on the contrary, having matured in a climate of sacrifice and in preparation for the future, it should stimulate and strengthen our spirit to transform this moment into the most fruitful. Countries, like men, mature. They are cleansed and enriched through sacrifice.

We are one people. Geographically we see Cuba divided in two: the Cuba inside and the Cuba outside — the island and exile. One million exiles from a population of ten million is a very high percentage, especially if we keep in mind that we are referring to a people who are genuinely attached to their country and do not have a tradition of emigration; those who have departed have only done so through force of circumstances, risking a hard and uncertain exile without benefit of anything. What is noticeable is that the great majority of the people who have left most recently are persons from the less privileged classes, including young people under thirty. Many who remain are struggling to leave due to the enormous ideological pressures and because they wish to breathe the air of freedom.

Notwithstanding, we must not allow a simple accident of geography to divide us because we are all one people and we must stretch the fundamental bonds that unite us and share equally in our pain, joy, suffering, expectation, struggle, and hope.

For those who stayed and those in exile:

a). *We share the same faith*, which we inherited from our ancestors. We are believers and Christians and, despite the superficiality and deviation of some, we want to continue being Christian. For a number of us keeping alive that faith demands struggle and effort. With Marxist materialism on the one hand and capitalistic materialism on the other, it is difficult for us to keep that faith alive. It demands our energy to keep from giving up and to keep from being absorbed by what surrounds us. In our devotion to Our Lady of Charity, if we understand it clearly, some of us have a source of light that brings us close to Christ and helps us maintain our values and spirit.

b). *We share the same culture*, which is anchored in our language, whose purity we want to preserve, even if in or away from our country we are exposed to the influences of other languages; we are one in our traditions, customs, music, family values, our openness, in all those values which we do not want to lose despite the vicissitudes that life brings us. Whether in or away from our country, we are still one people who, like the Nicaraguan poet Rubén Darío said, wants to continue "praying to Christ and speaking in Spanish."

c). *We share the same history,* of which we are very proud. We must continue to learn from the great lessons it teaches us about our past to help us through the present. It is a history solid with heroism and martyrs of yesterday and today. It is a history that is ours to carry on.

d). *We share the same suffering.* Inside Cuba there is suffering today, not so much because of the lack of material goods, but above all because of the lack of freedom. Those in exile also suffer. They suffer immensely, not only because of difficulties in earning a living and material uncertainties, but particularly because of the immense vacuum which is the absence of the homeland that nothing else can fill. For some, this is a hard and difficult moment in which we should embrace each other with the cross.

e). *But we have a shared optimism and hope* because Cuba is a country with a vocation for freedom and we must open new paths, conducting ourselves without hate or vengeance, staying focused on the positive and always seeking unity, as did [José] Martí [Cuba's national hero].

Monsignor Eduardo Boza Masvidal and Monsignor Agustín A. Román, "Mensajes: Cuba ayer, hoy y siempre" (Miami, 1982), 24–25, provided by the Archdiocese of Miami. Trans. Dora Elizondo Guerra. Printed by permission.

55. Founding of the Christian Democratic Party of Cuba, 1991

The Cuban Movimiento Demócrata Cristiano (MDC; Christian Democratic Movement) emerged in Cuba during the 1950s. Drawing from the ideals of the Latin American Christian Democratic parties, the MDC was among the first civic movements that questioned Fidel Castro's refusal to call for elections in 1959. As a result, MDC quickly became a clandestine movement dedicated to resisting the radical leftward movement of the Cuban Revolution that eventually took it to Communism. Most MDC leaders left Cuba during 1960 to enlist in the exile anti-Castro movements that led to the April 1961 Bay of Pigs invasion, which ended disastrously for the exiles. Though they continued clandestine activities with an organized military wing, they failed to achieve their goals of creating effective armed insurrection in Cuba against the government. After the 1989 collapse of the Soviet Union, Cuban exiles prepared for what they considered was the inevitable demise of Cuban Communism. Since the end of the 1960s, the MDC had abandoned its attempt to revolutionize Cuba through armed struggle and spent most of its energies on educational and political activities. During 1990, however, the MDC entered a new phase by turning itself into a formal political party. Believing that the Castro government would soon fall, Christian Democrats felt the time had arrived to prepare an organization that could help regenerate multiparty politics on the island. At its founding gathering in Miami during February 1991, the Christian Democratic Party of Cuba ratified a document which included the following selection (Partido Demócrata Cristiano de Cuba 7–10).

Those of us with deep democratic convictions, conscious of the feeling of solidarity that unites us, inspired and strengthened by the Christian principles that are a part of our lives, hereby establish the Christian Democratic Party of Cuba (Partido Demócrata Cristiano, or PDC) in an effort to achieve the liberation and democratization of our homeland.

Therefore, we wish to announce our message to the people of Cuba, that the party is founded on the teachings that humanity has received from Christianity throughout the centuries and on the heroic example bequeathed to us by our patriots and thinkers — men and women who dedicated themselves to the task of defending national interests and independence, ideals for which they gave up their lives. The stimulus, stamina, and teachings received have given us the necessary tools to create and propose to all Cubans a political scheme and strategy with great possibility for success, that has the common good in mind, and that will help reintegrate our homeland into the universal concert of free, sovereign, and democratic nations. In this manner, we, in conjunction with the members of the Christian Democratic Party living in Cuba who cannot speak freely due to the intense repression Cubans suffer, have at our disposal the ability to create and put into practice the mechanisms necessary toward that end.

The Christian Democratic Party will exist in Cuba and in exile as part of a whole; in exile it will assume the role of "Delegation" and represent the voice of those Christian Democrats in Cuba who have consecrated themselves to the search for avenues of democratization of society, continuing the individual and pluralistic efforts achieved in the course of our history, in and out of Cuba. We have decided to found the PDC because we will not resign ourselves to being permanent victims of injustice and tyranny nor surrender to the easy temptation of pessimism. We have the moral obligation to create an instrument of struggle in accordance with our beliefs and the demands of this historic moment.

We believe that there are certain basic principles that are immutable and inalienable, that are the foundation of our political action, such as respect for the *dignity of the person* who is subject and object of all political action and the *primacy of moral order* in every facet of human activity. From this *conviction of the importance of the individual* emerges the recognition of certain undeniable individual and social rights that are not within the purview of the state but are part of the very essence of man, as defined by our Creator.

In addition and in harmony with the above, we believe that the common good should take precedence over all other interests but, as important as this idea appears, always with the respect due to each person and all minorities, and always open to all opinions without discrimination due to creed, gender, race, political affiliation, or any other affiliations typical of participatory societies where the principles of authority and liberty come together and are practiced in balance.

We aspire to establish a democratic, participatory, and representative system based on a civil government, along with the social justice that acknowledges the spiritual and material needs of humanity and society as proclaimed by

Christian humanism. These Christian-inspired ideas now constitute universal ethical values accepted around the world; they include equality, fraternity, liberty, goodness, justice, and truth, and supersede materialistic ideas that promote privilege or discrimination. Accepting these ideas does not constitute a personal religious conviction. We are convinced that in order to achieve our objective of a better society, it is indispensable to join with similar spiritual, cultural, political, and social forces that are also determined to work toward a free, just, and democratic homeland in solidarity with other nations.

> Partido Demócrata Cristiano de Cuba, *Convocatoria: Primer congreso del Partido Demócrata Cristiano de Cuba,* 16 and 17 February 1991 (Coconut Grove, Fla., 1991), 11–13, Laureano Batista Collection, box 16, folder 361, Cuban Heritage Collection, Otto G. Richter Library, University of Miami. Trans. Dora Elizondo Guerra. Courtesy of the Cuban Heritage Collection, Otto G. Richter Library, University of Miami.

56. Returning Home: Excerpts from Cuban Exile Document, CRECED, 1993

In a visit to Haiti in 1983, Pope John Paul II recommended that the church in the Americas enter a period of reflection in preparation for the commemoration "of the quincentenary of the discovery and evangelization of the New World." He asked for a new evangelization effort in the Americas (CRECED iii). In 1989 the Fraternidad del Clero y Religiosos de Cuba en la Diaspora, an exile organization of Cuban priests and religious, held their Fifteenth Encounter in Puerto Rico and concluded that Cubans who had fled their homeland should also have the opportunity to participate in the reflections associated with the upcoming quincentenary. They decided to prepare a program "in which Catholic Cuban exiles would have the opportunity ... to come into contact with their Cuban roots" (CRECED iv). The following year in Miami, the Fraternidad launched the Comité de Reflexión Eclesiales Cubanas en la Diaspora (CRECED) under the guidance of Cuban exile bishops Eduardo Boza Masvidal, Agustín Román, and Enrique San Pedro (1926–1994). CRECED identified as many Cuban Catholics as possible who were willing to participate in the reflection and developed a questionnaire that was distributed to gather ideas and a sense of Cuban aspirations in exile. With that information CRECED produced a working document that was discussed at a gathering of Cuban Catholics from nineteen countries in St. Augustine, Florida, during August 1992. The final version of this wide-ranging theological reflection appeared in 1993 (CRECED i–v). The following selection from the document focuses on the issue of returning home. This was particularly on the minds of exiles in 1992 when most thought the Castro regime could not survive the economic devastation following the collapse of the Soviet Union. The reflection asks Cuban exiles to prepare for the return by meditating on their exile condition in relation to the Babylonian exile, emphasizing communion, reconciliation, and evangelization.

Hope and Preparation for Return

223. The spiritual climate of the Babylonian exile is the yearning for the fatherland, both bitter and sweet at once; together with it, as the years go by,

the urgency of preparing for return is a part of that climate. These sentiments are those which lend lilts of elegy to the most beautiful Psalm 137:

> By the streams of Babylon
> We sat and wept
> when we remembered Zion.
> On the aspens of that land
> we hung up our harps.
> (Psalm 137:1–2)

The same feelings inspire in the anonymous prophet of the exile the magnificent poems of the return: "Comfort, give comfort to my people, says your God. Speak tenderly to Jerusalem, and proclaim to her that her service is at an end, her guilt is expiated" (Isaiah 40:1–2).

224. These same sentiments must encourage the members of the Cuban Diaspora. Translated into a less lyrical language, we can say that we exiles must reaffirm — perhaps rediscover — the dimension of the church as communion, and prepare for the day of liberation and return through a conscious and sincere effort to reconcile among ourselves....

230. This vision of the church as communion is in a strong contrast with our reality of a people dispersed and divided. This makes us more conscious of the tragic conditions of injustice and suffering in our Americas, which are referred to in the Santo Domingo document (Document of the Fourth General Conference of the Latin American Episcopate, Santo Domingo, 1992), and in which we also participate. In order, then, to rebuild the Cuban nation in Diaspora it becomes necessary to have a healing and a reconstruction that permeate very deeply, to the point of reaching the very heart of the Cuban; of he/she who is a pilgrim in the world and of he/she who has remained on the island. We cannot aspire to a new fatherland without men and women who are new, and there is only One Who can make all things new: Jesus Christ.

231. He, and only He, is our salvation, our justice, our peace, and our reconciliation. In Him we were reconciled with God, and through Him we were entrusted the "message of Reconciliation" (2 Corinthians 5:19). He demolishes every wall that separates men and peoples (see Ephesians 2:14). That is why now, in this time of New Evangelization, we want to repeat with the Apostle St. Paul: "Be reconciled to God" (2 Corinthians 5:20).

232. Cuban Catholics must adopt St. Paul's exhortation as their own and convert it into a life experience. We must let ourselves be reconciled to God, which translates into a reconciliation with all the brethren. We must create communion, as Jesus did in the complex cultural context that was His to live. In the same manner that He is a sacrament of the Father, we must recognize ourselves as a sacrament of the Risen One in the midst of human beings, working for unity in the light of evangelical values; struggling to overcome all hate, resentment, and vengeful attitudes; and promoting, from the faith, reconciliation, justice, and forgiveness. We must give testimony that in Jesus Christ there is true liberation, full liberation, that we achieve as individuals and as a people.

233. Being our only mediator with the Father, Jesus Christ calls us to His church, a necessary means that safeguards, celebrates, and shares the faith. Jesus calls us to His church because it is a space for conversion, a reconciling instrument, a sacrament of communion where we can live unity by love and in love.

Program for Restoration

234. The great prophets of the exile, Ezekiel and the so-called Deutero-Isaiah, devoted a great deal of their activity to preparing for the return with programs and slogans that would help the restoration of the dispersed of Israel as the people of God returned to the promised land. That prophetic activity was continued by Aggeus, Zechariah, and Malachi, the prophets of the return, as well as by the leaders of the people, Ezra and Nehemiah.

235. Although the hoped-for hour has not yet rung for the Cuban exile to return to the fatherland, we would be remiss in our duty if we did not begin, right now, to prepare with prayer and concrete plans. These plans have a name in the present vocabulary of the Church: The New Evangelization.

236. Upon calling, with a sense of urgency, for a *New Evangelization* in Latin America, 500 years after the "first Evangelization," John Paul II committed the church in this continent to study the signs of the times and to listen to the outcry of peoples submerged in tragic situations of injustice and suffering. Those peoples ask for answers which could be given only by a church that will be a sign of reconciliation, and a bearer of the life and hope that spring from the Gospel....

239. Today we can, despite the distance and separation imposed by Diaspora and exile, feel ourselves called, before God and our brethren, to proclaim with enthusiasm the mission to which we feel committed, as the Cuban people of God in the Diaspora. It is the mission of calling all Cuban Catholics scattered around the world to commit ourselves to a New Evangelization. It is a new evangelization which has as its starting point the certainty that in Christ there are "unfathomable riches" (Ephesians 3:8) that do not exhaust any culture or any era — and much less the distance and the time that separates us, the Cubans — because of which all men and women will always be able to resort to His abundance to enrich them....

243. Evangelizing the culture means impregnating it with Christianity and directing it in a manner that will serve the good, and also will prevent it being used as an instrument of evil. To introduce the Gospel into a culture is to adapt it to the society in which it is preached, without altering the correct doctrine, but only vesting it in a local garb that will make it intelligible and familiar to those evangelized. It is presenting the Gospel in a way and manner that it will be easy to understand, in accordance with the culture of the evangelized. And it is also preaching the evangelical message garbed in the culture of those to whom it is conveyed, accepting and leaning upon everything that said culture may have of a positive nature and that may be compatible with the Gospel, so that the listeners will understand and accept it. An opening

must be maintained to accept the good from every culture, rejecting with love and without hurting whatever may be evil in it, and transfiguring everything according to the spirit of Jesus and the perspective of the kingdom of God.

244. Our people passionately love the human word. We have been criticized at times, and we have also criticized ourselves, for "talking too much." This, however, offers unlimited possibilities for the introduction of faith into a culture. The human word is a symbol and a hesitant spark of the Word par excellence. As the Word of God never falls in the void, but always gives life, thus the human word, judiciously and reflectively pronounced, can also induce to change and conversion, can originate new life. Our people love good rhetoric, sincere and authentically spoken words. Despite how much we may hear brethren in the Diaspora affirm that "much is spoken and nothing gets done," our love for the word is a cultural symbol with a great evangelizing power.

245. The Diaspora, when reflecting on the introduction of the Gospel into the rich Cuban culture, must recall that language is always an indispensable element. Language expresses culture, as the inexhaustible place abounding in springs of the human spirit that manifests itself through the language, which is articulated by feelings, ideas, instruments, institutions, actions, and poetry. Reflection about the language ought to lead the thinkers of the Diaspora to investigate the history — philosophically and theologically interpreted — of the Cuban identity — that identity which developed through a language that became Castillian-Cuban, not so much because of the diverse pronunciations or lilts, but because of the life and existence that it conveyed.

246. It is of a special significance — many times recognized, but not reflected upon — that the architects of Cuban expressions and customs were men so diverse as Arango y Parreño, Father José Agustín Caballero, Luz y Caballero, and, of course, Father [Félix] Varela [document 41], who was "the first that taught us how to think." It is extraordinary that the founding light of Cuban thought may have been the last one, a churchman recognized as "Servant of God" in the process of canonization, a priest who was a pedagogue and philosopher, a man of letters of the first rate, a constitutionalist and public man with a spotless vocation for service and prophetic vision; in short, a man with a universal culture who always sought "good logic and Christian charity."

247. The Diaspora has always been at the crossroads of two cultures: its own and the "acquired" one that always threatens to submerge it. It would be tragic for this to take place; it would be tantamount to a mutilation of the cultural foundations, by which the Gospel takes root and is proclaimed. But it would be equally tragic to despise, to refuse integration, creatively and responsibly, with the most authentic elements offered by the "adoptive cultures." Nothing that may be true and good must be alien to the experience of the Catholic faith. The authentic Christian tradition does not fear, it rather embraces all of the positive that can be offered by its own cultural wealth, and also by the foreigner's. We believe, for instance, that we can learn from the institutional discipline of other peoples and societies. It must be recalled that the whole organic nature of a true democracy depends upon the strength of inter-

mediate institutions and organisms. Without efficient intermediate institutions or bodies, democracy is but a masked anarchy.

248. The evangelization of the Diaspora demands deep attention to and theological-pastoral reflection on popular religiosity. Its perennially valid elements must be revitalized and incorporated, as much as possible, into the proclamation and the customs of our culture. But committed pastors, theologians, and Catholics of the Diaspora must always purify the faith from those aggregated elements (Santería, diverse modes of syncretism, etc.) that limit and at times distort the faith testimony of our church, within and outside of the island. These elements are deeply rooted in many sectors of our community. That is why there is no substitute for a deep and intelligent catechetic-pastoral education at all levels. The sects and Santería usually enter through either of these two vacuums: that of the head (ignorance) or that of the stomach (conditions of social injustice and oppression)....

251. The Catholic Cubans...convened at St. Augustine, upon pointing out the challenges that emanated from the analysis of reality, united ourselves to the project to propose a vision of a world in solidarity, in which we will be able to grow as human beings and recognize ourselves as brethren. We were also in agreement to the necessity that the Cuban exiles must form themselves solidly in their faith. This we stated by petitioning religious education for adults, in order to lead to a Catholicism that will be not only militant, but also intellectual and informed, as well as competent to assume the responsibility of instilling the Gospel into the culture.

Our Lady of Charity of El Cobre, the Mother of the Cuban People

252. In confirming the faith of our people, we want to proclaim that the Virgin Mary, the mother of Christ and of the church, is the first redeemed and the first believer. Mary, a woman of faith, has been fully evangelized, is the most perfect disciple and evangelizer (see John 2:1–12)....Her maternal image was decisive for men and women in Latin America to recognize in themselves their dignity as children of God. Mary is the distinctive seal of our continent's culture (Document of the Fourth General Conference of the Latin American Episcopate, Santo Domingo, 1992)....

256. Mary was and continues to be the key element in the evangelization of our people. Her presence from the dawn of the Gospel in our island has recovered, and will continue to recover, the tradition of Catholic faith in our Americas. Her presence in the new evangelizing mission, in the New Evangelization, guarantees the gift of the Spirit and of the continuing renewing action of Jesus Christ in His paschal mystery. With Her as guide and protector, we will continue our pilgrimage, until the arrival of final liberation.

CRECED, *CRECED: Final Document,* trans. José Roig and Archbishop Edward A. McCarthy (Miami: Shrine of Our Lady of Charity, 1996), 118–31. Printed by permission.

Latinas and Latinos often engage religious images like the crucified Jesus and Our Lady of Guadalupe in their public rituals and struggles for justice, as in this photo from a pilgrimage march in New Mexico, ca. 1980s. Courtesy Moises Sandoval.

Part 5

TWENTIETH-CENTURY STRUGGLES FOR JUSTICE

Creemos que las aguas del Río Grande y del Mar del Caribe son medios de unión, que al traernos aquí nos permiten ser instrumentos de Dios para fertilizar y enriquecer esta tierra que nos ha recibido.

Creemos que Dios está renovando su Iglesia en los Estados Unidos por medio del entusiasmo, espíritu misionero y voz profética del pueblo Hispano católico. . . .

Sabemos lo que significa ser profético, es escuchar y pasar adelante la voz de Dios que da esperanza y dirección a su Iglesia; es denunciar los valores contrarios al Reino y trabajar activamente para que reine el Amor.

We believe that the waters of the Rio Grande and the Caribbean Sea are a unifying source, for as we cross over them to come here, they allow us to become instruments of God for fertilizing and enriching the land that received us.

We believe that God is renewing his Church in the United States through the enthusiasm, missionary spirit, and prophetic voice of the Catholic Hispanic people. . . .

We know what being prophetic means: listening to and then passing on to others God's voice, which gives hope and guidance to his Church; denouncing values contrary to the Kingdom; and working actively so that love may reign.

> From the Credo of the Third Encuentro (see document 69), in *Prophetic Voices: The Document on the Process of the III Encuentro Nacional Hispano de Pastoral* (Washington, D.C.: United States Catholic Conference, 1986), 17–18. Printed by permission.

Introduction

Whether entering the United States as the result of U.S. territorial expansion or as immigrants or exiles, all Latinas and Latinos face the common challenge of adapting to life in a new country. One of the most defining challenges has been confronting the persistent racism and rejection of the dominant society. Latinos in the United States have consistently had to defend themselves from a generally aggressive anti–Latin American attitude in the United States. Whether Mexicans, Puerto Ricans, Cubans, or others, Latinos have felt the effects of Euro-American supremacist attitudes. Sometimes this has been expressed racially, and at other times the expression is culturally defined. In either case, persons of Latin American origin note that they have been (and often still are) viewed as inferior; this has contributed to a shared sense of outrage and struggle. The North American rejection of Latinos has been based on culture, class, and race, or perhaps more broadly speaking, "civilization." On the one hand, as one North American scholar observed, "We, meaning most Americans most of the time, like to see ourselves as prime exemplars of all that it means to be civilized." North Americans like to think of themselves as scientific, believers in linear progress measured by material achievements, and morally superior to most other peoples. On the other hand, the same scholar notes, "Latin Americans, as we are wont to see them, remain static; they are trapped in a primitive state of nature, the victims rather than the masters of nature" (Pike xiii).

At a very practical level, the dominant society's derisive stereotypes and prejudicial attitudes led to discriminatory practices that have been historically debilitating and isolating and have had severe implications for daily life. Latinos have more often than not been marginalized politically, economically, and socially in the United States, and frequently they have struggled to organize themselves and overcome this reality. We have seen (in part 2) how the annexed communities in the Southwest were subjugated. Mexican, Puerto Rican, and Cuban émigrés in the late nineteenth and early twentieth centuries also faced similar discrimination and marginalization. In fact, Mexicans were systematically deported during the 1930s. Since World War II, as immigration increased from throughout Latin America, so did North American anxiety, fear, and xenophobia.

As a result of this historical reality, both émigrés and native-born Hispanics have had to actively combat racism, poverty, and other social maladies. Through their community organizations and activism, which included mutual aid societies, newspapers, labor unions, political organizations, and civil rights groups, Latinos throughout the twentieth century have struggled to ensure dignity, self-determination, and the right of full participation in U.S. society. For example, after migrants to the mainland established the Porto Rican Brotherhood of America in 1923, organization members defended their people in efforts like the 1926 release of four compatriots erroneously detained as aliens at Ellis Island (Sánchez Korrol 147–53). Five years later, Mexican parents at Lemon Grove, California (near San Diego), won a landmark desegregation lawsuit after local school board officials sought to impose an all-Mexican school on their children (Acuña 236). In Tampa during the first decades of the twentieth century, Cuban and Spanish cigar makers struggled to maintain their unions in the face of violent efforts to crush them. Vigilantes often kidnapped, intimidated, expelled, and even lynched strike leaders (Ingalls).

In other instances, U.S.-born Hispanics led efforts to combat discrimination and prejudice, at times excluding their immigrant counterparts for political expediency. Organizations like the League of United Latin American Citizens (LULAC), founded in 1929, restricted their membership to U.S. citizens of Mexican or Spanish descent. Although LULAC promoted good citizenship, the use of the English language, and even "Americanization," it also focused considerable attention on issues like school reform, increased Mexican American representation for juries and other public duties, and an end to discrimination (Márquez). Similarly, in the wake of World War II, Mexican American veterans formed the American G.I. Forum; while primarily intended to lobby for the rights of veterans, forum members also promoted social and political reforms that benefited their fellow Mexican American citizens (Allsup).

Like the struggles of African Americans and other "minority" groups, Latino activism increased dramatically during the 1960s. While Latino activism was most visible to the general public in the efforts of Chicano leaders César Chávez, Dolores Huerta, and the United Farm Workers (UFW), it was also evident in Puerto Rican–led organizations like the Young Lords and the Puerto Rican Forum (Stevens-Arroyo 98, 277), as well as predominantly Chicano groups like the Mexican American Youth Organization (MAYO), La Raza Unida Party, and the Crusade for Justice (Rosales). This increased activism, along with the reforms of Vatican II and the inspiration of Latin American liberation theology, influenced many U.S. Hispanic church leaders who consequently initiated efforts for ecclesial and social reform. No doubt the expanding Latino population and the growing number of Hispanic leaders and professionals also facilitated Latino activist efforts that have shaped both church and society in the United States over the past three decades.

Not surprisingly, Latinos often hold divergent views on specific concerns and issues. In combating prejudice and asserting their rights in church and society, they have also reinforced, defended, and reformulated diverse expressions of religious and cultural identity. Moreover, the Latino struggle has entailed various strategies like resistance to conquest and its effects, demanding equal treatment and representation in the church and governmental bodies, and reconstructing power by calling for radical changes in ecclesial and social structures. While these strategies are not mutually exclusive, each of them has tended to mediate distinct expressions of Hispanic and Catholic identities that serve the struggle for justice.

Resistance to Conquest

As was mentioned in part 2, various nineteenth-century Hispanic residents in what is now the Southwest articulated a Hispanic Catholic preconquest heritage as they struggled to resist the effects of U.S. conquest. Similarly, Puerto Ricans like Pedro Albizu Campos, who to this day enjoys the respect of Puerto Ricans on both the island and the mainland, drew on their people's preconquest heritage in defending their dignity after the 1898 U.S. takeover of their homeland in the Spanish-American War. In a famous 1933 speech delivered in Ponce, Puerto Rico, on El Día de la Raza (The Day of Our Race, or Columbus Day), Albizu rallied his hearers around the cause of Puerto Rican nationalism. Calling on his compatriots "to demand respect for the symbols of your origins," he contrasted Puerto Rico's rich Iberian Catholic patrimony with the racism, imperialism, and materialism of the United States. His analysis included the conclusion that "in the United States there is no Christianity" because if it existed "there would be no lynchings." Puerto Ricans, on the other hand, descended from great and noble heroes like Isabella the Catholic, King Ferdinand, and Simón Bolívar. Albizu also condemned the "orgy of the golden calf" in the United States, which he declared a perverted alternative to "the values of the soul of our race." Faced with the challenge of striking out for Puerto Rican independence, he urged his compatriots that they "not abandon our people to those who do not know the grandeur of the civilization that courses through our veins" (document 57).

The strategy of claiming a preconquest heritage to reinforce group pride and enhance the struggle for rights has not been limited to the decades immediately following U.S. conquests. Since the late 1960s, for example, Chicano activists have acclaimed Aztlán as the land of their Native American ancestors before *both* the Spanish and the U.S. conquests, asserting an indigenous heritage that enabled them to promote their identity, dignity, and the Chicano Movement's demand for justice (Anaya and Lomelí). Similarly, during the early 1970s, Puerto Rican youth in New York enhanced their cultural pride and struggle for liberation by developing a group they named Naborí. This Taíno name recalled their indigenous background; it refers to a class of Taíno worker-warriors "whose job was to be workers in the fields and — in moments of danger — to defend their homeland" (document 67).

For this study of Latino Catholic identities, it is significant to note that in these (and some other) contemporary movements and organizations the preconquest heritage that is invoked antedates the Spanish Catholic subjugation of indigenous peoples. Many Latinas and Latinos who embrace their indigenous ancestry as central to their core identity sharply criticize Catholicism for its oppressive role in the Americas. Unlike the Civil Rights Movement among African Americans, which was born and nurtured in Christian churches, Chicano Movement leaders and other Latino activists frequently have disregarded the church as a potential ally in their struggle. In fact, during the 1960s they did so to such an extent that in 1968 César Chávez chided his fellow activists for not assisting the "hundreds of thousands of our people who desperately need some help from that powerful institution, the church" (document 60). Nonetheless, like the Spanish-speaking residents who lived through the conquests of northern Mexico and Puerto Rico, more contemporary proponents of Latinos' indigenous heritage acclaim their preconquest origins as a strategy for formulating identity and demanding justice.

Representation and Equality

Latino struggles for justice have often entailed promoting equal treatment and representation in civic and ecclesial bodies. One common strategy in the struggle for equality, especially among groups formed in the first half of the twentieth century like LULAC and the American G.I. Forum, was to extol the U.S. citizenship and loyalties of Latino residents. For example, in 1947 when the manager at a Texas restaurant ordered three Mexican American women to sit in a designated section for Mexicans, the Lay Council for the Spanish Speaking of the San Antonio archdiocese condemned this discriminatory action. Accentuating the outstanding character of the three women as well as enumerating the women's relatives who fought and died in World War II, council members asserted that "such acts of discrimination cause all good Americans to hang their heads in shame. As loyal Americans we feel it our bounden duty to see that discrimination such as this is given all possible attention to the end that this disgraceful blight on our way of life be eliminated once and for all" (document 59b). While not denying their Hispanic heritage or their pride in it, these proponents of equal rights accentuated their U.S. identity and allegiance as a rationale for demanding that their compatriots not treat Latin Americans as second-class citizens.

In other instances, Latinos engaged in political activism have asserted their ongoing national identity despite their residence in the United States. Such claims are particularly strong among Puerto Ricans on the mainland like Antonio Stevens-Arroyo, who was born in Philadelphia and spent much of his adult life in New York. In a 1979 editorial about the question of Puerto Rico's political status (commonwealth, statehood, or independence), Stevens-Arroyo insisted that Puerto Ricans on the mainland do not want to be "perceived as 'Newyoricans' [New York Puerto Ricans] if that implies that we are second-class Puerto Ricans." Moreover, he demanded that, because of their standing as true Puerto Ricans, "any change in the island's status must respect the rights of the thousands of Puerto Ricans" on the mainland who retained a strong bond with their homeland (document 70).

Within the church, Hispanic émigrés have made similar claims about their status as loyal and committed Catholics. Protesting the removal of Spanish-speaking priests from their parishes in 1939, Mexican Catholics in the diocese of San Diego, California, stated that they were not "dissidents" as their detractors had claimed but "conscientious Catholics" who were "struggling to defend their religious rights" (document 58). A 1972 editorial criticizing the treatment of Cuban priests in the Miami archdiocese opined that the persecution directed at these "worthy soldiers of Christ" was particularly offensive in light of the many North American priests who dedicated themselves to "spreading doctrines contrary to the church and the democratic system" (document 65). In these and other instances, Hispanic Catholics have highlighted their unwavering Catholic allegiance and identity in the process of demanding that church leaders respect them and respond to their protests and needs.

Over the past three decades Latino Catholics have increasingly advocated for greater cultural sensitivity in ministry; in the process they have frequently forged and accentuated their cultural identity. For example, a 1977 brochure of the Mexican American Cultural Center in San Antonio addressed various critical needs for ministry among Mexican Americans and other Hispanics. Reflecting on the founding of the center five years earlier, the brochure summarized the need for the center and its advocacy of culturally sensitive ministry: "As Mexican Americans, we were well aware that we were not typical white Anglo-Saxon middle class North Americans but we also became critically conscious that we were not the same as Mexicans living in Mexico or Latin Americans in Latin America. We have a unique identity of our own, for we have maintained our language, religion, and many of our customs and traditions in an English-speaking environment" (document 66). In 1988 the Confraternidad de Diaconos Hispanos de la Arquidiócesis de Nueva York (Confraternity of the Hispanic Deacons of the Archdiocese of New York) wrote Cardinal John O'Connor with several complaints, primarily the absorption of the Spanish formation program for permanent deacons into a parallel English-language program. The Hispanic deacons contended that "the burden of having to study in English spells the end of the Hispanic diaconate in the church of New York." They also stated that "the new program does not take into account our culture, our liturgy, our tradition and values; it can only produce infertile and confused hybrids with serious identity problems" (document 72). In instances like these, advocacy of respect for Hispanics' language, culture, and faith traditions entailed an expression of a distinct cultural identity and an implicit (and at times explicit) rejection of a monolingual and monocultural approach to church ministry.

Besides promoting cultural sensitivity in ministry, contemporary Hispanic Catholics have advocated for more Latino appointees to ecclesial posts, particularly Hispanic bishops. The first group to issue a national call for greater episcopal representation was PADRES (Padres Asociados por los Derechos Religiosos, Educativos, y Sociales, or Priests Associated for Religious, Educational, and Social Rights), who articulated their demand for more Latino bishops at their first national congress in February 1970 and subsequently continued their demand for increased Latino leadership in the church (document 62b). In 1972, Puerto Rican and other Hispanic leaders in the New York archdiocese called on Cardinal Terence Cooke to appoint a Hispanic bishop and a Spanish-speaking vicar general and episcopal vicar for the Spanish-speaking (document 64). Similarly, at the 1977 Segundo Encuentro Nacional Hispano de Pastoral (Second National Hispanic Pastoral Encounter), Bishop (later Archbishop) Patricio Flores applauded Hispanic advances in both church and society, but also called for "25 times more representation and participation at all levels of life" (document 69). Significantly, such demands for leadership parity reflect the increased use of the terms "Latino" or "Hispanic" over the past three decades as Latinos from the various groups have recognized their common struggle in the United States and have had more frequent occasions to work collaboratively at the local and national levels.

Lay Catholic leaders have raised similar cries of protest regarding their lack of representation within Hispanic Catholic groups. One such leader was Puerto Rican Haydée Borges, who voiced a strong critique when she perceived that women religious had usurped control of the planning process for a 1976 conference on Hispanic women in the northeast United States. Decrying the consistent oppression of Hispanic laywomen, she stated: "Three or four people are making the plans for the conference and this is not democratic, since a conference of this kind in the Northeast should take grassroots laywomen into account, and not be planned only according to a vision seen from the ideas of three religious women" (document 68).

Significantly, statements like these that call for equal representation within U.S. Catholicism frequently apply the principles of U.S. democracy to the church. Like many of their co-religionists in the United States, these Latino Catholics implicitly (and at times explicitly) embrace U.S. political ideals in articulating their demands for access to ecclesial leadership and decision-making bodies. In doing so they express an identity that weds their Hispanic ethnic consciousness, a contemporary Catholic theology of the laity, and their experience living in the political democracy of the United States. Drawing on all three of these sources, they formulate a U.S. Hispanic Catholic identity suited to the struggle for achieving leadership parity in U.S. Catholicism.

Recent Hispanic Catholic participation in civic life reflects this tendency to interweave elements of the Latino, Catholic, and U.S. experience in the expression of a single identity. In a 1986 pastoral statement, Bishops Agustín Román and Enríque San Pedro called attention to the plight of their fellow Cuban exiles who languished in federal prisons because of their ambiguous legal status. As Catholic leaders, the prelates declared it was fitting that they intercede for their imprisoned co-religionists who "look to the church as a source of hope." As Cubans, they contended that the exile community was best suited to offer their compatriots "understanding and help" since together they had "known the uprooting and uncertainty which political exile entails." As U.S. residents, they contrasted the "cruelty of the Cuban government" with the "generosity of this country." They also pledged themselves to work "within the channels of the democratic government" to alleviate the suffering of their incarcerated sisters and brothers (document 71). Similarly, in his 1994 speech to the Los Angeles County School Board urging the rejection of California's controversial Proposition 187, which denies government services to undocumented immigrants, Bishop Gabino Zavala introduced himself as "an American, a person who embraces a constitution that guarantees life, liberty, and the pursuit of happiness." The son of Mexican Catholic immigrants, he also went on to state that he is "the product of an immigrant's hope and an immigrant's dream" and "a leader in the Catholic church community." These pronouncements on his own background formed the basis for his denouncement of Proposition 187 as a contradiction to the U.S. creed, a defilement of the nation's immigrant heritage, and a scandalous transgression of Judeo-Christian ethics (document 73).

Restructuring of Power

While many Latino efforts for justice have focused on obtaining equal rights, some organizations have called for more radical changes in ecclesial and social institutions. Unlike their counterparts who promote reforms in the church and civic life, these more radical activists tend to reject their U.S. residence or citizenship as an integral part of their identity. Instead, they decry the forces of assimilation that can impede Latinos' full identification with their cultural heritage. Many of these activists also perceive Catholicism as an "Americanizing" institution that poses a further obstacle to acquiring liberation and an authentic Latino identity.

At times some of the aforementioned groups that sought equal representation and treatment also proposed more radical changes. For example, at the 1971 PADRES national convention, Alberto Carrillo outlined the numerous injustices Chicanos endured and concluded that their problem was "not a matter of rights" but "a matter of opportunity for self-determination." Denouncing the assimilationist melting pot in U.S. society and the "Irish-church melting pot" in U.S. Catholicism, he concluded that the best ecclesial solution for Chicanos was to divorce themselves from U.S. hierarchical control and form a national church directly under the auspices of the Propagation of the Faith in Rome (document 62a).

A group that had an explicitly transformative vision from its inception was Católicos por la Raza (Catholics for the Race). In a 1969 press release distributed shortly after the organization's founding, members declared that they had one goal: "the return of the Catholic church to the oppressed Chicano community" (document 61a). During the first days of 1970, the organization held a communal fast. In their public announcement for this event they identified themselves as Catholics who were committed to the lives of the poor, devoted to Our Lady of Guadalupe, and determined to "no longer sit idly while our church degenerates into a partnership with racist ideologies and governments of reaction." At the same time, they pronounced that they were Chicanos who sought to "radically reform our church and the whole of society" and who could "no longer endure the piteous paternalism of those *padres* whose only goal is the Americanization of a people whose culture and language is richer and more ancient than the vacuous alternative they strive to impose upon us" (document 61b).

As was previously mentioned, members of the youth group Naborí looked to their Taíno heritage as a source of strength and identity. Naborí members also deemed their organization a *comunidad de base* (base community), connecting themselves with the Latin American liberationist effort to restructure Catholicism and society at large. They further declared that "in Naborí, there is no distinction according to class. We are all equals. We have no president, no dues, nor do we look for prestige or privileges" (document 67). These statements reflect a revolutionary approach to Catholicism, rooted both in an indigenous Puerto Rican heritage and a radical communitarian vision of the gospel.

Although both Católicos por la Raza and Naborí had a relatively short-lived existence, the radical sentiment of their vision continues among some Latinas and Latinos and in organizations like Las Hermanas (The Sisters). Formed in 1971 as an association of Chicana women religious, Las Hermanas initially sought to enhance the members' ministry and make it "more relevant to our people" who lacked equality both in church and society (document 63a). As the organization evolved, Mexican American sisters welcomed other Latina religious and then laywomen into their membership, forging a national network that challenged the overt discrimination Latinas and Latinos faced (document 63b). By the 1980s the organization's membership developed a new vision for Las Hermanas, one more explicitly focused on Hispanic women's concerns. As women, Las Hermanas had limited access to hierarchical power; hence it is not surprising that they eventually defined their primary mission as separate from the struggle for institutional access. Instead, they perceived their core mission as building an empowering Latina network outside hierarchical control and affecting changes in the lives of Latinas themselves (document 63c).

In their promotion of substantive changes in church and society, members of Las Hermanas, Naborí, Católicos por la Raza, and other activists operative in the Catholic sphere identify with Catholicism as a spiritual force of liberation for oppressed groups like the poor, the colonized, the indigenous, and Hispanic women. They also emphatically embrace their Latino or even indigenous heritage while condemning "Americanization" as a paternalistic, dehumanizing, and racist ideology. Though they live within the U.S. realm and have varying degrees of contact with the official structures of U.S. Catholicism, their identities as Latina and Latino Catholics are formed in contradistinction to the dominant cultures of both church and society.

Struggle and Identity

The diverse strategies in the Latino struggle for justice mediate different visions of what it means to be Hispanic, Catholic, and a resident of the United States. In the course of these struggles, Latinos have defined themselves in such varied ways as both loyal "American" citizens and victims of Americanization, as faithful Catholics and second- (or third-) class members of the church, as a conquered people and as *mestizos* who unite their Latino heritage and their U.S. homeland, as immigrants and exiles, as members of specific national groups and as broader "Latino" or "Hispanic" coalitions comprised of various national groups. The documents in this part illustrate these complex and varied expressions of Hispanic Catholic identity which have emerged from Latinas' and Latinos' attempts to promote their dignity, equality, and liberty in the U.S. church and society.

57. Día de la Raza Speech, Ponce, Puerto Rico, 1933

Pedro Albizu Campos (1891–1965), founder of the Puerto Rican Nationalist Party, studied at Harvard University, where he became disillusioned with U.S. claims to leadership in the world struggle for democracy. At the same time he rediscovered his Catholic faith through the works of the nineteenth-century

Catalan philosopher Jaime Balmes and came to understand Puerto Rico as a nation whose Iberian Catholic civilization was superior to U.S. Anglo-Saxon Protestant civilization. "Americanization" was therefore to be resisted, including the Americanization efforts of U.S. bishops assigned to Puerto Rico, and independence was to be pursued as the only acceptable goal for the Puerto Rican people. Albizu's 1933 speech on the Día de la Raza (Day of Our Race — i.e., Columbus Day), given in the shadow of the cathedral at Ponce, illuminates his sharp distinction between Puerto Rico's heritage and ethos and that of the United States. Although many Puerto Ricans did not accept Albizu's eventual use of violence in the cause of Puerto Rican independence, he is widely acclaimed for his courage and ideals, as is evident from the fact that New York Puerto Ricans named a public school in his honor (Díaz-Stevens 1993a: 53, 96–97; Vidal 1994: 30–31, 48).

Do you wish to be worthy of a celebration like this one? You have to demand respect for the symbols of your origins. You have to punish severely those who come to disrupt an event such as this. And it is only this kind of event that will win respect from our enemy, because it shows the enemy that you're not completely hopeless.

Do you want to be respected by your own brothers and sisters? Stand here in this plaza surrounded by the sacred heroes of our race, by Isabella the Catholic, by [King] Ferdinand, by patriots like Bolívar, Sucre, Ríus Rivera, Betances. Then you will understand what these flags stand for. You will understand what a flag is and what a day of *la raza* is....

The fundamental principles of which I speak constitute the Christian aspiration of a people. In the United States there is no Christianity. So when a black man sits down on the train where he is not supposed to, the Yankees simply grab him by his rear end and drag him off so that the other blacks can see what awaits them. (*Laughter and applause.*) Don't laugh! Silence! That is what ruins our people. They are forever being dragged around by the feet and they don't defend themselves.

If Christianity existed in the United States, there would be no lynchings, because if there were a Catholic priest there, he would defend the black person. They admire this; the best of the Yankees are surprised at these things in Puerto Rico. (*Gesture to the church.*) They admire our interior peace — they say "interior peace" — but we tell them it is the renovation of our soul and blood. And we tell them that we are the depository of their salvation.

And now our hour begins. We must not abandon our people to those who do not know the grandeur of the civilization that courses through our veins. Even as the Spaniards saved the Iberian Peninsula [in their long struggle to expel the Muslims], we will save our lands from profane hands. Puerto Rico must begin to yank out by the roots this economic invasion, this political and cultural invasion: nationalism involves every aspect of nationhood....

We have something good to breathe into America. Let us begin by assuring our own civilization to our posterity in Puerto Rico. And let us, together with the other people of the Antilles, carry our civilization to North America, so that it will cover the world from pole to pole. Thus will we be forever affirmed on this planet.

Nationalism postulates four beautiful principles: the independence of Puerto Rico, the Antillean Confederation, Pan-American unity, and the hegemony of the Iberoamerican people for the glory of all of us before history. In the Tribunal of the Hague they have just finished rendering homage to the greatest jurist of the modern age, the father of international law, the priest Friar Vitoria [whose sixteenth-century legal defense of the Indians laid the foundation for modern theories of international law].

Spanish art, all the science of our race, above all the spiritual values, the values of the soul of our race are our aspirations, the supreme aspirations in a welter of material ambitions. The orgy of the golden calf is carrying humanity toward chaos and destruction. And I tell you that it will carry us to a world war as disastrous and fatal as the last one.

Puerto Rico has to play its role in history, and in order to look posterity in the face, it has to be free.

There then is our history, our flag, the flag of our forebears, the flag of our brothers and sisters. There is our flag that is also the flag of the future of Puerto Rico! Unfurl the flag and die shoulder to shoulder for it!

> Pedro Albizu Campos, Día de la Raza speech, 12 October 1933, as translated and cited in Antonio M. Stevens-Arroyo, *Prophets Denied Honor: An Anthology on the Hispano Church in the United States* (Maryknoll, N.Y.: Orbis Books, 1980), 61–63. Printed by permission.

58. Demand for Spanish-Speaking Clergy, San Diego, 1939

Mexican parishioners in the San Diego diocese contested Bishop Charles F. Buddy's (1887–1966) decision to remove Spanish priests of the Augustinian Recollects order from two parishes dedicated to Our Lady of Guadalupe, one in San Bernardino and the other in San Diego. After parishioner protests to the prelate and then directly to Pope Pius XII, Bishop Buddy asked several priests to encourage a countermovement. This effort resulted in the formation of a "spontaneous committee of Mexican Catholics" in San Bernardino. The committee sent the bishop an open letter acknowledging their respect and obedience. They also claimed that the dissidents opposing the bishop were a small group that did not represent the vast majority of Mexican Catholics in the diocese. In response, the protesting group wrote the following statement directed both at the bishop and the detractors among their Mexican co-religionists (Pulido 1991b).

A small, anonymous group that calls itself the "Spontaneous Committee" published an open letter to his excellency, Dr. Charles F. Buddy, D.D., bishop of our diocese, and it was distributed in San Bernardino on the third of this current month [December], in San Diego on the eighth, the feast of the Immaculate Conception, and in San Isidro on the fourteenth and fifteenth.

When in their name and in the name of all Mexican Catholics they presented the prelate with their letter of support, they also expressed, in less than

Christian terms, more than one invective at those whom they choose to call the "dissidents" of San Bernardino and San Diego.

One is left to wonder how the groups of San Isidro, National City, Escondido, Colton, and a few others escaped mention in what appears to be some very thorough research done from chancery sources.

It is fair to point out that the malcontents are not a small group; rather, they encompass a total of 85,000 Catholics who are struggling to defend their religious rights. They are conscientious Catholics who protest and regret the unjust removal of the priests who have identified themselves with their parishioners and who have worked at their side, understanding clearly their parishioners' situation and needs.

The importance of the Catholic communities in the San Diego diocese needs to be recognized and acknowledged, especially the importance of the immigrant communities. It's not as if they are requesting prerogatives that are beyond the boundaries of religion. What they request and deserve is that their priests be Spanish-speaking, that they not only speak and understand the language, but that they also have a spiritual connection that equips them with a deeper sense and understanding of the souls of the people they serve. Despite the accusations of the Committee, this is not a rebellion against his excellency, nor is it a threat from the Catholic petitioners of San Bernardino and San Diego.

They include in their letter (a letter that should have been a *closed* letter, so that the world would not have become aware of the Spontaneous Committee's jealousies and resentments) the following paragraph that expresses their aversion for the San Bernardino contingent. It says the following, "And now, your excellency, allow us publicly and in the name of the majority of the Mexican community, to inform you of how much we regret the aggravation caused by that small group of malcontents. We hope that they will recognize their mistake, feel genuine remorse, and ask forgiveness."

We were not aware, until now, that those who defend their rights are required to ask forgiveness; nor did we know that a group which views itself as being on the right track of righteousness needs to plead for the forgiveness of "the derailed."

All the Catholics who have not been blinded by passion are amply aware and have no doubt that the recent events and the disdain shown to the Mexican Catholics are sufficiently important affronts to be recorded and remembered in the history of Catholicism. What occurred was not simply a removal of some of God's representatives for the good of religion itself; rather, the steps taken were like darts plunged into the hearts of this area's Mexican Catholics.

We all feel that the state of spiritual disharmony within the community is the fault of his excellency, Bishop Charles F. Buddy, who removed the Spanish-speaking priests from their parishes. The first indication of this harmful disposition, which was interpreted as contempt directed at Mexican Catholics, occurred in the Catholic city of San Bernardino, where our number of Catholics is not only greater than all the other immigrant communities, but also outnumbers the American Catholics. This decision was an unwarranted blow that filled our countrymen with sorrow.

That decision is what initiated the split among Catholics, the intervention of ecclesiastical authorities, and a rigorous, religious investigation conducted by three highly placed prelates of great distinction in the chancery. Archbishop [John J.] Cantwell of Los Angeles, California, and the distinguished apostolic delegate in Washington were fully aware of those investigations.

As a result of orders from the chancery, Spanish-speaking priests began to disappear, including many who had founded parishes to honor the blessed Virgin of Guadalupe, as did the distinguished Augustinian Recollect Fathers, who were so loved and mourned by the parishioners of the San Diego diocese. In light of this, we agreed to organize in an effort to try to at least save San Diego County from the same fate.

In the midst of our struggle the *Southern Cross*, the chancery's weekly newspaper, came out with the news, in broad outline, of the imminent arrival of the Irish priests who were to fill the posts left vacant by those able and efficient Spanish-speaking priests, who knew their work, who had rapport with all social classes, and who were known for their organizational skills and administration of everything placed in their charge. This news created great consternation among the Mexican Catholic communities, as well as among the Italian, Portuguese, and others whose languages are akin to ours.

It was then that the last two Spanish-speaking priests were removed, having spent many years in the service of San Diego's Our Lady of Guadalupe parish (which they had founded). When that happened, things took on greater proportions and emotions exploded, resulting in a written expression of protest signed and supported by fifteen hundred people, which was then submitted to the bishop. It was a respectful protest and, perhaps, it is this protest that the Committee characterizes as being insulting and threatening.

Local newspapers covered all these issues during the first week of November, since the bishop's decision took vigorous effect on the first day of that month. The protest was filed away, and the Spanish-speaking priests were removed — the Augustinian Recollects — despite the religious clamor from Catholics in San Diego, who felt offended and despised.

The Committee seems to want to incite discord and to deepen the conflict, applauding the loss of our priests, who speak our language and touch our hearts through their sermons. It's the Committee who, without cause, has labeled as "dissidents" persons who have not acted rebelliously nor in disobedience, but rather who have struggled and will continue to struggle with all due respect and order, because justice is on their side. The Committee ignores the fact that the movement is supported by thousands of Catholics whose religious loyalty is impeccable. Local authorities have always respected matters of religion, and every Mexican who has supported the several and different petitions submitted has every legal right to live in this country and has the same rights as do the author or authors of the Committee.

Finally, hoping that the Committee justifies its honor by identifying itself before the public tribunal, it should be understood, at least for now, that its attitude of hate and lack of solidarity concerns and harms more than 85,000 Catholics in Southern California.

To all of the above points that reveal the Catholic communities' motives for feeling dismay at the personnel changes of priests, we need to add that the pain this decision has caused extends to the children of the community, who are now denied the warmth and kindness of the Mexican nuns, since the bishop has also prohibited them from continuing to enlighten the minds of these children and implanting religion in their hearts.

> Mexican Catholics of the San Diego Diocese, "Contestación de los Católicos Mexicanos de la Diócesis de San Diego, a una carta abierta dirigida al Ilmo. Sr. Obispo Carlos F. Buddy, D.D.," December 1939, Archives of the San Bernardino Diocese. Trans. Dora Elizondo Guerra. Printed by permission.

59. Protests against Discrimination and Segregation, Texas, 1947

Citizens of Latin American descent have vigorously contested segregation and the practice of discrimination. As the following two documents illustrate, in the wake of World War II they frequently buttressed their protests with the argument that soldiers who fought tyranny abroad should not return home to the prejudice they and their families often endured (Perales).

59a. Affidavit of Henrietta A. Castillo

The following affidavit protests an instance of segregation at a restaurant in New Braunfels, Texas. At the time of the incident Henrietta A. Castillo was a field worker of the Bishops' Committee for the Spanish Speaking, an episcopal effort for Hispanic ministry founded in 1945 under the guiding influence of San Antonio's archbishop, Robert E. Lucey (1891–1977).

Friday, February 14, at 3:00 P.M., Mrs. Anita Gomez, President of the Mother's Club of San Alphonsus Center, Lucy Elizondo, student of Our Lady of the Lake College and I, Henrietta Castillo, Field Worker of the Bishops' Committee for the Spanish Speaking, after buying $60 worth of materials at the New Braunfels Textile Mills went to the P. K. Cafe, 165 W. San Antonio Street at New Braunfels to dine. As we entered we sat at the first table in the cafe. The waitress came over to our table and told us if we wished to be served to go around the back. Mrs. Gomez got up immediately and walked out. Miss Elizondo walked out too. I got up, picked up my coat, walked to the back where the waitress was standing and asked her why we should go to the back when there was so much room in front. She told me that those were her orders and that I could talk to the manager. I asked her who the manager was and she pointed out a lady who was sewing the hem to a dress at the counter near the door and the cash register. I walked up to her and told her the waitress had refused to serve us in front where we were sitting. She said: "We'll serve you people but you have to go to the back, behind the screen." When I asked why, she said: "The lady with you is obviously a Mexican and that is where we serve them." By that time Miss Elizondo had walked back into the cafe and I said: "We are Mexicans, too." The manager answered: "Well, that's where we serve you people."

Even though we were hungry, we came straight to San Antonio for fear of running into more of such discrimination.

> Further affiant sayeth not. (Signed) Henrietta A. Castillo
> 21st day of February, A.D. 1947

> Henrietta A. Castillo, affidavit, 21 February 1947, as cited in Alonso S. Perales, *Are We Good Neighbors?* (San Antonio: Artes Graficas, 1948), 152–53. Printed by permission.

59b. Letter of Support from the Lay Council for the Spanish Speaking

In support of Henrietta A. Castillo's protest, the Lay Council for the Spanish Speaking of the San Antonio archdiocese wrote a letter that twenty church and civic leaders endorsed. The president of San Antonio's Lay Council for the Spanish Speaking was Henry B. González, who later served on the San Antonio city council, in the Texas senate, and for eighteen terms in the U.S. House of Representatives.

San Antonio, 28 February 1947

Lay Council for the Spanish Speaking
Archdiocese of San Antonio

Mr. Henry B. González, Pres.   Miss Mary Estelle Daunoy, Secy.
Dr. John L. McMahon, Vice-Pres.   Mr. Luis E. Gamez, Treas.

To whom it may concern:

In view of the facts presented in the accompanying affidavit [see document 59a], we the members of the Lay Council for the Spanish Speaking of the Archdiocese of San Antonio, hereby vigorously protest the act of discrimination of the manager of the P. K. Cafe at 165 W. San Antonio Street in New Braunfels. We declare that this action is not only un-American but it is un-Christian. We heartily agree that a business firm may refuse service to people on the grounds that they are unclean or disorderly but when American citizens of whatever descent who are neat and clean and conduct themselves in a manner that is above reproach are refused service because their parents or grandparents were born in another country, we feel that it is high time to cry out against it.

The persons involved in this case happen to be outstanding representatives of the group of people known as Latin Americans. One of them, for example, is a senior student at Our Lady of the Lake College. Another possesses two Master's Degrees, one granted by the University of Texas and the other by St. Mary's University of San Antonio. The third is president of a women's church group in San Antonio. The brother of Miss Castillo died in the service of his country. He was a member of the Army Air Forces during the last war. Mrs. Gomez's son is still in the U.S. Navy, having served in combat during the war. The brother and seventeen close relatives of Miss Elizondo served in the armed forces of this country during World War II. All three women have records of unquestioned caliber of patriotism to the country of their birth, the United States of America. They were deeply hurt by this discrimination and we feel that they deserve at least an apology.

The action of this person discriminating against these three women is contrary to the principles on which our country was founded. Such acts of discrimination cause all good Americans to hang their heads in shame. As loyal Americans we feel it our bounden duty to see that discrimination such as this is given all possible attention to the end that this disgraceful blight on our way of life be eliminated once and for all.

Signatures of twenty church and civic leaders

Lay Council for the Spanish Speaking, Archdiocese of San Antonio, letter of support for the affidavit of Henrietta A. Castillo, 28 February 1947, as cited in Alonso S. Perales, *Are We Good Neighbors?* (San Antonio: Artes Graficas, 1948), 149–52. Printed by permission.

60. César Chávez's Speech on the Mexican American and the Church, 1968

César Estrada Chávez (1927–1993) is arguably the most renowned figure in Chicano history. Born near Yuma, Arizona, he moved with his family to California in 1939. There he followed in his parents' footsteps, laboring as a farm worker in the San Joaquin Valley. In 1952, Chávez began organizing with the Community Service Organization (CSO) at San Jose, California, where his family lived when they were not working the fields. During the 1960s, he collaborated with Dolores Huerta to establish the National Farm Workers Association (later known as the United Farm Workers), the first union to secure contracts and official recognition from California growers. This union's significance extended far beyond the fields, as the efforts to gain farm workers' rights helped ignite the Chicano struggle in many other areas of church and society. In 1965, Chávez, Huerta, and other union leaders began their first major strike. Focused on the grape crop in the Delano area, they organized a national boycott of table grapes and a 1966 march on the state capital. Despite initial reluctance from Catholic bishops and priests, the union leaders also garnered support from church and civic leaders. While union officials successfully negotiated contracts with some growers beginning in 1967, as the campaign continued the brutality of the growers led to instances of retaliatory violence among union members. In February 1968, Chávez began a twenty-five-day fast to promote the principle of nonviolence in the farm workers' struggle. The following month, he delivered the presentation below to the Second Annual Mexican American Congress (Griswold del Castillo and García; Ferriss and Sandoval).

The place to begin is with our own experience with the church in the strike that has gone on for thirty-one months in Delano. For in Delano the church has been involved with the poor in a unique way which should stand as a symbol to other communities. Of course, when we refer to the church we should define the word a little. We mean the whole church, the church as an ecumenical body spread around the world, and not just its particular form in a parish in a local community. The church we are talking about is a tremendously powerful institution in our society, and in the world. That church is one form of the presence of God on earth, and so naturally it is powerful. It is powerful by definition. It is a powerful moral and spiritual force which cannot be ignored by any movement. Furthermore, it is an organization with tremendous wealth. Since the church is to be servant to the poor, it is *our* fault if that wealth is not channeled to help the poor in our world.

In a small way we have been able, in the Delano strike, to work together with the church in such a way as to bring some of its moral and economic power to bear on those who want to maintain the status quo, keeping farm workers in virtual enslavement. In brief, here is what happened in Delano.

Some years ago, when some of us were working with the Community Service Organization, we began to realize the powerful effect that the church can have on the conscience of the opposition. In scattered instances, in San Jose, Sacramento, Oakland, Los Angeles, and other places, priests would speak out loudly and clearly against specific instances of oppression, and, in some cases, stand with the people who were being hurt. Furthermore, a small group of priests, Frs. McDonald, McCollough, Duggan, and others, began to pinpoint attention on the terrible situation of the farm workers in our state.

At about that same time, we began to run into the California Migrant Ministry in the camps and fields. They were about the only ones there, and a lot of us were very suspicious, since we were Catholics and they were Protestants. However, they had developed a very clear conception of the church. It was called to serve, to be at the mercy of the poor, and not try to use them. After a while this made a lot of sense to us, and we began to find ourselves working side by side with them. In fact, it forced us to raise the question why *our* church was not doing the same. We would ask, "Why do the Protestants come out here and help the people, demand nothing, and give all their time to serving farm workers, while our own parish priests stay in their churches, where only a few people come, and usually feel uncomfortable?"

It was not until some of us moved to Delano and began working to build the National Farm Workers Association that we really saw how far removed from the people the parish church was. In fact, we could not get any help at all from the priests of Delano. When the strike began, they told us we could not even use the church's auditorium for the meetings. The farm workers' money helped build that auditorium! But the Protestants were there again, in the form of the California Migrant Ministry, and they began to help in little ways, here and there.

When the strike started in 1965, most of our "friends" forsook us for a while. They ran — or were just too busy to help. But the California Migrant Ministry held a meeting with its staff and decided that the strike was a matter of life or death for farm workers everywhere, and that even if it meant the end of the Migrant Ministry they would turn over their resources to the strikers. The political pressure on the Protestant Churches was tremendous and the Migrant Ministry lost a lot of money. But they stuck it out, and they began to point the way to the rest of the church. In fact, when 30 of the strikers were arrested for shouting "¡Huelga!" [Strike!], 11 ministers went to jail with them. They were in Delano that day at the request of Chris Hartmire, director of the California Migrant Ministry.

Then the workers began to raise the question: "Why ministers? Why not priests? What does the bishop say?" But the bishop said nothing. But slowly the pressure of the people grew, until finally we have in Delano a priest sent by the new bishop, Timothy Manning, who is there to help minister to the needs of farm workers. His name is Father Mark Day and he is the union's chaplain. *Finally,* our own Catholic Church has decided to recognize that we have our own peculiar needs, just as the growers have theirs.

But outside of the local diocese, the pressure built up on growers to negotiate was tremendous. Though we were not allowed to have our own priest, the power of the ecumenical body of the church was tremendous. The work of the church, for example, in the Schenley, Di Giorgio, Perelli-Minetti strikes was fantastic. They applied pressure — and they mediated.

When poor people get involved in a long conflict, such as a strike, or a civil rights drive, and the pressure increases each day, there is a deep need for spiritual advice. Without it we see families crumble, leadership weaken, and hard workers grow tired. And in such a situation the spiritual advice must be given by a friend, not by the opposition. What sense does it make to go to Mass on Sunday and reach for spiritual help, and instead get sermons about the wickedness of your cause? That only drives one to question and to despair. The growers in Delano have their spiritual problems...we do not deny that. They have every right to have priests and ministers who serve their needs. *But we have different needs, and so we needed a friendly spiritual guide.* And this is true in every community in this state where the poor face tremendous problems.

But the opposition raises a tremendous howl about this. They don't want us to have our spiritual advisors, friendly to our needs. Why is this? Why indeed except that *there is tremendous spiritual and economic power in the church.* The rich know it, and for that reason they choose to keep it from the people.

The leadership of the Mexican American community must admit that we have fallen far short in our task of helping provide spiritual guidance for our people. We may say, "I don't feel any such need. I can get along." But that is a poor excuse for not helping provide such help for others. For we can also say, "I don't need any welfare help. I can take care of my own problems." But we are willing to fight like hell for welfare aid for those who truly need it, who would starve without it. Likewise we may have gotten an education and not care about scholarship money for ourselves, or our children. But we would, we should, fight like hell to see to it that our state provides aid for any child needing it so that he can get the education he desires. *Likewise we can say we don't need the church. That is our business. But there are hundreds of thousands of our people who desperately need some help from that powerful institution, the church, and we are foolish not to help them get it.*

For example, the Catholic Charities agencies of the Catholic Church have millions of dollars earmarked for the poor. But often the money is spent for food baskets for the needy instead of for effective action to eradicate the causes of poverty. The men and women who administer this money sincerely want to help their brothers. It should be our duty to help direct the attention to the basic needs of the Mexican Americans in our society...needs which cannot be satisfied with baskets of food, but rather with effective organizing at the grassroots level.

Therefore, I am calling for Mexican American groups to stop ignoring this source of power. It is not just our right to appeal to the church to use its power effectively for the poor, it is our duty to do so. It should be as natural as appealing to government...and we do that often enough.

Furthermore, we should be prepared to come to the defense of that priest, rabbi, minister, or layman of the church, who out of commitment to truth and justice gets into a tight place with his pastor or bishop. It behooves us to stand with that man and help him see his trial through. It is our duty to see to it that his rights of conscience are respected and that no bishop, pastor, or other higher body takes that God-given, human right away.

Finally, in a nutshell, what do we want the church to do? We don't ask for more cathedrals. We don't ask for bigger churches or fine gifts. We ask for its presence with us, beside us, as Christ among us. We ask the church to *sacrifice with the people* for social change, for justice, and for love of brother. We don't ask for words. We ask for deeds. We don't ask for paternalism. We ask for servanthood.

> César Chávez, speech on the Mexican American and the church, March 1968, as cited in Antonio M. Stevens-Arroyo, *Prophets Denied Honor: An Anthology on the Hispano Church in the United States* (Maryknoll, N.Y.: Orbis Books, 1980), 118–21. Printed by permission.

61. Católicos por la Raza

Activists from the Chicano Law Students Association at Loyola University (now Loyola Marymount University), the United Mexican American Students (UMAS) at Los Angeles City College, and members of La Raza *newspaper were the principal organizers of Católicos por la Raza (Catholics for the Race). Led by Loyola law student Ricardo Cruz, they established Católicos at Los Angeles in the fall of 1969. As the group's title suggests, Católicos was an attempt to link the Catholic identity of Chicanos with the Chicano Movement's push for renewed ethnic pride and solidarity. Organization leaders also demanded that, in imitation of Jesus, the Catholic Church in Los Angeles do far more to uplift the socioeconomic conditions of Chicanos and involve the Chicano community in ecclesial decision-making processes. The organization's conflicts with Los Angeles cardinal James Francis McIntyre (1886–1979) brought it notoriety, particularly a dramatic 1969 confrontation during the cardinal's Christmas Eve Mass at the newly built St. Basil's Church, which resulted in several injuries and arrests. Although short-lived, Católicos helped initiate efforts to make U.S. Catholic leaders more responsive to the Latino Catholic population (Pulido 1991a; M. T. García).*

— this section contributed by Mario T. García

61a. Press Release, 1969

After contentious initial contacts with Cardinal McIntyre, organization leaders issued the following press release that included a letter to the cardinal. In it they outlined the reasons for organizing Católicos, as well as the group's vision and concerns.

December 4, 1969

Católicos por la Raza (CPLR) is a coalition of Mexican American Catholics working within the framework of the Congress on Mexican American Unity. We have committed ourselves to one goal: the return of the Catholic church to the oppressed Chicano community. We have today delivered the following message to the Roman Catholic Archdiocese of Los Angeles:

Dear Cardinal McIntyre and members of the Catholic clergy:

Mexican Americans have been most faithful to Catholicism and its traditions. We have produced saints and martyrs, have given and continue to give truly sacrificial donations to our Catholic Church, and for the most part have attempted to live up to Christ's mandate that we love our brother. We believe that you, our spiritual leaders, know these things to be true.

We are confused, however, because while we have cherished Christ's words "blessed are the poor," have lived in barrios and slums, have received on the average an eighth-grade education in the United States, and while we are treated as beasts of burden for the betterment of agribusiness, we know that, paradoxically, the Catholic Church is one of the richest and most powerful institutions in the world and the United States. We know, for example, that in Los Angeles County alone property owned by the Catholic Church is valued in excess of one billion dollars ($1,000,000,000). We know that the stained glass in Los Angeles' newest Catholic church is worth approximately two hundred and fifty thousand dollars ($250,000). We know of this wealth; yet Chicanitos are praying to La Virgen de Guadalupe as they go to bed hungry and will not be able to afford decent educations.

We are confused our dear priests, nuns, and brothers because when we have attempted to discuss our desperate needs at the chancery office, we were lied to and had the police called upon us. Indeed, when we finally did obtain an audience with you, Cardinal McIntyre, our spiritual leader, you told us to "say what you have to say or get out."

Thus, because we are Catholics, because we know that Christ was born in a manger, washed and kissed the feet of the poor, and ultimately gave his life for the needs of poor people, and because we are Chicanos, we are left with no choice but to publicly demand that the Catholic institution in Los Angeles practice what it preaches and channel its tremendous spiritual and economic power to meet the needs of its most faithful servants. After all, it is the Catholic priest, nun, and brother, and not the Mexican American, who have taken the vow of poverty.

Understand that, unlike other peoples, we need not demand specific sums of money. Our demands are more basic. We are demanding that the Catholic Church be *Christian*. For you see, if it is Christian it cannot in conscience retain its fabulous wealth while Chicanos have to beg, plead, borrow, and steal for better housing, education, legal defense, and other critical needs. Indeed, a Christian Catholic Church would not allow the Chicanito to go uneducated for lack of funds; it would channel its wealth through community-controlled housing agencies to rid our society of barrios and projects; and it would allow members of the Mexican American community to participate in all church activities which are not of a purely religious nature. Clearly, a Christian Catholic Church would publicly commit itself, its influence and wealth, to all social issues in which Chicanos are presently involved: the farm worker, the high school walkouts, racist judges and grand juries, and the fact that 20% of those dying in the immoral Vietnam War are Chicanos. These are but a few examples of the business of a Christian Catholic Church.

Further understand that we shall enforce our demands with whatever spiritual and physical powers we possess even if it means we must be jailed. Because as Catholics and Christians we cannot and will not anymore ignore the mockery the church, as an institution and as the embodiment of Christ on earth, has made of the words "I come not to be served, but to serve" (Matthew 20:28).

> Católicos por la Raza, press release, 4 December 1969, Ricardo Cruz/Católicos por la Raza Papers, California Ethnic and Multicultural Archives, University of California at Santa Barbara. Printed by permission.

61b. Announcement of a Communal Fast, 1970

The week following a highly publicized protest and confrontation during Cardinal McIntyre's Christmas Eve Mass at St. Basil's Church, Ricardo Cruz announced on behalf of Católicos that the group would conduct a three-day fast to call further attention to their grievances. In this document, Cruz clearly links the Catholic faith of Católicos with the newfound expression of pride in Chicano identity.

We, Católicos Por La Raza, have chosen to begin the year 1970 by a public fast at St. Basil's to demonstrate our convictions to our people, the Chicano, and to our Catholic brothers whose support we seek in our struggle with the hierarchy of the church.

We are Catholics who have identified ourselves and committed our lives to the poor of all races, and more specifically to the situation of our people, the Mexican American, whose condition is one of oppression and manipulation by the forces of indifference, greed, and racism.

We are Catholics who approach this demonstration of our faith in the spirit of Christ and under the banner of our patron saint, La Virgen de Guadalupe. She is our only power and only source of wisdom, and the staff of La Virgen de Bronze shall be our only weapon.

We are Catholics who shall no longer sit idly while our church degenerates into a partnership with racist ideologies and governments of reaction. Too long has the philosophy of the hierarchy been that of accommodation to the existing government, whether for good or for evil; too long has their primary concern been one of corporate power at the expense of the kingdom of God; too long has the economic enrichment of the hierarchy taken precedence over the needs for the daily bread without which no man can meaningfully worship God.

We are Chicanos: La Raza can no longer endure the piteous paternalism of those *padres* whose only goal is the Americanization of a people whose culture and language is richer and more ancient than the vacuous alternative they strive to impose upon us.

We are Chicanos: We seek peaceful means to radically reform our church and the whole of society. We shall not allow the hierarchy or their army under the guise of law enforcement officers, to disrupt our demonstrations of faith.

We are Chicanos: We shall protect ourselves and defend our women and children even to the death ... Ya Basta!

Ricardo Cruz
Co-Chairman
Católicos Por La Raza

Ricardo Cruz, "The Fast of Católicos por la Raza" (typescript), 1970, Ricardo Cruz/Católicos por la Raza Papers, California Ethnic and Multicultural Archives, University of California at Santa Barbara. Printed by permission.

62. PADRES

PADRES (Padres Asociados por los Derechos Religiosos, Educativos, y Sociales; Priests Associated for Religious, Educational, and Social Rights) emerged out of a Chicano priests' support group in San Antonio, Texas. The first PADRES national congress met at Tucson, Arizona, in February 1970. Although a relatively small group, PADRES quickly took an active role in vital causes and organizations such as the National Chicano Moratorium, the United Farm Workers (see document 60), Communities Organized for Public Service (COPS) in San Antonio, and the United Neighborhoods Organization (UNO) in Los Angeles. In 1975 PADRES extended full membership to all Latino priests, deacons, and religious brothers. The organization lasted for two decades and played a major role in advancing Latino leadership and concerns within both church and society (Romero 1990; Matovina 1999).

62a. Proposal for a National Chicano Church, 1971

While PADRES at times took prophetic stands on social issues, their most con-sistent activism was within the church itself. In the following speech from PADRES's 1971 national congress in Los Angeles, Alberto Carrillo announced one of the organization's most radical proposals: a national Chicano church re-moved from U.S. episcopal control and placed directly under the Propagation of the Faith in Rome.

As everyone at this congress well knows, the Chicano and Spanish-surnamed Catholic is by far the largest Catholic minority. We constitute 25 percent of the Catholic population. Yet it is interesting to note that of the 25 percent of the Catholic population that is Spanish-surnamed, the Chicano is the most un-educated person in the United States. He becomes "illiterate in two languages." Economically, he is disadvantaged, averaging less than $5,000 a year income. Politically, he is legally disfranchised. In the courts he faces a system of double-standard justice. Being less than 5 percent of the national population, he is nevertheless representative of 21 percent of the casualties in Vietnam. Yet, when he returns, he lives in the worst housing; he lives under a system of educational abortion and economic atrocity. He is more welcome in jail than in a college classroom. He has been programmed to poverty — because indeed opportunity and poverty in this country are ethnic.

All these things are made possible because institutions demand cultural sui-cide and self-negation as a ransom for acceptance and success. This is made possible with stereotype images of the Chicano as lazy, cruel, indifferent, violent, fatalistic by the image-makers, so that the country might salve its conscience in the perpetuation of the Chicano as its cheap labor force.

We know the problems. Let us ask why, why do they exist? It is not a matter of rights, and we should not get into a rhetoric of rights. No one denies that Chicanos have rights. It is a matter of opportunity for self-determination. We do not need a Civil Rights Act — we need an Opportunity of Self-determination Act, educationally, economically, politically, and yes, ecclesiastically. Why? Because of discrimination.

Again, let us make a distinction in rhetoric. We do not feel that it is the discrimination of hatred, of a KKK, of an overt nature that is dangerous. It is recognizable and consequently easy to fight. However, the discrimination the Chicano feels is the systematic, the inadvertent, one that is not based on hatred or malice, but on a system, a systematic discrimination.

It is important to recognize this, so one cannot say, "Because I can go into any motel or restaurant, there is no problem." It is important because the church has discriminated in this way against our people, and we cannot accuse the church of hatred or malice, because that is just simply not true.

Inadvertently, discrimination is based on four reasons — human reasons, if you like — or four principles. This has happened in every conquest in the history of the world, or any clash of cultural values: man/woman, youth/adult, Norman/Saxon, Spanish/Aztec, Anglo/Chicano. Here's what happens:

1. The majority culture makes the policies that affect the minority; also, they establish the qualifications for those who shall make policy.

2. The majority culture assumes that the problems are the fault of the minority.

3. The majority culture assumes there is no problem until it affects the majority peoples.

4. The majority culture assumes that their way is the superior and only way because it is the majority way.

Politically, economically, and educationally these are the reasons that have excluded minority peoples from opportunity. We could spell these out at another time. Let us just apply these things to the church. The church is no different from a political system, an educational system; it is sociologically human and capable of reflecting the same failings of other human institutions that have failed Chicanos for the same reasons. There is no need to prove the church's failure to meet the needs of the Chicano, but let us try to understand why this has happened.

1. *The majority culture makes the policies:* In the United States 81 percent of the hierarchy is of either Irish or Germanic descent, and so come from a different value system; they make the policy for our people. How many provincials, mothers superior, representatives in priest senates and chanceries are Chicano? There are reasons why there are none, but the point is that people who do not even know the problems cannot be expected to find their solutions. Bishops who do not know the educational problem of the Chicano cannot be expected to put bilingual education into their schools.

2. *The majority culture assumes that the problems are the fault of the minority:* How many times have you been asked, "Why don't the Mexicans give more money?" "Why are they lazy?" "Why don't they have the initiative to go to college?" "Why are there no more Mexican priests?" When only 1 percent of our kids get to college, how can they possibly survive the academic and cultural shock of a seminary? How can people be blamed for being poor? How can people be blamed for being deprived of education, religious as well as secular? How can a person be blamed for not wanting to become "Irish" and prefer to celebrate Guadalupe rather than St. Patrick's day? Our people are not in the mainstream of Catholicism in this country because the church has not been relevant to them; they have not been given the dignity of being accepted for what they are, what they wish to be, why God made them. So it is not a Chicano problem; it is an Anglo problem, it is with education, etc.

3. *The majority culture assumes that there is no problem until it affects the majority culture:* Let us be honest even though it is painful. What would the official church attitude be if the grape pickers had been Irish? What would the official attitude of the church be if 60 percent of the Catholic kids dropped out of school because they were Catholic? What if all the problems that Chicanos faced were faced by Anglo Catholics? This is natural. This is human. Drugs were not a problem as long as they were confined to the barrios and ghettos, but now that the drugs are hurting the middle-class youth, we have a drug problem.

4. *The majority culture assumes that there is only one way to do things —their way:* Humanly speaking again, the church has assumed, with the rest of American society, that we are a melting pot. Ecclesiastically we are an Irish-church melting pot. In general, cultural differences in religious expression have not been allowed because it was assumed they did not exist. A "good" Catholic was one who accepted the Irish ecclesiastical value system.

Yet there is a vast cultural difference in expressing religious sentiments and practices. Vatican II spelled this out quite clearly. The Chicano has a different view and different insights into the interpretation of law, liturgy, and moral theology, and these have been suppressed. And when one's values are suppressed, a person has two choices: cultural suicide, or rejection of the institution. Both phenomena are normal for the Spanish-speaking person in the United States toward his church.

How about Solutions?

Sociologically, solutions can be found by a complete reversal of the four causes or reasons for inadvertent discrimination in any institution. Witness the Civil Rights Commission demanding racial parity in policy-making, in cultural input, in obvious social injustice. Can the church come up with a voluntary plan of compliance? Here are some of the things that would be necessary now:

- equitable (25 percent) representation in the hierarchy, provincialates, seminaries, chanceries, councils, senates to allow a just sharing of policy-making that touches our people
- a massive educational program to make a bicultural clergy
- Chicano studies in the seminaries
- lay leadership courses, lay diaconate among the Spanish speaking
- admission of innovative cultural programs from Chicano clergy without fear
- participation in the Chicano struggle for equal opportunity in every sphere where the struggle exists
- a drastic change in Catholic education to make it relevant to Chicano students
- opening of Catholic higher education to Chicanos in equitable numbers
- development of Chicano seminaries
- development of Chicano liturgy, moral theology, canon law interpretation

Alternatives

These general solutions mentioned are not luxuries, but necessities for the religious survival of our people in this country. Patience and time in this case are vices and real obstacles to the message of Christ and must be treated so. If the redemptive act of Christ is a value that must reach our people, we must then heed the words of Pope Paul VI: "to take up a double task of inspiring and of innovation in order to make structures evolve, so as to adapt them to the real needs of today."

Solutions can be found only with the admission of two premises: (a) the Chicano in the church is at a missionary status (when the ratio is one bishop for 7 million people and less that 200 priests); (b) Catholicism encourages cultural difference and development.

If, indeed, the Chicano church is in the state of a mission, it cannot survive with normal pastoral practice, it must be served by a mission concept as outlined very clearly in the distinction made in *Ad Gentes* [*Decree on the Mission Activity of the Church*, Vatican II].

Historical precedent in the United States articulates that similar problems were solved by national churches which allowed the faithful the right to practice Catholicism in their own cultures and not make acculturation blackmail to receive the redemptive act of Christ.

The entire document "On the Care of Migrants" by Pope Paul, insists on episcopal vicars, personal parishes, special concern for youth in colleges, and all necessary innovative means to end cultural shock, economic atrocity, and educational abortion within society and the church.

If solutions are to be found before it is too late, there can be only one answer: *a national Chicano Church under the Propagation of the Faith in Rome.*

> Alberto Carillo, presentation to the PADRES national congress, October 1971, as cited in Antonio M. Stevens-Arroyo, *Prophets Denied Honor: An Anthology on the Hispano Church in the United States* (Maryknoll, N.Y.: Orbis Books, 1980), 154–57. Printed by permission.

62b. Circular Letter Promoting the Appointment of Hispanic Bishops, 1978

Although PADRES leaders like Alberto Carillo advocated more radical stances such as a separate Chicano church, PADRES members typically lobbied within existing ecclesial structures, particularly to advocate for more Latino bishops. For example, when the Vatican formed the new diocese of San Bernardino-Riverside in 1978 and appointed Philip Straling as the first ordinary to this heavily Latino see, PADRES and Las Hermanas (documents 63a–63c) sent a letter of protest to apostolic delegate Jean Jadot. Subsequently PADRES executive director Trinidad Sánchez distributed the circular letter reprinted below, asking concerned parties to write California's two archbishops and demand action on PADRES proposals for episcopal appointments.

San Antonio, 20 October 1978

Estimado Amigo/a:

You may be aware of the situation in San Bernardino, California. The Hispanic community has publicly voiced its concern over the process of appointment of bishops in dioceses with large populations of Spanish speaking.

Several PADRES and Hermanas at our National Encuentro, August 14–18, 1978, wrote a letter to the apostolic delegate addressing themselves to the four points listed below:

1. That in all dioceses of the United States wherein exists an Hispanic Catholic population of 50 percent or more, an Hispanic ordinary committed to the development of all the people be named as there be an opening;

2. That Hispanic religious order priests truly committed to the development and liberation of the people be considered and named ordinaries for some of these dioceses;

3. That any diocese with 20% or more Hispano Catholic population have an Hispano episcopal vicar for the Spanish Speaking, who has true authority over personnel matters and financial resources insofar as they effect the quality and effectiveness of Hispanic ministry;

4. That in the process for the selection of bishops, the voice of the local people be heard and have influence, especially in regards to the qualities and characteristics they desire their next bishop to possess.

This being a national concern, the local people have asked for our support in writing to the following: Cardinal Timothy Manning, Archbishop of Los Angeles, and Most Rev. John R. Quinn, Archbishop of San Francisco, asking them to support the Hispanic community and the four points listed above. Please send a copy to PADRES office. This has become a national issue, *so it is imperative que nuestros hermanos y hermanas* in San Bernardino receive our support. We also ask that you encourage two or three other local Hispanic leaders or groups to write letters of support.

Please send your letter as soon as possible and before November 6, 1978.

Thanking you in advance for you cooperation, I remain,

Sincerely yours,
Trinidad Sánchez, SJ, Bro.
Executive Director

Trinidad Sánchez, circular letter promoting the appointment of Hispanic bishops, 20 October 1978, PADRES Collection, personal files of Juan Romero, Santa Monica, California. Printed by permission.

63. Las Hermanas

Las Hermanas is the only national Catholic organization of Chicana/Latina women. Like Católicos por la Raza (documents 61a, 61b) and PADRES (documents 62a, 62b), Hermanas mobilized during the Chicano Movement for civil rights. The organization's foundresses were Sister Gregoria Ortega, a Victoryknoll sister and community activist from El Paso, Texas, and Sister Gloria Graciela Gallardo, a Holy Ghost sister from San Antonio who worked as a catechist and community organizer. These two leaders convened fifty sisters at Houston in April 1971 and established Las Hermanas. The charter membership declared that the organization's purpose was "to meet the needs of the Spanish-speaking people of God, using our unique resources as Spanish-speaking religious women." Within six months membership expanded to seven hundred representing twenty-one states. Attendance at national conferences averaged two hundred in succeeding years. The three documents in this section illuminate Las Hermanas's founding vision, resolute activism, and evolution into an organization primarily focused on the concerns and leadership development of Latina women (Tarango and Matovina; Medina 1998).

— this section contributed by Lara Medina

63a. Circular Letter to Prospective Hermanas Members, 1970

*The following selection reflects Gregoria Ortega and Gloria Graciela Gallardo's
initial concerns in establishing a network of Mexican American women religious.
This letter from Gallardo sparked a response from other Chicana sisters who
had common experiences with discrimination and alienation in their religious
vocations, leading to the founding of Las Hermanas six months later.*

October 20, 1970

Dear Sister,

Times are changing rapidly and by necessity and nature the church must
also "change" so as to better meet the needs of her people. The "church" is
becoming more and more aware of the need there is to relate to people and to
become more relevant to the times and, therefore, is seeking ways and means
of identifying more closely with the people of God. This "identity role" must
also be ours.

We, as religious, exert much influence among our Spanish-speaking people
because of their deep seated religious principles. Many of us feel that we are
not doing this to our fullest capacity. On the other hand, there are some of
us who have tried to become more relevant to our people and, because of
this, find themselves in "trouble" with either our congregation or other members of the hierarchy. Then there are some of us who would like to be able
to do more among our people but cannot, either because they are not yet
quite sure of themselves or because they are being constrained by the lack of
understanding or communication in their congregation. For these and many
other reasons, some of us have felt for some time that we should unite closer,
not just for strength and support, but to educate ourselves as to who we are,
where we're going, why we're going, and how. Sister Gregoria Ortega and
I would like to hear your opinion on uniting throughout the country. We
have thought much about this and thought it might be best to unite Mexican
American sisters first so as to give us the opportunity of establishing our own
self-identity, and then asking other sisters, who are and have been working
with our Spanish-speaking people, to join us. What do you think? Are you
interested?

Sister Gregoria is a Victoryknoll and I am a Holy Ghost sister based in San
Antonio, but working in Houston. (With the Holy Ghost, we can't help but
have Victory–knoll?)

Tu hermana en Cristo,
Sister Gloria Graciela Gallardo, S.H.G.

Gloria Graciela Gallardo, circular letter to prospective Hermanas members,
20 October 1970, Las Hermanas Papers, Our Lady of the Lake University, San
Antonio, Tex. Printed by permission.

63b. Presentation on U.S. Bishops' Proposed Pastoral Letter on Women, 1985

*While Las Hermanas was initially comprised primarily of Mexican American
sisters, soon laywomen and other Latina religious, particularly those of Carib-*

bean heritage, joined their Chicana counterparts in the organization. Uniting members from diverse ethnicities and locales across the United States, particularly regions with a large Hispanic population, enabled Las Hermanas to form an organization that collectively challenged the overt discrimination toward Latinas and Latinos in the church and in society at large. Within the church, Las Hermanas influenced the policy decisions of major ecclesial bodies like the National Conference of Catholic Bishops Secretariat for Hispanic Affairs and the Leadership Conference of Women Religious. The following report from Informes, *Las Hermanas's periodic newsletter, recounts the presentation of four Hermanas to an episcopal committee overseeing consultations for a proposed U.S. bishops' pastoral letter on women in church and society. Widespread protest and criticism of the proposed letter eventually led the bishops to abandon this project.*

The U.S. Bishops voted in November 1983 to write a pastoral letter on Women in the Church and Society. On March 4–5, 1985, representatives of major national organizations of women were consulted on what approach to take. More than half of the women's groups testifying, including Las Hermanas, asked the bishops to write a pastoral on sexism or on patriarchy rather than on women. The problem is not women but sexism. Furthermore, it would be presumptuous or foolish for an all male group of bishops to write a pastoral on women. Why not one on men? Formerly, the bishops wrote on racism, not on black people. Nevertheless, work has continued and many dioceses have sponsored "hearings" on women's concerns.

The following is a report of Las Hermanas' presentation to the bishops. It was part of the national coordinating team's report at the national meeting in August 1985, but many of you were not present. We feel it is important for you to know Las Hermanas' position as you hear of or participate in local "hearings."

On the 4th and 5th of March, 1985, the committee of bishops in charge of writing the Pastoral Letter on Women held several public hearings at the Washington Plaza Hotel in Washington, D.C. Las Hermanas were invited to testify on the 5th of March at 1:30 p.m. Las Hermanas were represented by Beatriz Díaz-Taveras, state coordinator for New York; María Teresa Garza, national coordinator living in Indiana; Ada María Isasi-Díaz, New York; and Carmen Villegas, national coordinator living in New York.

The bishops had eight female consultants, none of whom was Hispanic.

The four representatives were bent on being realistic in their presentations and decided to testify before the bishops as prophets, keeping in mind the pain of the women whom they represented, as well as their own. Their theme was, "We Are the Voice of the Voiceless." They took as their mentor the late Archbishop Oscar Romero, a Christian who lived the Gospel fully.

The presentation began with an introduction reflecting the Hispanic woman's reality. *Example:* We are representing the single mother, the woman who has been a victim of machismo, the mother who has lost her sons and daughters to drugs and to many other social problems, and the women who lack a role of leadership in the church. Beatriz then presented her reality as a young, Catholic, Hispanic woman who belongs to a church that has almost never given her support nor educated her about sexuality. The last to testify was María Teresa Garza, who presented her reality as a divorced, Catholic, Hispanic woman. She declared very clearly that she did not want her daughter or any other woman to go through what she had.

The presentation concluded with each bishop receiving a stone while Matthew 7:9–12 was read. The bishops were told, "We have asked for bread, and you have given us a stone. If you truly seek reconciliation, place these stones on the altar and remember the Hispanic woman struggling for her liberation and the liberation of her people."

> "Las Hermanas y la carta pastoral sobre las mujeres," *Informes* (May 1986): 2, Las Hermanas Papers, Our Lady of the Lake University, San Antonio, Tex. Trans. Dora Elizondo Guerra. Printed by permission.

63c. Reflections on Las Hermanas National Conference, 1991

While originally formed to empower Chicana women religious and advance Hispanic ministry and social concerns, by 1980 Las Hermanas evolved into an organization that focused more specifically on the leadership development and concerns of grassroots Latinas. Las Hermanas's current constitution states that "the expressed priority of the organization is the promotion of the Hispanic woman." The following document reflects Hermanas's role as an organization that empowers grassroots Latinas; it contains the reflections of Teresa Almeda, an Hermanas member from Colorado, who attended her first Hermanas national conference at Albuquerque in November 1991 after joining the organization earlier that year.

I would like to share an emotional high point of my first year as a member of Las Hermanas. I had the wonderful opportunity to attend the 20th anniversary conference in Albuquerque, New Mexico, November 1–3. For me, this experience has become a landmark in my personal history of being "Mexicana." Despite growing up with no experience of women in positions of worldly authority, I had learned that individual women could be competent, courageous, and loyal to each other. Albuquerque proved to me that Hispanic women as a group are proficient, resourceful, effective, and here to stay! There were women representing every group of Hermanas: Mexicans, Puerto Ricans, Cubans, Chilenas, Españolas, who together forged a shared resolution. We met in discussion groups of 8–10 that followed the dynamic and inspirational lectures. We described the common experiences of women of color while preserving the special issues of each group. These discussions were profoundly consciousness-raising, sincere, and gave us a chance to hear feelings confirmed. In my particular group there was enough energy, intelligence, skill, anger, and humor for a revolution. My two biggest rewards were a sense of making a difference and the sharing of ideas. The first would be enough in itself, for that is how we know we are alive, but the second is magic! It was gratifying to know that a roomful of Hispanic women can dialogue and set off a chain of thought that leads us all to a new place. There was an explosion of understanding, empathy, unity, and pride! I am filled with the spirit! I have totally committed myself to the endeavors of Las Hermanas.

Teresa Almeda, "Reflections on Albuquerque," *Informes* (January 1992): 5, Las Hermanas Papers, Our Lady of the Lake University, San Antonio, Tex. Printed by permission.

64. Call for Increased Hispanic Leadership in the Archdiocese of New York, 1972

Hispanic leaders in the New York archdiocese convened a series of gatherings to prepare for the First National Hispanic Encuentro (see document 69). On 13 March 1972, participants in these gatherings wrote a letter to Cardinal Terrence Cooke (1921–1983) requesting a meeting with him and asking for a greater representation of Hispanics at the decision-making levels of the archdiocese. The 159 signers of this letter encompassed the Puerto Rican, Dominican, Cuban, and other Hispanic groups living in New York and included priests, sisters, and lay leaders. Two weeks later the cardinal met with eleven delegates from this group in an exchange that several signatories described as tense. Subsequently archdiocesan officials appointed more Hispanics to positions in the chancery office, but the Office for the Spanish-Speaking Apostolate, which had sponsored the Encuentro process, lost considerable influence within the archdiocesan structure (Stevens Arroyo 208–13).

Our migration to New York is the first great non-European migration and the first to come unaccompanied by a native clergy. Historically, in former migrations that clergy assumed a role of natural leadership for the migrant community, not only with regards to the religious ministry, but in the whole process of the development of the migrant. The present structures of the New York Church were developed in response to the needs of a particular people and in the past served well that people. Our presence in New York without our own clergy has presented a new challenge to this church, one that to date has not been adequately responded to.

We are Hispano Americans and we are Catholics. We believe that, although what has been done thus far is insufficient, it is possible to mobilize the resources of the church in the city to further the development of our people as human beings and as children of God. As a first step towards achieving this goal and as a sign of hope and leadership in the Hispanic Church we ask the following:

1. That an episcopal vicar for the Spanish speaking be appointed with the consultation of the Coordinating Committee of the Spanish-Speaking Apostolate and that the person chosen be Spanish-speaking, totally identified with the Spanish people and their culture, and have all those faculties expressed and implied by such a position in accordance with Canon Law.

2. That on the next occasion of appointment of a vicar general a Spanish-speaking priest be named.

3. That the vicar general and the episcopal vicar for the Spanish speaking consult and work closely with the Coordinating Committee of the Spanish-

Speaking Apostolate in all matters affecting the Spanish-speaking community of the archdiocese.

4. That on the next occasion of appointment of new auxiliary bishops in recognition of the Spanish-speaking community at least one of them be of Hispanic origin and experienced in pastoral work in New York and that this appointment be made with the consultation of the Spanish-speaking community through the Coordinating Committee of the Spanish-Speaking Apostolate.

> Spanish-speaking apostolate leaders, letter to Cardinal Terence Cooke, 13 March 1972, as cited in Robert L. Stern, "Evolution of Hispanic Ministry in the New York Archdiocese," in Ruth T. Doyle et al., *Hispanics in New York: Religious, Cultural, and Social Experiences* (New York: Archdiocese of New York Office of Pastoral Research, 1982), 2:334–35. Printed by permission.

65. Cuban Exiles Denounce Archbishop for Discrimination, Miami, 1972

The Cuban Revolution of 1959 resulted in a sharp confrontation between Fidel Castro's government and the Cuban Catholic Church. Thousands of Catholics fled the island, including a large proportion of the clergy and religious, many of whom were deported. On arriving in the United States many Cuban priests became vocal activists against the Communist regime in their homeland; two Cuban priests and a Protestant minister even accompanied the Cuban brigade that landed at the Bay of Pigs in 1961. This crusading spirit of the Cuban Catholics alarmed a number of U.S. church officials. These leaders felt uncomfortable with the Cubans' highly vocal and activist exile identity, which they boldly promoted within the church. The following document reveals a conflict that developed between Cuban Catholics and Archbishop Coleman Carroll (1905–1977) of Miami. This editorial from a Spanish-language Miami newspaper illustrates the deep resentment of many Cubans who felt that U.S. church officials not only had little sympathy for their situation but openly discriminated against Cuban exiles for their strong anti-Communist attitudes and desire to maintain exile consciousness among their people.

The Cuban Catholic priests of Miami are the object of a severe and unprecedented discrimination on the part of this city's archbishop, Monsignor Coleman Carroll, according to information learned by *Alerta*. As a result, priests who are being singled out have gone silent or abandoned the priesthood, while others have been transferred outside of Miami.

The persecution became even more evident when a few days ago Archbishop Carroll prohibited Father Ramón O'Farrill — a prestigious, high profile, and greatly respected and admired priest in the Cuban community — from giving the religious invocation in Spanish to an ecumenical meeting celebrated by the Republican Party in the early morning hours of August 20th at the Carrillon Hotel.

According to what we have been able to learn unofficially, Monsignor Brian Walsh, Archbishop Carroll's advisor, informed Father O'Farrill of the archbishop's order forbidding him from attending the aforementioned function.

The cause of the disagreement stemmed from the fact that Carroll was not invited to give the invocation, as he had at the Democratic Party convention.

This is the latest in a long chain of discrimination against Cuban priests carried out by Monsignor Carroll. But what is more unusual is that, while this is happening, some North American priests preach communist-like slogans from the pulpit, dare to celebrate Mass in short sleeves, and many of them sport long hair, looking like Hippies, while the archbishop looks the other way without a word of reproach.

Even more surprising, not too long ago, Monsignor Brian Walsh gave the religious invocation at a political meeting organized by Chicano labor leader César Chávez, a well-known leftist militant.

The first priest to fall victim to Monsignor Carroll's anti-Cuban attitude was Father Daniel Sánchez, who in 1962 was ordained into the priesthood by the late archbishop of New York, Cardinal Francis Spellman. The ordination took place amid great pomp and celebration at the Miami Beach Convention Hall. Sánchez was the first Cuban ordained in exile. That ordination was Cardinal Spellman's response to the brutal repression being carried out by Castro's tyranny against the Catholic Church in Cuba.

Today, Father Daniel Sánchez is pumping gas at the corner of Collins Avenue and 14th Street in Miami Beach. He was forced to ask for a leave after Archbishop Carroll, refusing to leave him alone, transferred him from one parish to another.

Another of Monsignor Carroll's victims was Father Eugenio del Busto, who had been secretary of Hispanic affairs for the archdiocese. He was removed from that post without a single explanation and assigned to St. Robert Bellarmine parish, a very poor parish on 27th Avenue and N.W. 34th. Finding himself without resources, Father del Busto organized a festival to raise funds for rebuilding the parish.

Several discrepancies in viewpoint about the festival caused a very disagreeable incident that led Father del Busto to leave the church and renounce the priesthood.

On the archbishop of Miami's hit list was the Congregation of the Brothers of La Salle who Carroll persecuted until they all left Miami.

The next victim was Father Martínez, a Jesuit whose noble task was providing spiritual support for the prisoners at the county jail.

Due to differences of opinion surrounding his apostolic services with the prisoners at the county jail, Father Martínez was banished from Miami despite the opposition of Martínez's superiors in the Jesuit order.

Next it was Father José B. Chabebe's turn. He was removed as assistant at the parish of St. John Bosco and transferred to New York. Even though Father Chabebe, according to some, was controversial, he nonetheless denounced communism and firmly supported Cuba's cause.

The last victim was Father O'Farrill. *Alerta* tried to interview the distinguished Cuban priest, but he politely declined from making any comments to the journalist.

It is time for the archbishop of Miami, Monsignor Coleman Carroll, to explain his discriminatory attitude toward the Cuban clergy. Instead of persecuting these worthy soldiers of Christ, Monsignor Carroll ought to be regulating the activities of many North American priests who, with their insulting attitudes toward the traditions of the priesthood, are spreading doctrines contrary to the church and the democratic system.

Monsignor Coleman F. Carroll, archbishop of Miami, has the floor.

Alerta (Miami), 1 September 1972. Trans. Dora Elizondo Guerra. Courtesy of the Cuban Heritage Collection, Otto G. Richter Library, University of Miami.

66. Reflections on the 1972 Founding of the Mexican American Cultural Center

Hispanic pastoral centers have served for decades as language and pastoral training institutes, as well as advocates for Hispanic ministry and justice in church and society. The first such center was the Institute of Intercultural Communication (initially called the Institute of Missionary Formation) established for the New York archdiocese with an immersion program at the Catholic University of Puerto Rico in Ponce. Founded in 1957 by Father Ivan Illich, during its fifteen-year existence the institute prepared numerous priests and religious in the Spanish language as well as cultural awareness in Hispanic ministry (Vidal 1994: 101–5). Four years after the institute's closing another center opened in New York, the Northeast Catholic Pastoral Center for Hispanics. Other pastoral centers include the highly regarded Southeast Pastoral Institute (SEPI) in Miami, which collaborates with all twenty-six dioceses in the southeast United States; Cuban priest Mario Vizcaíno, SchP, helped found this institute in 1978 and has led it ever since.

In the Southwest, the Mexican American Cultural Center (MACC) emerged as a pastoral center for Hispanic and multicultural ministry in San Antonio. While primarily focused on Mexican American Catholics, since its 1972 founding the staff at MACC has engaged in an ongoing ecumenical, interethnic effort to train leaders for cross-cultural work in a variety of contexts. MACC has also played a leading role in advocating for Hispanic ministry and rights and publishing groundbreaking research about Latino liturgy, faith expressions, history, and theology. The dream of establishing a pastoral center for Mexican Americans emerged at a February 1971 PADRES (see documents 62a, 62b) retreat and workshop in Santa Fe, New Mexico. PADRES member Virgilio Elizondo served as MACC's founding president from 1972 to 1987; Las Hermanas (see documents 63a–63c) and lay leaders joined Elizondo and other PADRES members in establishing the center. A 1977 brochure that articulated the center's purpose and activities included the following reflection on the reasons for establishing MACC (Elizondo 1997b; Rodríguez 230–34).

The Mexican American Cultural Center is a response to the struggles, frustration, and disappointments of many of the native-born Spanish-speaking priests of the United States. As we started to meet for the first time in our history and that of the United States, it became very evident that no one of a minority group, alone and isolated, could respond to the multiple pastoral needs of our people. It was equally evident that none of the existing institutions in this country, whether in the Catholic universities, seminaries, or other centers of learning, were addressing the needs of approximately 15 million Spanish-speaking Catholics in the United States. Not only were they not responding to this definite pastoral crisis, but for the most part they were not — and are not today — even aware that there is a need.

Many of the Hispanic people were leaving the Roman Catholic Church. In disappointment and frustration some joined Protestant Churches. Others saw any church as totally alienating. Growing numbers accepted Karl Marx's accusation that religion is the very opium that keeps the people from taking themselves seriously and thus making an effort to develop and transform society.

Five years ago we Spanish-speaking priests [and sisters] could see the cultural exasperation of our people. There were no pastoral materials available for relevant instruction or liturgical celebration for the Spanish speaking in the United States. Materials published in English and in Spanish in Spain were foreign to our situation. As Mexican Americans, we were well aware that we were not typical white Anglo-Saxon middle class North Americans but we also became critically conscious that we were not the same as Mexicans living in Mexico or Latin Americans in Latin America. We have a unique identity of our own, for we have maintained our language, religion, and many of our customs and traditions in an English-speaking environment.

We painfully discovered that we were, in effect, a people without a land, without a country, without a psychological nationality, and, in a way, even without a language. In the United States we are seen as second-class citizens by the dominant society. Many cruel stereotypes were imposed upon our people, who were considered a problem and a burden. Economically, the only possibility open to us was to be a cheap labor force.

In Latin America we were not accepted either. There we were called "pochos." Latin Americans laughed at our Spanish, our customs, as tainted by the U.S. lifestyle and we were seen as funny or quaint. Hence, we were not at home either in the United States or in Latin America.

These and many other events motivated the Spanish-speaking priests of the United States to decide that a center of learning was needed where persons could be educated and culturally attuned, and where materials could be prepared to respond to the immediate and specific needs of the Spanish-speaking people in this country. In the beginning we focused on language. If our people did not understand English they should be able to worship in the language of their birth. Many of our own Hispanic priests were not fluent in Spanish because all our theological education had been in English. We had become foreigners to our own people. The first efforts of MACC were, then, to start a pastoral language program to prepare leaders to speak the language of the people.

From language we went to the deeper question of education, economics, and politics. To be ministers of the Gospel meant not only to be interested in the salvation of souls but also in the salvation of a whole people. Our people had to become familiar with the institutions that controlled their lives. In addition to religious programs, our center had to be a center for organizing and speaking out against an economic system that enslaved our people. Ignorance would keep us in slavery; knowledge would be a power for liberation.

Mexican American Cultural Center brochure, 1977. Archives of the Mexican American Cultural Center, San Antonio. Printed by permission.

67. Presentation of Puerto Rican Youth, Northeast Regional Encuentro, 1974

While the median age of the U.S. Hispanic population is significantly lower than that of the population at large, effective ministerial initiatives among Latino youth (as well as among young people of other backgrounds) are rare. One noteworthy effort at Latino youth ministry was Naborí, a group of Puerto Rican university students influenced by Antonio Stevens-Arroyo in the 1970s. Representatives from this organization made the following presentation at the Northeast Regional Pastoral Encuentro held in November 1974 (Stevens-Arroyo 341).

Today, unfortunately, in spite of the great number of Hispano youth in our cities, their presence in the church is minimal. Even among those who go to church, there is a rapid and continuous drop off. We ask where the fault lies: is it that the community of the faithful has stopped being a visible witness or is it that the goings-on of the modern world do not let us hear the call? It is certain that once our youth leave the parochial school, once beyond childhood, adolescence, puberty — the enthusiasm also ends. Sometimes it seems that they forget God. Certainly this is not a local problem, nor a regional one: it is a universal phenomenon. But we live in this region of the Northeast of the United States and it is very important for us to face up to the situation in which we live to remedy it. Youth is the hope of the future. But if this youth does not return to the church, what church will be left for us tomorrow? For example, in the city of New York, half of the Puerto Rican population is nineteen years old or less. But, brothers and sisters, does our church dedicate half of its attention and its resources to us? Does the church commit half of its money for use in programs for us? Are our Hispano children, let alone half of them, admitted to Catholic schools, or to Catholic high schools? The answer to these questions is a firm "No!" We young people wish to share with you our Christian concern for the Christian development of Hispano youth in our region. But first we would like to introduce ourselves.

Some of us are university students and, as such, we know the problems of youth — our problems — by their scientific names. We suffer from social disintegration, from alienation, from exploitation, from a family structure that has been destroyed, etc. But we also know these sad realities because we have felt them in our own flesh. And so we prefer to speak of them in terminology common to everyone; we want to speak *tú a tú* [person to person] of our personal experiences.

I am a member of Naborí. Naborí is a Taíno name, from the tribes of the Indians of the Antilles; that is, of the islands of Boriké, Haití, and Cubanacán, today known as Puerto Rico, the Dominican Republic, and the Socialist Republic of Cuba. On these islands lived a class of Indians whose job was to be workers in the fields and — in moments of danger — to defend their homeland. To this class of Indians, a worker-warrior, was given the name "Naborí."

Recognizing our Taíno heritage and accepting the responsibility of struggling and working for our values, we have adopted this name. Naborí functions as a *comunidad de base* [base community]. Among its principal elements, we would like to point out the following ones to you.

1. We are a family, we love one another mutually, showing affection and interest in the needs, worries, and projects of the members of the group. We study and work together for the good of our community.

2. We have used group dynamics and psychological games to deepen our personal commitment.

3. In Naborí we are all Puerto Ricans. It is not our intention to look down on other nationalities, but we have thought that it was very important that the bonds that join us in this *comunidad de base* should be common to everyone by the similarity in our lived experience, in the ambient and the cultural background from which we come.

4. We are all of us poor, children of *jíbaros* [peasants], and we are proud of it. [*Applause.*] We do not feel ashamed at all of having been born outside of our land in poverty, because in like condition was born in Bethlehem the Child of Mary of Nazareth.

5. In Naborí, there is no distinction according to class. We are all equals. We have no president, no dues, nor do we look for prestige or privileges. Once we asked help from a parish and it was denied us. Instead they offered us basketball games and participation in bingo as the apostolic programs of the parish.

6. We study our culture and the history of our Puerto Rican people. We are interested in poetry, theater, literature, and music.

7. We try to keep abreast of all movements which are focused on the destiny of our people.

8. We share our ideas and even the little we have and seek to make life a little more friendly for all of us.

Naborí, presentation at Northeast Regional Encuentro, 1974, as cited in Antonio M. Stevens-Arroyo, *Prophets Denied Honor: An Anthology on the Hispano Church in the United States* (Maryknoll, N.Y.: Orbis Books, 1980), 342–43. Printed by permission.

68. A Laywoman Calls for Justice, Northeast Pastoral Region, 1976

Haydée Borges, a Puerto Rican Cursillo (see document 34b) leader from the New York area, expressed Hispanic laywomen's impatience with the triple oppression they experienced in the church as Hispanics, as women, and as laypersons in the following excerpt from an article in El Pueblo Pide, *the newsletter of Cristanos Hispano Americanos por Justicia (CHAPJ). The occasion for Borges's article was her criticism that women religious had excluded her and other laywomen from the planning process for a conference on Hispanic women in the northeast United States (Stevens-Arroyo 288–89).*

On May 5, 1976, the Regional Pastoral Center for Hispanos in the Northeast called a woman's meeting for a small group of ten lay and religious women involved in the Hispano apostolate. The director of the center wanted to hear the women's opinion about how to establish a communications network with all of the Northeast of the United States — something of great importance, since the church is made up of men and women, although men are always the ones who have a voice in what is going on. It is then a rare occasion when we women are asked for our opinion in order to form a more exact vision of what the church is. They asked us for written suggestions and said that these would be taken into consideration in the planning of a pastoral approach for the center. I personally sent my written suggestions, some of which are already being taken care of. For the second meeting, they asked each one of us to invite another person beside ourselves.

On June 9 we met again, the ten women, and talked about how to organize ourselves as women and as Northeast. We decided to continue meeting as a women's group at the regional center and thus offer our suggestions and ideas for the better operation of the center. On July 6, thirteen lay and religious women came to the monthly meeting and, with a lot of enthusiasm, agreed among ourselves to plan a conference on the Hispana woman of the Northeast. Each one of us agreed to do some "homework" with an eye to organizing the conference. It was agreed that the theme of the conference would be "The Ministries of the Woman in the Church," and the following topics would be treated, four topics by two key speakers: (1) Woman Historically, Considered in the Past (biblically, Mary) and the Present (Scripture); (2) The Pastoral Issue of Today (pastoral dynamics in small groups); (3) The Woman in the Apostolate Today (a panel for each need); and (4) Cultural and Religious Obstacles Which the Woman Faces in the Church (group dynamics).

Women from the Northeast were to be sought for the principal presentations. On September 8, 1976, another meeting was held where different laywomen from the grassroots were excluded for reasons that were scarcely convincing, and in that meeting three committees were formed: (1) Committee for the Program, on which there were only three religious and an American laywoman (who quit); (2) Publicity Committee, formed by three laywomen from Brooklyn and a sister; (3) Committee for Hospitality, formed by three religious women.

It is ironic to think that those left out were lay persons from New York! Those who were not informed of the meeting and thus were absent could join any of the committees. Now, in accord with parliamentary law, committees are named to plan and to study, but then their work should be presented to the whole assembly or group in order to be approved, with changes or additions. Here, the committees plan and it's done! What two or three say is the decision! A meeting was called for each group and only four persons came to continue what had not been either reviewed or approved by a majority. Although the presentations shall be those that the committee had prepared, what happens? Three or four people are making the plans for the conference and this is not democratic, since a conference of this kind in the Northeast should take grassroots laywomen into account, and not be planned only according to a vision seen from the ideas of three religious women. I think that the church is made up of religious men and women, lay persons and priests, etc.

Here can be very clearly seen the third-class role that is given to the woman who is not a member of any religious order. We are discriminated against, first because we are Hispanas, second for being women, and third for being lay persons who do not belong to any religious order. The religious woman — nun — lives a reality very different from ours since she has been lucky enough to get a good education with a great academic title. And, speaking of justice, this does not give them the right to speak for all women in the church, since they have to recognize that we nonreligious women live a very different reality. As a laywoman and as a leader, I ask that the voice of all the women in the church be heard. If we want unity, we should respect each other as true sisters, daughters of the same Father God, redeemed by one Lord, Jesus Christ. We don't want a conference where they tell us the problems to challenge us. But let our voice be heard with all united in love to help each other, to look upon ourselves as equals, the women of the church!

We women of the grassroots serve God by a divine vocation through our baptism, without any limitations or bonds to the structures that oppress and stifle the spirit. I, as a single laywoman committed completely to the service of the church, wish to publicly raise my voice from these pages of *El Pueblo Pide* since they don't pay any attention when you speak privately. Two years ago grassroots women asked for a movement of Hispana women in the church and nobody showed great interest in it. This conference offered great hope, but we see with great sadness that the conference — if it is carried out — will be a resounding failure, since they have not taken into account the grassroots women. In order to free others, we first have to be free ourselves from the bonds of selfishness and pride, from complexes of all kinds, and above all be free in Christ, who is the Truth and Justice for all....

As a free woman in Jesus, I speak out loud for the equality of rights of the woman in the church, and as a Christian I ask and demand that our dignity as daughters of God be respected in our diverse states — single women, married, widows, divorcees. We serve the total church — without pay — by vocation and love for God and neighbor, and as laywomen we carry the royal priesthood of Christ, consecrating our femininity day after day on the altars of service to the people of God — church — and in the church we work so that in this world there may be found peace, love, understanding, happiness, and, above all, sisterhood and justice for all — equally.

Haydée Borges, "The Voice of the Laywoman in the Church of the Northeast of the United States of America," *El Pueblo Pide,* December 1976, as translated and cited in Antonio M. Stevens-Arroyo, *Prophets Denied Honor: An Anthology on the Hispano Church in the United States* (Maryknoll, N.Y.: Orbis Books, 1980), 289–91. Printed by permission.

69. Bishop Patricio Flores's Address at the Segundo Encuentro, 1977

Patricio Flores was ordained for the diocese of Houston in 1956 and during the 1960s was instrumental in spreading the Cursillo (document 34b) throughout Texas (and beyond). On 5 May 1970, he became the first Chicano bishop in the United States; subsequently he served as an auxiliary bishop of San Antonio (1970–1978), the bishop of El Paso (1978–1979), and the archbishop of San Antonio (1979–present). His numerous accomplishments and contributions include the establishment of the National Hispanic Scholarship Fund and the leading role he played in founding organizations such as the Mexican American Cultural Center (document 66) and Communities Organized for Public Service (COPS) (McMurtrey). Flores's role as a prophetic spokesperson for Hispanic Catholics is illustrated in the following closing address he gave at the Segundo Encuentro Nacional Hispano de Pastoral (Second National Hispanic Pastoral Encounter) in Washington, D.C., during August 1977. This historic event was the second of three national Encuentros (others were held in 1972 and 1985) that gathered Hispanic Catholic leaders from across the United States (Davis 1995; Sandoval 1994: 141–46). As this book goes to press, Latinos are also playing a leading role in convening Encuentro 2000, a national gathering of the diverse ethnic and racial groups that comprise U.S. Catholicism.

This Second National Hispanic Pastoral Encuentro is a new sun which with its ray of light marks the beginning of a new age for all Hispanics in the United States. The fact that more than 800 of us from diverse backgrounds were able to gather in Washington, D.C., is in itself a notable accomplishment. In addition, the fact that more than 40 cardinals, archbishops, and bishops are here today marks this conference as a historic event in this country. That at present there are eight Hispanic bishops in the United States, and that all are present, is marvelous. That my brothers and sisters who toil in the fields are here side by side with the church hierarchy, with clergymen and religious, as well as with businessmen and professionals, marks the beginning of a new age.

Five years ago the First Encuentro was celebrated. On that occasion only 250 people participated in the proceedings. Only one Hispanic bishop was present. Only five archbishops and bishops attended. This year several thousand Hispanics wanted to attend. But due to the lack of lodgings we were obliged to limit the number of participants to 800.

In years past it had been said of the Hispanic people that it was a sleeping giant. Now no one believes that. We are a gigantic group, but we are not asleep. We are on our feet, we have begun our march toward assuming a position of leadership in our society, in our church, in our neighborhoods, in our places of employment, in politics, in education and in the defense of our homeland. In all places we are to be found with our arms open, ready to love, to serve and to share.

This community, which has been oppressed, excluded and discriminated against, harbors no ill will. It is eager to contribute even though that demands a great deal of sacrifice. It was very difficult for each of us to come here but we will go wherever the Lord bids us so as to share Christ's Gospel with others and to give assistance to our afflicted and oppressed brothers in their struggle toward self-betterment.

We are not an insecure people but rather one which possesses great strength. We are a young people filled with new life, with creativity and initiative. Our strength is not destructive, rather it is a force which has the capacity to give meaning and value to the life of this country and to the life of this church.

For more than 100 years we have suffered and we continue to suffer. This is a common bond which we all share — Puerto Ricans, Cubans, Central and South Americans, Mexicans, and Mexican Americans. We know that, in the end, good will spring from the evils which we have endured. We also believe that God is present among all who suffer. Slaves and oppressed persons will liberate themselves and in so doing will liberate their oppressors.

We have struggled against many forces so as to not lose our identity, our Spanish language, our sense of religion, our attitudes toward family, mothers and children, our customs, our social and religious traditions and practices. Our resistance to the "melting pot" philosophy has caused us much hardship. Since we have retained our identity, we are able to appreciate the values and mores of our brothers in the United States.

Without doubt we are the only oppressed people which has borne so much abuse and which has least resorted to violence, because violence is not a child of God. Vengeance is not ours, it is God's. In our efforts to eliminate oppression we do not want to become oppressors.

What we have accomplished is the source of our hope:

1. We have succeeded somewhat in improving the living conditions and salaries of farm workers and these will continue to improve.

2. Bilingual, bicultural education is a reality. Hispanics stand above all in their efforts to accomplish this.

3. By means of the Civil Rights Commission, MALDEF [Mexican American Legal Defense and Education Fund], Equal Opportunity Employment, etc., we had been able to destroy some of the barriers and to open some of the doors to opportunity.

4. The Voting Rights Act has recognized the fact that we had been excluded from exercising our right to vote. Thanks to Congressman Herman Badillo and other brave individuals who used their leadership to accomplish this goal, this legislation has been extended to almost all areas throughout the country where large numbers of Hispanics reside.

In the [past] we had neither voice nor power in civic or religious matters. However, in the last few years, we have had:

1. Two state governors;

2. Numerous small town mayors;

3. City councilmen;

4. Members of school boards;

5. State congressmen and senators, as well as judges on the state and local level;

6. Commissioner Leonel Castillo, the first Hispanic to be named as national director of I.N.S. (Immigration and Naturalization Service);

7. Eight Hispanic bishops, and a growing number of Hispanic priests and nuns; and

8. A national Secretariat for Hispanic Affairs with regional offices as well.

The major part of the growth of representation has taken place in the last eight or nine years. We are happy about what has been accomplished, but we are not satisfied!

We will continue our struggle in a peaceful and Christian manner, so as to obtain 25 times more representation and participation at all levels of life. The great deal which has been accomplished should neither confuse nor placate us. It should fill our hearts with hope. This hope will encourage our struggle that much more for the self-development of our Hispanic communities. Full of hope we should continue to be united in prayer and in our fight for the kingdom of God — so that that kingdom may be one of justice and peace for all. Fighting in unison, with a mature sense of responsibility, the seed of our hope will slowly emerge as a tangible reality. Our united struggle will give glory and praise to the God of all consolation and in this united brotherhood we will find the moral strength to continue our efficacious march forward. If up until now we have seen but a ray of light, we await that day in the near future when we will be allowed to see all the grandeur of the sun.

Patricio F. Flores, "A People Filled with Hope," in *Proceedings of the II Encuentro Nacional Hispano de Pastoral* (Washington, D.C.: United States Catholic Conference, 1978), 60–61. Printed with the permission of the United States Catholic Conference.

70. Essay on Mainland Puerto Ricans' Aspirations for the Island, 1979

In 1979 politicians in Puerto Rico proposed, as a political maneuver, a plebiscite to definitively decide the status of the island (commonwealth, statehood, or independence). Their proposal caused great uneasiness among mainland Puerto Ricans, since their identity as true Puerto Ricans depends to a great extent on Puerto Rico's ambiguous status as a U.S. possession that nonetheless maintains a national identity and consciousness. For many mainland Puerto Ricans, statehood would mean there was no such thing as a Puerto Rican nationality; independence would force them to choose between being Puerto Ricans and being "Americanos." Passionist priest Antonio Stevens-Arroyo, a young Philadelphia-born Puerto Rican leader, articulated some concerns of his compatriots on the mainland in an editorial that included the following excerpt. Stevens-Arroyo accentuated mainland Puerto Ricans' earnest desire to have a voice and a vote in the island's fate. He also underscored mainland Puerto

> Ricans' insistence that politicians in San Juan and Washington recognize the mainlanders' legitimate interest in the ultimate status of the island, which they still considered their country. The plebiscite, as usual, had no serious results, but the sentiments it provoked are a useful indicator of mainland Puerto Ricans' perception of their identity.

On the occasion of his recent visit to Poland, our Holy Father John Paul II pointed out that love of one's country is a Christian obligation, and that it infuses a prophetic vision into the field of politics. The Puerto Rican population of the United States — which at this point makes up 40% of the world's Puerto Ricans — is a living witness to how migrants are transformed into fervent apostles of patriotism. The example of our Polish pope is relevant to the heart of Puerto Ricans, since it appears that political forces within the island of Puerto Rico may drag our dear homeland into a definitive change in its political status [i.e., from commonwealth to statehood or independence].

It may be that 1980 will be to us what 1910 was to the Mexicans in Los Angeles or San Antonio, or what 1895 was to the Cubans in Tampa or New York. In the face of this challenge we must do some serious reflecting on the shared aspirations which unite us as a community with reference to the destiny of Puerto Rico.

In the first place, we do not want to be perceived as "Newyoricans" [New York Puerto Ricans] if that implies that we are second-class Puerto Ricans. Whatever changes in the status of the island may ensue, our love for that small island, the emerald of the Caribbean, will not change. We all want to be able to return, if only to visit and to be proud of belonging to Puerto Rico.

In the second place, any change in the island's status must respect the rights of the thousands of Puerto Ricans who still hold as a patrimony an acre or two of their native soil, and who hope to return there to build a modest home and live out their declining years. Since the progress of the island's economy was partly based on the circumstances that forced us to leave, we must be allowed some input in the solving of the problem of the island's status. The example of some emerging nations in the British Commonwealth, where emigrants were given a vote on the issue of their homeland's status, must be seriously considered. After all, let's not forget that those [resettled Anglo Americans and Cuban exiles] who now occupy our places in Puerto Rico are "foreigners" there and therefore will not be as genuinely Puerto Rican as we are — even if they live on the island and we do not.

In the third place, it is only fair that after so many years of work and service we should not lose our benefits — our social security, our pensions, and our veterans' benefits — no matter what changes may occur in the status of the island. Those who advocate a new relationship [between Puerto Rico and the United States] must also address these basic issues of "our daily bread."

In the fourth place, we look askance at the childish squabbles and divisiveness that reign in our island's political scene. It's time for that kind of thing to end. We have learned how power works, and the catty gossip and petty resentments that spread in the island's political scene are well beneath the dignity of our people. With regard to this last point, I feel there are a few things that have to be taken into serious consideration. (1) We don't want a Puerto Rico so impoverished that it will become the new version of a "Polish joke." To be classified as the most backward state in the Union, whatever material benefits this may bring, is to suffer an indignity and a shame. (2) We do not want to be stripped of the symbols that represent the best values of Puerto Rico: its flag, its music, its language, its customs, and its culture. (3) We don't want a civil war in which Puerto Ricans will shed each other's blood. (4) We don't want "another Hawaii, another Cambodia, another Northern Ireland" — one more banana republic. We want a new Puerto Rico.

> Antonio Stevens-Arroyo, "Siete aspiraciones de Puertorriqueños en los Estados Unidos," *El Visitante Dominical*, 29 July 1979. Trans. Jaime R. Vidal. Printed by permission.

71. In Defense of Cuban Prisoners in the Atlanta Federal Penitentiary, 1986

From March through May 1980, about 125,000 Cubans arrived in the United States after the Cuban government opened the port of Mariel, on Cuba's northern coast, for exiles wishing to pick up family members. As the boats arrived from Florida, Cuban authorities filled them with people who wanted to leave but also with others who were forcibly deported (Masud-Piloto 128–37). While most of these new arrivals integrated into life in the United States, a significant number were never released into the community because of criminal records or psychiatric problems. Many others who initially gained their freedom subsequently committed crimes, were arrested, and served prison terms, but under U.S. immigration law they remained in prison even after serving their time. Hoping to send these prisoners back to Cuba, the United States opened immigration talks with Cuban authorities in 1984. Subsequently Auxiliary Bishops Agustín Román of the Miami archdiocese and Enríque San Pedro, SJ (1926– 1994), of the Galveston-Houston diocese issued the following statement. As the only two Cuban exile bishops in the United States, they expressed their grave concerns about the government's handling of the prisoners' cases. Their concerns were well placed because the next year, after an agreement between U.S. and Cuban authorities resulted in the return of some imprisoned Cubans to the island, major prison rebellions erupted. Some twenty-seven hundred Cuban prisoners in two federal prisons rioted and initiated a standoff with federal officials. Bishop Román played a crucial role in negotiating a solution, convincing the prisoners to release their hostages and lay down their arms in return for a government promise to consider the prisoners' cases individually and ensure due process. Many of these prisoners continue detained (Hamm).

In Advent we celebrate another anniversary of the encyclical "Dives in Misericordia" ("On the Mercy of God"), in which the Holy Father John Paul II, wishing to show us how merciful our Father in heaven is, also teaches us the importance of mercy in matters of justice. In the light of this document and in the family atmosphere in which we gather to thank God for so many blessings, and as we prepare for celebrating Jesus' birth, let us examine our consciences and meditate on the situation of those members of our large Cuban family who are imprisoned in the federal penitentiary in Atlanta and in other federal prisons. They place their hope in the Church, as evidenced by the large number of letters that have been received and that we bishops, as well as priests, still receive every day. Letters full of sufferings reach us from different prisons, expressing the feelings and needs of those persons, some of whom have been incarcerated for more than six years and whose future grows more uncertain each day.

The majority of the prisoners in Atlanta and in other prisons arrived in this country with the massive immigration of 1980, when more than 125,000 Cubans left the island through the Mariel Port in search of freedom. The Cuban government, in its effort to conceal the damage to its image which that desperate exodus entailed, forced departures in small boats and deported, as if they were so many simple objects, hundreds of human beings suffering from mental illness as well as hundreds of persons who were serving their sentences in Cuban jails for common crimes. Thus did the Cuban government try to alter the reality of Mariel and discredit the exile from Cuba. The intended purpose was for the press around the world to report on the arrival of the "criminals from Mariel" and not on the failure of the communist totalitarian system which was the cause of the mass exodus.

We have witnessed how, in just a few short years, the great majority of the immigrants who left through Mariel have made a life for themselves, whether on their own or with the help of their family and friends, and are today productive members of our society. However, we cannot allow the success of the majority to make us forget the pain still felt by those forsaken few who have been classified as "undesirables" and remain in prison. Specifically, in April 1986 the Subcommittee on the Administration of Justice of the House Committee on the Judiciary identified 1,929 Cubans incarcerated in the federal penitentiary in Atlanta who are not serving criminal sentences. In spite of numerous appeals to appellate courts, these individuals remain in prison, without so much as the most elementary legal rights granted to them. The courts have ruled that, due to the fact that these people were never officially accepted in this country or else have violated the conditions of their parole, they are "excludable" and have no right to individual hearings with legal representation nor to many other rights which would be considered as elementary for persons who are legal residents of this country.

Among the Atlanta prisoners, at least four groups can be distinguished. The first one consists of those suffering from mental illness. The second group includes persons who were never granted entry permits to this country because they had committed serious crimes in Cuba. The third group is made up of those who, upon arrival, were granted parole and subsequently committed crimes in this country and have already served their sentences. Last, we have those who, having been granted parole upon arrival in this country, subsequently committed crimes here and are serving their sentences.

It is important to note that the first two groups did not come voluntarily, but were forced to board the ships by Cuban government officials, representatives of that same government which now denies their return.

The U.S. Congress has authority over the admitting of foreigners into this country. The federal judges have ruled that, under current laws, those who were never officially admitted to the country and are considered to be a threat to national security should be deported (and in cases when it is not possible, imprisoned). We have no quarrel with this argument. On the contrary, we would be greatly saddened if one of the prisoners who is not well enough to live freely in our society were prematurely set free, thus causing a mishap. However, the indiscriminate application of the law of exclusion as regards the Cuban prisoners in Atlanta results in a situation we cannot accept. The indefinite imprisonment of human beings who are not serving sentences due to crimes they have committed cannot be justified. Any person who, having undergone a fair trial, has been sentenced for a crime he committed, should serve his or her sentence. But it is a basic human right that after a man or woman has paid his or her debt to society, his or her freedom should be restored. We cannot accept that those persons who committed crimes in this country remain indefinitely imprisoned after serving their sentences. Yes, we know that technically the fact that they committed a crime after arriving in this country constitutes a violation of parole, thus making them subject to deportation. Such is the law. However, since deportation is not an alternative due to the fact that the Cuban government will not take them back, the application of the law in the case of Cuban prisoners results in indefinite imprisonment. This is not acceptable. It is obvious that the law does not contemplate a situation such as the present one. Therefore, this "legality" must give way to other alternatives that adhere more closely to reality and have a firm moral and humane basis.

Persons who have not been granted permission to enter the country are "excludable" and have no right under the law to individual hearings, legal representation, and many other proceedings which would be considered basic rights of any resident or citizen of this country. Again, the law does not conform to these persons' reality. Some have been incarcerated for many years and their legal situation does not seem any closer to being resolved than on the day they reached these shores. The Cubans in Atlanta are such a diverse group that each case must be analyzed in individual hearings, where each person would have the opportunity, with the help of the appropriate legal counsel, of stating his case in the most favorable way possible.

The mentally ill deserve to be looked upon with mercy and understanding. We cannot keep these people indefinitely in jails that are not equipped to help them with their problems. We understand that this represents the taking on of a great public burden by this country. But this burden, in the long run, shall be much lighter than the weight of the moral burden on our consciences that would come from an indefinite prolongation of the present situation. The whole world shall be able to contrast the cruelty of the Cuban government, which deposited these ill men and women on this country's shores, and the generosity of this country, which gives them adequate treatment, not because it has the obligation to do so, but because it is the correct and humane way to treat those ill individuals.

The cases of those who committed crimes in Cuba should be reviewed to determine if they were duly judged. We all know the characteristics of the Cuban judicial system.

Those who committed crimes in this country but who have already served their sentences should be freed if it is determined that they do not constitute a threat to our society.

Those who are still serving their sentences should do so in adequate facilities.

All of them should be provided participation in rehabilitation programs that would allow them to be reincorporated into our society. Let us not forget that within this mass of immigrants there were some who, victims of the moral relativism and the poor integral development that the totalitarian communist system favors, where human creativity is repressed to follow the dictates of only those in power, or who due to the lack of training on the part of relatives or institutions upon arriving in a free country where a foreign language is spoken, or simply due to their own mistakes, went astray. These people should be strengthened, giving them a moral base and principles that would allow them to recover their dignity as human beings and coexist in a free society.

The deportation of these persons is not a satisfactory solution to the problem. It has been seen that the Cuban government is not willing to have these Cubans return. We cannot have these people imprisoned indefinitely until the Cuban government changes its mind. Meanwhile, each day that goes by, these persons, still in jail, grow roots in this country. Many have their families here. Others have married here and have children from said marriages. For all these reasons, the intended deportation of these persons has never represented a solution — and it is even less so today — since it would imply a painful separation from the family.

We reiterate that we are not advocating the immediate release of all the Cubans imprisoned in Atlanta and in other prisons. We do not pretend to ignore the judicial system which governs. But we are asking, in keeping with the best tradition of this same judicial system, that all these prisoners be given the opportunity to be heard on an individual basis by the competent judicial officers so that the most just procedure may be established in each case, thus putting an end to the inhumane situation of uncertainty and indefinite incarceration.

It is proper that the church should intercede in favor of those who are most forsaken. From what institution other than the church of the God of Love, who is Christ, can these children of God expect support so that the uncharitable manner in which they are being treated may be corrected? From what other group of people can they expect understanding and help in recovering their dignity (and their freedom, when they so deserve it), if not from their countrymen who have known the uprooting and uncertainty which political exile entails? We cannot overlook the fact that an overwhelming majority of the prisoners are Roman Catholics by profession or culture, and that they look to the church as a source of hope.

Lastly, in remembrance of the fact that Mary, the mother of God, chose to talk to the people of Cuba through Our Lady of Charity, we wish to exhort everyone to practice that divine virtue of charity in serving the suffering

Christ who waits for us in expectation at the federal penitentiary in Atlanta and in other prisons. And let us do so not only with our prayers, which are a very important part of the solution to this whole sad situation, but also with our actions as citizens, working within the channels of the democratic government which rules in this nation blessed by God.

> Agustín A. Román and Enríque San Pedro, SJ, statement on Cuban exiles in federal penitentiaries, 21 December 1986 (typescript), Archdiocese of Miami Archives. Printed by permission.

72. Hispanic Deacons' Statement to Cardinal John O'Connor, New York, 1988

In August 1988 the Confraternidad de Diáconos Hispanos de la Arquidiócesis de Nueva York (Confraternity of the Hispanic Deacons of the Archdiocese of New York) protested changes that Cardinal John O'Connor (1920–2000) had recently mandated for diaconal ministry in the archdiocese. They particularly decried the abolition of a long-standing, Spanish-language diaconal training program that addressed the needs of the Latinos whom Hispanic deacons would predominantly serve. Other contested policy changes included a prohibition on permanent deacons' use of the Roman collar and a severe curtailment of the deacons' opportunities to vest and appear as a body for major liturgical events such as ordinations, the Chrism Mass, and the patronal celebrations of various Hispanic nations. No immediate action was taken on the confraternity's protest to the cardinal. However, when the single English-language program proved ineffective, Cardinal O'Connor reestablished the Hispanic training program, although many Hispanic leaders assert the restored program is merely a Spanish-language version of the English program and gives scant consideration to the different needs of Hispanics.

Hispanic deacons in their great majority come from this humble base [of society]. All of them identify themselves as true neighbors and friends of the laity. It is needless to mention the joy experienced by our Hispanic community as they saw some of their own being called to orders leading to a much desired *native* Hispanic clergy. At last the Hispanic community could provide its own ordained ministers. What a disappointment as they saw their "ordained" deacons reduced to function as altar boys in many parishes as preference was given to extraordinary ministers of the Eucharist and other lay ministers or as priests took over diaconal functions in the presence of deacons.

To make things worse, by recent mandate, we have now been ordered out of the sanctuary, out of our liturgical vesture, and physically removed from the body of the clergy. We are indeed clerics incardinated in this archdiocese (canon 266), the symbols removed and others substituted, change the reality, our being; as Hispanics they effectively remove us from the native clergy in the eyes of our people....

For us Hispanics the symbol of attending as a body is an essential one. Hispanics view life in symbolic rather than abstract terms, and the ordination of neighbors and fellow workers to the ministry of Word and Sacrament is a powerful symbol of their own worth and validity "in medio Ecclesiae" [in the midst of the Church]. When these ordained ministers are ejected from the sanctuary and told to dress like the laity and sit among the laity, this too is a powerful symbol — but a powerful *negative* symbol. It may not mean to tell them, but it *does* effectively tell them that "you do not belong with us," and to the Hispanic deacons in particular, "you are not *really* clergy but only glorified lay ministers." No amount of *verbal* explanation will undo the damage of this negative symbol, because Hispanics do not take words seriously when behavior, and especially symbolic behavior, goes counter to the words being said. . . .

Another area of grave concern lies with the changes in the formation program for Hispanic permanent deacons. At the precise time when other dioceses are establishing diaconate programs in the Spanish language and have requested from New York Hispanic deacons copies of their Spanish program, our Hispanic candidates to the diaconate are now asked to be literate in English so that they may study in English with the native speakers, as the Spanish program has now been absorbed by the English program. Unless these candidates come from the more advantaged and academically oriented Hispanic classes, which our church hardly reaches, the good candidates that come from our parishes will never be able to get through the program. One thing is to be able to communicate in English and another is to read books and attend classes, much less write papers and take examinations in English. Classes in English have been tried before, ending in failure.

As the tides of immigration continue to arrive, Spanish is here to stay; it cannot be wished away. It is a fact that demands action from our part for, as younger generations learn English, the adults remain monolingual in Spanish and the new arrivals are overwhelmingly Spanish speakers: their spiritual needs must be met in Spanish. The diaconate, coming from the same social strata, can minister to them even in ways the priests cannot. But in order to do so we need Spanish-speaking, Spanish-trained deacons.

The new program does not take into account our culture, our liturgy, our tradition and values; it can only produce infertile and confused hybrids with serious identity problems. This program does not take into account that our deacons have to counteract sectarian proselytism where trinitarian, christological, as well as ecclesiological issues are central. While an English-speaking deacon may not need to know what Arianism is, a Hispanic confronts it on a daily basis in the Jehovah's Witnesses. Need we say anything about the divine maternity of the Blessed Virgin Mary? How are our deacons going to deal with *santería* [a religion of African roots that draws from Christian traditions] and Spiritism? Further, how can our deacons speak, teach, argue, or preach without the facile use of theological, biblical, and ecclesial vocabulary in Spanish? This vocabulary cannot be given through a program in English. In fact, the burden of having to study in English spells the end of the Hispanic diaconate in the church of New York.

Confraternidad de Diáconos Hispanos de la Arquidiócesis de Nueva York, statement to Cardinal John O'Connor, 15 August 1988, photocopy from personal archives of Jaime R. Vidal. Printed by permission.

73. Bishop Zavala's Address on Proposition 187, Los Angeles, 1994

While still an infant, Mexican-born Gabino Zavala came to the United States with his family after a tragic Tijuana fire took the lives of his father and a sister. His widowed mother raised her remaining five children in southern California. He delivered the following address to the Los Angeles County School Board on 18 August 1994, shortly after his ordination as auxiliary bishop for the Los Angeles archdiocese. Despite the strong opposition of Zavala and other church and civic leaders, Proposition 187 passed by a wide margin. This controversial proposition denies public education and medical care to undocumented immigrants and their families; its passage sparked an ongoing series of court battles regarding its constitutionality and galvanized Latino immigrants to apply for citizenship and become active as voters.

Good afternoon! Thank you for inviting me to share my thoughts on Proposition 187, otherwise known as SOS or Save Our State. I hasten to add that the slightest notion of even entertaining this motion for legislation indicates that our state is in need of salvation. However, not of the makings proposed here.

I accepted your invitation because of my deep convictions that the proposed initiative is unconscionable. I stand before you not as a bishop, a priest or even a Catholic, but as a human being who is experiencing deep moral outrage and a sense of profound disappointment in the ways we choose to address societal ills. The attitude and stance which chooses to "blame the victim" again prevails. The creation of a subculture which thrives on suspicion and uses public service personnel as "watchdogs" is cloaking discrimination (in what amounts to blatant racism) on the basis of color, by the abuse of the legal system.

I stand before you as a man who values human life and human rights. Every person despite status — legal, documented/undocumented, immigrant/citizen — deserves dignity and respect. Every person has the right to food, shelter, education, employment, and health care.

I stand before you as an American, a person who embraces a Constitution that guarantees life, liberty, and the pursuit of happiness, as minimal in terms of rights and freedoms, and excludes no one, but thrives on generations of immigrant peoples to give this document credibility and make this democratic nation a reality. A nation that extends an invitation to the poor, the tired, the huddled masses, a welcome that is inscribed on the monument to our liberty and immigration status. A welcome that, as far as I am aware of, has not been rescinded.

I stand before you as a man of principle and intelligence, one who cannot turn from the truth. The truth of this situation is that Proposition 187 is a reactionary document. It is a response to a growing anger and frustration over the state's economic woes, and its over-taxed service programs and population. In truth, given the present social/economic environment of California, legislation of this nature is not an honest or appropriate response to the situation. It is a reaction to fear.

I stand before you as the youngest son of an immigrant widow — a woman who raised and educated five children, who struggled to feed, house and clothe them — to provide them with a solid moral base and a healthy sense of self. Each of these five children and their children have contributed to society here. Each has enhanced the common good. I am the product of an immigrant's hope and an immigrant's dream.

What is so particularly reprehensible about this bill is that it targets the powerless, children, those who are ill or differently abled. It robs human beings of hope, the opportunity to make a difference and a contribution. It reduces those of us committed to human services to being screening agents — a far cry from what we ever desired. It creates an atmosphere of fear and suspicion in every essential element of life, and we all know what fear does to the human psyche and spirit — it is a death knell.

I am a Catholic, a universal Christian man, and I am a bishop, a leader in the Catholic church community. I oppose this proposition for all the above reasons and for one more — the greatest. It is against the law of God. From my faith tradition, rooted in the Judeo-Christian code of ethics, it is imperative that the "alien, the widow, and the orphan" be cared for and treated justly, and that we love as God has loved us, welcoming all as brother and sister. This proposition leaves none who uphold this faith tradition free to live "rightly" before their God.

I commend you on your motion of July 18th and support the passage of your resolution to oppose the SOS initiative. I did not cite the adverse effects of Proposition 187 in my comments. You noted them well in your resolution. Each system in our society, health, social welfare, and legal as well, will experience similar adverse effects if this proposition is enacted into law — not to mention the backlog of lawsuits for wrongful questioning of status that will more than likely begin to appear, as well as the proposition's lack of constitutionality.

Gabino Zavala, address to the Los Angeles County School Board, 18 August 1994, personal files of Gabino Zavala, Irwindale, Calif. Printed by permission.

University students discuss Latino spirituality with theologian Virgilio Elizondo (document 75) at Loyola Marymount University, Los Angeles, April 2000. Courtesy Cecilia González-Andrieu.

Part 6

CONTEMPORARY
THEOLOGICAL VOICES

Latinos, *nosotros*, vivimos sobre un puente que se extiende entre dos mundos: el
    de ellos y el nuestro.
Y el dolor nos llena al acercarnos más a un lado y apartarnos del otro,
porque al caminar, tenemos que cortar los hilos antiguos
que unen estos dos mundos en nosotros.
Sabemos en nuestras entrañas, que caminar hacia un lado del puente es
    imposible,
y al mismo tiempo quedarnos del otro lado traería nuestra muerte.
Porque el mundo que vemos a nuestros pies ya no es un mundo sin
    conquistadores
y el otro lado del puente solo nos ofrece una vida sin poetas,
sin *nicahuman* y las canciones de amor de nuestra cultura.

Pero desde aquí, podemos ver el panorama distante, y el paisaje....

Latinos, *nosotros,* live on the suspension bridge of two realities; theirs and ours.
It is painful to come to either end of the bridge,
because in that journey, we must sever the already frayed strands of rope
which have kept our two worlds together for so long.
We know in our hearts that going to one end of the bridge is impossible,
while remaining on the other is certain annihilation.
For the world at our feet is no longer a place without conquerors
and the end of the bridge means living in a world without the poets,
without *nicahuman* and the love songs of our culture.
Yet from this vantage point, we can see the distant panorama, the landscape....

> José Roberto Gutiérrez, "A Journey of Faith, a Search for Dignity," presentation
> given at Fordham University, New York, 1992. Trans. Cecilia González-Andrieu.
> Printed by permission.

Introduction

Latina and Latino Catholics have engaged in profound reflection on and analysis of their faith experience for generations. The documents in this book
reveal some of this rich theological tradition as expressed in diverse sources
like rituals and devotions, sermons, letters, petitions, speeches, editorials, testimonials, and prayers. However, only over the past three decades have U.S.
Hispanics produced a body of published theological literature. These writings

of U.S. Latino theologians reveal significant insights for the study of Latino Catholic identities.

Like the expanded Latino struggle for justice over the past three decades examined in the previous chapter, various social forces facilitated the emergence of Latino theologies. Vatican II and subsequent papal teaching, especially the call for theological reflection adapted to particular local contexts in documents like the conciliar decree *Ad gentes* (1965) and Paul VI's *Evangelii nuntiandi* (1975), provided impetus and official support for the work of Hispanic theologians. The growing number of university-educated Hispanics and the noteworthy population increase among Latinos generally enhanced the pool of potential theologians and accentuated the need for a theology that addressed Hispanic faith expressions and pastoral needs. Additionally, Latin American liberation theology inspired many Hispanic theologians in their work, although from early on Latino theologians in the United States recognized they had to develop an original theology grounded in their unique historical experience and social reality (Deck; Medina 1994: 10–13).

The spark that ignited a theological movement and new school of thought to emerge from these conducive historical conditions was the groundbreaking work of Virgilio Elizondo (see documents 66, 75), who published his first essay from a distinctly Mexican American perspective in 1972 (Elizondo 2000: 58–61). In the years that followed, both Protestant and Catholic Hispanic colleagues joined Elizondo in a collaborative effort to construct theologies from a U.S. Latino perspective, most notably Justo González, a Cuban Methodist leader in theological education who has been the most prolific writer among Latino theologians. By the end of the 1980s, the number of Hispanic Catholic theologians was sufficient for them to form their own professional association. Led by Arturo Bañuelas and Allan Figueroa Deck, both noted theologians and widely recognized analysts and practitioners of Hispanic ministry, in 1988 U.S. Hispanic theologians formed the Academy of Catholic Hispanic Theologians of the United States (ACHTUS). The following summer, they convened the organization's first annual meeting. While ecumenical both in its membership and its mission, ACHTUS is largely a Hispanic Catholic organization that provides a forum for professional Hispanic theologians to develop their ideas and projects (Deck xxi–xxiv). In 1993, ACHTUS leader Orlando Espín led the academy's initiative to establish the quarterly *Journal of Hispanic/Latino Theology*. Since its inception the journal has enhanced scholarly, ecumenical, and interdisciplinary exchange on topics pertinent to U.S. Latino theology, as well as promoted "the Latino/Hispanic struggle for justice" (Espín 4). The *Journal of Hispanic/Latino Theology*, its Hispanic Protestant counterpart *Apuntes* (begun in 1981), and the dramatic increase in books and articles that Latina and Latino theologians publish in a wide variety of venues have provided a major new voice and perspective in the theological landscape of the United States and beyond.

Latino theologies are by no means univocal and monolithic, thus the use of the plural form theolog*ies* in this chapter. However, Latina and Latino writers have noted several common themes and issues in Hispanic theological works, such as conquest, *mestizaje* (the mixing of cultures), the engagement of popular Hispanic expressions of faith as a primary source for theology, cultural analysis, and, particularly in the work of Hispanic women theologians, a concomitant attention to gender and class analysis. Moreover, Latinas and Latinos articulate passionate, advocacy theologies that are linked to Hispanic communities' faith-filled struggles for survival, life, justice, and liberation (Bañuelas 72–80; Deck ix–xxi; Fernández 2000; Medina 1994: 13–31).

For the purposes of this study on Latino Catholic identities, one further salient feature of Hispanic theologians and their writings is particularly important: the tendency for these thinkers to critically engage their personal histories as well as the communal history of Hispanic groups in the United States. The five documents that follow, for example, successively mirror the major historical experiences and topics explored in this volume's previous five parts: the legacy of Spanish colonization, the enduring faith of conquered Hispanic Catholics in the Southwest, immigration, exile, and the struggle for justice. In their reflections on these respective topics, each author uncovers significant insights on theological issues and themes such as conversion, Christology, devotional traditions, and the prophetic demand for justice. Together these select writings illustrate contemporary Latina and Latino theologians' conscious attempt to develop their work from a specified social location and lived experience such as that of *mestizaje,* the "diaspora" of exile, or the *mujerista* (Hispanic women's) struggle for liberation. These and other writings of Hispanic theologians encompass an implicit (and often explicit) critique of Euro-American theologians who ignore the particular context out of which their theology arises and uncritically presume their work is "objective" and therefore normative for all. Most importantly for this study, the documents that follow illuminate the fascinating scholarly and pastoral contribution that has emerged out of Hispanic theologians' efforts to critically assess their personal and collective histories and articulate their sense of identity.

74. Conversion: Embracing an Indigenous Heritage

Alvaro Dávila left his native Guatemala in 1981 and lived in Honduras and El Salvador until 1983, when he resettled in Chicago. He has served as associate director of the Chicago archdiocese's Instituto de Liderazgo Pastoral and as a pastoral associate at Nuestra Señora de la Merced (Our Lady of Mercy) parish. Currently he is the domestic violence project coordinator at the Counseling Center of Lake View, as well as the director of religious education at St. Francis of Assisi parish, where his primary work is family-based catechesis. He is also pursuing a master's degree at Catholic Theological Union and is a frequent lecturer and animator of Hispanic ministry groups. The following passage, an excerpt from Dávila's contribution for a book on Latino spirituality, reveals his profound theological reflection on conversion in light of his struggle to appreciate and embrace his indigenous roots.

I never had to read *Popol Vuh* (the holy book of the Mayas) as part of my education. This would have helped me to understand better why I eat so many tortillas, corn stew, tamales, and corn drinks. Who knows, I might have even considered becoming a farmer and learned to respect mother nature. But instead I had to eat ham sandwiches in school to be considered "normal." Only the rejected, the poor, the Indian, or the lowly, as we tend to describe them, eat tortillas and beans.

Now that I remember, it brings tears to my eyes when I hear my mother, with her immense unconditional love, telling me so often not to say that she was my mother, so that I wouldn't feel tied to a "peasant reality," which in the capital city would only serve to make me part of a rejected heritage and which would prevent me from advancing "in the civilized world of the Ladinos [mixed-blood or Hispanicized indigenous Guatemalans]." In fact, I even learned to insult others by saying, "You look like an Indian."

I remember the tears in my father's eyes when I took down all his photos from his living room wall and put them in a box sealed with tape and tied with twine, as if to make sure that they wouldn't get out. I was ashamed of them when my school friends came to visit me. Those time-yellowed photographs reflect the little that my father knows of his history. They show the faces of the people who helped my father and the efforts that he had made to "get ahead" in his life. They speak of the suffering of being orphaned, but also of the joys and the pride of being father of a family of nine. Today my father has those same photos on the walls of his room. Every time I go home those pictures remind me of what I did.

Mine is a history of constant denial of what I am, a *mestizo* [mixed blood] with a beard, the product of a raped Indian culture who has had to spend most of his life denying who he is. Finally, after being confronted, I have begun to recognize the identity that "Tata Chus" (Father of Jesus) gave me.

My background has helped me to learn to value what we often deny. I remember that when I arrived in the United States and I began to wash dishes, I felt so happy the first day because I was working. But as the days went by, it became depressing to realize that this was what I would do for the rest of my life. But what else could I do? I came to this country to work.

Then, after my first week of work, they couldn't pay me because they didn't have my Social Security number to make out the check. In my naïveté I told them: "Just make out the check to my name and that's enough." They responded: "Don't be a . . . it's not your name we care about, but your number." How sad, I said to myself! In order to be someone in life it is not enough just to quit being rural, to stop eating beans, to have no mother, but now not even my name mattered. I could go by any name, since it no longer made any difference.

In the midst of all this rejection something happened. It was during Advent in 1986 in our parish (Nuestra Señora de la Merced in Chicago). We were invited those four Sundays to wear the typical clothing of our countries. It was something very colorful, wonderful, and joyful to see a whole world of people arrive each Sunday who were celebrating their life with their colors, their clothing, and the fragrance that those give off, and all of it in the name of the God who gave us that life, that face, that fragrance, and that color.

Suddenly, just like when children discover their shadows and see themselves without realizing that it is them, I asked myself two questions. First, on this occasion not only the children dressed in their special clothing, but so did the adults. That didn't happen in our native countries. We had never wanted to be indigenous people. The only time indigenous dress was allowed during the religious celebration of the town was for the festivals of the Virgin of Guadalupe, for which the boys and girls dressed as "little Indians," but the adults never dressed up. What was happening here, I asked myself? We were celebrating what we had rejected our entire lives. How is that possible?

A second and more profound question occurred to me later. I started thinking that my people, when they came to this country, brought with them those indigenous things that they had rejected for generations. It didn't matter how many rivers we had to cross; it didn't matter that we had never worn them; it didn't matter that we might never wear them. Nevertheless we brought them with us and we hung them up on the walls of our homes, and we gave them to our new neighbors in other countries as a sign of our love for them. How can it be that we would bring that which we rejected, I asked myself? My answer was laughter, pleasure, and also anxiety. I trembled because I saw my children dressed up like "Tona," the Indian woman who used to sell me corn drink every day. I trembled because I didn't know what was happening.

Years after that experience I realize that our life, along with our language, with our medicinal plants, with our good customs, with its beautiful and rich culture, this life is good enough to enable us to be in harmony with God and with God's creation. Today I have learned to be free. Today I have learned to be spiritual because I have reconnected with my roots, with the source of my life. Today I have a clearer idea of where I'm going. Today I have learned to call myself a child of God. Today I have learned to see God in my brothers and sisters and, although I don't wear a hat with which I could greet people respectfully as my father does, I have learned to stand up and give them my hand.

That's why when I was asked to write my experience of spirituality as a Latin American man, as the Christian I profess to be, the word "conversion" came to mind. Conversion to what, I asked myself? Well, being a man I was told that I would be the provider for a family and for that reason I had to go to school and educate myself and learn. For that reason I do believe that to speak of the spirituality of the Latin American male is also to speak of conversion. The only difference is that this time we are talking about a conversion to recognize ourselves as God made us.

Alvaro Dávila, "Re-discovering My Spiritual History: Exodus and Exile," in Arturo Pérez, Consuelo Covarrubias, and Edward Foley, eds., *Así es: Stories of Hispanic Spirituality* (Collegeville, Minn.: Liturgical Press, 1994), 89–92. Printed by permission.

75. A Galilean Christology: *Mestizaje* and the New Humanity

Virgilio Elizondo is internationally known as a writer, speaker, and pastor, particularly for his visionary work on the Mexican American religious experience. A Mexican American native of San Antonio and a priest of the San Antonio archdiocese, his numerous leadership positions include his service from 1972 to 1987 as the founding president of the Mexican American Cultural Center (see document 66) and his tenure as rector of San Fernando Cathedral (see documents 4, 43) from 1983 to 1995. Currently he is director of the San Antonio archdiocesan television ministry. As the following selection illustrates, Elizondo consistently enjoins his fellow mestizos not to identify themselves in a negative way as "not Mexican" or "not American" but to claim the positive identity of mestizos who, despite frequent experiences of rejection, have the advantage of knowing two (or more) cultures. Drawing on his fascinating insights about Jesus' Galilean identity, Elizondo insists that a mestizo identity entails a calling and mission; despite the pain of rejection, those who know multiple cultures can lead others in building a "new humanity" that transcends the divisive barriers between peoples (Elizondo 1983, 1988, 1997a, 2000).

During my boyhood days there were no questions whatsoever about my identity or belonging. We grew up at home wherever we went — playgrounds, school, church. The whole atmosphere was Mexican and there was no doubt in our minds about the pride of being Mexican. Radio stations provided us with good Mexican music and the local Mexican theaters kept us in contact with the dances, folklore, romance, and daily life of Mexico. The poverty of Mexico, which was always evident in the movies, was completely surpassed by the natural simplicity, ingenuity, graciousness, and joy of the Mexican people. The United States was so efficient, but Mexico was so human. The contrasts were clear. We might be living outside the political boundaries of Mexico, but Mexico was not outside of us. We continued to interiorize it with great pride.

Como México no hay dos — there is nothing else like Mexico. Being Mexican was the greatest gift of God's grace. We loved it, lived it, and celebrated it. In many ways, we felt sorry for the people who were not so lucky as to be Mexican. In those early years I never thought of myself as a native-born U.S. citizen of Mexican descent. My U.S. identity was quite secondary to my Mexican identity. Yet I was happy living in the United States. We belonged to this land called the United States and this land belonged to us. In those early days, I never experienced being Mexican as not belonging. This was my home. I was born here and I belonged here.

Little did I think in those early years that the foundations of a new identity were already being formed within me. I was living a new identity that had not yet been defined and that would take many years to emerge. The new identity was beginning to emerge, not as a theory of evolution or as a political ideology of one type or another. It was rather a life lived not just by me, but by thousands of others who were living a similar experience. We were the first of the new human group that was beginning to emerge.

The paradise existence of the neighborhood came to a halt the first day I went to a Catholic grade school operated by German nuns in what had been a German parish. There the pastor still told Mexicans to go away because it wasn't their church. My parents had sent me there because it was the nearest Catholic school. Mexicans were tolerated but not very welcome.

The next few years would be a real purgatory. The new language was completely foreign to me and everything was strange. The food in the cafeteria was horrible — sauerkraut and other foods that I only remember as weird. We were not allowed to speak Spanish and were punished when we got caught doing so. The sisters and lay teachers were strict disciplinarians. I don't think I ever saw them smile but I remember well them hitting us frequently with a ruler or a stick. They were the exact opposite of the Mexican sisters around our home who were always happy, joking, and smiling and formed us carefully through counsels, suggestions, and rewards. In one system we were punished for bad things we did while in the other we were rewarded for our good accomplishments.

Mass was so different. Everything was orderly and stern. People seemed to be in pain and even afraid of being there. It was a church of discipline, but it was not one of joy. In fact, joy seemed to be out of place. Mass was recited, not celebrated. People went because they had to, not because they wanted to. It seemed like a totally different religion.

It was hard going to school in a language that was almost completely unknown and in surroundings that were so foreign and alienating. Things did not make sense. I used to get very bored. The school hours seemed eternal; the clock appeared not even to move during those horribly unintelligible hours. My parents had to force me to study and it was very difficult for me even to make passing grades. Going to school was so different that it was like crossing the border every day, like going to another country to go to school, even though it was only a few blocks from our home.

It was during these days that I first started to get a feeling of being a foreigner in the very country in which I had been born and raised. Guilt started to develop within me: why wasn't I like the other children who spoke English and ate sandwiches rather than *tortillas*? I started to feel different and mixed-up about who I was. But the mixture and the bad feelings came to a quick end every day at three o'clock when school was dismissed and I returned home. It was the beginning of life in two countries that were worlds apart.

I wanted to become what I felt I had to be, for it was my parents, whose authority and wisdom I never questioned, who had sent me to that school. Yet it meant not so much developing myself as ceasing to be who I was in order to become another person. Those three years in primary school were awful. I was afraid to mix with the kids and often felt better going off by myself. The teachers were constantly getting after me for daydreaming. That was my natural escape mechanism or, better yet, my instinct to survive. The dreams were my spontaneous efforts to create an existence of my own, thus refusing to accept the existence that was being imposed on me.

As I look into the past and try to understand it from my present perspective many years later, I re-experience the original pain, sadness, embarrassment, ambiguity, frustration, and the sense of seeking refuge by being alone. Yet I can also see that it was already the beginning of the formation of the consciousness of a new existence — of a new *mestizaje* ("the process through which two totally different peoples mix biologically and culturally so that a new people begins to emerge"). The daily border crossing was having its effect on me. I didn't know what it meant. I didn't even know why it had to be. But that constant crossing became the most ordinary thing in my life. In spite of the contradictions at school, there was never any serious doubt in my mind that my original home experience in a Mexican neighborhood was the core of my existence and identity; there my belonging was never questioned. There I did not seek to go off by myself but was developing into quite an outgoing person....

Yet this certitude of being Mexican began to be questioned whenever we visited our relatives in Mexico. Even though they loved us and we loved to visit them, in many ways they would let us know that we were *pochos* — Mexicans from the United States. To this day, it is not uncommon to hear someone in Mexico say about a Mexican American's Spanish, "For a *norteamericano*, your Spanish is not so bad." Yet it is not uncommon for an Anglo American from the United States to say about a Mexican American speaking perfect English, "For a Mexican American your English is pretty good." Whether in Mexico or the United States we are always the distant and different "other." The core of our existence is to be "other" or to "not be" in relation to those who are. Yet being called *pocho* in Mexico was not insulting, for we were fully accepted. There was always rejoicing when our families visited us in San Antonio or when we visited them in Mexico. *Pocho* was simply a reality. Even though the United States was our home, it was in Mexico that we felt more and more at home. The label marked distance and difference but not separation or rejection.

This was an experience totally different from being called "Meskins," "Greasers," or "wetbacks" in the United States. The titles were used to remind us that we were different — meaning that we were backward, ignorant, inferior, scum. We were not wanted in the United States, merely tolerated and exploited. Our people were consistently subjected to multiple injustices. The movies depicted us as treacherous bandits or drunken fools and our women as wanting nothing better in life than to go to bed with one of the white masters. Anglo-American society had no doubts that it alone was the Master Race! Indians, Mexican "half-breeds," and Blacks were inferior and therefore to be kept down for the good of humanity....

The Galilean identity of Jesus and of his first followers is one of the constants of the New Testament. As I started exploring the socio-cultural imagery of Galilee I became more intrigued. It was a borderland, the great border region between the Greeks and the Jews of Judea. People of all nationalities came along the caravan routes on their way to and from Egypt. There was abundant agriculture and commerce and a flourishing Greek society. The Jews were in the minority and were forced to mix with their Gentile neighbors. It was a land of great mixture and of an ongoing *mestizaje* — similar to our own

Southwest of the United States. The Galilean Jews spoke with a very marked accent and most likely mixed their language quite readily with the Greek of the dominant culture and the Latin of the Roman Empire. Peter could deny Jesus, but there was no way he could deny he was a Galilean. The moment he opened his mouth he revealed his Galilean identity.

The more I discovered about Galilee, the more I felt at home there and the more Jesus truly became my flesh-and-blood brother. He was not just a religious icon, but a living partner in the human struggle for life. He too had lived the experience of human distance and ridicule. Being a Jew in Galilee was very much like being a Mexican American in Texas. As the Jews in Galilee were too Jewish to be accepted by the Gentile population and too contaminated with pagan ways to be accepted by the pure-minded Jews of Jerusalem, so have the Mexican Americans in the Southwest been rejected by two groups....

In his *mestizo* existence Jesus breaks the barriers of separation, as does every *mestizo*, and already begins to live a new unity. That is both the threat and the greatness of a *mestizo* existence. *Mestizos* may struggle to become one or the other of the great traditions out of which they are born, but even if they were to succeed, that would be a mere return to the previous divisions of society. We usher in new life for the betterment of everyone when we freely and consciously assume the great traditions flowing through our veins and transcend them, not by denying either but by synthesizing them into something new.

The *mestizo* is the biblical stone, rejected by the builders of this world, that God has chosen to be the cornerstone of a new creation, not chosen for honor and privilege, but for a sacred mission. Having been marginated and misunderstood, we know the suffering of separation by our own experiences; we know that this type of existence is wrong and it must change. But change does not mean that we now take over and impose our ways upon all. This would simply be a new conquest, a new domination, and nothing would really change. The *mestizo* affirms both the identities received while offering something new to both. Being an insider-outsider and an outsider-insider to two worlds at the same time, we have the unique privilege of seeing and appreciating both worlds. It is from this position that we begin to combine the elements of both to form something new.

In the *mestizaje* and mission of Jesus our own *mestizaje* is transformed and redeemed. What appears to be a curse to some now appears for what it truly is — a blessing. What humanly speaking is the basis of margination and rejection is now discovered to be the basis of divine election. What appeared to be at the furthest outposts of the frontiers of nationality and race, now is recognized as the cradle of a new humanity.

Virgilio Elizondo, *The Future Is Mestizo: Life Where Cultures Meet* (Bloomington, Ind.: Meyer Stone, 1988; reprint, San Antonio: Mexican American Cultural Center Press, 1998), 12–17, 20–21, 76–77, 84–85. Printed by permission.

76. Immigrant Traditions: The Religion of the Mountains on Fifth Avenue

Ana María Díaz-Stevens (née Díaz-Ramírez) was born in Moca, Puerto Rico; at the age of eleven she moved with her family to New York. As a young woman she joined the Maryknoll sisters, but left before final vows because of an illness; later on she joined the Puerto Rican congregation of the Hermanas Dominicas de Fátima. After four years of ministry in the Puerto Rican countryside she left in order to care for her ailing parents. Subsequently she worked as administrative coordinator of the Office for the Spanish-Speaking Apostolate of the New York Archdiocese and at the Board of Global Ministries of the United Methodist Church. She also attended City College, New York University, and Fordham University, where she earned a Ph.D. in sociology. Díaz-Stevens has taught at Fordham and Rutgers Universities and currently is a full professor in the Department of Church and Society at Union Theological Seminary. In the following passage, she relates her childhood experience in the rural world of a devout Puerto Rican family and compares that experience to her adult life in the urban setting of New York and its archdiocese (Díaz-Stevens 1993a; Díaz-Stevens and Stevens-Arroyo 1994, 1998).

Religion in that mountain town of my childhood was part of daily life despite the fact that some of us saw the priest and visited the town church sparingly. The day would always begin with my mother opening up the windows and doors and proclaiming: "May God's grace enter upon this house and those therein and may it remain with us always." When we left home to help in the fields or to go to school, we always asked for a blessing from our parents. The same was done upon returning. Passing a place marked with a cross, we knew someone had met an untimely death there; we said a quick prayer for the repose of that person's soul. And, upon entering a crossway we remembered the agony of Jesus on the cross and the souls in purgatory. A statue or an icon of the Blessed Mother made the rounds to the dwellings of the mountain town, where it was kept overnight. There was a prayer to greet the statue and a prayer to take leave of it. We prayed the holy rosary promptly after sunset every night, and no one in the family was excused from this obligation. On special feast days like *la Candelaria*, or Candlemas day, each family prepared bonfires, which were set ablaze at sunset. The families got together to recite the rosary, sing hymns, and tell stories of bygone days. All Souls' Day was a time for pranks but also for prayer for the departed souls of relatives, friends, and neighbors. On the feast of St. John the Baptist, the patron saint of the island, everyone made a special effort to go to church and then to the closest town near the ocean to take the ritual baths. Oftentimes modesty only allowed walking, fully dressed, knee-high into the water and sprinkling the face and arms. People believed that because on that day Jesus was baptized in the River Jordan, all the waters, especially ocean waters, were blessed. There was a prayer for every hour of need: when you left the house, when you returned, when it rained too much, when it would not rain enough, for the living, for the dying, for the dead, to find a good husband, to straighten out the one you already had, to be blessed with a child, to stop having so many, and so on.

Holy Week was a time of penance. No one was allowed to sing, dance, shout, do unnecessary work, or make noise. It was a time of prayer and recollection. My father would bring out one of our most precious possessions, the old *Camino recto y seguro para subir al cielo* [Straight and Sure Way to Heaven], an old prayer book yellowed with age and the tropical weather. He would read aloud to us all kinds of mysterious prayers about the passion of Jesus before our humble home altar of *Santos de palos* [folk carvings of saints] and the imported Santa Teresita, which my grandmother had secured after her youngest son, missing in action in World War II, was found, wounded but alive.

My father had a reputation for being a good *rezador* [prayer leader]. That coupled to the fact that he had a magnificent voice made him the most sought-after *cantador* [song leader] as well. For Christmas *parrandas* [a Puerto Rican caroling tradition], for the *rosarios de cruz* in May [hymn services in honor of the Holy Cross], for *bakinés* and *velorios* (child and adult wakes), my father was always present. People from neighboring towns would seek his services. He brought this reputation to the United States; it carried him into many Puerto Rican households on both sides of the Hudson River until age and cancer no longer allowed him to move his aching body. Perhaps that was the one thing he regretted most. In an interview on his eightieth birthday, he told a priest he missed being able to provide this service and that he hoped one day he would be well enough to continue his mission among his people.

Back in our hometown my father had inherited, by public acclamation, the post of catechist after my uncle's departure [to the mainland]. He and my mother instilled in us the belief that we should pray at home when we could not go to church on Sundays and that each member of the family should at least go the one Sunday a month assigned to the sodality to which each one belonged. For the girls in the family, it meant inviting all the girls from the neighboring farms to sleep over (in a house barely big enough for a ten-member family). It also meant getting up before the crack of dawn, getting dressed in the white uniform of the *Congregación de Hijas de María* [Daughters of Mary], walking miles to the paved road (crossing two streams of water on the way), and then boarding a *público* [public transportation vehicle], in which we literally felt like we were packed in a can like sardines. This was a three to four hour expedition. If we were lucky some gallant young fellow would give up his only day of rest to take us in an oxcart to the public transportation. Our pale, youthful faces were a perfect match for the white uniforms (the venerable curate frowned and even prohibited the use of "that worldly, almost satanical use of *esencias y colorines*," that is, perfumes and makeup!). Upon arriving at church, everyone had to go to confession. The lines were interminable, and since church law at that time prohibited the consumption of water or any other food from the previous midnight on, many became dizzy and suffered fainting spells.

To be a churchgoer was indeed a very hard task. To be religious, however, was something else. This was expected; it was as natural as being a Puerto Rican mountain dweller. Everyone we knew was a Catholic. In my town there was no other religion practiced or believed, except for the exceptional occasion when someone consulted a *curandera* [healer] in case of emergency or when the doctor's medicine did not have the expected results. No one asked if a person was Catholic, only if he or she was religious. This meant, were you and your children baptized? If so, did you truly believe in the Creator and live as if your life depended on him? Did you pray and meet your obligations as a parent, a son, a neighbor?

As an employee of the Roman Catholic Archdiocese of New York, after my tenure with the Maryknoll Sisters of St. Dominic at Ossining, New York, and *La Congregación Dominica de Hermanas de Fátima* in Puerto Rico, I would pass by St. Patrick's Cathedral on my way to work. To this day I cannot make up my mind if I find the cathedral on Fifth Avenue beautiful or simply awesome. I do know that more often than not I felt lost in its vastness. I also often wondered if the feeling would some day go away forever, but I can honestly say that it has not. The imposing St. Patrick's on New York's Fifth Avenue is a far cry from my village's *Nuestra Señora de la Monserrate*, just as downtown Manhattan, with its magnificent skyscrapers, its sophistication, and its hurried existence, is a far cry from my hometown of Moca in the northwestern plateau of Puerto Rico. And although at times I could almost hear the irreverent whisper, "You've come a long way, baby," deep in my heart I knew (and still know) that I cannot help preferring the hills to the skyscrapers, or the church of my youth to the cathedral of my adult life, or my native tongue, in which my most fervent prayers are always said, to the language of the metropolis, which is mostly reserved for professional purposes.

Ana Maria Díaz-Stevens, *Oxcart Catholicism on Fifth Avenue: The Impact of the Puerto Rican Migration upon the Archdiocese of New York* (Notre Dame, Ind.: University of Notre Dame Press, 1993), 6–9. © 1993 by University of Notre Dame Press. Used by permission of the publisher.

77. Diaspora Theology: Journeying through Exile

Cuban exile Fernando Segovia completed his advanced studies in theology at the University of Notre Dame and is now professor of New Testament and early Christianity at the Divinity School of Vanderbilt University in Nashville. Among Latino and other colleagues he is esteemed for his outstanding leadership in professional associations and his dedication as an advocate for "minorities" in the academy. A highly acclaimed scholar of Johannine literature and biblical hermeneutics, Segovia has consistently challenged his fellow scholars to recognize the vital significance of an interpreter's social location for theology, biblical studies, and other disciplines (Segovia and Tolbert 1995, 1998; Isasi-Díaz and Segovia). In writings like the following excerpt from a 1996 essay, he illustrates the importance of social location as he draws on his own experience of displacement and "otherness" to initiate his reflections on theology constructed in the diaspora of exile.

From a personal point of view, this rather typical day [July 10, 1961] of the Cold War era proved to be, with the benefit of over thirty years of hindsight, the most important day of my life. For it was on that day that I embarked on my journey of exile, a journey of mythic proportions across the Florida

Straits — that great divide between worlds that so many have dreamed of crossing, where so many have lost their lives while doing so, and through which so
many others have had their lives transformed beyond recognition. In effect,
this divide signified a cosmic journey involving a variety of highly complex
and imbricated worlds: (1) from the world of Latin American civilization, by
way of its Caribbean version, to the world of Western civilization, in terms of
its North American variant; (2) from East to West, from the world of state-
controlled communism to the world of capitalist liberal democracy; (3) from
South to North, from the traditional world of the colonized, with honor and
shame as dominant cultural values, to the industrialized world of the colonizers, with the dollar as its core value; (4) from a world that was mine, which
I knew and to which I belonged without question, to a world where I represented the "other" — the alien and the foreigner. While the actual journey
as such was over rather quickly (waking up early in La Habana, so that my
mother and I could make the late morning flight on KLM to Miami; a flight of
approximately an hour; and going to sleep that night in Miami at the house of
friends of friends of the family), the journey of exile has never ended; indeed,
exile has become my permanent land and home — the diaspora.

I still recall that journey as if it had taken place but yesterday or last week,
although I was only thirteen at the time. Indeed, it is only now, with the
advantage and disadvantage of time, that I can see the symbolic and highly
ritualistic dimensions of the entire proceedings, properly marking such a tran-
scending occasion and transition in my life in a quasi-sacramental way — a
re-birth of water and the spirit, the waters of the Gulf Stream and the spirit
of "otherness."

Preparations for the Journey. I recall the preparations for the journey itself.
The efforts to get me out of the country, for fear that I would be sent to
Eastern Europe for study — standard procedure in the colonies of the Soviet
Empire and not at all surprising, given the logic of empires and the weight
attached to the center vis-à-vis the margins. The frantic search for a missing passport — sent through mysterious channels for the procurement of the
waiver visa necessary to enter the United States, lost in the hectic diplomatic
world of the capital, and finally found quite by chance at the embassy of the
Dominican Republic. The surprise call on a Friday to the effect that I would
be leaving on the following Monday, alone — as so many others did, though in
the end a seat came open for my mother as well. The final weekend of visits
to family, friends, places — the exchange of good-byes, *sotto voce* in case somebody might wish to do us harm; the preparation of the one piece of baggage
per-person allowed, a sack that came to be known affectionately as *el chorizo*
(the sausage) and that was stuffed with clothing for an unspecified period of
time in the unknown *el norte.* (I often wonder nowadays what we must have
looked like as we donned our distinctive tropical attire in the streets of New
York.) And throughout, quite ironically, my own gleeful anticipation of the
voyage.

That anticipation of flying for the first time and visiting the United States
remained uppermost in my mind. Little did I understand what was going on

around me — about what was in the mind of my parents, who were separating for my own sake; about my family, some of whom would never cross the divide; and about our friends, many of whom we never saw or heard from again. I must confess that exile for me had, on the whole, a rather joyous beginning. It was a terrific adventure and, besides, nobody expected it to last very long. Soon we would all be back — next year in La Habana!

Crossing the Divide. I distinctly recall the flight over the divide. The final glance at the house where we lived, as we set off for the airport — faces staring out of the windows, one hand waving goodbye while the other held a wet handkerchief. The long wait at the airport itself in what came to be known as *la pecera* (the fishbowl), where those about to depart were kept together, separated from their families by a thick glass partition from ground to ceiling — sitting there for hours, subject to repeated interrogations, baggage searches, body and even strip searches. The long walk to the plane itself, the taking of seats, the takeoff — and throughout hardly a word on the part of anyone, for fear that next to you or behind you or in front of you someone might be listening, indeed for fear that the plane itself might be called back. Then, all of a sudden, the announcement from the cockpit to the effect that we were now out of Cuban waters and in international waters — pandemonium! I remember the explosion: the clapping, the embracing, and the conversation à la Latin style — emotional, boisterous, heartfelt. The people who had not dared to exchange a word before now proceeded to tell their life story, their apprehensions for the immediate future, their dreams of freedom, and their hopes for a quick return. Finally, the sign from the window that read "Welcome to Miami" and a long walk along endless and curved corridors, leading to the immigration office — more questions, more papers, more information.

Arrival in the Promised Land. I recall our arrival in the United States, our exit into the waiting area, and our first days in Miami. We had no money whatsoever, for those who left were allowed to take nothing out but the one *chorizo* — exiles were completely dependent on the goodwill of family and friends who had already made the journey and who would be waiting for the new arrivals at the airport. Actually, two other items were allowed, a bottle of rum and a box of cigars, which we, like everybody else, dutifully carried — such items would fetch our first earnings at the airport itself. It was our introduction to American culture and capitalism. The opened doors and the avalanche of two different groups of people: those who were there to receive us, speaking in our tongue and giving us as warm a greeting as the good-byes we had received hours earlier; and those who were there to buy goods, speaking in another tongue and angling for the best deal — we sold it all for ten dollars, the sum total of our wealth, aside from the offer of a room for the next few nights. The room at the inn — I had never experienced such surroundings: carpeting, air-conditioning, color television, a large and well-groomed patio.

Indeed, my earliest memories of the United States have to do with its wealth, a wealth I had never encountered before in my life, a wealth conveyed to me at that time by way of vivid and concrete images: air-conditioned churches with cushioned kneelers; enormous supermarkets with an endless variety of products, stacked to the hilt, row upon row; suburbia, with enormous distances between houses, immaculate lawns and streets, and nobody to be seen anywhere.

In one day, indeed in the space of a few hours, my whole life had changed — my life in Cuba (=Latin American civilization; the East; the colonized; my world) had come to an end, and my life in the United States (=Western civilization; the West; the colonizer; somebody else's world) had begun.... Thirty-some years later, this cosmic journey of mine into exile and this long experience of exile continue to ground, inform, and shape my theological reflection about the world, the otherworld, and the relationship between the two. It is a reflection with "otherness" at its very core, as if suspended in the air somewhere over the great divide, over the waters of the Florida Straits, looking — like Janus — in various directions at the same time: a part of both worlds and yet of none; at home in two cultures and in neither one; speaking in two tongues with none to call my own; in the world but not of it. Such is the locus and voice of my theology of the diaspora.

> Fernando F. Segovia, "In the World But Not of It: Exile as Locus for a Theology of the Diaspora," in Ada María Isasi-Díaz and Fernando F. Segovia, eds., *Hispanic/Latino Theology: Challenge and Promise* (Minneapolis: Fortress, 1996), 209–12. Reproduced from *Hispanic/Latino Theology* by Ada María Isasi-Díaz and Fernando Segovia, copyright © 1996 Augsburg Fortress.

78. *Mujerista* Theology: The Struggle for Liberation

Ada María Isasi-Díaz was born and raised in La Habana, Cuba, earned graduate degrees at Union Theological Seminary in New York, and is currently professor of Christian ethics and theology at Drew University in Madison, New Jersey. A popular author and lecturer, she has extensive experience in pastoral work, particularly through her activism with Hispanic women in the United States and different oppressed groups here and in other countries. Significantly, her activism and scholarly endeavors are inextricably bound, as her grassroots work and research among Latinas across the United States are the primary sources for her acclaimed and ongoing project to articulate a Hispanic women's mujerista theology (Isasi-Díaz and Tarango; Isasi-Díaz 1993, 1996). In the process of developing mujerista *theology, Isasi-Díaz has offered an insistent challenge to Euro-American theologians who fail to identify their social location and lived experience in articulating their supposedly "objective" theological perspectives. The following excerpt is from an article published in a collection of essays that explored how women's theological enterprise is rooted in their lived experience and the way they have "inherited their mothers' gardens."*

I was born a feminist on Thanksgiving weekend, 1975, when over one thousand Roman Catholic women met to insist on the right of women to be ordained to a renewed priestly ministry in our church. Failing, as the overwhelming majority of humans do, to remember my bodily birth, I am privileged to remember every detail of this birth to the struggle for liberation. But the process of "giving birth to myself" was not an all-of-a-sudden experience; in many ways the process had started years before.

I spent the early part of my life in Cuba, where I belonged to the dominant race and the middle class. Growing up in the 1950s, I did not pay much attention to the oppressive structures of sexism operative in my country. But I was always attracted to struggling along with those "who had less than I did" — as I thought of the oppressed then. As a matter of fact, it was precisely that attraction which made me come to understand my vocation to the ministry. It was that attraction which I now understand as the seed of my commitment to the struggle for liberation.

At age eighteen I entered the convent, a protected way of life that used to carry with it much prestige and privilege. Therefore, the few times I came into contact with the broader society during the first eight years of my adulthood, I was treated with deference, respect, and even reverence. My life within the convent walls was very difficult, and at the time I did not have the lenses needed to understand ethnic prejudice. I was greatly misunderstood and suffered much because of it, but I did not have a good analysis of what was happening to me and how I was being treated by the other nuns.

By 1975, therefore, the only oppression I was aware of was the one I suffer within the church simply because I am a woman. It is no surprise, then, that it was in relation to church teaching and practice that I came to understand the dynamics of personal oppression and joined the struggle for liberation. The 1975 Women's Ordination Conference was such an intense experience that when I emerged from the hotel where we had held the three-day conference, I realized I was perceiving the world in a different way. It took a few months before I realized what the difference was that I was seeing. My eyes had been opened to the reality of sexism. My whole life had been affected; how I saw myself and what I was to do with my life had changed radically.

The struggle against sexism in the Roman Catholic Church has been the school where I learned about feminism, as well as the main arena in which I carried out my struggle for liberation between 1975 and 1988. I rejoice in the sisterhood in whose creation I participated and am grateful for all that I learned from the women involved in the Womanchurch movement. This became my home. Soon I proceeded to plant my own garden there; however, that brought me into conflict with the sisterhood. As long as I toiled in the garden of Euro-American feminism, I was welcomed. But as I started to claim a space in the garden to plant my own flowers, the ethnic/racist prejudice prevalent in society reared its head within the Womanchurch movement.

The issue was and is power. Somewhat naively I had thought that together we would decide not only how to garden but what the garden was to look like, what it would be. But the Euro-American feminists, being part of the dominant culture, deal with Hispanic women — and other racial/ethnic women — differently from the way they deal with each other. They take for granted that feminism in the United States is their garden, and therefore they will decide what manner of work racial/ethnic women will do there.

By the time I began to experience all this, I had learned much about the dynamics of oppression and prejudice and I could understand what was going on. However, what took me totally by surprise was the inability or unwillingness of the Euro-American feminists to acknowledge their prejudice. Most feminists believe that, because they are feminists, they cannot be racists. Euro-American feminists, like all liberals, sooner or later, have come to the point at which they are willing to acknowledge that racism exists, reluctantly of course, but nobody admits to being a racist. While whitewashing — pun intended — their personal sins of racism/ethnic prejudice in the restful waters of guilt, they continue to control access to power within the movement. Euro-American feminists need to understand that as long as they refuse to recognize that oppressive power-over is an intrinsic element of their racism/ethnic prejudice, they will continue to do violence to feminism. As a liberative praxis, feminism has to do with radically changing the patriarchal understanding of power, which is operative even in the feminist movement. Euro-American feminists need to remember that, in order to undo patriarchy, we must create societies in which people can be self-defining and self-determining. To achieve that, power has to be transformed and shared.

True sharing of power leads to mutuality, and that is what we *mujeristas* ask of Euro-American feminists. It is not a matter of their allowing us to share in what they define as good. Nor is it only a matter of each one of us respecting what the other says and defending her right to say it. Mutuality asks us to give a serious consideration to what the other is saying, not only to respect it but to be willing to accept it as good for all. *Mujerista* understandings must be included in what is normative for all feminists. Our priorities must be considered to be just as important as the priorities of the Euro-American feminists. All women committed to liberation must work together on deciding the priorities for the movement....

As a Hispanic I belong to a marginalized group in this society and have had to struggle to understand and deal with the siege mentality we suffer. The need to protect ourselves against discrimination is such an integral part of our lives that we are unable or unwilling to critique ourselves. It is difficult to see criticism as constructive when we are not valued by society. Those of us who as *mujeristas* criticize sexism in the Hispanic culture are often belittled and accused of selling out to the Euro-American women. But Euro-American feminists call into question our integrity and praxis as *mujerista* feminists when we are not willing to criticize Hispanic men and culture in public. I would like to suggest that this kind of horizontal violence is linked to both internalized oppression and the siege mentality.

The challenge that lies before me has many different facets. I must struggle to convince myself and other Hispanics that our goal has to be liberation and not participation in oppressive situations and societies. We must not give in to internalized oppression and a siege mentality. We must be willing to look at ourselves and examine our experiences in view of our liberation and continue to insist, no matter where we are, on being included in setting the norm of the feminist movement. Then I have to find renewed strength and commitment to struggle with Euro-American feminists over the issue of sharing power with all involved in the women's liberation movement. Finally, I have to challenge myself and others to understand that, as women committed to liberation, the changes we are advocating will change the world radically and that we need to begin to live out those changes so they can become a reality. The only way we can move ahead is by living the reality we envision; our preferred future will flower only if we allow it to be firmly rooted in us and among us. It is up to us to change our lives radically if we want our world to change.

I plow ahead, aware that I must not idealize what I have inherited from my mother — especially because we have been transplanted and in that process have lost some of our roots and have not always correctly reinvented them. I must be careful because as transplants we often have to defend ourselves, and that can easily distort the truth. What I have received from my mother, as well as what I have gained on my own, must be subjected to the critical lens of liberation; that is the only way I can be faithful to myself and to other Hispanic women and men. The task is not easy, but the community of my family provides for me a safety net — it gives me an immense sense of security. This is one of the main reasons why, for me, hope is guaranteed and I always see possibilities. That is why I keep trying to plant my garden. That it has been uprooted several times does not keep me from trying again. Though often it is a painful struggle, I believe the struggle for women's liberation is the best of struggles, and this is why that struggle is my life. *¡La vida es la lucha!*

"A Hispanic Garden in a Foreign Land," by Ada María Isasi-Díaz. Adapted from Letty M. Russell, Kwok Pui-lan, Ada María Isasi-Díaz, and Katie Geneva Cannon, eds., *Inheriting Our Mothers' Gardens: Feminist Theology in Third World Perspective* (Philadelphia: Westminster, 1988), 94–97, 103–4; reprint, Ada María Isasi-Díaz, *Mujerista Theology: A Theology for the Twenty-First Century* (Maryknoll, N.Y.: Orbis Books, 1996), 16–19, 25–27. © 1988 Letty M. Russell. Used by permission of Westminster John Knox Press.

LIST OF WORKS CITED

Abrahamson, Eric A. 1989. *Historic Monterey: California's Forgotten First Capital.* N.p.: California Department of Parks and Recreation.

Acuña, Rodolfo. 1988. *Occupied America: A History of Chicanos.* 3d ed. New York: Harper and Row.

Allsup, Carl. 1982. *The American G.I. Forum: Origins and Evolution.* Austin: University of Texas Press and the Center for Mexican American Studies at the University of Texas.

Almaráz, Félix D. 1998. "Transplanting 'Deep, Living Roots': Franciscan Missionaries and the Colonization of New Mexico — the Fledgling Years, 1598-1616." In *Seeds of Struggle/Harvest of Faith: The Papers of the Archdiocese of Santa Fe Catholic Cuarto Centennial Conference on the History of the Church in New Mexico,* edited by Thomas J. Steele, SJ, Paul Rhetts, and Barbe Awalt, 1-26. Albuquerque: LPD Press.

Anaya, Rudolfo A., and Francisco A. Lomelí, eds. 1991. *Aztlán: Essays on the Chicano Homeland.* Albuquerque: University of New Mexico Press.

Badillo, David A. 1994. "The Catholic Church and the Making of Mexican-American Parish Communities in the Midwest." In *Mexican Americans and the Catholic Church, 1900-1965,* edited by Jay P. Dolan and Gilberto M. Hinojosa, 235-308. Notre Dame, Ind.: University of Notre Dame Press.

Bañuelas, Arturo J., ed. 1995. *Mestizo Christianity: Theology from the Latino Perspective.* Maryknoll, N.Y.: Orbis Books.

Baylies, Francis. 1851. *A Narrative of Major General Wool's Campaign in Mexico, in the Years 1846, 1847 & 1848.* Albany, N.Y.: Little.

Boza Masvidal, Eduardo, and Agustín Román. 1982. "Cuba ayer, hoy y siempre." Miami: n.p.

Brewer, William H. 1966. *Up and Down California in 1860-1864: The Journal of William H. Brewer, Professor of Agriculture in the Sheffield Scientific School from 1864-1903.* Edited by Francis P. Farquhar. Berkeley: University of California Press.

Burns, Jeffrey M. 1994. "The Mexican Catholic Community in California." In *Mexican Americans and the Catholic Church, 1900-1965,* edited by Jay P. Dolan and Gilberto M. Hinojosa, 129-233. Notre Dame, Ind.: University of Notre Dame Press.

Camarillo, Albert. 1979. *Chicanos in a Changing Society: From Mexican Pueblos to American Barrios in Santa Barbara and Southern California, 1848-1930.* Cambridge, Mass.: Harvard University Press.

Cardoso, Lawrence A. 1980. *Mexican Emigration to the United States, 1897-1931.* Tucson: University of Arizona Press.

Chipman, Donald E. 1992. *Spanish Texas, 1519-1821.* Austin: University of Texas Press.

Colton, Walter. 1949. *Three Years in California.* With an introduction by Marguerite Eyer Wilbur. Stanford, Calif.: Stanford University Press.

Covington, James W., ed. 1963. *Pirates, Indians, and Spaniards: Father Escobedo's "La Florida."* Translated by A. F. Falcones. St. Petersburg, Fla.: Great Outdoors Press.

CRECED. 1996. *CRECED: Final Document.* Translated by José Roig and Edward A. McCarthy. Miami: Shrine of Our Lady of Charity.

Cruz, Gilbert R. 1988. *Let There Be Towns: Spanish Municipal Origins in the American Southwest, 1610–1810.* College Station: Texas A&M University Press.

Davis, Kenneth G. 1995. "Encuentros." In *New Catholic Encyclopedia,* supplementary volume 19, edited by Berard Marthaler, 117–19. Washington, D.C.: Catholic University of America Press.

———. 1999. "Cursillo de Cristiandad: Gift of the Hispanic Church." *Chicago Studies* 38 (fall/winter): 318–28.

Deck, Allan Figueroa, ed. 1992. *Frontiers of Hispanic Theology in the United States.* Maryknoll, N.Y.: Orbis Books.

De la Guerra, Pablo. 26 April 1856. Speech to the California legislature. In *El Grito: A Journal of Contemporary Mexican-American Thought* 5 (fall 1971): 19–22.

De León, Arnoldo. 1982, 1997. *The Tejano Community, 1836–1900.* Dallas: Southern Methodist University Press.

Deulofeu, Manuel. 1904. *Héroes del destierro: La emigración: Notas históricas.* Cienfuegos, Cuba: Imprenta de M. Mestre.

Díaz-Stevens, Ana María. 1987. "A Concept of Mission: The National Parish and Francis Cardinal Spellman." *Migration World* 15, no. 1: 22–26.

———. 1990. "From Puerto Rican to Hispanic: The Politics of the Fiestas Patronales in New York." *Latino Studies Journal* 1 (January): 28–47.

———. 1993a. *Oxcart Catholicism on Fifth Avenue: The Impact of the Puerto Rican Migration upon the Archdiocese of New York.* Notre Dame, Ind.: University of Notre Dame Press.

———. 1993b. "The Saving Grace: The Matriarchal Core of Latino Catholicism." *Latino Studies Journal* 4 (September): 60–78.

Díaz-Stevens, Ana María, and Anthony M. Stevens-Arroyo, eds. 1994. *An Enduring Flame: Studies on Latino Popular Religiosity.* New York: Bildner Center for Western Hemisphere Studies.

———. 1998. *Recognizing the Latino Resurgence in U.S. Religion: The Emmaus Paradigm.* Boulder, Colo.: Westview Press.

Din, Gilbert C. 1988. *The Canary Islanders of Louisiana.* Baton Rouge: Louisiana State University Press.

———. 1996. *The New Orleans Cabildo: Colonial Louisiana's First City Government, 1769–1803.* Baton Rouge: Louisiana State University Press.

Dolan, Jay P., and Allan Figueroa Deck, eds. 1994. *Hispanic Catholic Culture in the U.S.: Issues and Concerns.* Notre Dame, Ind.: University of Notre Dame Press.

Dolan, Jay P., and Gilberto M. Hinojosa, eds. 1994. *Mexican Americans and the Catholic Church, 1900–1965.* Notre Dame, Ind.: University of Notre Dame Press.

Dolan, Jay P., and Jaime R. Vidal, eds. 1994. *Puerto Rican and Cuban Catholics in the U.S., 1900–1965.* Notre Dame, Ind.: University of Notre Dame Press.

Doyle, Ruth T., et al. 1982. *Hispanics in New York: Religious, Cultural and Social Experiences.* 2 volumes. New York: Archdiocese of New York Office of Pastoral Research.

Elizondo, Virgilio. 1983. *Galilean Journey: The Mexican-American Promise.* Maryknoll, N.Y.: Orbis Books.

————. 1988. *The Future Is Mestizo: Life Where Cultures Meet.* Bloomington, Ind.: Meyer Stone; reprint, San Antonio: Mexican American Cultural Center Press, 1998.

————. 1997a. *Guadalupe: Mother of the New Creation.* Maryknoll, N.Y.: Orbis Books.

————. 1997b. "The Mexican American Cultural Center Story." *Listening: Journal of Religion and Culture* 32 (fall): 152–60.

————. 2000. *Beyond Borders: Writings of Virgilio Elizondo and Friends.* Edited by Timothy Matovina. Maryknoll, N.Y.: Orbis Books.

Engh, Michael E. 1992. *Frontier Faiths: Church, Temple, and Synagogue in Los Angeles, 1846–1888.* Albuquerque: University of New Mexico Press.

————. 1994. "From *Frontera* Faith to Roman Rubrics: Altering Hispanic Religious Customs in Los Angeles, 1855–1880." *U.S. Catholic Historian* 12 (fall): 85–105.

————. 1997. "Companion of the Immigrants: Devotion to Our Lady of Guadalupe among Mexicans in the Los Angeles Area, 1900–1940." *Journal of Hispanic/Latino Theology* 5 (August): 37–47.

Espín, Orlando O. 1993. "From the Editor." *Journal of Hispanic/Latino Theology* 1 (November 1993): 3–4.

Espinosa, J. Manuel. 1993. "The Origins of the Penitentes of New Mexico: Separating Fact from Fiction." *Catholic Historical Review* 79 (July): 454–77.

Fernández, Eduardo C. 1998. "The Contributions of the Jesuit Order in the New Mexico–Colorado–West Texas Area as the Rocky Mountain Mission, 1867–1919." In *Seeds of Struggle/Harvest of Faith: The Papers of the Archdiocese of Santa Fe Catholic Cuarto Centennial Conference on the History of the Church in New Mexico,* edited by Thomas J. Steele, SJ, Paul Rhetts, and Barbe Awalt, 135–48. Albuquerque: LPD Press.

————. 2000. *La Cosecha: Harvesting Contemporary United States Hispanic Theology (1972–1998).* With a foreword by Ada María Isasi-Díaz. Collegeville, Minn.: Liturgical Press.

Ferrée, William, Ivan Illich, and Joseph P. Fitzpatrick, eds. 1980. *Spiritual Care of Puerto Rican Migrants: Report on the First Conference, Held in San Juan, Puerto Rico, April 11th to 16th, 1955.* New York: Arno.

Ferriss, Susan, and Ricardo Sandoval. 1997. *The Fight in the Fields: César Chávez and the Farmworkers Movement.* Edited by Michele McKenzie. New York: Harcourt Brace and Co.

Fitzpatrick, Joseph P. 1987. *Puerto Rican Americans: The Meaning of Migration to the Mainland.* 2d ed. With a foreword by Milton M. Gordon. Englewood Cliffs, N.J.: Prentice-Hall.

Gannon, Michael V. 1965. *The Cross in the Sand: The Early Catholic Church in Florida, 1513–1870.* Gainesville: University of Florida Press.

García, Juan R. 1996. *Mexicans in the Midwest, 1900–1932.* Tucson: University of Arizona Press.

García, María Cristina. 1997. *Havana USA: Cubans and Cuban Americans in Miami.* Berkeley: University of California Press.

García, Mario T. Forthcoming. "Religion and the Chicano Movement: The Case of Católicos por la Raza." In *Chicano Religions: Essays on the Mexican American Experience,* edited by Mario T. García and Gastón Espinosa. Berkeley: University of California Press.

Gleason, Philip. 1987. *Keeping the Faith: American Catholicism Past and Present.* Notre Dame, Ind.: University of Notre Dame Press.

Gonzales, Manuel G. 1999. *Mexicanos: A History of Mexicans in the United States.* Bloomington: Indiana University Press.

Granjon, Henry. 1986. *Along the Rio Grande: A Pastoral Visit to Southwest New Mexico in 1902.* Edited by Michael Romero Taylor. Translated by Mary W. de López. Albuquerque: University of New Mexico Press.

Griswold del Castillo, Richard. 1979. *The Los Angeles Barrio, 1850–1890: A Social History.* Berkeley: University of California Press.

———. 1984. *La Familia: Chicano Families in the Urban Southwest, 1848 to the Present.* Notre Dame, Ind.: University of Notre Dame Press.

———. 1990. *The Treaty of Guadalupe Hidalgo: A Legacy of Conflict.* Norman: University of Oklahoma Press.

Griswold del Castillo, Richard, and Richard A. García. 1995. *César Chávez: A Triumph of Spirit.* Norman: University of Oklahoma Press.

Gutiérrez, Gabriel. 1999. "*Con sus calzones al réves,* With His Underpants on Inside Out: Cultural Economy and Patriarchy in Pablo de la Guerra's Letters to Josefa Moreno de la Guerra, 1851–1872." *JSRI Occasional Paper,* no. 60. Julian Samora Research Institute, Michigan State University, East Lansing, Mich.

Gutiérrez, Ramón A. 1995. "El santuario de Chimayó: A Syncretic Shrine in New Mexico." In *Feasts and Celebrations in North American Ethnic Communities,* edited by Ramón A. Gutiérrez and Geneviève Fabre, 71–86. Albuquerque: University of New Mexico Press.

Hall, Thomas D. 1989. *Social Change in the Southwest, 1350–1880.* Lawrence: University Press of Kansas.

Hamm, Mark S. 1995. *The Abandoned Ones: The Imprisonment and Uprising of the Mariel Boat People.* Boston: Northeastern University Press.

Hawley, Walter A. 1987. *Early Days of Santa Barbara, California: From the First Discoveries by Europeans to December, 1846.* Edited by John C. Woodward. Santa Barbara, Calif.: Santa Barbara Heritage.

Hennesey, James. 1981. *American Catholics: A History of the Roman Catholic Community in the United States.* With a foreword by John Tracy Ellis. New York: Oxford University Press.

Hernandez Travieso, Antonio. 1984. *El Padre Varela: Biografía del forjador de la conciencia Cubana.* 2d ed. Miami: Ediciones Universal.

Herrera, María Cristina. 1998. Oral Interviews with Gerald E. Poyo.

Hinojosa, Gilberto M. 1990. "The Enduring Hispanic Faith Communities: Spanish and Texas Church Historiography." *Journal of Texas Catholic History and Culture* 1 (March): 20–41.

———. 1994. "Mexican-American Faith Communities in Texas and the Southwest." In *Mexican Americans and the Catholic Church, 1900–1965,* edited by Jay P. Dolan and Gilberto M. Hinojosa, 9–125. Notre Dame, Ind.: University of Notre Dame Press.

Hispanic Catholics: Historical Explorations and Cultural Analysis. 1990. Double issue of the *U.S. Catholic Historian* 9 (winter/spring).

Ingalls, Robert P. 1988. *Urban Vigilantes in the New South: Tampa, 1882–1936.* Knoxville: University of Tennessee Press.

Isasi-Díaz, Ada María. 1993. *En la lucha: A Hispanic Women's Liberation Theology.* Minneapolis: Fortress.

———. 1996. *Mujerista Theology: A Theology for the Twenty-first Century.* Maryknoll, N.Y.: Orbis Books.

Isasi-Díaz, Ada María, and Fernando F. Segovia, eds. 1996. *Hispanic/Latino Theology: Challenge and Promise.* Minneapolis: Fortress.

Isasi-Díaz, Ada María, and Yolanda Tarango. 1988. *Hispanic Women: Prophetic Voice in the Church.* San Francisco: Harper and Row; reprint, Minneapolis: Fortress, 1992.

Juárez, José Roberto. 1973. "La iglesia Católica y el Chicano en sud Texas, 1836–1911." *Aztlán* 4 (fall): 217–55.

Kanellos, Nicolás, and Bryan Ryan. 1996. *Hispanic American Chronology.* New York: U.X.L.

Kirk, John M. 1989. *Between God and the Party: Religion and Politics in Revolutionary Cuba.* Tampa: University of South Florida Press.

Koch, Joan. 1991. "Selections from *Nuestra Señora de la Soledad: A Study of a Church and Hospital Site in Colonial St. Augustine.*" In *America's Ancient City: Spanish St. Augustine, 1565–1763,* edited by Kathleen A. Deagan, 94–145. New York: Garland.

Lummis, Charles F. 1893. *The Land of Poco Tiempo.* New York: C. Scribner's Sons.

Mainwaring, Scott, and Alexander Wilde. 1989. "The Progressive Church in Latin America: An Interpretation." In *The Progressive Church in Latin America,* edited by Scott Mainwaring and Alexander Wilde, 1–37. Notre Dame, Ind.: University of Notre Dame Press.

Márquez, Benjamin. 1993. *LULAC: The Evolution of a Mexican American Political Organization.* Austin: University of Texas Press.

Marriott, Alice. 1948. *María: The Potter of San Ildefonso.* Norman: University of Oklahoma Press.

Masud-Piloto, Félix. 1996. *From Welcomed Exiles to Illegal Immigrants: Cuban Migration to the United States, 1959–1995.* Boston: Rowman and Littlefield.

Matovina, Timothy. 1994. "Lay Initiatives in Worship on the Texas *Frontera,* 1830–1860." *U.S. Catholic Historian* 12 (fall): 107–20.

———. 1995. *Tejano Religion and Ethnicity: San Antonio, 1821–1860.* Austin: University of Texas Press.

———. 1996. "Guadalupan Devotion in a Borderlands Community." *Journal of Hispanic/Latino Theology* 4 (August): 6–26.

———. 1997a. "New Frontiers of Guadalupanismo." *Journal of Hispanic/Latino Theology* 5 (August): 20–36.

———. 1997b. "Sacred Place and Collective Memory: San Fernando Cathedral, San Antonio, Texas." *U.S. Catholic Historian* 15 (winter): 33–50.

———. 1999. "Representation and the Reconstruction of Power: The Rise of PADRES and Las Hermanas." In *What's Left? Liberal American Catholics,* edited by Mary Jo Weaver, 220–37. Bloomington: Indiana University Press.

McMurtrey, Martin. 1987. *Mariachi Bishop: The Life Story of Patrick Flores.* San Antonio: Corona.

Medina, Lara. 1994. "Broadening the Discourse at the Theological Table: An Overview of Latino Theology, 1968–1993." *Latino Studies Journal* 5 (September): 10–36.

———. 1998. "Las Hermanas: Chicana/Latina Religious-Political Activism, 1971–1997." Ph.D. diss., Claremont Graduate University, Claremont, Calif.

Meyer, Jean A. 1976. *The Cristero Rebellion: The Mexican People between Church and State, 1926–1929.* Cambridge: Cambridge University Press.

Montejano, David. 1987. *Anglos and Mexicans in the Making of Texas, 1836–1986.* Austin: University of Texas Press.

Navarro, José Antonio. 1995. *Defending Mexican Valor in Texas: José Antonio Navarro's Historical Writings, 1853–1857.* Edited by David R. McDonald and Timothy Matovina. Austin, Tex.: State House.

Neri, Michael Charles. 1997. *Hispanic Catholicism in Transitional California: The Life of José González Rubio, O.F.M. (1804–1875)*. Berkeley, Calif.: Academy of American Franciscan History.

Osio, Antonio María. 1996. *The History of Alta California: A Memoir of Mexican California*. Translated by Rose Marie Beebe and Robert M. Senkewicz. Madison: University of Wisconsin Press.

Owens, Lilliana. 1951. *Reverend Carlos M. Pinto, SJ, Apostle of El Paso, 1892–1919*. El Paso, Tex.: Revista Católica.

Padilla, Félix M. 1987. *Puerto Rican Chicago*. Notre Dame, Ind.: University of Notre Dame Press.

Partido Demócrata Cristiano de Cuba. 1991. *Primer congreso del Partido Demócrata Cristiano*. Coconut Grove, Fla.: n.p.

Perales, Alonso S. 1948. *Are We Good Neighbors?* San Antonio: Artes Graficas.

Pérez, Lisandro. 1994. "Cuban Catholics in the United States." In *Puerto Rican and Cuban Catholics in the U.S., 1900–1965*, edited by Jay P. Dolan and Jaime R. Vidal, 145–208. Notre Dame, Ind.: University of Notre Dame Press.

Pérez, Louis A., Jr. 1988. *Cuba: Between Reform and Revolution*. New York: Oxford University Press.

Pike, Fredrick B. 1992. *The United States and Latin America: Myths and Stereotypes of Civilization and Nature*. Austin: University of Texas Press.

Pitt, Leonard. 1966. *The Decline of the Californios: A Social History of the Spanish-Speaking Californians, 1846–1890*. Berkeley: University of California Press.

Poyo, Gerald E. 1989. *"With All, and for the Good of All": The Emergence of Popular Nationalism in the Cuban Communities of the United States, 1848–1898*. Durham, N.C.: Duke University Press.

Poyo, Gerald E., and Gilberto M. Hinojosa, eds. 1991. *Tejano Origins in Eighteenth-Century San Antonio*. Austin: University of Texas Press for the University of Texas Institute of Texan Cultures at San Antonio.

Pulido, Alberto L. 1991a. "Are You an Emissary of Jesus Christ? Justice, the Catholic Church, and the Chicano Movement." *Explorations in Ethnic Studies* 14 (January): 17–34.

———. 1991b. "Nuestra Señora de Guadalupe: The Mexican Catholic Experience in San Diego." *Journal of San Diego History* 37 (fall): 236–54.

Quinn, Jane. 1975. *Minorcans in Florida: Their History and Heritage*. St. Augustine, Fla.: Mission Press.

Quirk, Robert E. 1973. *The Mexican Revolution and the Catholic Church, 1910–1929*. Bloomington: Indiana University Press.

Recinos, Harold J. 1997. *Who Comes in the Name of the Lord? Jesus at the Margins*. Nashville: Abingdon.

Reimers, David M. 1992. *Still the Golden Door: The Third World Comes to America*. 2d ed. New York: Columbia University Press.

Rodríguez, Edmundo. 1994. "The Hispanic Community and Church Movements: Schools of Leadership." In *Hispanic Catholic Culture in the U.S.: Issues and Concerns*, edited by Jay P. Dolan and Allan Figueroa Deck, 206–39. Notre Dame, Ind.: University of Notre Dame Press.

Romero, Juan. 1976. *Reluctant Dawn: Historia del Padre A. J. Martínez, Cura de Taos*. With Moises Sandoval. San Antonio: Mexican American Cultural Center Press.

———. 1990. "Charism and Power: An Essay on the History of PADRES." *U.S. Catholic Historian* 9 (winter/spring): 147–63.

————. 1998. "Begetting the Mexican American: Padre Martínez and the 1847 Rebellion." In *Seeds of Struggle/Harvest of Faith: The Papers of the Archdiocese of Santa Fe Catholic Cuarto Centennial Conference on the History of the Church in New Mexico,* edited by Thomas J. Steele, SJ, Paul Rhetts, and Barbe Awalt, 345–71. Albuquerque: LPD Press.

Rosales, F. Arturo. 1996. *Chicano! The History of the Mexican American Civil Rights Movement.* Houston: University of Houston Press.

Ruiz, Vicki L. 1998. *From Out of the Shadows: Mexican Women in Twentieth-Century America.* New York: Oxford University Press.

Samora, Julian, and Patricia Vandel Simon. 1993. *A History of the Mexican-American People.* Revised edition. Notre Dame, Ind.: University of Notre Dame Press.

Sánchez, George G. 1993. *Becoming Mexican American: Ethnicity, Culture, and Identity in Chicano Los Angeles, 1900–1945.* New York: Oxford University Press.

Sánchez, Rosaura, Beatrice Pita, and Bárbara Reyes, eds. 1994. *Nineteenth Century Californio Testimonials.* San Diego: Crítica Monograph Series, UCSD Ethnic Studies/Third World Studies.

Sánchez Korrol, Virginia E. 1983. *From Colonia to Community: The History of Puerto Ricans in New York City, 1917–1948.* Westport, Conn.: Greenwood.

Sandoval, Moises. 1990. *On the Move: A History of the Hispanic Church in the United States.* Maryknoll, N.Y.: Orbis Books.

————. 1994. "The Organization of a Hispanic Church." In *Hispanic Catholic Culture in the U.S.: Issues and Concerns,* edited by Jay P. Dolan and Allan Figueroa Deck, 131–65. Notre Dame, Ind.: University of Notre Dame Press.

———— , ed. 1983. *Fronteras: A History of the Latin American Church in the USA since 1513.* San Antonio: Mexican American Cultural Center Press.

Scholes, Frances V. 1971. "An Overview of the Colonial Church." In *The Roman Catholic Church in Colonial Latin America,* edited by Richard E. Greenleaf, 19–29. New York: Alfred A. Knopf.

Segovia, Fernando F., and Mary Ann Tolbert, eds. 1995. *Reading from This Place.* 2 volumes. Minneapolis: Fortress.

————. 1998. *Teaching the Bible: The Discourses and Politics of Biblical Pedagogy.* Maryknoll, N.Y.: Orbis Books.

Seguín, Juan N. 1991. *A Revolution Remembered: The Memoirs and Selected Correspondence of Juan N. Seguín.* Edited by Jesús F. de la Teja. Austin, Tex.: State House.

Sheridan, Thomas E. 1986. *Los Tucsonenses: The Mexican Community in Tucson, 1854–1941.* Tucson: University of Arizona Press.

Steele, Thomas J., ed. 1997. *New Mexican Spanish Religious Oratory, 1800–1900.* Albuquerque: University of New Mexico Press.

Stevens-Arroyo, Antonio M. 1980. *Prophets Denied Honor: An Anthology on the Hispano Church in the United States.* Maryknoll, N.Y.: Orbis Books.

St. Mary Star of the Sea. 1996. *A History of St. Mary Star of the Sea Catholic Church: The Oldest Roman Catholic Parish in the Diocese of Miami.* [Key West: n.p.].

Stoller, Marianne L., and Thomas J. Steele, eds. 1982. *Diary of the Jesuit Residence of Our Lady of Guadalupe Parish, Conejos, Colorado: December 1871–December 1875.* Translated by José B. Fernández. Colorado Springs: Colorado College.

Tarango, Yolanda, and Timothy Matovina. 1994. "Las Hermanas." In *Hispanics in the Church: Up from the Cellar,* edited by Philip E. Lampe, 95–120. San Francisco: Catholic Scholars Press.

Taylor, Mary D. 1990. "Cura de la frontera, Ramón Ortiz." *U.S. Catholic Historian* 9 (winter/spring): 67–85.

TePaske, John Jay. 1964. *The Governorship of Spanish Florida, 1700–1763.* Durham, N.C.: Duke University Press.

Thompson, Joseph A. 1961. *El Gran Capitán, José De la Guerra: A Historical Biographical Study.* Los Angeles: Cabrera and Sons.

Tijerina, Andrés. 1998. *Tejano Empire: Life on the South Texas Ranchos.* College Station: Texas A & M University Press.

Timmons, W. H. 1990. *El Paso: A Borderlands History.* With a foreword by David J. Weber. El Paso: Texas Western Press.

Torres-Saillant, Silvio, and Ramona Hernández. 1998. *The Dominican Americans.* Westport, Conn.: Greenwood.

Tweed, Thomas A. 1997. *Our Lady of the Exile: Diasporic Religion at a Cuban Catholic Shrine in Miami.* Oxford: Oxford University Press.

"UCE." 1978. *Cuba diaspora, 1978: Anuario de la iglesia Cubana.* Caracas, Venezuela: n.p.

Vargas, Zaragosa, ed. 1999. *Major Problems in Mexican American History.* Boston: Houghton Mifflin.

Vidal, Jaime R. 1990. "The American Church and the Puerto Rican People." *U.S. Catholic Historian* 9 (winter/spring): 119–35.

———. 1994. "Citizens Yet Strangers: The Puerto Rican Experience." In *Puerto Rican and Cuban Catholics in the U.S., 1900–1965,* edited by Jay P. Dolan and Jaime R. Vidal, 9–143. Notre Dame, Ind.: University of Notre Dame Press.

La voz de la iglesia en Cuba: 100 documentos episcopales. 1995. Mexico City: Obra Nacional de la Buena Prensa, A.C.

Walsh, Bryan O. 1975. "The Spanish Impact Here: How the Archdiocese Is Meeting the Challenge." *The Voice* (18 July).

Weber, David J. 1979. " 'Scarce More Than Apes': Historical Roots of Anglo American Stereotypes of Mexicans in the Border Region." In *New Spain's Far Northern Frontier: Essays on Spain in the American West, 1540–1821,* edited by David J. Weber, 295–307. Albuquerque: University of New Mexico Press.

———. 1982. *The Mexican Frontier, 1821–1846: The American Southwest under Mexico.* Albuquerque: University of New Mexico Press.

———. 1992. *The Spanish Frontier in North America.* New Haven, Conn.: Yale University Press.

———, ed. 1999. *What Caused the Pueblo Revolt of 1680?* Boston: Bedford/St. Martin's.

Weigle, Marta, and Peter White. 1988. *The Lore of New Mexico.* Albuquerque: University of New Mexico Press.

Wright, Robert E. 1990. "Local Church Emergence and Mission Decline: The Historiography of the Catholic Church in the Southwest during the Spanish and Mexican Periods." *U.S. Catholic Historian* 9 (winter/spring): 27–48.

———. 1998. "How Many Are 'A Few'? Catholic Clergy in Central and Northern New Mexico, 1780–1851." In *Seeds of Struggle/Harvest of Faith: The Papers of the Archdiocese of Santa Fe Catholic Cuarto Centennial Conference on the History of the Church in New Mexico,* edited by Thomas J. Steele, SJ, Paul Rhetts, and Barbe Awalt, 219–61. Albuquerque: LPD Press.

COLLABORATORS

CECILIA GONZÁLEZ-ANDRIEU is a writer and media producer whose artistic and scholarly work centers on the intersection between the arts and theology. Her documentary and dramatic radio and television projects feature U.S. Latino culture and religion with an emphasis on social justice and the liberating power of art.

TIMOTHY MATOVINA is an associate professor of theology at the University of Notre Dame. He is the author of numerous articles and seven books on Latino religion and history, including *Tejano Religion and Ethnicity* (1995) and *Beyond Borders* (1999).

GERALD E. POYO is professor of Latin American and U.S. Latino history at St. Mary's University in San Antonio. He has written widely on both Cubans and Mexican Americans, including *With All, and for the Good of All* (1989), *Tejano Journey* (1996), and, with Gilberto Hinojosa, *Tejano Origins in Eighteenth-Century San Antonio* (1991).

STEVEN P. RODRÍGUEZ is a graduate student in Latin American and U.S. Latino history at St. Mary's University in San Antonio. He is also a member of an Aztec dance group that works in the local community to maintain and realize a sense of indigenous history, spirituality, and culture.

JAIME R. VIDAL is director of the Franciscan Press at Quincy University in Quincy, Illinois. He served as coordinator of the Notre Dame study on U.S. Hispanic Catholics and coedited *Puerto Rican and Cuban Catholics in the U.S.* (1994), the second volume of that three-volume study. Vidal is a nationally recognized expert on Puerto Rican Catholicism.

INDEX

Academy of Catholic Hispanic Theologians of the United States, 244
Acción Católica (Catholic Action), 144. *See also* Spanish Catholic Action Office
activism. *See* justice struggles
Ad gentes, 244
Agrupación Católica Universitaria (Catholic University Group), 144, 176–78
Albizu Campos, Pedro, 193–94, 199–201
Albuquerque, New Mexico, 9
Alemany, Joseph, 48, 49, 52, 101
Alexander VI, Pope, 2
Alianza Hispano-Americana (Hispanic-American Alliance), 51
All Souls Day, 118
Almeda, Teresa, 220
Amat, Thaddeus, 48, 49, 52, 57, 71, 72
American G.I. Forum, 193, 194
Americanization, 197–201. *See also* assimilation
anarchism, 143, 153
anticlericalism, 143, 145–47, 160–63
anti-Communism, 143–44, 145, 174–78
anti-Semitism, 32
Apaches, 12–14
Apuntes, 244
Arce, G. L., 165–68
Argentineans, 134
Arizona, 106–7. *See also specific cities and towns*
Arroyo Hondo, New Mexico, 82–85
Asociación Católica Juventud Mexicana (Mexican Catholic Youth Association), 165
Asociación Nacional de los Vasallos de Cristo Rey (National Association of the Vassals of Christ the King), 149, 156–58
assimilation, 99–100, 197–99. *See also* Americanization
Assumption, the, 71

Augustinian Recollects, 201, 203
Aztecs, 2

Balmes, Jaime, 200
Bañuelas, Arturo, 244
Bardeck, Phillip, 97
Baylies, Francis, 46
Bay of Pigs invasion, 144, 145, 183, 222
Benavides, Alonso de, 6, 12
bishops
   call for more Hispanic, 196, 216–17, 222
   Las Hermanas and, 219–20
   Medellín conference and, 142
   pastoral letter on Hispanics, xviii
"Black Legend," the, 46
borderlands Catholicism, 106–8
Borges, Haydée, 196, 227
Boza Masvidal, Eduardo, 144, 148, 150, 171–74, 180, 182–83, 185
Bracero Program, 94
Buddy, Charles F., 201, 202

Caballeros de San Juan Bautista (Knights of St. John the Baptist), 97, 115–16
Cabeza de Vaca, Alvar Núñez, 10
California
   colonial period in, 7
   effects of U.S. annexation of, 48
   missions in, 23–25, 37–43
   Proposition 187 and, 240–41
   See also specific cities and towns
California Migrant Ministry, 207
Calles, Plutarco Elías, 146, 147, 160–61, 163, 167
Canary Islanders, 7
Cantwell, John J., 165, 166–67, 203
Capilla de los Milagros, La (San Antonio), 87–89
Cárdenas, Lázaro, 146, 165
"On the Care of Migrants" (Pope Paul VI), 216
Carrillo, Alberto, 198, 212, 216

271